WORKS ISSUED BY
THE HAKLUYT SOCIETY

———

THE VOYAGE OF
SEMEN DEZHNEV IN 1648

SECOND SERIES
NO. 159

THE VOYAGE OF
SEMEN DEZHNEV IN 1648:

BERING'S PRECURSOR

WITH SELECTED DOCUMENTS

by

RAYMOND H. FISHER

THE HAKLUYT SOCIETY

LONDON

1981

ISBN 0 904180 07 7

Printed in Great Britain at the
University Press, Cambridge

Published by the Hakluyt Society
c/o The Map Room,
British Library Reference Division
London WC1B 3DG

For
Raymond
and
Deborah

CONTENTS

MAPS

ILLUSTRATIONS

PREFACE

The name of Semen Dezhnev is not a well-known one in the history of geographical exploration, though it is better known in the Soviet Union than outside it, as might be expected. He was an illiterate Siberian cossack who was the surviving leader of a party of petty entrepreneurs, originally numbering ninety persons, which sailed in the summer of 1648 around the eastern tip of Asia, from the Kolyma River, which empties into the Arctic Ocean, to a point south of the mouth of the Anadyr´ River, which empties into the Pacific, thus anticipating by eighty years almost to the month the voyage of Vitus Bering through the strait separating Asia and America and now bearing his name.

No logbook or ship's journal was kept on this voyage, and what is known of it is found in brief remarks about it in later reports by Dezhnev and some of his associates. Thus, in treating the voyage here it has not been feasible to follow the customary format of the volumes published by the Hakluyt Society in which a consecutive narrative of a voyage is presented, in English translation if not originally written in English, carefully edited and with comments by the editor. Instead I have had to substitute some 34 selected documents which bear on the voyage and some of the questions raised by it. To give coherence to the information contained in these documents it has been necessary to depend upon and expand the commentary, with the result that it constitutes the larger part of this volume.

All of the documents have been published; I have not had access to unpublished archival materials. Consequently my purpose has not been to present new or expanded materials about the voyage, but rather to draw together what earlier scholars, mostly Russian and Soviet, have uncovered and what interpretations and explanations they have advanced concerning the voyage and particularly certain controversial questions. More specifically, a major instigating motive has been to counteract the scepticism expressed by the American scholar, Frank A. Golder, whose discussion of the voyage has been the most widely disseminated account in English. Modern Soviet research has rendered

xi

it badly out of date. Mere compilation has not, on the other hand, been my intention. I have felt free to expand some of the arguments on controversial matters, to present my own conclusions in certain instances, and to take sides on disputed points or to suspend judgement where I think the evidence does not warrant firm conclusions. The final evaluation of the significance of the voyage is my own.

The voyage of Dezhnev first came to my attention in the course of working on my doctoral dissertation on the Russian fur trade in the 1930s. It was brought more sharply to my attention while on sabbatical leave in 1955 when I came across an article by I. I. Ogryzko, 'Otkrytiye kuril'skikh ostrovov' (see the Bibliography) in which he claimed that some of the participants in the voyage of Dezhnev were the Russians first to discover Kamchatka and the Kuril Islands. Though that view is now discredited, it had gained some acceptance then. Previously I had read an article by A. E. Sokol, 'Russian Expansion and Exploration in the Pacific', in *The American Slavic and East European Review* (Vol. IX, pp. 84–105), which was based on materials published outside Russia and the Soviet Union, mostly in English. This article was a sign for me that western scholars really knew very little about what scholars in the Soviet Union had done and were doing on Russian exploration and discovery in the Pacific. The immediate post-World War II years saw a kind of quantum leap in Soviet research on Russian exploration and discovery there and elsewhere, of which western scholars seemed unaware. Between Ogryzko on the one side and Sokol on the other I was led to investigate further the unusual voyage of Dezhnev, which led me to Frank A. Golder, Dezhnev's chief detractor, Gerhard F. Müller, Mikhail I. Belov, and then to others, not the least of whom is Boris P. Polevoy. As a first step I wrote an article analysing Golder's arguments of rejection, which was published in 1956. But then other academic interests and activities diverted me from a continuous pursuit of this subject. It was finally energised into a thorough-going examination by an invitation from the Hakluyt Society to present the manuscript now manifested in this book. Forty-five years from insemination to maturity are an unconscionably long time for a work of this sort, but advantages have accrued: judgements have not been hasty, and what Soviet scholars have produced over these years make the book a better one than if I had pushed it out into the world a decade or two sooner.

Over the many years during which I have worked on this topic I have received financial support most of all from the Research Committee of the Academic Senate of the University of California, Los Angeles, but also from the American Philosophical Society in Philadelphia and from the Russian and East European Studies Center of the University of California, Berkeley. I welcome this opportunity to express publicly my appreciation for their support. Recognition is also due to Dr Boris P. Polevoy of the Institute of Ethnography of the Soviet Academy of Sciences for his assistance in dealing with the antique and regional vocabulary found in the documents translated herein and for his comments on some disputed points; and to Professors Vladimir Markov and Dean S. Worth of the University of California, Los Angeles, to Professor Anatole G. Mazour of Stanford University, and to the late Professor Oleg Maslenikov of the University of California, Berkeley, for assistance in translating difficult passages in the documents. My thanks are due too to my cousin, Edwin J. Maile, for his assistance in proof reading.

A number of maps of 17th- and 18th-century origin have been included in translation for the elucidation of certain points. Though a few of them have been reproduced intact, in most of them details irrelevant to the point under discussion have been omitted. Thus they are much modified and simplified. They and the drawings of a koch were prepared by Mr Noel L. Diaz, cartographer in the Department of Geography, University of California, Los Angeles.

RAYMOND H. FISHER

ABBREVIATIONS

AAN	Arkhiv Akademii nauk [Archive of the Academy of Sciences]
AN SSSR	Akademiya nauk, Soyuz sovetskikh sotsialisticheskikh respublik [Academy of Sciences, Union of Soviet Socialist Republics]
DAI	*Dopolneniye k aktam istoricheskim* [Supplement to the historical documents] (see Russia, Arkheograficheskaya kommissiya in the Bibliography)
LOII	Leningradskoye otdeleniye Instituta istorii [Leningrad division of the Institute of History]
ORZPM	*Otkrytiya russkikh zemleprokhodtsev i polyarnykh morekhodov v XVII veka* [Discoveries of Russian land and polar sea farers in the 17th century]
RAE	*Russkiye arkticheskiye ekspeditsii XVII–XIX vv....* [Russian Arctic expeditions of the 17th–19th centuries]
RM	*Russkiye morekhody v ledovitom i tikhom okeanakh...* [Russian seafarers in the Frozen and Pacific oceans]
TsGADA	Tsentral'nyy gosudarstvennyy arkhiv drevnikh aktov [Central State Archive of Historical Documents]
VGO	Vsesoyuznoye geograficheskoye obshchestvo [All-Union Geographical Society]
YaA	Yakutskiye akty [Yakutsk documents]
YaPI	Yakutskaya prikaznaya izba [Yakutsk voyevoda's chancellery]

CHAPTER I

THE RECOVERY OF A DISCOVERY

In the summer of 1648 a party of Siberian cossacks, traders, and hunters assembled by Fedot Alekseyev, a merchant's agent, and placed under the authority of Semen Ivanov Dezhnev, a cossack, sailed from the Kolyma River, which flows into the Arctic Ocean, to a point south of the mouth of the Anadyr′ River, which empties into the Pacific Ocean. In so doing Dezhnev and his associates became the first Europeans to sail through the strait separating northeastern Asia from northwestern America, eighty years before Captain Vitus Jonassen Bering and his crew sailed through that same strait, to which his, not Dezhnev's, name was later given. Bering's voyage through and discovery of the strait became known in the west almost immediately after his return to St Petersburg in 1730, whereas Dezhnev's voyage did not become known in European Russia and the west until after Bering's voyage, for it was with Bering's first expedition to Kamchatka that the recovery of Dezhnev's discovery began. The fact is that Dezhnev's discovery itself had to be discovered.

Shortly after Bering returned to St Petersburg at the beginning of March 1730, the first public notice of his voyage in 1728 appeared in the *St. Petersburg Gazette* (March 16).[1] In that notice was a brief statement that Bering had 'learned from the local inhabitants that fifty or sixty years before a vessel arrived in Kamchatka from the Lena'.[2] This statement can be seen as a reference, inaccurate and incomplete, only to the voyage of Dezhnev. So where did Bering pick up this bit of information?

Though there is no evidence of knowledge in St Petersburg of such a voyage prior to Bering's return, it does appear that there was knowledge of it in Moscow and northern maritime Russia and Siberia.[3] Most likely Bering encountered it first in Tobol′sk, his first major stop en route to Kamchatka. Correspondence from the rest of Siberia to Moscow and St Petersburg was channelled through this main administrative centre in western Siberia. The Swedish military officer

[1] *Sanktpeterburgskiya vedomosti.*
[2] Vadim I. Grekov, 'Naiboleye ranneye pechatnoye izvestiye o pervoy kamchatskoy ekspeditsii (1725–30 gg.)', *Izvestiya AN SSSR, seriya geograficheskaya*, 1956, Vypusk 6, p. 109.   [3] See the discussion of this topic in Chapter 10, pp. 263–72.

and captive of war, Philip Tabbert von Strahlenberg, who spent nearly eleven years (1711–1721) in Tobolsk where he associated with the local officials and served the Russian government, picked up a similar report. After his departure from Russia he published in 1730 a detailed description of Russia and Siberia based on his research during his captivity.[1] In his discussion of Russian activities along the Arctic littoral he mentions a voyage from the Lena River to Kamchatka.[2]

It is pretty certain that Bering encountered this report also in Yakutsk. Upon arrival there in June 1726 he had a conversation with Ivan Kozyrevskiy, a cossack forcibly turned monk, who had explored Kamchatka and the northern Kuril Islands and who had drafted a map of Kamchatka, a copy of which he gave to Bering. On this map appears an inscription that men from Yakutsk came to Kamchatka by sea[3]

How much credence Bering gave to these reports then we do not know. It appears quite certain that when he sailed north from Kamchatka in July 1728 he expected to find an isthmus in the north connecting Asia with America. But on reaching the southeast corner of the Chukotskiy Peninsula he learned from the Chukchi there that the coast of that peninsula turned north and then west and was washed by the ocean all the way to the Kolyma River,[4] and a few days later he discovered that the coast did indeed not continue northward, but turned to the west. Thus, whether or not he had earlier believed the report of a voyage from the Lena River to Kamchatka, he thereafter must have taken the report seriously, as the statement in the St. Petersburg Gazette testifies.

Not long after his return to St Petersburg Bering presented to his superiors proposals for renewed and expanded exploration of the north Pacific and Arctic in order to open up trade with America and Japan. The officials in the Admiralty College and Administrative Senate adopted his proposals almost in toto in 1732 and expanded them into the most comprehensive programme of exploration yet witnessed in Europe, the Second Kamchatka Expedition. One of the projects added by the officials was the despatch to Siberia of a contingent of academicians from the recently established Academy of Sciences to survey that vast land as to its geography, history, ethnography,

[1] *Das nord und östliche Theil von Europa and Asia*...(Stockholm).
[2] See p. 269 below.
[3] See p. 193 below.
[4] Vadim I. Grekov, *Ocherki istorii russkikh geograficheskikh issledovaniy v 1725–1765 gg.* (Moscow, 1960), p. 33; Raymond H. Fisher, *Bering's voyages: Whither and why* (Seattle, 1977), pp. 81–2.

antiquities, and resources. At the head of this contingent was placed Gerhard Friedrich Müller, who was to become the founder of Siberian historiography and the discoverer of Semen Ivanov Dezhnev.

In 1725, when a young man of twenty, Müller had emigrated to St Petersburg from Germany after three years of university study at Rinteln and Leipzig. He was accepted in the year-old Academy of Sciences as an adjunct (assistant) in history. During the subsequent eight years he taught history, geography, and other subjects, performed administrative and library duties, edited and contributed to the Academy's publications[1] and published the first three parts of the first volume of his nine-volume compendium, *Sammlung russischer Geschichte*. By 1731 he had become a professor and member of the Academy. Two years later he accepted the assignment as co-leader of the academic contingent of the Second Kamchatka Expedition along with his fellow-countryman, the naturalist Johann Georg Gmelin. Gmelin soon bowed out as co-leader because of ill health, though he later returned to the contingent. This left Müller as sole head. In the decade 1733–43 he travelled the length and breadth of Siberia, visiting important settlements there as far east as Nerchinsk and Yakutsk. With the aid of a corps of assistants he examined some twenty local government archives, from which he selected, and had copied or extracted, a wealth of documents, transporting them in his 'campaign sledge' (*pokhodnyy vozok*), which he called his 'Siberian archives'.[2] In addition, he interviewed old natives, explored possible locations of mineral resources, studied the trade of Siberia, and made some archeological explorations. During his decade in Siberia and after his return to St Petersburg he wrote and published several essays on that country and its past, as well as his pioneer history of Siberia, *Description of the Siberian Kingdom*.[3] Except perhaps for Gmelin, Müller became

[1] *Commentarii Academiae scientarum petropolitanae* (14 vols.; St Petersburg, 1726–46); *Sanktpeterburgskiya vedomosti* (189 vols.; St Petersburg, 1726–1816, 1854–1917); *Primechaniya k sanktpeterburgskim vedomostiyam* (St Petersburg, 1732–42).

[2] In the archives of the Soviet Academy of Sciences (*fond* 21, *opis'* 4) are 36 folio volumes, bound in leather, with copies of the documents from the Siberian repositories. Those from Yakutsk comprise five volumes and total several thousand pages (G. A. Knyazev and B. A. Mal'kevich in introduction to 'Otpiska Semena Dezhneva yakutskomu voyevode Ivanu Pavlovichu Akinfiyevu o morskom pokhode yego s ust'ya r. Kolymy do ust'ya r. Anadyr', *Izvestiya VGO*, Tom LXXX [1948], Vypusk 6, p. 577 and note 1).

[3] *Opisaniye sibirskago tsarstva* (St Petersburg). Tom I was published in Russian in 1750 and reissued in 1787; Tom II was published in full only in German in *Sammlung russischer Geschichte*; separate chapters were published in Russian in *Sochineniya i perevody... (Ezhemesyachnyye sochineniya)*; Tom III remained in manuscript. Tomy I and II were again published in Russian in 1937 and 1941 as *Istoriya Sibiri* (Moscow and Leningrad) with various appendices and essays by A. I. Andreyev, S. V. Bakhrushin, and others.

probably the best informed person of his time, 'the authority', on Siberia.[1]

In the months of planning the Second Kamchatka Expedition, before leaving St Petersburg in 1733, Müller talked at length with Bering about his voyage of 1728.[2] It is quite reasonable to assume that the report of a voyage from the Lena to Kamchatka was one of the topics the two men discussed. Thus as Müller went through the local archives in eastern Siberia, he must have been on the lookout for information about the purported Lena–Kamchatka voyage. In August 1736 he arrived in Yakutsk, the administrative centre of northeastern Siberia, and it was there that he found confirmation of the voyage. In the archives he found several documents that related to Dezhnev's voyage in 1648, particularly two reports sent by Dezhnev in 1655 from Anadyrsk to Yakutsk, which gave some of the specifics as to the origin, participants, course, and termination of the voyage. Other documents provided background information.

Müller communicated this information to the authorities in St. Petersburg in the spring of 1737 in an historical sketch, 'Information about the Northern Sea Passage from the Mouth of the Lena River for the Exploration of the Eastern Regions' (document 1). One of the assignments of the Second Kamchatka Expedition was to discover whether there was a sea passage from the Lena River to the Pacific and Kamchatka. The first attempt was made in 1735 in a vessel commanded by Petr Lassenius. It failed, and most of the crew perished. A second attempt under Lieutenant Dmitriy Ya. Laptev in 1736 was made, and it too failed.[3] Uncertain whether the Admiralty College and Senate wanted a third attempt, Bering, who was then stationed at Yakutsk and was supervising these voyages from there,[4] wrote in April 1737 to St Petersburg for further instructions. With it went Müller's 'Information about the Northern Sea Passage', for its information would help to explain the conditions prevailing along the Arctic coast

[1] Gerhard F. Müller, 'Avtobiografiya...' in his 1937, pp. 147–9; Grekov, 1960, pp. 131–4, 361, note 124; Anatole G. Mazour, *Modern Russian historiography* (Princeton, 1958), pp. 16–22; Sergey V. Bakhrushin, 'G. F. Miller kak istorik Sibiri', in Müller, 1937, pp. 5–55; AN SSSR, Institut istorii yestestvoznaniya i tekhniki, *Istoriya Akademii nauk SSSR* (Moscow and Leningrad, 1958), Tom I, pp. 126–8.

[2] 'Lettre d'un officier de la marine russienne à un seigneur de la cour...', *Nouvelle bibliothèque germanique...*, Vol. XIII, Part I (1753), p. 53; *A letter from a Russian sea-officer, to a person of distinction at the court of St. Petersburgh...* (London, 1754), p. 7.

[3] Aleksandr P. Sokolov, 'Severnaya ekspeditsiya, 1733–43 goda', *Zapiski Gidrografi-cheskago departamenta Morskago ministerstva*, Chast' IX (1851), pp. 309–10, 311–13; Belov, 1956, pp. 315–17.

[4] Petr P. Pekarskiy, *Istoriya Imperatorskoy akademii nauk* (2 vols.; St Petersburg, 1870), Tom I, p. 326.

of eastern Siberia.[1] Five years later, in 1742, Müller's account appeared anonymously in *Notes to the St Petersburg Gazette*[2] under a slightly different title, 'Information about the Northern Sea Passage of the Russians from the Mouths of Several Rivers Which Empty into the Frozen Sea for the Discovery of the Eastern Regions'.[3] In this account is found the first published statement of the voyage of Dezhnev. It does not, however, appear to have attracted much attention, probably because the journal in which it appeared had a limited circulation and was printed in Russian.

Effective and widespread dissemination of the story of Dezhnev's voyage began sixteen years later with the publication by the Academy of Sciences of Müller's account of Russian voyages in the Arctic and north Pacific in the period 1636–1742. In 1751–2 Gmelin had published a four-volume account of his travels in Siberia from 1733 to 1743,[4] and in 1750 Joseph N. Delisle, the French astronomer-geographer, brother of the famous Guillaume Delisle and member of the Russian Academy of Sciences, as well as adviser to the Admiralty College and Senate, presented a map and paper in April 1750 before the French Academy of Sciences in Paris, which described the new knowledge of the north Pacific as he understood it at the time of his departure from Russia in 1747. The paper was published two years later in expanded form along with the map.[5] The Russian authorities found errors in Gmelin's account and considered Delisle's map and memoir to be 'full of gross inaccuracies and unfounded opinions and judgements'. Whereupon Müller was commissioned to prepare a refutation.[6] His first step was to publish anonymously in 1753 a 'Lettre d'un officier de la marine russienne à un seigneur de la court concernant la carte des nouvelles découvertes au nord de la mer du Sud, et le mémoire qui y sert d'explication publié par M. de l'Isle', which was then translated into English.[7] His next step was the preparation under his supervision of a map in the Academy. Several copies were printed in 1754, but not published then, for he decided to make a few revisions.[8]

[1] Aleksandr I. Andreyev, 'Trudy G. F. Millera o Sibiri' in Müller, 1937, p. 69; *Ocherki po istochnikovedeniya Sibiri*, Vypusk 2: *XVIII vek (pervaya polovina)* (Moscow and Leningrad, 1965), pp. 86–7.

[2] *Primechaniya k sanktpeterburgskim vedomostyam*.　　　　　[3] See pp. 24–5 below.

[4] *Reise durch Sibirien, von dem Jahr 1733 bis 1743…*(Göttingen, 1751–2).

[5] *Explication de la carte des nouvelles découvertes au nord de la mer du Sud* (Paris, 1752).

[6] Aleksandr I. Andreyev, 'Trudy G. F. Millera o vtoroy kamchatskoy ekspeditsii', *Izvestiya VGO*, Tom XCI (1959), Vypusk 1, pp. 3–8 *passim*.

[7] See p. 4, note 2 above.

[8] Müller, 1758a, p. 279; 1758b, Tom VIII, pp. 402–3. The map is titled 'Nouvelle carte des découvertes faites par des vaisseaux russiens aux côtes inconnues de l'Amérique

Publication of the map came in 1758 and was accompanied by the publication of a monograph entitled *Nachrichten von Seereisen, und zur See gemachten Entdeckungen, die von Russland aus längst den Küsten des Eismeeres und auf dem östlichen Weltmeere gegen Japon und Amerika geschehen sind*, which was to serve as an explication of the map. The monograph appeared in two versions, Müller's original German, in Volume III of his *Sammlung russischer Geschichte*,[1] and a Russian translation also issued in 1758, 'Description of the Ocean Voyages in the Icy and Eastern Seas Made from the Russian Side'.[2] From the German version a somewhat abridged and not always accurate English translation was made and published by Thomas Jefferys in 1761 and again in 1764.[3] A French translation followed in 1766.[4] The account of Dezhnev's voyage in *Nachrichten von Seereisen* is much longer than those of 1737 and 1742.[5] It became for the next century or so the basic and only original treatment of the voyage.

To one in a less interested age it is surprising how much importance was attached to Dezhnev's voyage, how often the story of it was retold or discussed. To be sure, it was not retold or discussed independently just for its own sake. Until more recent times the known details about Dezhnev and about it were too sparse to invite independent treatment. Rather, it appeared as part of the larger story of Russian exploration in the Arctic and north Pacific, particularly as the voyage bore on the question of a northeast passage to the orient. Interest in finding a northeast or northwest passage to the Pacific had developed almost as soon as it was realized that Columbus had discovered not a direct route westward to the riches of the Indies, China, and Japan, but a two-continent barrier foreclosing such a route. From the early 16th century on, the Dutch and English especially had been trying to find a northeastern passage around Asia to the Pacific, a route free of Spanish and Portuguese interference; but by the 18th century no western Europeans had succeeded in proceeding beyond the Yamal Peninsula,

septentrionale avec les paies adjacents...' (St Petersburg). An English translation of the map appears in Gerhard F. Müller, *Voyages from Asia to America, for the completion of the discoveries of the northwest coast of America...*(London, 1761; 1764), frontispiece.
    [1] (St Petersburg, 1758a), pp. 1–304. Because it takes up almost all of Volume III of the *Sammlung*, the *Nachrichten* is treated in citation as a separate work.
    [2] 'Opisaniye morskikh puteshestviy po ledovitomu i po vostochnomu moryu s rossiyskoy storony uchinennykh', *Sochineniya i perevody, k pol'ze i uveseleniyu sluzhashchiya* (St Petersburg), 1758b, Tomy VII, VIII.
    [3] See p. 5, note above.
    [4] *Voyages et découvertes faites par les Russes le long des côtes de la mer glaciale et sur l'océan oriental, tant vers le Japon que vers l'Amérique* (Amsterdam).
    [5] Pages 7–20.

which extends northward from the Ural Mountains.[1] Eastward advance beyond that point by non-Russians was blocked not only by the natural obstacles of ice and storm, but by enforcement of decrees by Muscovite authorities in 1616 and 1619 closing the sea route around the Yamal Peninsula.[2] Thus by the 18th century western Europeans did not know whether a northern sea route around Asia was possible, a possibility which rested on the assumption, of course, that Asia and America are separated. The matter therefore remained a question very much alive in both learned and commercial circles.[3] The only people situated to answer it were the Russians since they held dominion over practically all of the Arctic coast of Eurasia and barred passage east along the Siberian part of that coast. Hence in time Peter the Great was urged by such eminent figures as Gottfried W. Leibnitz, the German philosopher, to pursue an answer to this question;[4] and the Bering voyages served to sustain foreign interest in Russian exploration and discovery in the Arctic and north Pacific. Thus there was generated a particular interest in Dezhnev's voyage.

One of the first to publicize further the voyage was the Swiss geographer and economist, Samuel Engel. Certain that a northern water passage to India was possible, he rejected in 1765 and again in 1772 the then current contention that the cape at the eastern end of Asia was impassable, and there was no stronger support for his argument than the voyage of Dezhnev, of which he presented a condensed version.[5] In fact, he was convinced that for Russia's own selfish interest Müller and his fellow academicians were suppressing information confirming his views, and he kept up a long-running polemic with Müller, which served to keep attention on Dezhnev's voyage.

About the same time the German philologist, Johann Christoph

[1] James Burney, *A chronological history of north-eastern voyages of discovery; and of the early eastern navigations of the Russians* (London, 1819), pp. 77–83.

[2] *Russkaya istoricheskaya biblioteka* (St Petersburg, 1875), Tom II, columns 1048–95 contain the orders and reports accompanying the closure; *ORZPM*, pp. 54–5; Mikhail I. Belov, *Arkticheskoye moreplavaniye s drevneyshikh vremen do serediny XIX veka* (Moscow, 1956), pp. 116, 118; Raymond H. Fisher, *The Russian fur trade, 1550–1700* (Berkeley and Los Angeles, 1943; reprint, Millwood, New York, 1974), p. 78.

[3] Müller, 1758a, pp. 1–3; 1758b, Tom VII, pp. 3–6; 1761, 1764, pp. iii–iv; Andreyev, 1956, pp. 9–11.

[4] Fisher, 1977, p. 9 and note 2.

[5] *Mémoires et observations géographiques et critiques sur la situation des pays septentrionaux de l'Asie et de l'Amérique, d'après les relations sur les plus récentes...* (Lausanne, 1756), pp. 236–8, 241. Reprinted as *Extraits raisonnés des voyages faits dans les parties septentrionales de l'Asie et de l'Amérique ou Nouvelles preuves de la possibilité d'un passage aus Indes par le nord* (Lausanne, 1779), pp. 333–4.

Adelung, a man of catholic intellectual interests, published in 1768 a history of the voyages and attempts to discover a northeastern route to Japan and China in the belief that they deserved systematic treatment and widespread attention. Paraphrasing Müller, he related Dezhnev's exploit in all its then known details.[1]

The English, as the leading maritime people of the 18th century, continued to maintain a very practical concern for a northeastern passage. In 1780 the English scholar, traveller, and divine, William Coxe, who visited Russia in 1778–9, published his *Account of Russian discoveries between Asia and America*, which in the next quarter of a century went into three more editions.[2] Coxe devoted more than passing attention to Dezhnev's voyage. Concerned over inaccuracies in the Jefferys translation of Müller's narrative, he enlisted the aid of Professor Simon S. Pallas while in St Petersburg and examined the documents on which Müller based his narrative. Coxe quoted at some length from them, providing a few elaborative details not mentioned by Müller.[3]

The voyage of Dezhnev came in for attention not only from publicists like Coxe, but from explorers as well. The first to give attention was the noted English explorer, Captain James Cook. In 1776 the British Admiralty commissioned Cook to make a third voyage into the Pacific, this time into the north Pacific to determine the practicability of a northern passage to Europe. The expedition of two vessels spent several weeks during the summers of 1778 and 1779 in the waters north and south of the Bering Strait, examining among other areas the coast northwest of the strait, the strait itself, and southwestward toward Kamchatka. Cook was particularly concerned with Müller's depiction on the map of 1758 of the great rocky promontory which Dezhnev describes in his reports on the voyage. The observations of Cook and Captain James King, who wrote the third volume of the account of the third Pacific voyage, led them to reject Müller's portrayal of the promontory and to identify it as Cape Dezhneva, which at that time Cook named East Cape. He did so after matching the features mentioned by Dezhnev with those he observed on the voyage.[4] It was

---

[1] *Geschichte der Schiffahrten und Versuche, welche zur Entdeckung des nordöstlichen Weges nach Japon und China von verschiedenen Nationen unternommen worden...* (Halle, 1768), pp 506–12.

[2] London, 1780; 2nd edition rev. and corrected, 1780; 3rd edition rev. and corrected, 1787; 4th edition considerably enlarged, 1804.

[3] 1780, pp. 313–23; 1787, pp. 251 (misnumbered 247)–62; 1804, pp. 376–85.

[4] See pp. 212–13 above and document 34. James Cook and James King, *A voyage to the Pacific ocean...* (London, 1784), Vol. II, pp. 471–2, 474; Vol. III p. 244; James Cook, *The*

this identification that was one of the reasons Coxe added a supplement to the third edition of his account in which he compared the Russian discoveries with those of Cook and noted Cook's identification of Dezhnev's promontory as East Cape and to single out this 'earliest and most important of the Russian voyages in these parts' for renewed discussion.[1] The conclusions reached by Cook and King mark an important step forward in the recovery of Dezhnev's discovery by not only correcting Müller's error, but in providing substantial support for Müller's conclusion that Dezhnev had sailed through the Bering Strait.

Even though Müller's *Nachrichten von Seereisen* aroused much interest in Russian Arctic and Pacific exploration, no further works on the subject were published by Russian authors until the next century. Müller continued to work on a history of this exploration, but he was now concerned with the period after Bering's second voyage, with which his published account ended.[2] At the same time a greater degree of interest was being displayed in the Russian discoveries in the Aleutian Islands. It was the 18th rather than the 17th century on which attention was now being focused. That does not mean, however, that Dezhnev's voyage and the question of a northern sea passage were totally ignored.

In 1763 Mikhail V. Lomonosov, the Russian polymath, prepared an unpublished treatise for the Academy of Sciences in which he sought to demonstrate the possibility of a northern route.[3] As part of his demonstration he briefly surveyed the Arctic coastal voyages of the Russian promyshlenniks[4] and cossacks and singled out the voyage of Dezhnev as one of the most important because it 'proved without doubt the sea passage from the Arctic Ocean to the Pacific'.[5] This treatise was not published, however, until some eighty years later and then in only five hundred copies.[6] In 1785 the Empress Catherine II issued orders for an expedition, to be led by Commodore Joseph Billings, an English sea captain who had served with Cook on his third voyage, to explore the coast of Siberia from the Kolyma River to East Cape

journals of Captain Cook on his voyages of discovery (ed. by J. C. Beaglehole; Cambridge, 1967), Vol. III, pp. 430–1, 433.

[1] *A comparative view of the Russian discoveries with those made by captains Cook and Clerke*...(London, 1787), pp. 11–14; Coxe, 1787, supplement, pp. 423–7.

[2] Raisa V. Makarova, *Russkiye na Tikhom okeane vo vtoroy polovine XVIII v.* (Moscow, 1968), pp. 11–12; *Russians on the Pacific, 1743–1799* (Kingston, Ont., 1975), p. 8.

[3] 'Kratkoye opisaniye raznykh puteshestviy po severnym moryam i pokazaniye vozmozhnogo prokhodu sibirskim okeanom v vostochnuyu Indiyu', *Polnoye sobraniye sochineniy (Moscow)*, Tom VI (1952), pp. 416–98.

[4] For an explanation of this term see chapter 3.

[5] Ibid., pp. 448–9; RM, p. 86.

[6] V. A. Perevalov, *Lomonosov i Arktika; iz istorii geograficheskikh nauk i geograficheskikh otkrytiy* (Moscow Leningrad, 1949), pp. 28, 33; cf. Andreyev, 1959, p. 13.

and the waters between Asia and America.[1] Command of that part of the expedition which was to explore the coast of Siberia east of the Kolyma was entrusted to a young Russian naval lieutenant, Gavriil A. Sarychev. So formidable, however, was the ice in the coastal waters that his vessel was able to advance only a short distance east of the river, well short of Cape Shelagskiy (July 1787).[2] A result of this experience, incidentally, was that Sarychev became one of the first to express doubt about Dezhnev's voyage. Except for the fact that the Billings expedition could hardly be kept secret from the rest of the world – it was a response to Cook's voyage into the north Pacific – the Russians communicated little of their interest to the outside world until the next century.

Cook's voyage and the Billings expedition proved to be the last attempts in the 18th century to obtain answers to the question of a northern sea passage between the Atlantic and Pacific oceans. Europe's preoccupation with the French Revolution and the Napoleonic wars scarcely afforded conditions for further Arctic exploration. But with the restoration of peace after 1815 interest in the question revived almost immediately, expressing itself in renewed speculation and exploration and further publication, particularly on the part of the Russians.

The first Russian effort in renewed exploration of the Arctic was directed like the Cook and Billings expeditions to the Arctic north of the Bering Strait. This was the expedition organized in 1815 and financed by Count Nikolay P. Rumyantsev, State Chancellor and former president of the State Council, and commanded by a young naval lieutenant, Otto von Kotzebue. His route took him past East Cape in the summer of 1816, and he made use of the opportunity to examine the cape from the sea. Nothing that he and his associates saw there led them to doubt Cook's and King's identification of this cape as Dezhnev's great rocky promontory.[2a]

Meanwhile, the post-bellum years witnessed the first major controversy over Dezhnev's voyage. The Englishman, James Burney, a lieutenant in Cook's third expedition came, forth many years later with a theory which questioned some of the particulars in Müller's account of the voyage. Burney, it should be noted, however, was not the first to challenge the Müller story. Others before him had expressed doubt, and not without reason.

[1] Gavriil A. Sarychev, *Account of a voyage of discovery to the north-east of Siberia, the Frozen ocean and the north-east sea* (London, 1806), Vol. I, p. 5; *Puteshestviye po severo-vostochnoy chasti Sibiri, ledovitomu moryu i vostochnomu okeanu* (Moscow, 1952), p. 31.
[2] Sarychev, 1806, Vol. I, p. 35; 1952, p. 84.   [3] See p. 216 below.

It must be remembered that there is no record of anyone after Dezhnev who succeeded in rounding Cape Dezhneva from the Kolyma River. One of his fellow cossacks, Mikhail V. Stadukhin, sailed eastward from the Kolyma for seven days in the summer of 1649, but was forced to return in face of a rugged shore and lack of provisions (documents 15 and 16).[1] Another Stadukhin, Taras, a trader, may have reached the vicinity of Cape Dezhneva in 1667 or 1668, but was forced to cross overland to reach the Gulf of Anadyr'.[2] A third Stadukhin, Vasiliy, may have got as far as Cape Shelagskiy in 1712, but then was blown out to sea.[3] In 1735 Lassenius and 1737 Laptev, we have seen, failed to advance much beyond the Kolyma River.[4] A Siberian merchant who came from Ustyug, Nikita Shalaurov, explored Chaunskaya Bay immediately southwest of Cape Shelagskiy in 1762 and two years later tried to round that cape, but disappeared in the attempt.[5] Sarychev's futile attempt to reach Cape Shelagskiy in 1787 we have already reported.

In light of these failures it is not surprising that Müller's conclusion that Dezhnev sailed through the Bering Strait should come under question. The first publicly to question this conclusion was the Scottish historian William Robertson. In his *History of America*, first published in 1777 (Cook had not yet reached the north Pacific), he made this comment in his remarks about Russian efforts to reach America from the Lena and Kolyma rivers:

[1] See p. 172 below.

[2] *Pamyatniki sibirskoy istorii* (St Petersburg, 1885), Kniga 2, pp. 500–1; Müller, 1758a, pp. 28–30; 1758b, Tom VII, pp. 100–2; *RM*, pp. 94–5. Below (*RM*, p. 63, note 2) believes Taras to have been a brother of Mikhail Stadukhin, but that is not certain. He also believes (1956, p. 169) that the 'impassable promontory' which Taras Stadukhin crossed on foot was not Cape Dezhneva at the end of the Chukotskiy Peninsula, but Cape Shelagskiy – so does Vrangel' (1840, p. 111) – though how he reached the Gulf of Anadyr' and the mouth of the Penzhina River, which empties into the Sea of Okhotsk, Belov does not explain. What makes Stadukhin's claim puzzling is that he goes on to say that after crossing the promontory he and his men built a koch and sailed to the Penzhina River. If they had started somewhere in the Gulf of Anadyr' and went all the way by water to the Penzhina, they would have had to sail around Kamchatka into the Sea of Okhotsk, and there is no record of such a voyage before Bering's time. Burney (1819, p. 90) assumes that they did. Müller (document 1; 1758a, pp. 28–30; 1758b, Tom VII, pp. 100–1), on the other hand, doubts that Stadukhin reached the Penzhina and does not say that he crossed Cape Dezhneva. The sole source of information on this voyage is a deposition made before the Yakutsk voyevoda in 1710 (Belov, 1956, p. 169).

[3] Document 1, pp. 30–1; Müller, 1758a, pp. 39–40; 1758b, Tom VII, pp. 109–10.

[4] Ferdinand P. Vrangel', *Narrative of an expedition to the Polar sea, in the years 1820, 1821, 1822, & 1823* (edited by Edward Sabine; London, 1840), pp. lxxvi–lxxxv; Vasiliy N. Berkh, *Khronologicheskaya istoriya vsekh puteshestviy v severnyya strany, s prisovokupleniyem obozreniya fizicheskikh svoystv togo kray* (St Petersburg), Chast' I (1821), pp. 97–9.

[5] Vrangel', 1840, pp. lxxxvii–xc; Berkh, 1821, pp. 144–5; Mikhail I. Belov, 'Novyye materialy o pokhodakh ustyuzhskogo kuptsa Nikity Shalaurova', *Geograficheskiy sbornik Geograficheskogo obshchestva SSSR*, Tom III (1954), pp. 168–77.

Muller seems to have believed, without sufficient evidence, that the cape had been doubled... But I am assured from undoubted authority [not specified], that no Russian vessel has ever sailed around that cape, and as the country of the Tschutki is not subject to the Russian empire, it is very imperfectly known.[1]

Twenty-five years later Sarychev expressed the same doubt in his account of the Billings expedition. His own failure to advance no more than a short distance east of the Kolyma together with the failure of earlier similar attempts and the reports of natives that that conditions of ice and fog were somewhat more favourable than usual that summer of 1787, led him to doubt not only Müller's conclusion, but Dezhnev's veracity:

But many still have their doubts about this and think that his voyage is a story invented by him to gain the glory of a new discovery and that the whole account by Dezhnev of the shores there [Pacific and Arctic oceans] is based entirely on information received from the Chukchi.[2]

So complete a rejection of the voyage was to remain a minority opinion, but it persists in some quarters even today.

Burney, now an admiral, did not dismiss the voyage as a piece of fiction, but his theory required him to deny that it was made all the way by sea. His theory posited an isthmus, an arching land bridge, which connected Asia and America and formed a mediterranean sea north of Bering Strait. Advanced in a paper read before the Royal Society of London in December 1817,[3] this theory, though quickly challenged,[4] was not just fantasy. Rumours of land and the discovery of islands in the Arctic had led to a Russian belief in the 17th and 18th centuries that a belt of land perhaps a westward extension of North America, lay north of Asia.[5] Reading the shallow depths of the ocean north of Bering Strait, which he observed during the Cook voyages there, and the absence of tides and currents in these waters as signs of land in the north, Burney postulated his land bridge theory.[6] Burney made Cape Shelagskiy, never doubled except allegedly by Dezhnev, the Asiatic anchor of his

---

[1] (London), Vol. I, p. 457, note XL. This appears as note XIV in Vol. II, Book IV, p. 421 in the 6th edition (London, 1792).

[2] 1806, p. 36; 1952, pp. 84–5. For criticism of Sarychev's attitude toward such seafarers as Dezhnev see Aleksandr I. Alekseyev, *Gavriil Andreyevich Sarychev* (Moscow, 1966), pp. 97–9.

[3] 'A memoir on the geography of the north-eastern part of Asia, and on the question whether Asia and America are contiguous, or are separated by the sea', *Philosophical transactions of the Royal society of London*, Vol. CVIII (1818), part I, pp. 9–23, especially pp. 17–20; Burney, 1819, pp. 297–310.

[4] *Quarterly review* (London), Vol. XVIII (1817–18), pp. 431–58.

[5] Fisher, 1977, p. 52. See also p. 175 below.

[6] Others on Cook's staff shared this view ('Samwell's journal' in Cook, 1967, p. 1268).

land bridge. He accepted Dezhnev's voyage as beginning at the Kolyma, rounding East Cape, and ending on the Pacific coast of Siberia; but he had, of course, to conclude that Dezhnev and his party crossed the land bridge on foot. Burney supported his conclusion by pointing out that Dezhnev says practically nothing about his voyage from the Kolyma to East Cape except to mention an unlocated Sacred Cape, and by misconstruing the type of vessel used by Dezhnev's party. He argued that they used not koches, but *shitiki*, small boats held together by thongs and easily disassembled and reassembled. Upon reaching the cape or isthmus, the boats were taken apart, hauled overland to the other side, and put together again to continue the long journey to the Pacific.[1] Thus Burney modified Müller's account by claiming that a short segment of Dezhnev's journey was by land.

Burney's theory did not endure very long. At the order of Alexander I, the Marine Ministry organized an expedition to explore the islands and coast of northeastern Siberia from the Yana River east. Because of the demonstrated difficulties of exploring the coast from the sea, the exploration was to be undertaken from the land, the freezing of the ocean in the winter making travel offshore feasible. A young Russian naval officer, Ferdinand P. Vrangel', then a lieutenant, was assigned to lead that part of the exploration from the Kolyma River to Cape Shelagskiy. Actually he proceeded considerably east of Cape Shelagskiy, reaching Cook's North Cape (now Cape Shmidta) and Kolyuchin Bay, 1,120 km (700 miles) east of the Kolyma.[2] His exploration in 1822 and 1823 clearly established that Cape Shelagskiy was not an isthmus, and by examining the coast from that cape to North Cape he filled in the one remaining gap in the scientific exploration of the Arctic coast of Russia and Siberia. Any theory about a land bridge connecting Asia and America was shattered.[3] Fifteen years later an account of the explorations of Vrangel' was published first in a German translation,[4] then in an English translation from the German.[5] Next came publication of the Russian original,[6] and finally a French translation from it.[7] Not

[1] 1819, pp. 64, 69, 298, 301–3; cf. also pp. 92–4.
[2] Vrangel'. 1840, pp. 361–370.
[3] Vrangel', 1840, pp. 109, 110, 113.
[4] *Reise des kaiserlich-russischen flotten-lieutenants Ferdinand v. Wrangel der Nordküste von Sibirien und auf dem Eismeere, in den Jahren 1820 bis 1824*...(ed. by C. Engelhardt; 2 vols.; Berlin, 1839).　　　　　　　　　　　　　　[5] See p. 11, note 4 above.

[6] *Puteshestviye po severnym beregam Sibiri i po ledovitomu moryu, sovershennoye v 1820, 1821, 1822, 1823, i 1824 gg.*, ekspeditsiyeyu, sostoyavsheyu pod nachal'stvom flota leytenanta Ferdinanda fon-Vrangelya (2 vols.; St Petersburg, 1841).

[7] *Le nord de la Sibérie; voyage parmi les peuplades de la Russie asiatique et dans la mer glaciale, entreprés par ordre du gouvernement russe et exécuté par M. M. de Wrangell...Matiouchkine et Kozmine* (translated by Prince Emanuel Galitzin; 2 vols. in 1; Paris, 1843).

only did this multiplicity of editions testify to continuing interest in Arctic exploration, but their publication sustained attention to Dezhnev's venture, for Vrangel′ prefaced his account with a long historical introduction narrating Arctic exploration from the 16th century to 1820, and in it he gave particular attention to Dezhnev, basing his treatment on Müller's account.[1]

While Vrangel′ was engaged in his Arctic explorations, two histories of Russian voyages and explorations in the Arctic were published, the first extensive accounts of such activity since the publication of Müller's account in 1758. One was by Vasiliy N. Berkh, the historian of Russian voyages, geographical discoveries, and fur trade in the north Pacific, who took issue with Burney and sided with Müller.[2] The other was by the historian of Siberia, Grigoriy I. Spasskiy.[3] Neither Berkh nor Spasskiy added any new information about Dezhnev's voyage, and the value of their accounts is weakened by the fact that neither of them saw fit to cite or mention his sources, though Berkh, at least, is known to have used original materials.[4]

Meanwhile, doubt about the actuality of Dezhnev's achievement was kept alive by Petr A. Slovtsov, an historian of Siberia. In the first volume of his historical survey of Siberia, published in 1838, he rejected the conclusion that Dezhnev had passed from the Arctic to the Pacific through the Bering Strait. The denials of Robertson and Sarychev had been made briefly and without elaboration. Burney had accepted Dezhnev's passage through the strait, but contended that the journey had been broken by a short land journey. Slovtsov went further, denying the passage through the strait and most of the sea voyage and doing so with the most detailed argument to date. He based his denial not on any new evidence, but on a different interpretation of the data in Müller's account, some of which he badly misconstrued. He contended that Dezhnev 'boasted audaciously' (bakhvalit s derzostiyu) and took the position that those geographical features which Dezhnev described as marking the great rocky promontory around which he had sailed applied to some other cape on the Arctic coast west of the eastern end of the Chukotskiy Peninsula, probably Cape Shelagskiy; that

[1] 1840, pp. xxiii–xxxiii.
[2] Berkh, 1821, p. 88; Fisher, 1977, p. 16 and note 18.
[3] 'Istoriya plavaniy Rossiyan iz rek sibirskikh v ledovitoye more', Sibirskiy vestnik, Chast′ xv (1821), pp. 26–42.
[4] Aleksandr I. Andreyev, ed., Russkiye otkrytiya v Tikhom okeane i severnoy Amerike v XVIII–XIX vekakh (Moscow and Leningrad, 1944), p. 8; Russian discoveries in the Pacific and in North America in the 18th and 19th centuries; a collection of materials (translated by Carl Ginsburg; Ann Arbor, 1952), p. 4.

instead of passing through the Bering Strait to reach the Anadyr´ River Dezhnev had crossed overland from the Arctic coast to that river, subsequently boasting that he had done otherwise. Slovtsov also argued that Fedot Alekseyev, not Dezhnev, had been the leader of the undertaking. In short, Slovtsov questioned Dezhnev's veracity and the accuracy of his statements, as well as the conclusions Müller drew from them. That Dezhnev accomplished what more experienced and better equipped mariners of later times like Laptev, Shalaurov, and Sarychev had failed to accomplish, or like Vrangel´ had not attempted, was more than Slovtsov could accept.[1] Perhaps it should be noted that Slovtsov reached his conclusion without benefit of any knowledge of the documents Müller had used, for they were not published until after Slovtsov's death.

The first major advance in further reconstructing Dezhnev's voyage, beyond the point to which Müller had carried it, came in the middle of the 19th century with the publication of several original documents relating directly and indirectly to the voyage. In 1836 the Ministry of Public Enlightenment formed the Archeographic Commission whose task it was to select, edit, and publish historical materials. One of its publications is the twelve-volume *Supplement to Historical Documents*.[2] The Commission included in the *Supplement* many of the documents which Müller had had copied in Siberia and are contained in what are called Müller's Portfolios. Among these in particular are Dezhnev's two reports of 1655,[3] as well as a number of other documents which provide information about the setting in which the voyage was initiated and developments which occurred after it.[4] Unfortunately, some of the documents as copied contain errors of transcription, a few of which are significant, as we shall have occasion to note.[5] Nevertheless, an opening had been made for going behind the scenes of Müller's narrative of Dezhnev's voyage.

For nearly a century and a half Müller was the major and virtually

---

[1] *Istoricheskoye obozreniye Sibiri* (2nd edition; 2 vols. in 1; St Petersburg, 1886), Tom I, pp. 57–9; Tom II, p. x. As the edition more available the second edition is the one usually cited. The first edition was published in two volumes in 1838–44. Interestingly enough, Slovtsov dedicated his work to Müller.

[2] *DAI* (12 vols.; St Petersburg, 1846–72). It is supplementary to the 5-volume *Akty istoricheskiye* (St Petersburg, 1841–2).

[3] Documents Nos. 7: I and II, pp. 16–27.

[4] Tom II (1846), No. 99; Tom III (1848), Nos. 24, 57, 75, 76, 76–80, 87, and 98; Tom IV (1848), Nos. 4–6, 30, 45, and 47.

[5] Cf. Nikolay N. Ogloblin, 'K russkoy istoriografii. Gerard Miller i yego otnosheniya v pervoistochnikam', *Bibliograf*, 1889a, No. 1, pp. 1–11; 'K voprosu ob istoriografe G. F. Millera', *Bibliograf*, 1889b, No. 8–9, pp. 161–6.

the only figure in the historiography of Dezhnev and his voyage. He found Dezhnev's reports and on the strength of their data first made known that voyage to the world. Those who questioned or rejected Müller's conclusions did so on the basis of the data made available by him. The documents relating to Dezhnev and the voyage published in the *Supplement to the Historical Documents* were of his original selection. Thus this century and a half may be regarded as the first stage, Müller's stage, in the recovery Dezhnev's discovery. A second stage began late in the 19th century.

It got under way with Nikolay N. Ogloblin, a Russian archivist and member of the Moscow Society of History and Antiquities, who later published a monumental guide to the archives of the Siberian Department.[1] In those archives he found four petitions submitted by Dezhnev to the tsar, three of them requesting compensation for nineteen years of service for which he had not been rewarded. The petitions provided new biographical information about Dezhnev and confirmed, in Ogloblin's judgment, Müller's conclusions about the voyage. The first petition was written and presented to the authorities at Yakutsk in 1662; the other three at Moscow between September 1664 and February 1665. Ogloblin published an article containing these petitions in 1890 as a separate,[2] as well as in the *Journal of the Ministry of Public Enlightenment*.[3] The article announced his discovery of the petitions, reviewed the previous knowledge about Dezhnev, stated his argument in support of the traditional interpretation of the voyage, and elaborated on the new biographical data. He also gave over several pages to a critique of Slovtsov's rejection of the voyage. This publication not only contained the most extensive discussion of Dezhnev and his venture up to that time, but presented the only other source material on the voyage to appear before the Soviet period, when a new generation of scholars began to probe the archives. It took its place alongside that of Müller.

Though one could wish that these petitions added more than they do about the voyage itself, they serve to substantiate rather than deny the voyage as Müller first presented it, and from then on Russian writers and scholars accepted that presentation.[4] Meanwhile in 1898 official

[1] *Obozreniye stolbtsov i knig sibirskago prikaza* (1592–1768 gg.) (4 vols.; Moscow, 1895–1900).

[2] *Semen Dezhnev* (1638–1671 gg.). *Novaya dannyya i peresmotr starykh* (St Petersburg).

[3] *Zhurnal Ministerstva narodnago prosveshcheniya*, Chast' CCLXXII, December 1890, Otdel 2, pp. 249–306.

[4] E.g. Nikolay N. Firsov, *Chteniya po istorii Sibiri* (2 vols. in 1; Moscow, 1920–1), Tom I, pp. 21–2; *Entsiklopedicheskiy slovar'* (St Petersburg, 1893), *sub nomine*; A. K–r

recognition of this acceptance came when, at the suggestion of Yuliy M. Shokal'skiy, president of the Imperial Russian Geographical Society, Emperor Nicholas II on June 18 of that year, 250 years after Dezhnev began his voyage, ordered the name of the northeastern tip of Siberia changed from East Cape to Cape Dezhneva (Mys Dezhneva).[1]

Shortly before the Revolution, however, one discordant voice was raised amidst the Russian chorus of agreement, that of the American scholar, Frank A. Golder. Golder was then professor of history at Washington State University – he later moved to Stanford University – and a pioneer in the study of Russian history in the United States. First in an article,[2] then in the third chapter of his *Russian Expansion on the Pacific, 1641–1850*[3] he rejected almost contemptuously the contention that Dezhnev had passed through the Bering Strait. In more detail than Dezhnev's earlier detractors Golder argued that the characteristics of Dezhnev's great rocky promontory do not apply to East Cape, but to Cape Shelagskiy, as Slovtsov had argued. With no other authority than Dezhnev himself and no confirmation by his contemporaries and by the immediately succeeding generations, with the climatic and ice conditions prevailing in the Arctic, the great distances involved, and the frailty of the craft used by cossacks and their ignorance of ocean navigation, it was impossible for him to believe that Dezhnev and his companions had made the voyage around East Cape. Better men than Dezhnev tried and failed to make the passage. He may have reached the Anadyr', but if so, part of the journey was by land after being shipwrecked on the Arctic coast. Golder's treatment of the voyage gained acceptance by a number of non-Russian scholars,[4] and over the years his work has been the principal source of several non-Russian accounts of Russian activity in the north Pacific. With the increased interest and writing about the voyage by Soviet scholars and writers

[A. A. Kruber], 'Semen Dezhnev i 250-letiye so vremeni otkrytiya proliva imenuyemago beringovym', *Zemlevedeniye*, 1898, Knizhka III–IV (Moscow, 1899), pp. 190–6; A. Zelenin, 'Yakutskiy kazak Semen Dezhnev. K 250 letnemu yubileyu otkrytiya beringova proliva', *Nauchnoye obozreniye* (St Petersburg), 1898, Kniga 12, pp. 2181–93.

[1] Yuliy M. Shokal'skiy, 'Semen Dezhnev i otkrytiye beringova proliva', *Izvestiya Imperatorskago russkago geograficheskago obshchestva*, Tom XXXIV (1898), p. 500; A. K–r, 1898, p. 196; Vyacheslav A. Samoylov, *Semen Dezhnev i yego vremenya...* (Moscow, 1945), pp. 114–15.

[2] 'Some reasons for doubting Dezhnev's voyage', *The geographical journal*, Vol. XXXVI (1910), No. 1, pp. 81–3.

[3] (Cleveland, 1914), pp. 77–95.

[4] E.g. John F. Baddeley, Review of Golder (1914), *The geographical journal*, Vol. XLVII (1916), pp. 469–70; John N. L. Baker, *A history of geographical discovery and exploration* (London, 1937), p. 156; Henry W. Clark, *History of Alaska* (New York, 1930), pp. 34–5; Leslie H. Neatby, *Discovery in Russian and Siberian waters* (Athens, Ohio, 1973), pp. 42–3.

that occurred after the Revolution, Golder's position has come in for much critical attention and rebuttal from them. Indeed, most of their umbrage over the questioning of Dezhnev's voyage falls on Golder,[1] yet Golder's case against Dezhnev is essentially that of Slovtsov, whom he cites, and most Soviet critics of Golder ignore Slovtsov.

But Robertson, Sarychev, Slovtsov, and Golder were a minority in their doubt, perhaps conspicuous because they were a minority. The fact remains that for most Russian and foreign scholars Dezhnev's voyage took place as he said it did, Müller's conclusion that the voyage took Dezhnev through Bering Strait being correct. This view prevailed and still prevails, strongly underpinned by considerable research and publication carried on by Soviet scholars since World War II. The degree of research carried on by them justifies designating the post-World War II years the third or modern stage in the historiography of Dezhnev's voyage.

Meanwhile, the first scholar to answer Golder was the geographer-historian, Lev S. Berg. In 1919 he published a long article 'The Bering Strait and Its Shores before Bering and Cook',[2] in which he devoted a couple of sections to the voyage, mainly to correcting what he regarded as errors by Ogloblin and to answering Golder's arguments. He agreed with Cook's and King's identification of Dezhnev's great rocky promontory as East Cape, now Cape Dezhneva. Most of this article was later incorporated into Berg's monograph on the discovery of Kamchatka and the Bering expeditions in both its second and third editions, published in 1935 and 1946.[3] With one exception no one besides Berg published anything of importance on the voyage until after World War II. The exception was Vyacheslav A. Samoylov, a journalist living in Khabarovsk after the Revolution who became interested in pre-Petrine Russia, especially Siberia. His book on Dezhnev and his times was published posthumously in 1945.[4] Of intermediate length, it was the only other separate besides Ogloblin's to appear before the 300th anniversary of Dezhnev's voyage. It is derivative in content, but goes beyond earlier accounts in that it presents the setting and times in which Dezhnev lived and carried out his voyage. It constitutes an assemblage of all that was then known on these matters.

[1] E.g. Aleksey V. Yefimov in introduction, ORZPM, p. 48; Berg, 1946, pp. 27, 34–8.
[2] 'Izvestiya o beringovym prolive i yego beregakh do Beringa i Kuka', Zapiski po gidrografii, Tom II (1919), Vypusk 2, pp. 77–141.
[3] Otkrytiye Kamchatki i ekspeditsii Beringa, 1725–1742 (2nd edition, Leningrad; 3rd edition, Moscow and Leningrad), pp. 28–40 and 27–34 respectively.
[4] See p. 17, note 1 above.

In addition it brought together all of Dezhnev's petitions and reports in an appendix. But it was soon to become outdated in several respects. The year 1948 marks the tricentennial anniversary of Dezhnev's voyage. This circumstance led the Geographical Society of the USSR, the Arctic Scientific Research Institute of the Northern Sea Route Administration,[1] and the Institute of Geography of the Academy of Sciences to sponsor a number of public lectures and scholarly papers in commemoration of the event, some of which were published. A short popular biography of Dezhnev by Sergey N. Markov also appeared.[2] These, however, were little more than restatments of accepted information. The major contribution and step forward, evidence that the third stage in the recovery of Dezhnev's discovery had got under way, was a monograph by Mikhail I. Belov, then a candidate in historical sciences at the Arctic Scientific Research Institute and until recently one of its senior researchers. Titled *Semen Dezhnev, 1648–1948: In Commemoration of the Discorvery of the Strait between Asia and America*,[3] this monograph was based on new documentary material, chiefly from Müller's Portfolios in the Academy of Sciences in Leningrad and the Yakutsk archives in the Central State Archive of Historical Documents in Moscow. An appendix of nineteen new documents was included. He followed this work by publishing the next year a rather long article, 'The Historical Voyage of Semen Dezhnev',[4] which presented new information about the voyage, its participants and antecedents. Belov took up where Ogloblin had left off. Meanwhile, this activity was not taking place in isolation. It was part of an investigation on an increasing scale by Soviet scholars of Russian expansion in Siberia and Russian exploration and discovery in the Arctic and north Pacific. Much of the impetus for this came from the Northern Sea Route Administration, the Arctic Scientific Research Institute being the research arm of that agency.

Belov's monograph was soon followed by the publication of two one-volume collections of archival documents dealing with Arctic exploration and discovery. The first was *The Discoveries of Russian Land and Polar Sea Farers of the 17th Century in Northeast Asia: A Collection of Documents*, compiled by N. S. Orlova, an archivist, and published

[1] Now the Arctic and Antarctic Scientific Research Institute.

[2] *Podvig Semena Dezhneva* (Moscow, 1948).

[3] *Semen Dezhnev, 1648–1948: K trekhsotletiyu otkrytiya proliva mezhdu Aziyey i Amerikoy* (Moscow and Leningrad, 1948).

[4] 'Istoricheskoye plavaniye Semena Dezhneva', *Izvestiya VGO*, Tom LXXXI (1949), Vypusk 5, pp. 459–72.

in 1951 by the Central State Archive of Ancient Documents.[1] The second was *Russian Seafarers in the Arctic and Pacific Oceans*, compiled by Belov and published by the Arctic Scientific Research Institute in 1952 as part of a project on the history of the northern sea route.[2] Though there is some overlapping of contents, the two volumes are for the most part discrete. Each devotes a section to documents related to Dezhnev's voyage, though that of the second work is the longer of the two. Neither compiler turned up, with one exception, any documents that provide new information about the voyage itself. Several documents do, however, add to our knowledge of the participants and their activities before the voyage. Perhaps equally important is the fact that the documents present a much more adequate picture of the activities of service-men, traders, and hunters, of the maritime activity east of the Lena River, and of relations with the natives. Drezhnev's undertaking becomes less unusual, more credible; it may be seen as part of a considerable on-going movement into northeastern Siberia in the middle of the 17th century. Had Dezhnev's detractors known what these documents tell us, their scepticism would have been greatly tempered, if not eliminated.

Seven years after the publication of his *Semen Dezhnev* Belov issued a new edition, considerably revised and expanded, but without the documents of the first edition, most of them having been included in *Russian Seafarers*.[3] Eighteen years later Belov rewrote much of his study and published it as a third edition under the title *The Exploit of Semen Dezhnev*.[4]

Another manifestation of the tricentennial celebration was the appearance of a redaction of the report authored by Dezhnev alone in 1655. Examining the report as published in volume IV (No. 7: II) of the *Supplement to Historical Documents*, taken from a copy of Müller's Portfolios, G. A. Knyazev and B. A. Mal'kevich found several omissions of undeciphered words and phrases, incorrect readings of several words, and digressions from the manuscript text. Their corrected text, with their introduction and with notes by Berg, was published by the Geographical Society in 1948.[5]

This redaction was, however, soon to be superseded. Not long after the end of World War II a large consignment of 17th-century documents from Yakutsk held in the archive of the Eastern Siberian

[1] ORZPM. [2] RM.
[3] *Semen Dezhnev* (2nd edition; Moscow, 1955).
[4] *Podvig Semena Dezhneva* (Moscow, 1973). [5] See citation on p. 3, note 2 above.

Division of the Geographical Society at Irkutsk and from other Siberian archives was transferred to the Central State Archive of Historical Documents. In 1951 archivist T. D. Lavrentsova found at the bottom of one of the cartons the long-lost and detailed report of 1655 by Dezhnev and Nikita Semenov in which they make a short statement about the voyage. Several years later archivist B. D. Kats found the original of Dezhnev's report, recently re-edited by Knyazev and Mal'kevich, with its more detailed information about the great rocky promontory. In 1957 Boris P. Polevoy, a member of the Institute of Ethnography of the Academy of Sciences, uncovered in the consignment the original of Dezhnev's first petition, the Müller copy of which Belov had published in his *Semen Dezhnev, 1648–1948* and which he dated as of 1654 and Polevoy as of 1655. Seven years later Polevoy found the original of the petition of Yemel'yan Vetochka and his associates, who corroborate some of the statements made by Dezhnev.[1] Thus were brought to light the originals of the four documents on the basis of which Müller drew his conclusion that Dezhnev and Alekseyev had sailed through the strait between Asia and America.

It was first thought that the documents added little or nothing to what was known from the copies already published. This is true of Dezhnev's petition of 1654 and of that of Vetochka and his companions. But comparison of the other two originals with their copies revealed important differences. Whereupon Lavrentsova set about establishing exact texts of the two originals. This was not easy for they were written in a spidery, barely legible script, which helps to explain the mistakes in copying made during Müller's stay in Yakutsk. A number of words were in doubt. Lavrentsova succeeded, nevertheless, in establishing authentic texts whose corrections, especially those in the report of Dezhnev alone, force a revision of our understanding of certain aspects of the voyage and the great rocky promontory, as we shall see later. It becomes apparent too from internal evidence that the report of Dezhnev and Semenov, which had been thought to have been written first and thus was placed in the *Supplement* ahead of the report authored by Dezhnev alone, was written after the latter. So when the two documents were published, as they were in 1964, their order of appearance and numbering were reversed.[2]

[1] Boris P. Polevoy, 'Nakhodka podlinnykh dokumentov S. I. Dezhneva o yego istoricheskom pokhode 1648 g.', *Vestnik Leningradskogo gosudarstvennogo universiteta*, 1962b, No. 6, pp. 145–6; 'O tochnom tekste dvukh otpisok Semena Dezhneva 1655 goda', *Izvestiya AN SSSR, seriya geograficheskaya*, 1965a, No. 2, p. 101.

[2] *RAE*, pp. 130–43.

In the meantime, within the last two decades, a second major scholar of Dezhnev, his exploit and times, has emerged. This is Polevoy. His research has been devoted to geographical exploration and discovery in northeastern Siberia, the Arctic and Pacific oceans and to the cartography of 17th- and 18th-century Siberia, resulting in the publication of a long list of articles. Some nine of them deal with various aspects of the voyage and its antecedents, with the Kolyma area where it originated, and with the Chukotskiy and Kamchatka peninsulas. His findings have led him to some new interpretations concerning the voyage, to the point that he has become the principal revisionist of the traditional views about the voyage. This has brought him into frequent disagreement with Belov, but it has also enlarged and improved our understanding of the episode. He has to be considered a leading 'recoverer' of Dezhnev's discovery. We shall draw much from his many articles.

And now it is time to move to a more detailed examination of Dezhnev's discovery. We begin with Müller, who began its recovery.

CHAPTER 2

MÜLLER'S ACCOUNTS

Unlike many voyages of exploration and discovery Dezhnev's voyage is without any major account prepared by a participant or contemporary, nor is it recorded in a commander's or ship's journal from which a consecutive account could be written. Such record-keeping was introduced into Russia only with the creation of a Russian navy by Peter the Great. Dezhnev himself was illiterate. For more than a century the major account of the voyage and other matters related to it was that published by Müller in his *Nachrichten von Seereisen* and 'Opisaniye morskikh puteshestviy' in 1758. It became, as we noted in the preceding chapter, the basic account, derived from original sources found at Yakutsk. Even when further research on Dezhnev and his voyage was resumed late in the 19th century and continued in this century, the results until recently were an elaboration, or sometimes, a revision of Müller's account. It is, therefore, appropriate that we begin our reconstruction and examination of Dezhnev's voyage by reproducing Müller's basic account as well as his earlier account, shorter and little known, that of 1737.

Müller wrote his account of 1737 at Yakutsk in his native German, though it has never been published in that language. It was sent to St Petersburg with an abstract in French in 1737. In his *Nachrichten von Seereisen* (pp. 155–6) he says this about the provenance of this article:

At that time [of the decision to leave it up to the Senate to decide the question of a third voyage in the Arctic from the Lena] I had already assembled from the archives of the city of Yakutsk the same information about the previous voyages through the Icy Sea, some of which I have mentioned at the beginning of this account. I brought it into order and added other information about the present condition of the Icy Sea, which I also learned from persons in Yakutsk who had been on the Icy Sea. In case another attempt should be made, in order now to advance the common good I turned my manuscript over to the Captain Commander, who sent it to St Petersburg where it was incorporated in the year 1742 in the St Petersburg Notes in the form of an abstract.[1]

[1] Translated in 1758b, Tom VII, pp. 24–5, and in somewhat abridged form in his 1761 and 1764, p. 64. Aleksey V. Yefimov, *Iz istorii velikikh russkikh geograficheskikh otkrytiy v*

Two years later it was translated into Russian by Il'ya Yakhontov, the Russian translator who accompanied Müller on his Siberian travels, and sent a second time to St Petersburg.[1] It was this translation which appeared anonymously in the *Notes* in 1742 with several minor modifications of text and title.[2] More than two hundred years later that part of the 1737 account dealing with Russian exploration in northeastern Siberia was published in the Russian translation under its original title by Aleksey V. Yefimov, first in his history of Russian expeditions on the Pacific Ocean (1948) and then in his history of the great Russian geographical discoveries in the Arctic and Pacific oceans in the 17th and first half of the 18th centuries (1950).[3] A little more than half of the extract is devoted to Dezhnev and his voyage. It is presented here for the first time in English translation.

Although Müller claimed that he was the author of the 1742 version, as we just saw, his authorship has been questioned. In his history of the Imperial Academy of Sciences Petr P. Pekarskiy states that Kristian N. Vinsgeim, a member of the Academy and editor of the *Notes*, claimed to have written the article, and Pekarskiy adds that it was based on information found by Müller in the Yakutsk archives.[4] Recently Belov, after first accepting Müller as the author,[5] declared in 1973 that he believed Vinsgeim probably to be the author on the ground that there are several differences between the 1742 and 1758 accounts.[6] Knyazev and Mal'kevich tell us, however, that among Müller's papers in the archives of the Academy there is a manuscript text of his 1737 account that is almost word for word the same as the account in the *Notes*, and they therefore conclude that Müller is the author of the 1742 account.[7] Vinsgeim's claim to authorship may technically be true in the sense of having actually written down the account that appears in the *Notes*, as we shall see. But Belov makes the mistake of comparing the shorter 1742 account with the longer 1758 account written many years later. There are indeed some differences between the two

severnom Ledovitom i Tikhom okeanakh XVII – pervaya polovina XVIII v. (Moscow, 1950), p. 258, states that it was sent to St Petersburg as an attachment to Bering's letter of 27 April 1737 to Admiral Golovin, a date Yefimov says is approximate. Andreyev (1937, p. 69; 1965, pp. 86–7) writes that Müller sent it to St Petersburg in September 1737, but cites no authority. Yefimov's statement is closer to Müller's than Andreyev's.

[1] Andreyev, 1965, pp. 86–7.
[2] *Chasti* 56–60 (12–19 July 1742), pp. 223–40.
[3] *Iz istorii russkikh ekspeditsiy na Tikhom okeane*, Chast' I: *Pervaya polovina XVIII veka* (Moscow, 1948), pp. 219–28, and 1950, pp. 258–64.
[4] *Istoriya Imperatorskoy akademii nauk* (St Petersburg, 1890), Tom I, p. 479.
[5] 1949, p. 466.
[6] 1973, p. 113.   [7] Dezhnev, 1948, p. 577.

accounts; but what scholar who restates his writing several years later has not changed his mind on particular matters? A microfilm copy of that part of the 1742 article that parallels the excerpt from the 1737 account published by Yefimov was obtained for me through the Leningrad Public Library. A comparison of the two texts leaves little or no doubt that Müller was the author of the 1742 version. There are, to be sure, a number of petty to minor differences between the two: differences in paragraphing and individual words; changes in punctuation; and rewording of phrases as well as of an occasional sentence. But nothing of the content is left out, nothing is added. The most convincing evidence, however, that Vinsgeim was not the author is the reference to 'the gospodin author' in the 1742 version. In two of three places where Müller used the pronoun 'I' in his 1737 original it has been changed in the 1742 version to 'the gospodin author' and in an instance where Müller used the impersonal 'one' it was replaced by the same phrase. The retention of the pronoun 'I' in one place must have been an oversight. And once again, at the beginning of the concluding instalment of the 1742 version, reference is made to 'the gospodin author', to the doubts which he had about certain despatches. These changes can best be explained, or even only explained, as the kind of changes an editor would make, not the author. Thus we have to conclude that someone edited the Russian translation of Müller's manuscript for publication, though only superficially, and since Vinsgeim was the editor of the *Notes*, it would be surprising to learn that it was not he who did the editing. If, when he claimed that he wrote it he meant that he rewrote or copied Müller's article, then in that very restricted sense he 'wrote' the 1742 version. We may remind ourselves that savants of the 18th century were not always scrupulous in matters of attribution, and alteration of an author's text without explanation was not viewed as harshly as it is today. Knyazev and Mal'kevich are right; Pekarskiy and Belov are wrong.

Because the two texts are almost identical, there is no point in reproducing the 1742 one here. However, I deem it desirable to indicate in the notes several of the deviations of the later text from the earlier by way of showing the character and degree of alteration. The omitted few are instances of the replacement of a word by a synonym.

Document 1

1737. Information about the northern sea passage from the mouth of the Lena River for the discovery of the eastern regions. ('Izvestiya o severnom morskim khode iz ust'ya Leny reki radi obretaniya vostochnym stran').

...One has to regret[1] that the regions east of the Kolyma River are not so well known by the Russians, not so thoroughly explored, as is evident from the foregoing description of the western regions, for there are very few instances of anyone who has gone by sea in the manner of the times, [or examples] of what are the dangers from the local Chukchi and Shelagi people, who still cannot be brought completely under Russian authority. Also the so-called Chukotskoy – the same as the Shelaginskoy or Shelatskoy – nos[2] stands in the way because this nos extends far into the sea from the most distant part of the continent in the northeast and causes the greatest difficulty in the circumnavigation of it.

The short journey of the above-mentioned boyar-son Fedot Amosov from the mouth of the Kolyma to the east here could not be regarded as of any consequence,[3] although an existing small island close to the mainland was made known by him. It was impossible to hope that after that time something notable might have followed when, the maritime movement on the Kolyma having ceased, the Yakutsk cossacks' own desire for new discoveries had passed. What has already been done occurred in early times. The very first voyage undertaken with that purpose was so successful that it proceeded around the Chukotskoy nos to the Anadyr' River, which empties into the Eastern Sea [Pacific Ocean]. No instances of this after that time are known.[4]

This information about the passage around the Chukotskoy nos is so important that it merits all the above-written remarks, for it is known that heretofore no one really knew whether Asia was joined with America at this place, this doubt having given rise to the original sending of Mr. Captain Commander Bering to Kamchatka. But now there is no longer any doubt in this matter. I cannot, however,

[1] 1742: 'the gospodin author says further'.
[2] Because the character and extent of this nos (literally 'nose') are the subject of later debate and discussion, I have chosen to retain the Russian term rather than presuppose the outcome of that debate by using one of the English equivalents, which are not precisely differentiated among themselves.
[3] A reference to the unsuccessful attempts in 1723–5 of Amosov to find an island near the mouth of the Kolyma River (Müller, 1758a, pp. 44–8; 1758b, Tom VII, pp. 112–17).
[4] 1742: 'were heard'.

introduce the information here word for word, some of which I obtained about this route, because it is very poorly written, but it is necessary to state from it briefly the following:[1]

When Yakutsk cossacks reached the mouth of the Kolyma River in 1646 [sic] in the above-described manner, one of them, Semen Ivanovich Dezhnev, later in another year purposed to carry out a voyage farther east, but he could not pass beyond the great amount of floating ice found in the sea that summer, and he had to turn back to the mouth of the Kolyma and spend the winter there.

On 20 July [sic] 1648 Dezhnev departed again by sea and with him went the two koches[2] of service-man Gerasim Ankudinov and the trader Fedot Alekseyev. They passed the mouth of some river which emptied into the Icy Sea and which Dezhnev called the Chukoch'ya because of the people living along it. On the eastern side of the river a nos extends into the sea. Nothing is mentioned in connection with this route about drifting ice, difficulty of passage, or any fear. Dezhnev[3] arrived safely at the great Chukotskoy or Shelaginskoy nos with the two other koches, but the koch of Gerasim Ankudinov was wrecked on this nos, and the men in it were transferred to the other two koches. Then, nevertheless, they went successfully around the nos mentioned even though it was late in the season, for in light of the other circumstances of the voyage it is not possible to conclude otherwise, except that it was done in the month of September.

For an authentic sign of this nos Dezhnev declared that a small river emptied into the Icy Sea near it on the western side and that at that place there was, as it were, a tower made of whalebones by the Chukchi. The nos first extended very far into the sea in a northeasterly direction, then turned to the south. Opposite the nos, maybe on the western side, he saw two islands and on them people of the Chukchi nation whose lips, it was said, were pierced and teeth from walrus tusks placed in them.

Either[4] many contrary winds opposed them or they stopped often

[1] This paragraph is the part of the 1737 version most extensively revised by Vinsgeim's editing. In the 1742 version it is compressed somewhat and the reference to Bering is omitted: 'This information about the passage around the Chukotskoy nos the gospodin author considers of such importance that it merits comment especially among the above-mentioned announcements for it was made known that in this place Asia is not joined with America. But because the little information which has been obtained about this route has been written in a varied and unorganized manner, he sets forth briefly the following:'.

[2] A kind of boat, described in chapter 8.

[3] 1742: 'Both Dezhnev and the other two koches'.

[4] 1742: Preceded by 'Maybe'.

to explore the coast of the mainland, so long did their voyage continue. On September 20 Dezhnev and Fedot Alekseyev pulled in at a place on the coast and had [a hard fight][1] with the Chukchi. After this Fedot Alekseyev was separated from Dezhnev without a word. Dezhnev was carried over the sea after the Feast Day of the Intercession of Our Holy Mother [October 1][2] and was thrown ashore beyond the Anadyr′ River, that is, to the south of that river or between the Anadyr′ and Olyutora rivers.

Dezhnev declares that the Anadyr′ River is no farther from the southern end of the Chukotskoy nos that the distance that can be run in a koch in three days-and-nights[3] with an enabling wind, but he may be mistaken[4] in this because he hoped that the Anadyr′ River lies farther to the north than its true position later gave reason for what might be undertaken from it by land. He went with 25 men from the place where his koch was wrecked into the mountains not knowing the way ahead of him because there was no guide, and they suffered great hardship from hunger and cold en route. For this reason they may have hunted animals on the way to obtain food and clothing; and on account of this their journey was much prolonged so that after a passage of ten weeks without guidance they came upon the Anadyr′ River near its mouth.

I[5] will not mention here the other circumstances of Dezhnev's journey, in particular his life on the Anadyr′ River, his construction of the tribute zimov′ye,[6] his subjugation of the local Yukagirs and the collection of tribute from them, etc., which do not belong here. These remarks are sufficient: in 1650 two parties of cossacks and promyshlenniks, which were commanded by Semen Motora and Mikhail Stadukhin, came to the Anadyr′ overland by way of the Anza [Anyuy][7] River, a tributary of the Kolyma. Dezhnev joined with the first of the two parties, and on Semen Motora's death he took command of it. In 1653 Dezhnev built on the upper Anadyr′ River two koches

---

[1] Supplied from 1742.
[2] 1742: 'until October'.
[3] The Russian language has a word, *sutki*, for the day as the 24-hour period as against 'day' (*den′*) as the lighted part of the day.
[4] 1742: 'deceived'.
[5] The one place where 'I' is retained in the 1742 version.
[6] The zimov′ye was primarily a winter shelter, a cabin or hut, though it was used the year around. The native hostages, taken to assure payment of tribute (*yasak*), were kept in them. In time other structures might be added and a stockade built around them, the resulting cluster thereby becoming an *ostrozhek* or *ostrog* and an administrative centre. In the absence of a good English equivalent I retain the Russian term.
[7] 1742: 'An′a'.

with *lodki*[1] carried on them, and it was his hope to return on them from the mouth of the Anadyr′ around the Chukotskoy nos to the Kolyma and Lena rivers with the tribute collected. He did not, however, dare to do this in the absence of strong sails, ropes, and anchors, for the distance by sea is much greater, and according to the natives' reports the sea is not free of ice every year.

In the meantime the koches that were built were suitable for exploring the places located around the mouth of the Anadyr′, whereupon in 1654 Dezhnev found Koryak habitations situated in the vicinity of the sea,[2] from which, upon seeing the Russians, the men fled with their 'best' wives. The other women and slaves remained. Among them Dezhnev found a Yakut woman who had previously lived with the above-mentioned Fedot Alekseyev. The woman said that Fedot's boat was wrecked nearby, that Fedot lived there for some time, died from scurvy, and that his companions were killed by the Koryaks; the others fled in lodki to parts unknown. In connection with this there is a rumour, which circulates among the inhabitants of Kamchatka and is supported by everyone who was there,[3] namely: they say that many[4] years before the arrival of Vladimir Atlasov in Kamchatka a certain Fedotov's son[5] lived there on the Kamchatka River at the mouth of a small river, which is now named Fedotovka after him, and he begat children with a Kamchadal, who were later killed by the Koryaks near Penzhina Bay where they had moved from Kamchatka. This Fedotov's son was in every respect the son of Fedot Alekseyev, who on death of his father at the time his companions were killed by the Koryaks fled in a lodka along the shore and settled on the Kamchatka River. In 1728 during Captain Commander Bering's sojourn in Kamchatka signs were seen of two zimov′yes in which Fedotov's son and companions lived.[6]

If there were voyages eastward from the mouth of the Kolyma River that long ago, then information about them was either much in doubt or lost. Soon after the discovery of the Kolyma River there circulated the rumour about a certain Pogycha River, which emptied into the Icy

[1] Boats with oars.
[2] 1742: 'situated rather near'.
[3] 1742: 'Here may be mentioned the oral report that was supported by everyone who was in Kamchatka.'
[4] 1742: 'several'.   [5] 1742: 'a certain man, son of Fedotov'.
[6] 1742: This marks the end of the instalment in parts 56–7. The next instalment in parts 58–60 is headed by this notation: 'Conclusion of the information on the northern sea passage of the Russians'. The text begins: 'The gospodin author mentions further several communications about which he has doubts when he writes in this fashion:'.

Sea on the eastern side of the Kolyma. In July 1649 the above-mentioned Mikhail Stadukhin set out to find this river. But he did not go as far as to find such a river. However, he and the others who went with him said about this trip that they went for seven days-and-night and an enabling wind without slackening sail. Stopping on shore, they looked for people. Although they found them, neither by kindness nor torture could they obtain any information about local rivers which emptied into the Icy Sea. Since they lacked grain supplies and it was impossible to catch fish because the coast was rocky and steep, Stadukhin turned back and reached the Kolyma on September 7.

The Pogycha River may have been the one Dezhnev called the Chukoch'ya, or, since in the latest information more began to be heard about rivers which emptied into the Icy Sea between the Kolyma River and the Chukotskoy nos, one of those rivers might be designated by that name. A rumour to that effect originated on the Kolyma River from the Chukchi, about some river on the eastern side of the Kolyma that emptied into the Icy Sea and which the Chukchi called simply the Big River.

There was mentioned above the oral information according to which a statement was taken in 1710 in the chancellery of the Yakutsk voyevoda about an island existing in the Icy Sea. In this statement the following information is found about a certain ocean voyage undertaken from the Kolyma to the east.

In past years the trader Taras Stadukhin went with ninety men by sea from the Kolyma to explore the Chukotskoy nos, which was called impassable in this deposition. But they could not go around it by water, and they crossed that nos to the other side. Making new koches on the eastern side of the nos, they went along the shore to the mouth of a certain river called the Penzhina. From there they marched against the local people and took a woman prisoner, through whom they obtained information about an island which is situated opposite the mouth of the Penzhina, that men with beards lived on that island; they wore long clothing and called the Russians brothers. The island is seen from the shore. Stadukhin and his comrades were not on that island. They went back, and during that time the local people killed 81 of his comrades. Only nine men arrived on the Kolyma with Stadukhin. The purveyor of this information, serviceman Nikifor Malchin [Malgin], said that he heard the above statements from Taras Stadukhin himself on the Kolyma River, but I impute to this information, which is not quite accurate in its details, the same [doubt] as previously,[1] for it is not likely that in going along the shore for seven days without slackening sails no river would be found.[2] Even less so could it happen that a koch was built on the Chukotskoy nos because according to all information no forests exist there. Most of all, it is not known what river one must take for the local Penzhina for [if he went] to the now known Penzhina River, which empties into Penzhina Bay, named after it, Taras Stadukhin would have had a much longer route, and he would have had first to go around all of Kamchatka. However, if one wishes to defend this information, one might recognize as the Penzhina River one of the three rivers which fall into the Eastern Ocean between the Chukotskoy nos and the Anadyr´ River because there are several of them and their names are not known...

★ ★ ★

Müller's later and longer account of Dezhnev's voyage, that of 1758, appears near the beginning of his *Nachrichten von Seereisen*...(pp. 5–20) and in 'Opisaniye morskikh puteshestviy...' (pp. 7–21). It is the second voyage narrated therein. Two translations of this account from the German into English have been made previously. The first is that found in Jefferys' Müller (1761 and 1764). It contains some errors and lacks the precision desired for scholarly work. The second was made by Golder, who published it along with the German original in an appendix in his *Russian Expansion on the Pacific* (1914). It lacks, however, two initial paragraphs belonging with the account. It too has some errors of detail and, made in quite free form, lacks the desired precision. Accordingly I have made my own translation for the presentation here.

Document 2

1758. Müller's basic account of the voyage of Dezhnev and related matters.

At that time neither at the imperial court nor in farthest Siberia itself was it known in this case what had occurred and was discovered more than seventy years earlier by means of voyages which had taken place from Yakutsk in the northeastern Siberian country. A long time ago

---

[1] 1742: 'but the gospodin author has his doubts about the information for the following reasons:'.

[2] Here it appears that Müller unwittingly borrowed a detail from the report of Mikhail Stadukhin of September 1649 (see document 15).

the northeastern corner of Siberia, commonly called the Chukotskoy Nos was circumnavigated. A long time ago the Russians reached Kamchatka on this voyage. Thus it had been determined that no connection existed between both continents [Asia and America]. However, the matter had fallen into oblivion. So remarkable an occurrence might have remained concealed, despite the hints encountered in the stories of the natives of Kamchatka, had I not had the good fortune in the year 1736 during my presence in Yakutsk to discover in the local city archives the written sources in which this voyage with its particulars is described, leaving no remaining doubts.

Navigation of the Icy Sea out of Yakutsk had begun with the year 1636. The rivers Yana, Indigirka, Alazeya, [and] Kolyma became known one after the other. The last one had hardly been reached when one wanted to know what kind of rivers lay beyond it, not only to subject the people living there to tribute, but to obtain profit from the anticipated sable hunting in that area. The first excursion to the east from the Kolyma River occurred in the year 1646 with a company of volunteers called promyshlenniks under the leadership of one Isay Ignat'yev, born in Mezen'. They found the sea full of ice, but also yet a free passage between the ice and the mainland in which they sailed continuously for two days and nights. A small bay amidst the cliffs at the water's edge induced them to enter it.[1] They encountered people from a tribe of Chukchi. They traded with them no differently than did the Sirrhae (*Seres*) with strangers who came to them with this purpose.[2] The goods were spread out at the water's edge, from which the Chukchi took what pleased them and left there walrus tusks or items which were made from walrus tusks. Never were they willing to hazard going ashore to the Chukchi. Moreover, they needed an interpreter to understand the Chukchi language. They were content to have made this discovery, and they sailed back to the Kolyma River.

With the return of these men the news of the walrus tusks encouraged several hunters to undertake a second expedition the following year. For that purpose Fedot Alekseyev, a native of Kholmogory and employee of Aleksey Usov, a Moscow merchant of

---

[1] In document 3 the adjective 'small' applies to 'place', not 'bay'. The bay may or may not have been amidst the cliffs.

[2] This is an allusion to the so-called dumb trade allegedly of the Chinese (Sirrhae) mentioned by Pliny the Elder in his *Natural History* (bk. 6, ch. [xxiv]). Herodotus (*Persian Wars*, bk. ix, ch. 196) recounts a similar kind of trade by the Carthaginians, which must be why the Russian translator from Müller's German rephrased the passage to: 'They traded with them in a way the ancient writers tell about the trade carried on with wild savages.' (1758b, Tom vii, p. 9.)

the *gostinaya sotnya*,[1] formed a group and was regarded likewise as head of it. He thought it advisable to petition the commandant on the Kolyma River for one of the service cossacks who might attend to the interests of the crown on the journey. A Simeon, or Semon, Ivanovich Dezhnev offered himself for this purpose and was provided with instructions by the commandant. Four boats, which are called koches, went together under sail from the Kolyma River in June 1647. There had been reports about a river Anadyr´, or Anandyr´ according to the speech of the time, which was inhabited by numerous foreign peoples. It was believed also to empty into the Icy Sea. Hence it was one of the purposes of this voyage to discover its mouth. However, not only this, but also everything else they had intended to do ended in failure because the sea was much too full of ice that summer to permit free passage.

Notwithstanding this the men did not abandon their aroused hopes. On the contrary the number of adventurers, cossacks as well as promyshlenniks, increased the following summer to such a degree that seven koches were outfitted, all of which had the same objective. Our information is silent about what happened to four of the boats. On the three remaining ones were Semon Dezhnev and Gerasim Ankudinov, the leaders of the cossacks, and Fedot Alekseyev, foremost among the promyshlenniks. The first two got into a quarrel even before departure, for Dezhnev became jealous over the fact that Ankudinov would share in the honour of future discovery as well as in the profits associated with it. Each boat may have been about thirty men strong. At least one finds that Ankudinov listed his boat thus. Previously Dezhnev had promised to deliver from the Anadyr´ River seven 'forties'[2] of sables as tribute for the treasury, so great was his confidence in reaching this river, which, to be sure, did finally come about, but not soon and with not so little trouble as he imagined.

The 20th of June 1648 was the day on which this remarkable voyage set forth from the Kolyma River. It is, in light of the very little information that we have of that country, very much to be regretted that not all of the circumstances of this voyage are recorded. Dezhnev, who himself tells of his deeds in a report to Yakutsk, seems to say in only an incidental manner what happened to him at sea. We find nothing at all mentioned about the events up to the great Chukchi cape. No obstructions from the ice are mentioned. Presumably there was

---

[1] The highest merchant guild in Russia at that time.
[2] Furs then were baled between two boards in lots of forty.

none. Later, on another occasion Dezhnev recalled that in not every year was the sea clear of ice as at that time. His narrative begins with the great cape, which also is the same feature that deserves the most attention. 'This cape', he says, 'is altogether different from the one that is found near the Chukoch'ya River (west of the Kolyma River). It lies between north and northeast and turns in a circle toward the Anadyr´. On its Russian (i.e., western) side a brook as a landmark empties into the sea, and near it the Chukchi had erected a scaffold, like a tower, of whalebones. Opposite the cape (it is not indicated on which side) are two islands in the sea on which people of the Chukchi nation were seen, through whose perforated lips [pieces of] walrus tusks protruded. With a good enough wind one can sail from the cape to the Anadyr´ River in three days-and-nights, and by land it is likewise no farther because the Anadyr´ empties into a bay.' Moreover, it happened also on this cape that Ankudinov's boat was wrecked and the men in it were stowed into the remaining two koches. Afterwards, on 20 September, Dezhnev and Fedot Alekseyev were on shore and had a fight with the Chukchi in which the latter was wounded. Then soon thereafter both koches lost sight of each other and did not come together again. Dezhnev was driven here and there by wind and weather until October. Finally he suffered shipwreck and that, as circumstances would have it, pretty far south of the Anadyr´ River somewhere in the vicinity of the Olyutora River. What happened to Fedot Alekseyev and his party will be told below.

Dezhnev was 25 men strong, with whom he set out to look for the Anadyr´. He found it despite the lack of any guide, only, however, after ten weeks during which he wandered on foot. The country where he reached the Anadyr´ was near its mouth, in an area devoid not only of inhabitants, but of forests. This circumstance imposed on him and his companions the greatest troubles. How could they feed themselves? They could do so only very ineffectively by hunting because of the absence of wild animals, which usually roam in the forest, and they lacked the necessary tackle for fishing. In view of this twelve men betook themselves up the Anadyr´. They encountered so few men in the course of twenty days as they moved about erratically that they saw themselves forced to turn back to Dezhnev's camp, which, however, only a very few reached because of hunger and exhaustion.

The following summer, in 1649, Dezhnev proceeded by water up the Anadyr´ with his men and found a people called Anauls, who then paid their first tribute on the Anadyr´ River. Since they were in any case not numerous, and yet stubborn, they were overcome in a short time. The Anadyrskiy fort was established at that time by Dezhnev as a zimov'ye. He adopted the place as his residence. He was concerned as to how to return to the Kolyma River in the future, or how he might transmit thereto just the information of his adventure when others, who arrived there overland on 25 April 1650, showed the way to him.

On the Kolyma River they had been busy since Dezhnev's departure organizing new departures, both by water and by land whereby, if hope for the former was not realized, the country lying farther to the east would not remain unexplored. Among them is one by sea which deserves to be mentioned, not only because of the discoveries it made, but also because of the circumstances that brought it about.

In 1644 Mikhaylo Stadukhin, a cossack from Yakutsk, had built the lower ostrog on the Kolyma River with several of his companions. Thereupon he had returned to Yakutsk with some information the accuracy of which seemed to merit investigation. A woman from the tribes inhabiting the Kolyma River is reported to have said to him that in the Icy Sea lies a big island that extends from the Yana to [a point] opposite the Kolyma and could be seen from the mainland. The Chukchi from the Chukoch'ya River, which empties into the Icy Sea west of the Kolyma River, were accustomed to going to this island with reindeer over the ice in the winter and of killing the walruses there, the heads of which, complete with the tusks, they brought back and worshipped. He had not, to be sure, himself seen these tusks among these people, but he heard from promyshlenniks that they were to be found among them and that certain rungs on their reindeer sleds were made of walrus tusks. The promyshlenniks also confirmed the actuality of such an island and regarded it as a continuation of the land Novaya Zemlya, which was customarily visited from Mezen'. In addition he had heard of a large Pogycha River, also called Kovycha, which empties into the Icy Sea three or more days' journey by sea in a good wind beyond the Kolyma. A great gain for the crown was to be hoped for if a large number of cossacks was sent there, etc.

On the strength of this information and proposal Stadukhin was sent on 5 June 1647 for a second time to the Kolyma River with the order to go from there to the Pogycha River, construct a zimov'ye there, subject the local people to tribute, and collect information about the alleged island in the Icy Sea. He spent the winter on the Yana, went at the end of the winter of 1648 with sleds to the Indigirka in seven weeks, built a koch there, and proceeded on it to the Kolyma River.

Thereupon in the summer of 1649 the voyage to find the Pogycha River took place. Stadukhin, who had with him another boat, which was wrecked on this voyage, proceeded under sail for seven days-and-nights without coming upon a river. He made a stop [and] reconnoitred in order to find people. However, they too could not tell of any river in that country. The coast was rocky so they could not fish, and they lacked a sufficient supply of provisions. Accordingly Stadukhin returned to the Kolyma River. They found no signs on this journey of the alleged island in the Icy Sea that they were to search for or might find. The entire profit consisted of some walrus tusks brought back, which Stadukhin sent to Yakutsk and recommended that more should be sought, that more men should be sent there for their collection.

It had become known now that the Pogycha River was the same river as the one called the Anandyr'. It was no longer believed that its mouth should be sought in the same region. It was learned from the heathen people that it was nearer by land. This provided opportunity for the subsequent expedition. Actually one had to thank an expedition which cossacks made at the beginning of the year 1650 from the Kolyma River up along the Anyuy River for the useful information of a route by land to the Anadyr' River. What was known previously consisted only of an uncertain rumour. But here a captive was taken from the Chodyntsy tribe who himself knew how to show the way.

Immediately volunteers, some of them cossacks, some of them promyshlenniks, joined together in a company which sought by means of a petition to the commandant of the Kolyma ostrog to be allowed to go to the Anadyr' River in order to subject the natives there to tribute. This happened. Semen Motora, as the leader of these men was named, got hold on 23 March on the upper Anyuy of a respected man captured from the Chodyntsy and took him along to the Anadyr'. It was Motora who arrived on the Anadyr' on 23 April, as reported above, where he joined forces with Dezhnev. Mikhaylo Stadukhin followed him and spent seven weeks on the way. When he reached the Anadyr', he went right by Dezhnev's zimov'ye, did as he pleased, and out of jealously lived in constant conflict with him. Dezhnev and Motora wanted to avoid him by undertaking to go to the Penzhina River. But since they lacked a guide, they found themselves forced to turn back from their route. Whereupon Stadukhin set out for the Penzhina River himself, and nothing more was heard of him from then on.

Dezhnev and Motora had built boats on the Anadyr' so as to go to sea with them and discover several more rivers when the death of the latter occurred. He died in action against the Anauls at the beginning of the year 1651. However, these boats made it possible for Dezhnev to go in the summer of 1652 to the mouth of the Anadyr´ River where he observed that a sandbank stretched far into the ocean on the northern side. Such sandbanks were known in Siberia as *korgi*.[1] Walruses were in the habit of frequenting this one at the mouth of the Anadyr´. Dezhnev obtained several of their tusks and considered his efforts sufficiently rewarded thereby.

In 1653 he had some lumber cut so as to build a koch in which the tribute collected up to that time could be forwarded to Yakutsk. Because, however, the rest of the required items were lacking, the project remained unfinished. Also it was heard that the sea around the Chukotskoy Nos was not free of ice every year.

A second trip to the korga for walrus tusks occurred in the year 1654. Participating in it also was Yushko Seliverstov, a newly arrived cossack from Yakutsk, who had accompanied Mikhaylo Stadukhin on his voyage. Since he had been sent by the latter to Yakutsk with the proposal to be allowed to look for walrus tusks for the benefit of the crown, he was now provided with an order to do that. In his instructions there was specified, besides the Anadyr´, also the Chendon,[2] a river which empties into the Penzhina Gulf, at both of which he was to impose tribute on the natives, for no one at Yakutsk had then been informed of Dezhnev's exploits. Disagreement over this arose again. Seliverstov wanted credit for the discovery of the korga for himself, as if this were the place where he had come with Stadukhin in the year 1649 by sea. Dezhnev, however, insisted that by no means had they reached the great Chukotskoy Nos, which consisted solely of rocks and was known only too well to him as the place where Ankudinov's koch was wrecked. 'This is not the first nos', he says, 'which comes under the name of "Svyatoy Nos [Sacred Cape]"'. The island lying opposite the Chukotskoy Nos, with their toothed men, whom we have mentioned above, are its true proofs. Dezhnev, but not Stadukhin and Seliverstov, have seen these men, and the korga at the mouth of the Anadir River is very far removed from it.'

Meanwhile, when Dezhnev was looking around along the coast, he came upon Koryak dwellings and the Yakut woman who had belonged to Fedot Alekseyev. He asked her where her master was. She

[1] It is now believed that the sandspit visited by Dezhnev is the one on the south side. See p. 242, note 4 below.   [2] See p. 83, note 1 below.

replied: 'Fedot and Gerasim (Ankudinov) died from scurvy. The others in his party were killed. A few had saved themselves by flight in small boats without its being known what further befell them.' Traces of these last ones have been discovered in Kamchatka to which, with favorable winds and weather, they must have come while following the coast and at last turning into the Kamchatka River.

When Vladimir Atlasov laid the groundwork in 1697 for the conquest of Kamchatka, the Russians were already known to the local inhabitants. It is one of the common Kamchadal stories that a certain Fedotov, who probably was Fedot Alekseyev's son, and some of his comrades lived among them and married their Kamchadal women. They pointed out the place of Russian dwellings at the mouth of the little Nikul River, which empties into the Kamchatka [and] which for that reason is called the Russian Fedoticha. But even at the time of Atlasov's arrival none of these first Russians remained. They are said to have been so viewed and honoured as almost to be defied. No one believed that the human hand could hurt them. But afterwards the Russians fell to quarrelling among themselves; afterwards one of them wounded another and the Kamchadals saw blood flowing from him; and afterwards they separated from one another, and some of them passed over to Penzhina Sea; then they were all killed, some by the Kamchadals, some by the Koryaks. The Fedoticha River empties into the Kamchatka River from the southern side 180 versts (120 miles) below Verkhne-Kamchatsk ostrog. At the time of the first Kamchatka Expedition there were to be seen at this place the remains of two zimov'yes where Fedotov is said to have lived with his companions. On the other hand, nothing has ever been known to have been said by what route these first Russians came to Kamchatka. That became known, as mentioned above, no earlier than the year 1736 through the Yakutsk archive documents.

★ ★ ★

The longer account, as is to be expected, contains more detail, especially about the activities of Dezhnev and his associates after the establishment of Russian authority on the Anadyr' River. Even so the earlier and shorter account contains several details not included in the later one. Since they enter later discussions, they are noted briefly here.

(1) Early in the shorter one Müller explains that he can not give a detailed account of the voyage because 'it [Dezhnev's report] is very poorly written'. Presumably he could treat the voyage and later events

in greater detail in his 1758 account because he had time after returning to St Petersburg to examine Dezhnev's reports from the copies he had brought with him. Meanwhile, this remark tells us that Müller and his copyists encountered the same difficulties as the modern archivists have encountered in reading these reports, difficulties which help to explain the presence of errors in Müller's copies.

(2) In repeating Dezhnev's description of the 'great rocky nos' Müller writes that it 'extended very far into the sea in a northeasterly direction, then turned to the south' (p. 27 above). The relevance of these two details, particularly the latter, will emerge when we discuss the identity of the nos in chapter 9. Likewise for the statement that the Anadyr' River lies no farther 'from the southern end' of the nos than a run of three days-and-nights in a koch.

(3) Müller speculates on why it took the expedition so long to reach the great rocky nos and to go from the point of shipwreck to the Anadyr' as he does not in his later account.

(4) Müller tells us in this account that Dezhnev built 'two koches with lodki attached to them' in the hope of returning to Yakutsk. The reference to the lodki, a kind of small boat propelled by oars, gives an indication of the size of the koches Dezhnev and his associates used.

CHAPTER 3

MÜLLER'S SOURCES

Müller's account of Dezhnev's voyage is, as he tells us, based on documents which he found in the government archives in Yakutsk, a large number of which were copied and taken back to St Petersburg and deposited with the Academy of Sciences. However, no more than any other scholar in the 18th century did he think of citing specific documents in support of his statements and conclusions. Thus we are left for the most part to figure out on our own from which particular documents he drew the information for his account. Since his account was not confined to the voyage alone, but touched on its antecedents and aftermath, as well as concurrent developments, the documents he used were not restricted to the voyage alone. Had they been, they would have been few indeed. To determine from which documents Müller drew his information one has to depend on their contents, and that is what we have done in selecting the documents for translation and presentation here.

Before proceeding to a discussion of these documents, however, certain explanation are in order. First, although all of the documents reproduced in this and the next chapter have been published (I have not had access to unpublished ones), I have thought it desirable to indicate the archival location of them, except, of course, in the case of six excerpts from secondary accounts, included here for the sake of convenience. These archival documents are found in four fonds (*fondy*) or record groups in Soviet depositories.[1] Two of the fonds and a part of a third are contained in the Central State Archive of Historical Documents in Moscow (TsGADA). The remaining part of the third is found in the Archive of the Academy of Sciences of the USSR (AAN). The fourth fond is housed in the archive of the Leningrad Division of the Institute of History of the Academy of Sciences (LOII).

[1] The *fond* is the basic and broadest organizational unit within Soviet repositories, a type of archival grouping which derives from the practice of some European archives. The closest, but not identical, technical equivalent in British archival terminology is the concept of the 'archive group', or in American usage the 'record group' (Patricia K. Grimsted, *Archives and manuscript repositories in the USSR, Moscow and Leningrad* [Princeton, 1972], p. 64 and note 2).

The collection in longest use is that of Müller's portfolios, divided between AAN and TsGADA.[1] As we noted in chapter 1, all of the documents in these two fonds are copies, still of much value because many of the originals have not yet been found or have been lost or destroyed. The documents from Müller's portfolios presented here, ten in number, are all from the AAN.

The second fond, from which an equal number of documents is presented, is that of the Yakutsk Prikaznaya Izba or voyevoda's chancellery (YaPI), found in TsGADA (*fond* 1177). According to Belov on the initiative of the local Yakutsk authorities the historical archives at Yakutsk were broken up between 1839 and 1845.[2] The more important materials from the founding of Yakutsk to the beginning of the 18th century were sent to the Archeographical Commission in St Petersburg. Meanwhile, in the 1840s and 1850s more than 8,000 rolls of the Yakutsk chancellery were burned.[3] The documents sent to the Archeographic Commission were, evidently, later transferred from it to TsGADA. In this century, after World War II, a large consignment of Yakutsk documents from the Eastern Siberia division of the Geographical Society of the USSR at Irkutsk and other archives were transferred to TsGADA.[4] It is from this consignment that the originals of Dezhnev's petitions and two reports and of Vetoshka's petition were recovered. No doubt a considerable number of the documents in the YaPI fond are duplicated by copies in Müller's portfolios, but the presence of the originals makes the copies less important.

The third fond is that of the Siberian Department (no. 214), from which Ogloblin drew Dezhnev's four petitions of 1662–5. This fond has remained intact since the early 18th century. In the 19th century it was placed in the archive of the Ministry of Justice, the most advanced of the government archives in that century. After the revolution it was transferred to TsGADA.[5]

The fourth fond, the Yakutskiye Akty (YaA) in the Leningrad Division of the Institute of History, has a somewhat different origin. In 1848 a Yakutsk citizen, one Mikhaylov by name, gave to the Archeographic Commission 49 cartons containing 1,116 rolls of

---

[1] The bulk of the documents which Müller brought back from Siberia are in his 'portfolios' in the Archive of the Academy of Sciences in Leningrad (AAN), *fond* 21, *opis'* 4, and in the Central State Archive of Historical Documents in Moscow (Tsentral'nyy Gosudarstvennyy Arkhiv Drevneyshikh Aktov or TsGADA), *fond* 199 (Andreyev, 1965, pp. 78–9; Müller, 1937, p. 543; Boris O. Dolgikh, *Rodovoy i plemennoy narodov Sibiri v XVII v.* [Moscow, 1960] p. 5). For those in AAN see p. 3, note 2 above.

[2] *RM*, pp. 20–1.   [3] *RM*, p. 21, note 3.

[4] Polevoy, 1965a, p. 101.   [5] Belov in *RM*, p. 20; Dolgikh, 1960, p. 4.

transactions of the Yakutsk chancellery.[1] These rolls along with the other records of the Archeographic Commission were placed in the main repository of the Academy in Leningrad after 1929 when several archives were consolidated there under LOII. They remain there in the oldest of Academy archives though the archival headquarters were transferred to Moscow in 1963.[2] Three of the documents translated here come from that fond.

Second, a word needs to be said about the calendar in use in Dezhnev's time, before its reform by Peter the Great in 1700, for the dates in the documents are expressed according to it. The calendar used by the Russians in the 17th century dates from the supposed year of the creation of the world, 5509/8 B.C. The years of the 17th century fell in century 7100. Customarily the years were expressed with the last three figures, the initial '7' being dropped. The year began on September 1. To arrive at the year according to our contemporary calendar one subtracts 5508 from the year of the old calendar if the month and day fall between January 1 and August 31; 5509 if between September 1 and December 31.[3] Thus Dezhnev's voyage got under way on 20 June [7]156 according to the old calendar, and he was thrown ashore some time after 1 October [7]157. We have retained the years of the dates in the documents according to the old calendar, showing the year according to the Julian calendar in brackets. The days and months in the text are according to the Julian, not the Gregorian calendar, which in the 17th century was ten days behind the latter calendar.

Third, it should be noted also that several kinds of documents appear in the translations. Most common are reports and petitions. The difference in purpose between the two should be self-evident, but the nature of the contents is often the same. Two of the documents selected are a travel document and customs declaration. Every Russian in Siberia had to account for the goods he carried, whether for sale or for his own use. Lists and receipts issued by customs agents, usually private traders or promyshlenniks pressed into government service for periods of two to four years and called 'sworn-men' (*tseloval'niki* – literally 'cross-kissers') by virtue of the oath they took (by kissing the cross and Bible) to carry out their duties responsibly.[4] A fourth kind of

---

[1] Belov in *RM*, p. 21. [2] Grimsted,

[3] *ORZPM*,

[4] Such men drawn from the business community were better qualified than the average service-man to deal with the sovereign's business and financial affairs. Also they afforded a kind of protection against financial abuses on the part of the voyevodas. In the smaller

document is the *rasprochnaya rech'* or deposition, containing information given by a man from the field under questioning by higher officials. Such documents, particularly the first two categories, were submitted both by the men in charge of the outposts, the *prikaznyye lyudi* or commandants below the rank of voyevoda,[1] by the voyevodas and other high officials at the major administrative centres like Yakutsk, and by the service-men or cossacks and promyshlenniks who carried out exploration, subjection of the natives, collection of tribute, and guarding of the hostages taken to assure payment of tribute.

Two classes of individuals provided the manpower for the Russian conquest of Siberia. (1) The service-men, comprising several ranks of military servitors – atamans, boyar-sons, *sotniki, pyatidesyatniki, desyatniki* (commanders of one hundred, fifty, and ten men respectively), and the rank and file cossacks.[2] Theirs was a military service of an often informal sort. It was they who searched for new lands and went out to collect the tribute from the natives. The cossack, the most common type of service-man, was not, it should be noted, the freebooting, semi-independent frontiersman associated in the popular mind with the rivers of southern Russia.[3] (2) Private individuals, comprised of merchants' agents (*prikazchiki*), traders, trappers and hunters, or *promyshlenniki*. The last-named engaged largely in the fur trade, the sable being the principal objective of most of them, as it was for the state. But reports of precious metals and the ivory of the walrus tusk, as we shall see, exerted an equally powerful attraction for them. Some promyshlenniks worked on their own with small amounts of capital (*svoyeuzhinniki*), though their transportation in Siberia might be provided by the state or wealthier merchants' agents. Others, without capital, hired out their labour as trappers and hunters (*pokruchenniki*).[4] There is no good English equivalent for the term promyshlennik so it is retained here in its Russian form and treated like an English word.

The important thing to bear in mind is that the distinction between these two classes of men was blurred, not at all sharp. Many service-men engaged in trade and trapping on their own, sometimes illegally, and

outlying outposts the sworn-man stood as second in command to the commandant, though with restricted authority. (George V. Lantzeff, *Siberia in the seventeenth century*...[Berkeley and Los Angeles, 1943], pp. 117–20.)

[1] Lantzeff, 1943, p. 60. The voyevoda was the chief town official with a wide range of authority. As the title suggests, he was a military governor with responsibility for both military and civil matters (Lantzeff, 1943, pp. 8, 47–53).

[2] Lantzeff, 1943, p. 12, note 44.

[3] For a short discussion of the Siberian cossack see Lantzeff, 1943, pp. 67–9.

[4] Vladimir Dal', *Slovar' zhivogo velikorusskago yazyka, sub nomine*.

so acquired wealth on their own. Conversely, many traders and promyshlenniks engaged in state service, sometimes as volunteers, sometimes at the request of local commandants, for manpower on the eastern frontier was often in short supply. Such service could be remunerative for the promyshlenniks.[1] The survivors in Dezhnev's party were promyshlenniks who rendered service for the state on the Anadyr's River (document 32). Such service did not preclude trade and hunting on their own. When operating independently promyshlenniks also searched out new unexploited lands for fur-bearing animals and not infrequently called attention of the authorities to lands open to conquest.[2] Socially the origins of the cossacks and promyshlenniks were much the same.

We turn now to the documents themselves. The first of the fifteen documents utilized by Müller and presented here is a report in 1647 from the commandant on the Kolyma River, Vtoroy Gavrilov, to the voyevoda at Yakutsk in which he briefly notes the expedition of Isay Ignat'yev in 1646 with the episode of dumb trade with the Chukchi and tells of authorizing the voyage of Dezhnev and Alekseyev to the Andyr' River that had to be aborted (document 3).

Document 3

After June 1647. Report of service-man Vtoroy Gavrilov and associates from the Kolyma River to Yakutsk voyevoda Petr Golovin about the voyage of Isay Ignat'yev and the first voyage of Semen Dezhnev and Fedot Alekseyev to the east.

From the Kovyma[3] ostrozhek service-man Ftorko Gavrilov and associates make obeisance to stol'nik[4] and voyevoda Petr Petrovich Golovin of sovereign tsar and grand prince of all Rus', Mikhail Fedorovich.

In the summer of the past year 154 [1645–6] nine promyshlenniks went to sea in a koch to sail onward from the mouth of the Kovyma River: Isayko Ignat'yev Mezenets, Semeyka Alekseyev Pustozerets, and companions. They returned to us on the Kovyma River [and] under questioning stated: They ran under sail for two days-and-nights over the great sea along the frozen shore alongside cliffs and reached a bay

---

[1] Fisher, 1943, p. 30; Lantzeff, 1943, pp. 70–1; Bakhrushin, 1951, p. 91.
[2] Fisher, 1943, pp. 32–3.
[3] 'Kovyma' rather than 'Kolyma' was a common spelling in Dezhnev's time.
[4] A court title meaning 'table attendant'; originally a court dignitary who attended the tsar's table.

in which were found people who are called Chukchi. They traded with them at a small place. Because they had no interpreter, they did not dare go to those on shore from the vessel. They carried goods to them on shore and [then] left. The natives placed fish tooth bone [i.e., walrus tusks] there, though not a whole tusk. Crowbars and axes were made from the tusks. They said that many of these animals lie in the ocean at that place.

On the...day of June of the present year 155 [1647] Fedotka Alekseyev of Kholmogory, agent of Moscow merchant of the gostinaya sotnya, Aleksey Usov, went to sea with twelve men, [his] employees. Other promyshlenniks, self-employed, got together, and more than fifty joined forces and went in four koches to search for fish tooth bone and sable hunting grounds. Fedotka Alekseyev and companions [came] to us in the main office (*s'ezzhaya izba*)[1] and made a request for a service-man [to go] with them. Service-man Semeyka Dezhnev of Yakutsk ostrog made his obeisance to the sovereign out of interest for profit and presented a petition in the main office. In the petition he pledged a return of seven forties of sables for the sovereign on the new river Anandyr'. We sent Semeyka Dezhnev with the trader Fedot Alekseyev for that profit and to look for other new rivers and any place where the sovereign's profit might be made. We gave them instructions that wherever they found people not paying tribute, they were to take hostages, collect tribute from them, and bring them under the sovereign's exalted hand, etc.

AAN, *fond* 21, *kniga* 30, *no.* 114. Copy. Also designated as Portfeli Millera, *no.* 30, *list* 303.

Published in: Belov, 1948, Appendix, pp. 134–5; *RM*, pp. 110–11.

★ ★ ★

The next three documents (nos. 4–6) relate to the provenance of the voyage of Dezhnev and Alekseyev the next year: no. 4 – the report of the local authorities on the Kolyma River stating that they had authorised a second attempt to sail to the Anadyr' River and had placed Dezhnev in charge; no. 5 – the petition of Gerasim Ankudinov to replace Dezhnev as the state's representative on the expedition; no. 6 – Dezhnev's petition in rebuttal.

[1] Lantzeff, 1943, p. 58.

Document 4

June 1648. Report of Lena service-man Vtoroy Gavrilov and sworn-man Tret'yak Ivanov Zaborets from the Kolyma River to the Yakutsk voyevodas Vasiliy Pushkin and Kiril Suponov and d'yak Petr Grigor'yevich Stenshin about the second expedition of Semen Dezhnev and Fedot Alekseyev to the Anadyr' River.

Lena service-man Ftorko Gavrilov and sworn-man Tren'ka Ivanov and associates make obeisance to voyevodas Vasiliy Nikitich and Kiril Osipovich and d'yak Petr Grigor'yevich of the sovereign tsar and grand prince of all Rus', Mikhail Fedorovich.

In the past year 155 [1646–7] Lena service-man Semeyka Ivanov Dezhnev made obeisance to the sovereign and submitted a petition [to go] to the new river Anandyr'. Semeyka did not reach the new river. He returned from the sea and spent the winter on the Kovyma River. In the present year 156 [1647–8] this same Semeyka Dezhnev made obeisance to the sovereign and submitted a petition to me, Ftorko, [to go] to the same new river Anandyr' in the interest of profit, and he pledged seven forties plus five sables from that new river from the natives. I released Semeyka to the new river Anandyr' from the Kovyma River in accordance with that petition and gave instructions to him as well as to the trader Fedot Alekseyev. For gifts to the natives he was given the sovereign's goods, ten heavy clubs.

AAN, *fond* 21, *kniga* 30, *no.* 148. Copy. Also designated as Portfeli Millera, *no.* 30, *list* 330 *oborot*.

Published in: Belov, 1948, Appendix, pp. 135–6; *RM*, p. 111.

Document 5

Before 20 June 1648. Petition of Lena service-man Gerasim Ankudinov to be sent instead of Semen Dezhnev from the Kolyma ostrog to the Anadyr' River for tribute collection.

Your sovereign's slave, service-man Gerasimko Ankidinov, makes obeisance to the sovereign tsar and grand prince of all Rus', Mikhail Fedorovich.

Merciful sovereign tsar and grand prince of all Rus', Mikhail Fedorovich, please order me your slave sent from the Kovyma ostrog to the new river Anandyr'. In this present year 156 [1647–8] Lena service-man Semen Ivanov [Dezhnev] submitted to you, sovereign, a petition for the same new river Anandyr´, and that service-man pledged to you, sovereign, returns of five forties plus ten [210] sables. I, your sovereign's slave, will take for you, sovereign, into the treasury seventy more sables than Semen's profit from the new non-tribute paying people from the new river Anandyr´. Altogether I will take for you, sovereign, seven forties of sables as tribute from the new non-tribute paying natives from the new river Anandyr´ and will seek profit for you, sovereign, along other adjacent rivers and will bring the non-tribute paying people under your sovereign's exalted and mighty hand. I, your sovereign's slave, will take my own possessions and boat on your sovereign's service, and I will take my own firearms, powder, and various pieces of equipment. Those promyshlennik volunteers who wish to serve you, sovereign, with me will be listed by name in the main office in the Kovyma ostrozhek.

Sovereign tsar, have mercy, please.

On the verso: service-man Rod'ka Grigor'yev appends his signature in place of service-man Gerasim Ankidinov according to his request.

TsGADA, YaPI, *stolbets 95, list 4.*

Published in: Yefimov, 1950, Appendix, Part I, pp. 241–2; *ORZPM,* pp. 253–4; *RM,* p. 112.

Document 6

Before 20 June 1648. Petition of Lena service-man Semen Ivanov Dezhnev about the lawless intentions of service-man Gerasim Ankudinov.

Your slave, Lena service-man Semeyka Ivanov Dezhnev, makes obeisance to the sovereign tsar and grand prince of all Rus´, Mikhail Fedorovich.

In the present year 156 [1647–8] I addressed the sovereign and submitted a petition in the Kovyma ostrozhek to Lena service-man Ftoroy Gavrilov and sworn-man Tret'yak Zaborets for purposes of profit, and I pledged to you, sovereign, a return of seven forties and ten sables from the new river Anandyr´. In the present year 156 Gerasim Ankudinov, wanting with larcenous intent to take over your sovereign's service and the profit which I, Semeyka, pledged, drew to himself about thirty outlaws. They want to assault the traders and promyshlenniks who will be going with me to the new river and to rob them of their possessions. They want also to assault the natives from whom I have pledged a profit. I, your slave, am the one who is to participate in your sovereign's service with these traders and promyshlenniks and to collect a profit. On account of their lawlessness, their desire to assault and rob, the traders and promyshlenniks do not dare to go to the new river because Gerasimko Ankudinov [and] his outlaw conspirators want to assault them and steal their property.

Merciful sovereign tsar and grand prince of all Rus', Mikhail Fedorovich, have mercy on me, your slave, and order voyevodas Vasiliy Nikitich Pushkin and Kiril Osipovich Suponev and d'yak Petr Griogoriyevich Stenshin at the Lena ostrog to accept this my pledge and to sign it so that they will know of the lawlessness by which these outlaws wish through your sovereign's service to take over the profit and so that in the end I do not perish from their outlawry [whereby] they wish to attack the traders and promyshlenniks and natives from whom I pledged a profit. Sovereign tsar, have mercy, please.

AAN, *fond* 21, *kniga* 30, *no.* 149. Copy.
Published in: Belov, 1948, Appendix, pp. 136–7; *RM*, pp. 113–14.

★ ★ ★

The seventh document is a petition from one Ivan Baranov, who is not mentioned by Müller, though a copy of the petition is in his portfolios. His petition mentions participating in an aborted voyage to the east, which suggests that he took part in the voyage of 1647. He appears not to have been a member of the expedition next year. His petition testifies to the drainage of manpower on the Kolyma River caused by the second voyage.

Document 7

After 20 June 1648. Excerpts from the petition of Yakutsk service-man Ivan Baranov about his service on the Lena, Yana, Indigirka, and Kolyma rivers; about his unsuccessful trip by sea to the Anadyr' River; and about his request to be accepted for service on the Kolyma River.

Your Lena service-man Ivashko Baranov makes obeisance to the sovereign tsar and grand prince of all Rus', Mikhail Fedorovich.

In the year 151 [1642–3] I, your slave, was sent from the Yakutsk ostrog to the Yanga [Yana] River on your sovereign's service with boyar-son Vasiliy Vlas'yev for your sovereign's collection of tribute. In the past year 151 we collected tribute with profit for you, sovereign, from the Yakut natives on the Yanga River. I, your slave, crossed over

from the Yanga to the Indigirka River with boyar-son Vasiliy Vlas'yev.
In the past year 153 [1644–5] I, your slave, crossed over from the
Yndigirka to the Kovyma River. For two years, the years 154 [1645–6]
and 155 [1646–7], I, your slave, participated in all sorts of your
sovereign's service for you, sovereign, together with the service-men
at the lower tribute zimov'ye on the Kovyma River. Tribute was
collected for you, sovereign, in full and with profit in those years 154
[1645–6] and 155 [1646–7] from the native Yukagirs. I, your slave,
performed all kinds of your sovereign's service on the Kovyma River
together with the service-men, and I went on expeditions...

In the past year 155 the natives made known to me, your slave, the
new river Anandyr' and other nearby rivers. I, your slave, went by sea
to that new river Anandyr' for exploration and subjection under your
sovereign tsar's exalted hand for your sovereign's tribute collection in
the new lands. On account of my sins there was at that time impassable
ice in the sea. I returned from the sea, sovereign, [and] wintered on
the Kovyma River, unaccepted by service-man Vtoroy Gavrilov.[1] In
the present year 156 [1647–8], sovereign, the promyshlenniks who serve
you, sovereign, on the Kovyma River, by virtue of petitions at the
tribute zimov'yes, went from the Kovyma River to the new Anandyr'
River, and others went to Rus'. There is no one at these tribute
zimov'yes, sovereign, to perform your sovereign's various services
because there are few service-men.

Merciful sovereign tsar and grand prince of all Rus', Mikhail
Fedorovich, please order me, your slave, to perform your sovereign's
various services on the Kovyma River.

AAN, *fond* 21, *kniga* 30, *no.* 147. Copy.
Published in *RM*, pp. 114–15.

★ ★ ★

Documents 8–10 are the petition and two reports authored by Dezhnev.
An illiterate, he did not write them himself, but dictated them to
someone else, presumably Nikita Semenov, his co-commandant on
the Anadyr' River and co-author of the second report.[2] Together with
documents 11 and 28 these three documents are the main sources concerning Dezhnev and his voyage.

[1] Belov (*RM*, p. 115) comments that if Baranov is to be believed, he was one of the
first to hear of the Anadyr' River and one of the first to try, in the summer of 1647, to
go there by sea. It is possible that Baranov is saying here that he participated in Dezhnev's
and Alekseyev's aborted expedition of that year.
[2] *ORZPM*, p. 46; Polevoy, 1965a, p. 101.

The petition, first and shortest of the three documents is brief. It requests compensation for the expenditures and hardships incurred while going by sea from the Kolyma to the Anadyr´ and while serving on the latter river. It is Dezhnev's first mention of the success of the voyage, but other than a reference to going 'by the great sea-ocean', it contains no other information about the voyage. The petition carries no date of writing, despatch, or delivery. Belov first dated the writing in February–March 1654, though without explanation.[1] Four years later he dated it as no later than the winter of 1654–5, probably in the autumn of 1654, on the assumption that service-man Danil Filipov, who carried it to Yakutsk for delivery, left the Anadyr´ that winter.[2] Lavrentsova states that the original of the petition, as against Müller's copy, indicates that Filipov left the Anadyr´ on 5 April 1655 (163).[3] Thus it had to have been written before that date, and it could have well been at the time Belov sets forth. Polevoy asserts, without explanation, that it was written in 1655.[4]

The petition was first published in 1948 and again in 1952 from the copy in Müller's portfolios. The original was found in 1956, but since it contained only a few discrepancies in spelling from the copy it has not been published. Neither Müller nor the editors of the Archeographic Commission seem to have attached importance to it, perhaps because Müller's conclusion had not yet been subject to enough attack to make this additional bit of evidence seem needed.

Document 8

Before 1 September 1654. Petition of Semen Dezhnev, commandant of the Anadyrsk zimov'ye, to tsar Aleksey Mikhaylovich about payment of his salary and his relief as commandant on the Anadyr´ River.

Your slave, service-man Semeyka Ivanov Dezhnev of Yakutsk ostrog, makes obeisance to the sovereign tsar and grand prince of all Rus´, Aleksey Mikhaylovich.

In the past when your sovereign's stol'nik and voyevoda Petr Petrovich Golovin came to the Lena ostrog [Yakutsk], he sent me, your

---

[1] 1948, p. 139. [2] RM, pp. 118–19.
[3] RAE, p. 128.
[4] 1965a, p. 101. There is one conflicting datum in this dating, however, Filipov, in a brief report from Zhigansk on the lower Lena, which he reached on August 16 – the year is not specified – and where he stopped because of freezing weather en route to Yakutsk with a pud of walrus tusks from Dezhnev and Semenov, states that he left the Anadyr´ 'in the year 162', which means that he departed before 1 September 1654, seven months or more before the time cited by Lavrentsova (RM, p. 133). Was this a slip of the pen?

slave, on your sovereign's service to the Yemekon River. From the Yemokon I went on to the Kovyma River by sea. On the Kovyma River I, your slave, captured hostages; and for these hostages their kinsmen paid tribute to you, sovereign, at that place in accordance with their numbers, permanently and regularly.

In the past year 155 [1647] I was sent on your sovereign's service to the new river Anandyr´ by the great sea-ocean, but that year the ice did not permit it. I, your slave, returned to the Kovyma River and spent the winter there. The winter having passed, I was sent again to the same new river Anandyr´ by way of the same great sea-ocean and accepted great want, impoverishment, and shipwreck, and in the course of these activities and shipwreck I reached the Anandyr´ River. [I served] for many years in your sovereign's service without your sovereign's grain and money salary. While on your sovereign's service on the Anandyr´ River I bought fishing tackle [and] salmon nets for thirty roubles, a skein of twine for five roubles, an arshin [28 inches] of canvas for two roubles, a pound of powder for five roubles, a pound of lead for one rouble. I, your slave, have become impoverished and have incurred many debts.

Merciful sovereign tsar and grand prince of all Rus´, Aleksey Mikhaylovich, grant me, your slave, your sovereign tsar's salary and a change of commandant on the Anandyr´ River so that I do not finally perish. Sovereign tsar, have mercy, please.

AAN, *fond* 21, *kniga* 31, *no.* 66. Copy. Original is in TsGADA, YaPI, *fond* 1177, *opis´* 3, 1656, *no.* 18, *list* 1.

Copy published in: Belov, 1948, Appendix, pp. 139–40; *RM*, p. 118.

★   ★   ★

The second of the three documents is the report from Dezhnev alone. It contains more details about his voyage than any other document. It and the next one are the indispensable documents about the voyage. Without them we would know little concerning it. It is from them that Müller drew his conclusion that by going all the way by sea from the Kolyma to the Anadyr´ Dezhnev had demonstrated that a sea separated Asia and America. One passage in it gives a lean account of his voyage up to the point at which his vessel was thrown ashore south of the Anadyr´. It is followed by just as lean an account of his wandering to the Anadyr´ and the fate of half of his party. A third passage describes in some detail the great rocky promontory which impressed Dezhnev and whose identification of it as the eastern tip of Asia is essential to

Müller's conclusion. A fourth passage tells briefly of the fate of Alekseyev and the cossack leader Ankudinov. Like the preceding document it carries no date of writing. Lavrentsova sets the period within which it must have been written as 1 September 1654 to 5 April 1655. In the report itself the latest year mentioned is '162' (1653–4), and it is referred to as 'the past year 162', which ended 31 August 1654. On the back of the last sheet is the notation that Danil Filipov delivered the report in Yakutsk 11 April 1656. Lavrentsova notes that another report, i.e., Dezhnev's petition, delivered with it carried the notation that Filipov was sent from the Anadyr' with a pud (36 pounds) of walrus tusks on 5 April '163' (1655).[1] The translation here was made from the original of Dezhnev's report as established by Lavrentsova, whose text supersedes the Müller copy published in 1851 in the Supplements to Historical Documents[2] and the version as edited by Knyazev and Mal'kevich in 1948.

Document 9

Between 1 September 1654 and 5 April 1655. Report of service-man Semen Dezhnev to Yakutsk voyevoda Ivan Petrovich Akinfiyev about a journey by sea to the Anadyr' River and the fate of his companions.

Service-man Semeyka Ivanov Dezhnev makes obeisance to voyevoda Ivan Pavlovich [Akinfiyev] and d'yak Osip Stepanovich, in the service of sovereign tsar and grand prince of all Rus', Aleksey Mikhaylovich, at the Lena ostrog.

In the past year 156 [1648] on the 20th day of June, I, Semeyka was sent from the Kovyma River to the new river Onandyr' to search for new people not paying tribute. On the 20th day of the month of September in the past year 156 [1648], while going by sea from the Kovyma River, the Chukchi wounded trader Fedot Alekseyev in a fight at a place of shelter. Fedot become separated from me, Semeyka, at sea without further news and after the Feast Day of the Intercession of the Holy Virgin [i.e., October 1] I was carried everywhere against my will and cast ashore on the forward end beyond the Onandyr' River.[3] There were twenty-five of us altogether in the koch. Cold and

---

[1] RAE, p. 128. Cf. preceding note.

[2] DAI, Tom IV, no. 7: II, pp. 25–6.

[3] The phrase 'forward end beyond the Onandyr' River' is ambiguous at best. Müller, and others after him, took it to refer to the Olyutora River (document 2). Ogloblin (1890, p. 21) thought that by it Dezhnev was referring to the shore of the Gulf of Anadyr', or the Bering Sea in general, which lay forward of the Anadyr' River. Whatever Dezhnev

hungry, naked and barefoot, we all went by land[1] by what routes we do not know. I, poor Semeyka, and my companions went to the Onandyr´ River in exactly ten weeks and came upon it down near the sea. We could catch no fish; there was no forest. Because of hunger we poor men went separate ways.

Twelve men went up the Anandyr´, and they journeyed for twenty days, but saw no people, traces of reindeer sleds, or native trails. They turned back, and within three days' travel to camp they stopped for the night and set about digging pits in the snow. Among our number was the promyshlennik Fomka Semenov Permyak, [who] tried to tell them that there was no point in spending the night there, that they should go on to camp and their companions. Only the promyshlenniks Sidorko Yemel´yanov and Ivashko Zyryanin went with Fomka, and the rest remained, unable to go on because of hunger. They directed Fomka to have me, Semeyka, send them sleeping pallets and old work parkas and for us to bring them food and help them to camp. Fomka and Sidorko reached camp and told me. I, Semeyka, sent my last pallet and an old blanket with Fomka to those in the mountains. He did not find the rest of them there, and it is not known [whether or not] the natives carried them off. Such possessions of the registered agents Bezson Ostaf´yev and Ofanasiy Andreyev as remained were ordered left with their employee, Yelfimko Merkur´yev. At this time we had no clerk to keep records for anyone.

Of the twenty-five only twelve of us were left, and the twelve of us went up the Onandyr´ in boats. We came to the Anauls [a Yukagir tribe] and captured two of them in a fight. I was badly wounded. We took tribute from them [recording] by name in the tribute books what was taken from whom and what was taken as the sovereign's tribute. I wanted to take more tribute from the Anauls for the sovereign, but they said: 'We have no sables; we do not live in the forest. However, the reindeer people visit us, and when they come, we will buy sables and bring tribute to the sovereign.'

Mikhaylo Stadukhin arrived, but did not come to the tribute zimov´ye. He plundered the Anauls. After that the Anauls Lok and Kolupay gave nothing for the year 159 [1650–1] and the year 160 [1651–2] because, they said, in the autumn of the year 160 Kolupay's father-in-law, Mekara, put to death Kolupay's father, Obytay, and

referred to, it had to be at some distance from the Anadyr´ since Dezhnev and his men spent ten weeks reaching the river.

[1] The words so translated here, *v goru*, are usually translated as 'uphill'.

Negovo and their kinsmen, and there was no one to hunt for the tribute. In the same present [sic] year 160 on the 15th day of April Kolupay and Lok went to the reindeer Khodyntsy in the mountains to trade for sables for the sovereign's tribute. The Khodyntsy [carried them away] into the mountains, and they were not at the tribute zimov'ye. Lok lived along the nearby rivers and was not at the zimov'ye. The Khodyntsy killed Kolupay. During that time Lok and Kolupay went into the mountains, and without them the Anaul chieftan Mikera put all their kinsmen to death.

In going by sea from the Kovyma River to the Anandyr' River there is a nos. It extends far into the sea, but it is not the nos that lies off the Chukoch'ya River [west of the Kolyma]. Mikhaylo Stadukhin did not reach this nos. Opposite the nos are two islands; Chukchi live on them. They have carved teeth, [in] holes in the lips [made from] fish tooth bone.[1] This nos lies between north and northeast, and on the Russian side there is a landmark: a little river emerges. The Chukchi set up a *stanov'ye*[2] there, which consists of a tower of whalebones. The nos turns southward abruptly toward the Onandyr' River. A good run from the nos to the Anandyr' River is three days-and-nights and no more. To go from the coast to the river is not far (*nedalet'*) because the Andir' [sic] River empties into a bay.

In the past year 162 [1653–4] I went on an expedition near the sea, and I captured Fedot Alekseyev's Yakut woman from the Koryaks. This woman said that Fedot and service-man Gerasim [Ankudinov] died from scurvy and some companions were killed. A few remained, who fled in boats (*lodki*) with only their souls, I do not know where.

I collected sables for the sovereign's tribute, and that sable treasury

---

[1] That is, labrets cut from walrus tusks. Captain Frederick W. Beechey, who sailed through the Bering Strait in 1826 and 1827 along the Alaskan coast gives this description of them. 'It was at Schismareff Inlet that we first saw the lip ornaments which are common to all the inhabitants of the coast thence as far as Point Barrow. These ornaments consist of pieces of ivory, stone, or glass, formed with a double head, like a sleeve button, one part of which is thrust through a hole bored in the under lip. Two of these holes are cut in a slanting direction about a half an inch below the corners of the mouth. The incision is made when about the age of puberty, and is at first the size of a quill; as they grow older the natives enlarge the orifice, and increase the size of the ornament accordingly, that it may hold its place: in adults, this orifice is about a half an inch in diameter, and will, if required, distend to three quarters of an inch. Some of these ornaments were made of granite, others of jade-stone, and a few of large blue glass beads let into a piece of ivory which formed a white ring around them. These are about an inch in diameter, but I afterwards got one of finely polished jade that was three inches in length, by an inch and a half in width' (*Narrative of a voyage to the Pacific and Bering's Strait*... [2 vols.; London, 1831], Vol. 1, p. 249).

[2] Because the meaning of this word is uncertain in this context and is discussed later on p. 233 below, it is not translated here, but is retained in its Russian form.

is at the Onandyr' River. Service-man Nikita Semenov has taken over the possessions of slain service-man Semen Motora. Service-man Yevseyko Pavlov, who deserted from the Lena ostrog, served with Mikhaylo Stadukhin, but then left Mikhaylo and served with me, Semeyka. The promyshlenniks suffered great harm at the hands of Yevseyko, and they submitted a petition against him on account of this harm; but he would not submit to trial. While on an expedition in the past year 161 [1652–3] promyshlennik Tereshka Nikitin filed a complaint against Yevseyko for a wrong committed. At the trial [Yevseyko] fell to speaking rudely, leaning on a staff, and I wanted to beat him with a stick for his rudeness, but he fled from the camp to captain (*yasaul*) Vetoshka Yemel'yanov and told the promyshlenniks on his own authority that it was a government affair. When Yur'ye Seliverstov arrived, Yevseyko ran away to him. Because of Yevseyko Pavlov there is much trouble between the service-men and promyshlenniks.

On the verso of sheet 2: The 11th day April of the year 164 [1656]. Service-man Danilko Filipov delivered the report.

TsGADA, YaPI, *opis'* 3, 1656, *no.* 18, *listy* 2–4.

Original published in: *RAE*, pp. 130–2; *Russkaya tikhookeanskaya epopeya* (Krasnoyarsk, 1979), pp. 77–9. Copy published in: *DAI*, Tom IV, no. 7: II, pp. 25–6; Samoylov, 1945, pp. 139–41; Knyazev and Mal'kevich, 1948, pp. 578–9; part of it in *RM*, pp. 130–2.

★ ★ ★

The third of the three documents of Dezhnev, much the longest of those presented here, is the one co-authored with Semenov. He was the officially designated commandant on the Anadyr' as against Dezhnev whose status as a commandant was de facto, but not official. This document contains two passages that add a few details about the voyage: a short one in which a proposal to return to the Kolyma and Yakutsk by sea is mentioned and a longer one describing the great rocky nos. The rest of the document has little or no direct connection with the voyage. We reproduce it in translation in full, however, because it is the most complete account of the activities of Dezhnev and his contemporaries on the Anadyr' from the time of establishing the zimov'ye there to early 1655, a period to which Müller gave considerable attention. Also it helps us to understand why Dezhnev described his voyage as he did and the importance he attached to it. Finally, it contains information that helps us to date not only the document itself, but the report of Dezhnev and the petition of Yemel'yan Vetoshka and others which follow. In a passage near the end it mentions the year 163 (1654–5) as the 'present year' and also a date as late as March 25.[1] There is reference in the passage to the writing of Dezhnev's report and this one, as well as the one of Vetoshka and his companions and four others. The final sentence of the report then states: 'The reports were sent April 4'. Thus it was written, or completed, sometime after March 25 and by April 4. This information confirms Lavrentsova's dating of Dezhnev's report and the petition of Vetoshka and his fellow promyshlenniks, or at least their completion. The report was delivered in Yakutsk on 26 September 1655 by service-man Sidorko Yemel'yanov. That it was delivered a half year before Dezhnev's report is explained evidently by Filipov's delay at Zhigansk because of freezing weather.

Document 10

No later than 4 April 1655. Report of the commandants of the Anadyrskiy ostrog, Semen Dezhnev and Nikita Semenov, to the Yakutsk voyevoda, Ivan Pavlovich Akinfiyev, about the expeditions to the Anadyr' River, walrus hunting, and relations with service-man Yuriy Seliverstov.

[From the new river Anandyr' service-men and promyshlenniks [sic] Semeyka Dezhnev and Mikita Semenov make their obeisance to stol'nik and voyevoda Ivan Pavlovich Akinfiyev and d'yak Osip Stepanov of the sovereign tsar [and] grand prince of all Rus', Aleksey Mikhaylovich. In the past year 156 [1647–8] I, Mikitko, was sent with companions, service-men and promyshlenniks, by boyar-son Vasiliy Vlas'yev and sworn-man Kiril Kotkin[2] from the Kolyma][3] to the upper Anyuy River to the non-tribute paying people. With the sovereign's good fortune we found non-tribute paying Khodyntsy and carried out

[1] It perhaps should be mentioned that in two places in this report Dezhnev and Semenov refer to 'the present year 160' [1652] as well as to 'the present year 163' [1655]. This led Polevoy (1962b, p. 148) to conjecture that the report was written in two parts, the first in 1652, which was not then sent to Yakutsk, and the second in 1655, which was added to the first because of a shortage of paper. Lavrentsova, however, states that the unchanged colour of ink used in the alleged two parts, the same peculiarities of spelling of certain words, and the same calligraphy throughout do not support that conjecture (RAE, p. 129). In face of this evidence, though the appearance of 'the present year 160' twice in the same document appears to be a bit too much of a coincidence, Polevoy accepts Lavrentsova's conclusion (letter to me of 24 September 1976).

[2] Commandant and customs agent respectively on the Kolyma, 1648–50.

[3] The beginning part of the text was restored from the published copy in DAI, Tom IV, no. 7: 1, p. 25 – Lavrentsova.

a raid against them. We captured a 'best'[1] man named Angara in that raid for purposes of the sovereign's tribute and sent [him] to the Kolyma River to boyar-son Vasiliy Vlas'yev and sworn-man Kiril Kotkin. Under interrogation this man stated, as did the captives from the raid, that the new river Anandyr´ is across the mountains, and this Anandyr´ River comes close to the upper part of the Anyuy River. On the basis of these remarks in the questioning promyshlennik volunteers joined together and made their obeisance to the sovereign tsar and grand prince of all Rus´, Aleksey Mikhaylovich, and submitted a petition to boyar-son Vasiliy Vlas'yev and sworn-man Kiril Kotkin on the Kolyma River that the sovereign grant them permission [and] send them to the new places on the new Anandyr´ River across the mountains in search of new non-tribute paying people and for their subjection under the tsar's exalted hand. The promyshlenniks promised 40 sables for the sovereign's treasury from this new place. The service-man Semen Motora, they said, should be sent with the promyshlenniks. The sovereign granted them this, and they went across the mountains to the Anadyr´ River. Other promyshlenniks submitted a petition to Semen Motora in the year [15]8 [1649–50] to serve with him according to that set of instructions. Service-men were also sent with him.

In the year 157 [1648–9] service-man Mikhaylo Stadukhin of the Lena ostrog went by sea from the Kolyma River on toward the Pogycha River. In the past year 158 [1649] on the 7th day of September he arrived back on the Kolyma River from the sea. Mikhaylo wrote from the Kolyma to voyevoda Vasiliy Nikitich Pushkin and associates that he and his comrades and fugitive service-men went forward by sea for seven days-and-nights and found a few Koryaks and took captives. Under questioning they stated that there were people farther on, but that they knew of no river there. Having heard these remarks from the questioning and purchased the captives from our raid, Mikhaylo set to thinking about the same new places, about the same Anandyr´ River where we were sent, service-men and promyshlenniks. With his comrades and with fugitive service-men Yarafeyka Kiselev and comrades Mikhaylo drove [people] away and made all sorts of threats and took by force food and arms and all the hunting and fishing equipment dogs, and sleds while on his way to the Anyuy and Anandyr´ rivers. He stirred up differences among us so as to interfere in our sovereign's service, not wanting in his jealousy to see us in the

[1] A term used to designate a prominent or wealthy man in a tribe, one of high rank (Lantzeff, 1943, p. 92).

sovereign's merciful care. On the Kolyma River Mikhaylo and fugitive service-men struck our comrades, promyshlenniks Matyushka Kalin and Kirilka Proklov, and wrongfully took a captive by force from Kirilka. We submitted a petition of complaint in the tribute zimov'ye on the Kolyma River to service-men Mokey Ignat'yev and Ivan Ivanov Permyak regarding Mikhaylo's offence and all his boasting.

When we went from the Kolyma River up the Anyuy, we came across the natives' reindeer tracks in the mountains and followed them on the march. With the sovereign's good fortune we seized a 'good' Khodynets as a hostage, Chekchoy by name. [He has] four brothers, and he is the fifth, and [there are] many other kinsmen. We captured [this] hostage on the 24th day of March [1650]. Chekchoy sent to his kinsmen and ordered them to our camp (kosh)[1] with the sovereign's tribute in four days. Mikhaylo Stadukhin arrived from the Kolyma River up the Anyuy River on the 26th day of March and set up his camp close by. When the natives reached us with the tribute, we took the sovereign's tribute of 9 sables for this hostage. At the very moment of tribute collection Mikhaylo and his comrades fired their guns, for what reason is not known, and drove off the natives. We [tried] to stop Mikhaylo. He would not listen to us. He expected that it was possible to collect even more of the sovereign's tribute because the natives were not few in number, some fifty or more.

When we were crossing over to the Anadyr', Mikhaylo, in keeping with his original boasting, while proceeding along the trail, seized commissioned service-man Semen Motora by surprise and held him for nine days. Semen reached us on the trail on the 10th day. Semen said: 'Mikhaylo [sat] me on a log, and Mikhaylo forced from me on the log a letter to the effect that no individual would engage in the sovereign's service on the Anadyr' for me and my comrades; he would be under the command only of Mikhaylo.'

On the 23rd day of April Semen Motora and his men arrived at the tribute zimov'ye of Semeyka Dezhnev and his men, 12 promyshlenniks on the Anandyr' River. From that date I, Semeyka Dezhnev, and my men began to engage in the sovereign's service together with Semen Motora and his men and joined in caring for the hostages. I and my men took 2 new Anaul hostages. Kolupay is the name of one, Negovo of the other. By-passing the tribute zimov'ye, Mikhaylo Stadukhin raided the Anauls and killed many of them in the raid and plundered the fathers and kinsmen of the tribute men Kolupay and

[1] A name for a Siberian nomadic camp with carts – Lavrentsova.

Negovo. I, Semeyka, and my men went to Mikhaylo and his men at the Anaul stockade and set about telling him that he was acting wrongfully and was killing natives indiscriminately.

Mikhaylo said: 'These people are not tribute payers, but only say they are. Get over there to them, call them out of the stockade and take the sovereign's tribute from them.' I, Semeyka, then told the natives that they should come out and give the sovereign's tribute. A kinsman of the hostages started to give to the sovereign sable aprons (*opolniki*) from the yurt as tribute. Mikhaylo struck me on the face and grabbed the aprons from my hands. It was for this reason that I began to participate in the sovereign's service jointly with Semen Motora and his men because we were not numerous and Mikhaylo grew angry with us and tried to drive us away by every means. We service-men and promyshlenniks, Semen Motora and I, Semeyka Dezhnev, with our comrade service-men and promyshlenniks, fleeing and seeking escape from Mikhaylo's abuse, went farther on in the autumn by the sled route across the mountains to the Penzhina River to find new non-tribute paying people and to bring them under the sovereign's exalted hand. There were no known guides for us on that river. We travelled for 3 weeks and did not find the river. Foreseeing certain cold and death by freezing, we turned back.

In the past year 159 [1650] in the autumn at half-water Mikhaylo sent 9 service-men and promyshlenniks down the Anandyr´ River to the Anauls. The Anauls killed all the service-men and promyshlenniks and fled far down the Anandyr´ River and did not come to the tribute zimov´ye with the sovereign's tribute. We went down the river to the Anauls. A stockade had been built in their midst. We called on them [to come] out of the stockade so that they might admit their guilt to the sovereign and pay the sovereign's tribute. The Anauls started fighting with us. When God helped us take the first outermost yurt, we climbed up on the stockade. We [fought] with them in single combat, grabbing one another by the hands. The Anauls were prepared for a stubborn fight at the stockade: [they had] sticks and axes with wooden handles seven feet long...and knives, for after the killing of the Russians they expected the Russians back against them. Of our men they killed service-man Sukhanka Prokop´yev and three promyshlenniks, Putil´ka Ofonas´yev, Yevtushka Materik, and Kirilka Proklov. Service-man Pashka Kokoulin was wounded in the head and arm by an axe and stick and was disabled all winter. Service-man Artyushka Saldatko was wounded in the forehead by an arrow. Promyshlennik

Tereshka Mikitin was wounded on the bridge of his nose by an arrow, and promyshlenniks Fomka Semenov and Titka Semenov were wounded by sticks at the beginning of the fight. God enabled us to take their stockade and to subdue the Anauls in a military fight. We took 'best' man Kaygonya for purposes of the sovereign's tribute. Kaygonya and his kinsmen said that previously they had not paid the sovereign's tribute. The fathers of the former Anaul hostages killed Kallin and Obyy, and their kinsmen set about living in their previous habitat, as of old. The Anaul Mekerka and his kinsmen arrived among them in the summer by a secret way, and he put to death the fathers and kinsmen of the hostages. In the month of November in the past year 160 [1651] this same Mekerka and his kinsmen arrived by the same secret way and put Kaygonya and all his kinsmen to death and ate them. On the 7th day of December the Anaul hostage Kolupay and his kinsman Lok petitioned the sovereign to grant that we service-men and promyshlenniks go against that Mekerka and subdue him by armed action because he killed their fathers and kinsmen and he wants in the future to kill us service-men and promyshlenniks by the same means. Semen Motora and I, Semeyka Dezhnev, and men went on an expedition against that Mekerka and his kinsmen and summoned him under the sovereign's exalted hand. Mekerka and his kinsmens did not listen and started shooting at us. They killed service-man Semen Motora and wounded service-man Pashka Kokoulin in the shoulder and thigh with arrows. They wounded Fedotka Vetoshka in the knee with an arrow and promyshlennik Sten'ka Sidorov in the arm. We captured all their women and children. Mekerka and his kinsmen fled; others were wounded.

Trader Onisimko Kostromin and promyshlennik Vas'ka Bugor and his companions made their obeisance to the sovereign tsar and grand prince of all Rus', Aleksey Mikhaylovich, and submitted a petition on their behalf to us, Semeyka and Mikitka, that your sovereign's treasury, hostages, and all the sovereign's business should be our [responsibility] in accordance with the instructions which were given to Semen Motora on the Kolyma River by boyar-son Vasiliy Vlas'yev and sworn-man Kiril Kotkin and that we should supervise the promyshlenniks.

On the 12th day of January in the year 159 [1651] our companions, promyshlenniks Mishka Zakharov and Yelfimko Merker'yev of Mezen', an employee of agents Bezsonka Ostaf'yev and Ofan'ka Ondreyev, agents of the merchant Vasiliy Gusel'nikov of the gostinaya sotnya, and Petrushka Mikhaylov [and] Fomka Semenov went from us on the lower Anandyr′ River to the upper Anandyr′ River to the tribute zimov′ye, to the sovereign's hostage Chekchoy and to our companions Semen Motora and his men with food, clothing, and various belongings. Our companions, who remained with the sovereign's treasury and hostages, were starving to death and ate cedar bark. There was a small place with fresh fish and that was stored and fed as much as possible to the sovereign's hostage so that he would not die from want and scurvy, and thus with nothing in the treasury [we would] be in the sovereign's disgrace. Hearing that our comrades had gone to the tribute zimov′ye, Mikhaylo Stadukhin, catching up with them on the road, robbed our comrades of their food, arms, clothing, dogs, sleds, and various articles and took their equipment by force. They killed our comrades. Petitions of complaint regarding their fighting and pillaging have been presented.

In the year 160 [1651–2] we collected the sovereign's tribute for the hostage Chekchoy. In the same year 160 we went to sea in boats where we might make a great profit for the sovereign. At the mouth of the Anadyr′ River we found a sandspit [that extended] beyond the bay into the sea. Many walruses stretch out on that sandspit, and on that sandspit are the dead tusks of that animal. We service-men and promyshlenniks searched for these animals and collected the dead tusks. A great many of the animals stretch out on the point itself around from the ocean side in a space of half a verst or more and on a slope for 30 or 40 sazhens [210 to 280 feet]. Not all of the animals came out of the ocean to stretch out on the land; a great many of the animals were in the ocean by the shore. We did not wait for all these animals on land because the tribute zimov′ye is on the upper Anandyr′ River, the fishing grounds are far up in the rapids, and we had no food; we ought not to spend time walrus hunting and be late and freeze to death. In the year 160[1] we arrived at the sandspit on the eve of the Day of the Chief Apostles Peter and Paul [June 29]. We went from the sandspit up the Anandyr′ on the 11th day of July. We went four times to hunt for the animals, and they soon came out on the land. In the year 162 [1653–4] they came out later; the first hunting was on Il′in day [July 20]. They came ashore because the ice was carried away from the shore. Those promyshlenniks who are from Pomor′ye said that in the Russian Pomor′ye there are not so many animals as that. We service-men and promyshlenniks put 3 puds [72 pounds] of walrus tusks into the sovereign's treasury, 14 in number.

[1] Mistakenly in the text '159-go'.

In the year 161 [1652–3] we, Semeyka and Mikita and companions, obtained lumber [to build a koch] and wanted to set out by sea with the sovereign's treasury for Yakutsk ostrog, but I, Semeyka, and my men know that the ocean is big and the eddies near the land strong, and we dared not go without good boat equipment, without a good sail and anchor. The natives told us that not every year is the ice carried from the shore out to sea. We dared not send the sovereign's treasury with a few men across the mountains through the many non-tribute paying natives of various tribes since service-men and promyshlenniks have been killed in the sovereign's service, and other promyshlenniks have gone off with Mikhaylo Stadkuhin: Matyushka Kal´in, Kalinka Kurop[ot, Ivashka] Vakhov, Ivashko Suvorov, Semeyka Zayko, Bogdashka Onisimov. As to who left and for what reason, there is the memorandum of the late Semen Motora and a copy from the memorandum in his report.

In the past year 161 we went on an expedition to the non-tribute paying people, the Chuvanzy.[1] They, a reindeer people, departed and carried away their wives and children. Some of them were small children. After that, gathering many men, they defended these children and killed service-man Ivashka Pulyayev and four promyshlenniks: Mishka Zakharov, and employee Yefimko Merkur´yev Mezen' of the merchant of the gostinaya sotnya Vasiliy Gusel´nikov, [and] Ivashka Nesterov, Fomka Kuz´min. They wounded Fil´ka Danilov in the shoulder, Vas´ka Markov in the thigh, and Platka Ivanov in the arm. Consequently the sovereign's treasury was not sent off lest it be lost or the tsar's majesty among the natives be defamed, or the service-men and promyshlenniks killed.

In the winter and spring of the past year 162 [1654] the tribute paying Khodyntsy, the hostage Chekchoy's brothers and kinsmen, said: 'In the year 163 [1654–5] we will transport the entire treasury of the sovereign on reindeer across the mountains to the Anyuy, only give our kinsmen useful ironwork for any kind of purpose.' On the 27th day of April of the same year 162 volunteer service-man Yur´ye Seliverstov arrived from the Kolyma River with volunteer service-men and promyshlenniks. After going a day's journey from the tribute zimov´ye to the tribute natives, Chekchoy's kinsmen, or when many natives arrived at the tribute zimov´ye for a whole day, Yur´ye, having circled around the tribute zimov´ye, put the natives to flight. He seized their provisions and all their working equipment, wounded them, and

---

[1] A Yukagir tribe – Lavrentsova.

killed others among them and took as hostages the blood brother of the tribute paying man Lulani and Chekchoy's...Keota.

In the same year 162, having come to the sea, Yur'ye provided promyshlennik Overko Martem'yanov with reports to Yakutsk ostrog on his own [and] secretly from us because of jealousy. Yur'ye did not wish to see us your sovereign's slaves and orphans in his tsar's merciful care. He wanted to gain the sovereign's salary for our service and exploration. Yur'ye wrote to the Yakutsk ostrog that he, not we service-men and promyshlenniks, found the sandspit, marine animals, and dead tusks of the animals...when earlier he was with Mikhaylo Stadukhin. He wrote falsely because, it is known that in the past year 158 [1649] Mikhaylo Stadukhin wrote from the Kolyma River that he and his men sailed seven days-and-nights by sea from the Kolyma River toward the Pogycha River, but he did not reach any kind of river. He found a few Koryaks and took captives. In the questioning the captives said that they did not know of any river farther on. Mikhaylo and his men and fugitive service-men returned to the Kolyma River. Yur'ye was with Mikhaylo. Yur'ye did not write the truth because he did not reach the great rocky nos. That nos extends very far into the sea, and a great many Chukchi people live on it. On the islands opposite the nos there live people called 'toothed' (*zubatyye*) because they pierce the lip with 2 teeth [made from] large bones. This is not the first sacred nos from the Kolyma. We, Semeyka and companions, know this great nos because the boat of Gerasim Ankudinov and his men was wrecked on it, and we took the shipwrecked men into our boats. We saw the 'toothed' people on an island (*na ostrovu*). The Anandyr' River and sandspit are far from that nos.

We, Semeyka and Mikita and men, service-men and promyshlenniks, gave to Yur'ye and his men for the sovereign's service two boats – koches built and ready with all the rigging and [a *karbas*[1] so that their sovereign's service would not come to a halt for the year without boats and rigging and that they not be delayed en route to the ocean hunting, and so that a big profit would be made for the sovereign's treasury. Accepting the boats, Yur'ye himself inspected them for ocean sailing and sent his men and comrades to look over the boats completely for ocean sailing...Yur'ye gave us a receipt for the boats, cordage, and karbas. Yur'ye lost one of the boats by his own carelessness. The season coming very late for that boat, he sent a small number of men in it. Water

[1] A small boat with oars.

from the mountains came under it, and it became impossible to turn it around, and he abandoned it. We divided those companions of Yur'ye who were on the boat among our other boats, and Yur'ye went maritime hunting with us.

On the 10th day of April of the same year 162 (1654) we took two men from the non-tribute paying Chuvanzy for purposes of the sovereign's tribute, one named Legonta, the other Pondozya. We took the sovereign's tribute from them]¹ of a sable and a sable strip (*plastina*). Their other kinsmen, who were with the tribute-paying Khodyntsy whom Yur'ye had despoiled, were together and wished to come with the sovereign's tribute to the tribute zimov'ye and to bring their sons for exchange. Fearing Yur'ye's pillaging...² they went far away to their other tribesmen, and so Yur'ye seized their yurts and lived in them for 3 weeks.

In the present year 163 [1654–5], when the tribute paying natives Chekchoy, his brothers, and kinsmen came to the tribute zimov'ye, we asked them about the Chuvanzy, why did they not come to the tribute zimov'ye with the sovereign's tribute. Chekchoy and his brothers said: 'We saw their tribesmen, small in number, two yurts, and they went to find others of their tribesmen, and they wished to come as a group with the sovereign's tribute.' This Chekchoy was sent to his tribesmen on the 16th day of November of the present year 163 [1654] so that they would go hunting and come to the tribute zimov'ye with the sovereign's tribute. He left in his place as hostages his wife and two sons. He came to the tribute zimov'ye on the 19th day of March [1655] with his kinsmen and brothers. He made his obeisance to the sovereign tsar and grand prince of all Rus', Aleksey Mikhaylovich, and submitted a petition to us, Semeyka and Mikita and companions, [stating]: 'In the fall of the present year 163 [1654] many hostile Koryak natives arrived from across the Pyanzhina River and killed many of our tribesmen. They raided us, took our wives and children, and drove off the reindeer; and there [was] every kind of injury, killing, and robbing of us by them. We cannot stand these people. The sovereign should authorize and send against these people every service-man together with the tribute paying natives to subdue these Koryak people.' In the present year 163 [1654–5], they said, 'We cannot go hunting for the sovereign's tribute and carry the sovereign's treasury across the

¹ Sheet missing; bracketed portion taken from the copy in *DAI*, Tom IV, no. 7: 1 – Lavrentsova.
² A few letters are missing from the next word – Lavrentsova.

mountains to the Anyuy River because two raids have befallen us this year: one from the Russians, from Yur'ye and his men, the other from the Koryaks. We transported', they said, 'the sovereign's treasury and paid the sovereign's tribute from the past year 162 [1653–4] through the year 164 [1655–6] with profit.'

In the past year 162 we went to the sandspit against the Koryaks because they live not far from the sandspit, and they came to the sandspit secretly for killing: they hunt the walrus for food. I, Semeyka, and my men went against them and came to 14 yurts within a strong stockade. God helped us, and we routed all the men and captured some wives and children, but they escaped and the 'best' men took away the wives and children because they are many and have large yurts. Ten families live in one yurt. Our men were not many; altogether there were 12 men. In that fight Pashka was wounded by an arrow. He killed a man [with a shot] in the temple from his musket.[1]

The Anadyr' River is not forested, and few sables are there. There is larch along its upper course for 6 or 7 days' travel, but there are no dense forests of any kind except birch and aspen, and from the Mayen [Mayn] there is no forest at all except willows...;[2] and the woods along the shore are not broad; all is tundra and rock. A sketch of this river: from the Anyuy River and across the mountains to the upper Anandyr' the rivers which empty into it, and to the ocean, to the sandspit where the animals stretch out, are large and small. Travel from the upper Anandyr', from the mountains, to the tribute zimov'ye with loaded sleds [takes] two weeks or more.

There is no means for writing about the sovereign's business; there is no writing paper. The sovereign should allot us fishing nets for catching fish for his sovereign's hostages, drag nets and stationary nets. Much of the fishing here is with stationary nets since the river is rocky and steep. In the autumn it is rainy, and in the autumn the weirs do not remain because [the volume of] water is great. Many red fish [salmon] arrive. The fish leave the ocean on the lower Anandyr' good and arrive on the upper course bad because the fish die on the upper Anandyr' River and do not swim back to sea. We obtain few white fish because we have no good nets. We get new nets on credit at a cost of 15 roubles or more. We dare not feed the sovereign's hostages the red fish lest they die from the need of food, developing scurvy, and for that reason we would be in disgrace with the sovereign and

---

[1] The fight in which Dezhnev captured Alekseyev's Yakut woman.
[2] Word missing – Lavrentsova.

contribute nothing to the treasury. We stored and fed them white fish as much as possible. Few people with equipment come among us; there is no one from whom to buy linen nets and various pieces of equipment on credit.

The sovereign's tribute collection from the year 158 [1649–50] and all that is written above: In the year 158 9 sables were taken as the sovereign's tribute for the hostage Chekchoy. In the year 159 [1650–1] the brothers and kinsmen of Chekchoy did not come to the tribute zimov´ye because, they said, they obtained no food and ranged far away hunting. In the year 160 [1651–2] tribute of 6 sables and 5 sable pieces were collected for the hostage. In the year 161 [1652–3] 7 sables and 5 sable pieces were collected. In the year 162 [1653–4] the sovereign's tribute of 14 sables and 12 sable pieces was taken. In the year 163 [1654–5] 7 sables were collected. In the year 161 [8 sables with bellies (*pupki*) were taken from the hunting of the promyshlenniks into the ten per cent sable treasury, and 2 sables and sable strips and 13 sable bellies as duties from boat business. In the year 163 ten per cent imposts of 3 sables and a sable belly and 5 sables and 3 sable bellies were collected from boat business. Our total money collection is 2 roubles, 14 altyns, 2 dengas; and the money collection of the late Semen Motora was 2 roubles, 29 altyns, 2 dengas. In the year 162 one sable was collected as customs duty. We have the books in the tribute zimov´ye on the Anandyr´ River for everything about the tribute collection: from whom what was taken, the kind of animals, and the year; the ten per cent tax collection and the purchased sables; the customs taxes collected in sables and the money for petitions.][1]

Service-man Ivan Pulyayev was killed in the sovereign's service. He left a sworn testament in his own hand in the tribute zimov´ye that upon his death he bequeathed his possessions to the sovereign's treasury. We took these possessions into the sovereign's treasury. We sent with this dispatch [a statement] as to what his possessions are and what is written in his testament and a copy of his testament.

Thirty sables were taken from promyshlennik Sudorko Yemel´yanov for his captive Ivanov. Four sables were taken from Tren´ka Kursov for a woman's leather kaftan. Three sables were taken from Pashka Kokoulin for old linen, 3 strands [?–*pasma*] of twine, a fur cap of reindeer calfskin, a small pouch, and remnant of net; and 5 sables for wax candles. A sable strip was taken from Stepanka Kakanin for berries,

[1] Sheet missing; bracketed portion taken from copy in *DAI*, Tom IV, no. 7: 1 – Lavrentsova.

a basket, and a flint. One sable and 2 grivnas in money were taken from Grishka Bukor for a tray. Two grivnas were collected from Sidorko Yemel'yanov for a piece of netting. Four young sables were collected from service-man Vas'ka Bugor for caviar and butter.[1] A sable strip was collected from Vas'ka Markov for trousers of reindeer hide, *taushkanin*,[2] and a remnant of netting. From the same Sidorko on a pledge of 14 sables a pud of bones, 7 tusks, and 3 sables were taken. From service-man Ivashka Yakovlev 33 pounds of tusks were taken for 8 roubles, 10 altyns;[3] 3 roubles were taken from him for a fur blanket and 5 roubles, 10 altyns for a kettle and 10 mukluks. On a pledge of six roubles Semeyka Dezhnev took an axe, a dog, and hair net. On a pledge of 7 roubles, half a grivna, trader Onisimko Kastromin took a piece of netting, a reindeer skin, 2 pounds of lead, a pewter dish, a pistol, a linen garment, and a basin. For a cross, 10 partridge traps, a dragnet, and a frying pan 3 roubles, 10 altyns were taken on a pledge from Artyushka Saldat. A pledge of 4 roubles was taken from Semeyka Dezhnev for a pound of lead, 2 balls of thread, a needle, twine, a linen kerchief, and a dog. From Fedotka Vetoshka and signatories a pledge of 8 roubles, 29 altyns was taken for 20 mukluks, a pound of lead, incense, 2 arshins of linen, a cap with a red top and band, balls of thread, and a line for stationary nets. Ivanov's 6 puds [216 pounds] of walrus tusks, numbering 43 tusks, remained. A list from his testament of other petty acquisitions taken is being sent.

On the 1st day of February of the year 159 [1651] Platonka Ivanov and Pashko Semenov came to Semen Motora and his companions at the tribute zimov'ye and informed Semen about Mikhail Stadukhin: that Mikhaylo wanted to go with his detachment to Semen's zimov'ye and attack it and kill the service-men. Platonko and Pavel, not wanting this, left Mikhaylo. Promyshlennik Ivashko Fedorov Kazanets wrote down their statements and service-man Yevseveyko Pavlov attached his signature to the statements in place of them. These remarks of theirs were not sent, but a copy of them was. Ivashko Kazanets and Yevseveyko Pavlov came from Mikhaylo and submitted petitions to us to engage in the sovereign's service with us. In the past year 162 [1654] when we went to the sea, that Yevsevey withdrew as guard

---

[1] Above (p. 60) Bugor is designated a promyshlennik as he is below (pp. 68, 69, 71), but here and on p. 68 he is called a service-man. Stadukhin (document 15, p. 80 and document 17, p. 84) refers to him as a fugitive service-man. Such being the case, it might explain the dual designation: when acting independently, he was considered a promyshlennik.

[2] Maybe a dark blue cloth.   [3] See p. 97, note 2 below.

of the sovereign's treasury and hostages so as to engage in the sovereign's service with service-man volunteer Yur'ye Seliverstov. Service-man Vas'ka Bugor came to us from Mikhaylo and without a petition engaged in the sovereign's service with us, in the various common [tasks]: he took over the hostages, their feeding and guarding. He arrived on the Anandyr' on the...day of February of that same year 159 [1651].

When they went up the Anyuy River, they went on a campaign and captured the sovereign's hostage Chekchoy. In that fight pyatides-yatnik Shalam Ivanov was mortally wounded, and he died on the Anandyr' River on the 5th day of July in the same year. Titko Semenov was wounded in the thigh by an arrow. Service-man [sic] Vetoshka killed a man in that fight and promyshlennik Vas'ka Bugor killed a man too. When they seized the Anaul yurts, Pashka Kokoulin was wounded in the head and arm in the fighting. Pashko killed a man with a lance,[1] and Tren'ka Kursov was wounded in the arm by an arrow.

In the past year 162 [1653–4] we went against the Koryaks from the sandspit by the sea. Semeyka killed a man with his musket in that fight. In the same fight Pashka Kokoulin was wounded in the side, and he killed [a man] with his musket.

On the 3rd day of May in the year 161 [1653] in the tribute zimov'ye on the Anandyr' River we service-men, Semenko Dezhnev and Mikitka Semenov, asked from trader Onisimko and from promyshlenniks Vas'ka Bugor and comrades for the sovereign's tribute and ten per cent sable treasury and for the effects of deceased service-man and sworn-man Ivashka Pulyayev. They refused the sworn-man; they gave nothing. We examined the effects of the late Yelfimko Merkur'yev of Mezen', the employee of the agents of Vasiliy Gusel'nikov, merchant of the gostinaya sotnya, and recorded [them] in person in the presence of others. No one took over these effects, and without your sovereign's order we did not take them into the sovereign's treasury, but placed them in the treasury storehouse under guard until [receipt of] the sovereign's order. When the sovereign issues an order regarding these effects, a list [will be sent] with this report.

On the 25th day of March of the present year 163 [1655] in the tribute zimov'ye we [ordered] service-men and promyshlenniks sent with the sovereign's treasury to the Yakutsk ostrog. They could not

[1] Made by fastening a knife to a staff (Sergey V. Bakhrushin, 'Snaryazheniye russkikh promyshlennikov v Sibiri v XVII veke', *Istoricheskiy pamyatnik russkogo arkticheskogo moreplavaniya XVII veka*...(Leningrad and Moscow, 1951), p. 89).

take the sovereign's treasury because, they said, 'we are cold, in need of food, eat dead salmon'. They submitted a signed petition in this matter. On the 26th day of March in the present year 163 at the tribute zimov'ye Yur'ye Seliverstov read the instructions which were sent to Mikhaylo Stadukhin. Those instructions ordered Mikhaylo to send service-men Semen Motora and comrades, trader Onisimko Kostromin, and promyshlenniks Ivan Bugor and comrades from the Anadyr'. I, Semeyko, did not release these men from the sovereign's treasury because we have served together with them in the sovereign's service and because the sovereign's treasury is being collected, and we will send off that sovereign's treasury all together. A list is being sent of who declared how many fish tooth bones in the hunting of the year 160 [1651–2] and the year 162 [1653–4]. A petition of service-men and promyshlenniks Fedotka Vetoshka and Onisimko Kostromin and comrades about their needs is being sent with this report. Another petition by them against Mit'ka Vasil'yev is being sent. A petition by service-man Mikita Semenov is being sent. A petition of service-men Pashka Kokoulin and Mitka Vasil'yev about their needs is being sent. A petition of complaint of volunteer serving promyshlennik Danilko Filipov, who came to the Anandyr' with Yur'ye Seliverstov and service volunteers, in which Danilko states the sovereign's case against Yur'ye, is being sent with this report. On the 10th day of February of the year 163 [1655] we, Semeyka and Mikitka, told the service-men and promyshlenniks that they should go with the sovereign's treasury. They said: 'Let us think about it.' On the 25th day of March we, Semeyka and Mikitka, told the service-men and promyshlenniks that they should depart two weeks after Easter Sunday. Service-man Vetoshka Yemel'yanov said: 'I, the sovereign's slave, am ready for the sovereign's service.' Service-man Mit'ka Vasil'yev said: 'If you try to send me out, I will go to Yur'ye Seliverstov; I cannot haul the treasuries.' Service-man Saldatko spoke and promyshlenniks Onisimko Kostromin and Vas'ka Bugor and companions spoke: 'We will sign a petition about our need and the scarcity of food.' Mit'ka said: 'I will make obeisance in peace.' From that time we set about writing reports because they said: 'Write the reports to Yakutsk ostrog, and we will submit a petition. Permit us to go below (naniz) with the reports to someone and send our petition to the Yakutsk ostrog with the report.' When the service-men and promyshlenniks had written the petition and Mit'ka learned that we had written the reports and that there was enough paper, he, with Yevseveyko's knowledge and intent, spoke: 'I have not refused to serve for you; I will haul the [sovereign's] treasury when the time comes. We have no iron for gifts to the natives, and we have no writing paper.'

On the 21st day of November in the present year 163 [1654–5] with volunteer service-man Yur'ye Seliverstov we took the sovereign's tribute of 5 sable strips from the Khodynets Keoto and his brother Lulaniya, and we engaged in various kinds of the sovereign's service with him. On the 22nd day of March of the present year 163, together with Yur'ye Seliverstov, we took hostages for the sovereign's tribute, the Khodynets named Meyagin and his own son. No tribute was collected from him in this current year 163 because the hostage was taken late, and the hostages say that his father is a good man.

The hostage Chekchoy, [serving] as guide, departed from us with the men Sidorko Yemel'yanov and Panfilko Lavrent'yev, and Chekchoy left his place. Sidorko and Panfil were sent with the reports to the Kolyma River. It was ordered to give these reports to service-men or traders and promyshlenniks who would be travelling.

The reports were sent on the 4th day of April.

On the verso of sheet 1: On the 26th day of September of the year 164 [1655] volunteer service-man Sidorko Yemel'yanov delivered the re[port].

TsGADA, YaPI, *opis'* 3, 1655, *no.* 1, *listy* 1–6, 8–11, 13–17. Original published in: *RAE*, pp. 133–43. Copy published in: *DAI*, Tom IV, no. 7: 1, pp. 16–25; Samoylov, 1945, pp. 124–38; part of it in *RM*, pp. 126–8.

★ ★ ★

The eleventh document is the fourth one from which Müller drew information about the voyage. It is a petition by Fedotka Yemel'yanov Vetoshka and several promyshlenniks, some of whom accompanied Dezhnev on the voyage and who performed the functions of service-men on the Anadyr'. It is for that reason they are requesting compensation for their expenditures and service. From this petition we learn the names of the promyshlenniks serving on the Anadyr'. It corroborates much that is contained in Dezhnev's reports, including the actions of Stadukhin and Yur'ye Seliverstov on the Anadyr'. It contains a passage, like document 10, repeating part of Dezhnev's description of the great rocky nos. In it, too, is an item of information found nowhere else, the month in which Stadukhin set out on his voyage in the summer of 1649. The date for this document is derived from the information given near the end of the preceding document, that is, between 25 March and 4 April 1655. Because it repeats much of what is in that document, only excerpts from it are presented here.

Document 11

Between 25 March and 4 April 1655. Excerpts from the petition of service-men and promyshlenniks Fedotko Yemel'yan Vetoshka and associates about granting them money and grain allotments for service on the Anadyr' River.

To the sovereign tsar and grand prince of all Rus', Aleksey Mikhaylovich, obeisance is made by your slaves and orphans, service-men and promyshlenniks who were sent from the Kolyma River by boyar-son Vasiliy Vlas'yev and sworn-man Kiril Kotkin, promyshlenniks who presented petitions on the Kolyma River at the mouth of the Anyuy River to service-man Semen Motora and performed your sovereign's service with Semen on the Anadyr' River and were service-men in the year...[1] on the Anadyr' River with Semen Dezhnev: Fedotko Yemel'yanov Vetoshka, Artushka Fedotov Saldatko, trader Onisim Kostromin, promyshlenniks Vaska Yermolayev Bugor, Tereshka Mikitin, Vaska Markov, Stenka Sidorov Vilyuy, Stenka Petrov Kakanin, Petryushka Mikhaylov, Sidorov Vilyuy, Stenka Petrov Kakanin, Ivashka Kazanets, Ontonka Andreyev, Grishka Ontonov, Tomilka Yelfimov, Titko Semenov, Morozko Malafayev, Drushinka Alekseyev, Sidorko Yemel'yanov, Pashko Maksimov, Fomka Semenov, Kirilko Stepanov, Ivashko Lavrent'yev, Trenka Kursov, Filka Danilov, Danilko Pankratov.

In the past year 157 [1648–9], sovereign, it was made known to boyar-son Vasiliy Vlas'yev and sworn-man Kiril Kotkin on the Kolyma River from the questioning of the Khodynets hostage Angara, whom we, your slaves and orphans, captured on the upper Anyuy River, and of the Khodyntsy captives in that same raid that the new transmontane river Anandyr' approaches close to the upper Anyuy River. In light of these statements we promyshlennik volunteers got together...[1] and made obeisance to you, sovereign tsar and grand prince of all Rus', and...[1] [presented] a petition to boyar-son Vasiliy Vlas'yev and swornman Kiril Kotkin for us promyshlennik volunteers to go to the new land, to the new river Anandyr' across the mountains to search out and to subject new non-tribute paying people under your tsar's exalted hand with our own capital and...[4] for us to pay forty sables into your sovereign's treasury. We, your orphans, were sent on your sovereign's service with service-man Semen Motora and companions.

On the...[5] day of July of that same year 157 [1649] service-man

---

[1] Omission is in the published document.

Mikhaylo Stadukhin and companions went forward by sea from the Kolyma River to the new river Pogycha. He arrived back from the sea on the Kolyma River on the 7th day of September of the year 158 [1649]... [There follows a long statement about Stadukhin's abuses and depredations against both natives and fellow Russians, his false charges, and the petitioners' efforts to avoid or resist Stadukhin and his party.]

In the past year 160 [1651–2] we, your slaves and orphans, went by sea in boats in order to find where a steady profit could be made for you, sovereign and [at] the mouth of the Anandyr′ River we found a sandspit beyond the bay, and it extended far into the sea. Many walruses crawl out onto the sandspit. Many dead tusks of that animal are on the sandspit, and we exploited that animal.

Mikhail Stadukhin and his men did not reach that [part of] the Anandyr′ River or that sandspit, which by your sovereign's good fortune we, your slaves and orphans, discovered, because, sovereign, it is known that in the year 157 [1649] Mikhail Stadukhin went from the Kolyma River by sea toward the Pogycha River and returned from the sea on the...[1] day of September in the year 158 [1649]. He wrote from the Kolyma to your sovereign's voyevoda at Yakutsk ostrog that he sailed onward by sea for seven days-and-nights and found no river at all. He found a few Koryaks and took some captives. Under questioning the captives said that farther on there were many people, but that they knew of no river. Mikhail and his men returned to the Kolyma River.

Beyond that place there is a great rocky nos. It extends far into the sea, and there are a great many people on it. There are islands in the sea opposite the nos, and on the islands are a great many people. We your orphans who were with Semen Dezhnev know that rocky nos and islands and saw the people. It is not the nos that is the first sacred nos from the Kolyma River. The Anandyr′ River is far from the great nos and islands.

In the past year 162 [1654] volunteer service-man Yur′ye Seliverstov, with promyshlennik Overko Martem′yanov, wrote to the Yakutsk ostrog from the Anandyr′, to your sovereign's voyevodas, that he, Yur′ye, discovered that place first, not we your slaves and orphans. Yur′ye wrote falsely and sent reports unbeknownst to us because of jealousy, wanting to receive your sovereign's remuneration for our service and discovery. He went forward by sea with Mikhail Stadukhin, but Mikhail fell short of the Anandyr′ River by a long distance...

[1] Omission is in the published document.

In the past year 162 [1654] we your slaves and orphans gave to Yur'ye Seliverstov and his companions two koches already built and ready to go with rigging and a karbas, but without sail and anchor, so that your sovereign's service for the year would not remain unperformed and the time become late for maritime enterprise.

We your slaves and orphans who are active in your sovereign's service on the Anandyr´ River since 1650 have held on to nets and all kinds of working equipment, nautical and mineral. We went heavily into debt for nets; we took new nets on credit at a cost of fifteen roubles or more. There was nothing to buy them with because, sovereign, the Anandyr´ River is not forested and there are few sables on it and a great many non-tribute paying natives. There is no one to borrow from henceforth...[1] few men with equipment came with us. We eat dead salmon. They come far up the lower Anandyr´ River from the sea and arrive in the upper reaches in poor condition because the fish die in the upper Anandyr´ and do not swim back to sea. We get few white fish, sovereign, because we do not have good nets, and what white fish we get we save and feed as much as possible to your sovereign's hostages. We dare not feed them that salmon lest they get scurvy from that food and die, and we your orphans and slaves would be disgraced before you and there would be nothing in the treasury.

Merciful sovereign tsar and grand prince of all Rus´, Aleksey Mikhaylovich, grant us your slaves your sovereign's salary as allotted in the past for our service, great needs, and debts; and order, sovereign, a *ukaz* to be issued for us your orphans about our sovereign's service, and order, sovereign, service-men Semen Dezhnev and Mikita Semenov to accept our petition in the tribute zimov'ye on the Anandyr´ and to send [it] with a report to your sovereign's voyevodas at Yakutsk. Sovereign tsar, have mercy, please.

In AAN, Spiski Yakutskoy arkhivy [sic], *chast'* 2, *v list, na* 344 l. (old archival designation). Copy.

Published in: *DAI*, Tom IV, pp. 12–16.

★ ★ ★

In his 1758 account Müller gives attention to the activities of Mikhail Stadukhin: his founding of an outpost on the Kolyma River, his return to Yakutsk with the report of an island opposite the mouth of the Kolyma on which walrus tusks could be obtained, his being com-

---

[1] Omission is in the published document.

missioned to look for the Pogycha River, his voyage in 1649 in search of that river, and his overland journey to the Anadyr´ where he quarrelled with Motora and Dezhnev. These activities have relatively little direct bearing on the voyage of Dezhnev and Alekseyev, yet they have their relevance to it. On the one hand, they are evidence of the the great interest aroused by reports of the Pogycha or Anadyr´ River and of the availability of highly valued walrus tusks along the Arctic seaboard. Alekseyev and Dezhnev are not the only ones interested in finding the Pogycha, or the only ones who tried to find it. On the other hand, the account of Stadukhin's voyage in the summer of 1649 is of the voyage on which Seliverstov based his claim to having found the sandspit occupied by walruses actually discovered by Dezhnev and his men. It was in part to counteract that claim that Dezhnev was led to mention his voyage and to describe the promontory he had circumnavigated. For these reasons we reproduce here six documents, some in excerpted form, relating to Stadukhin and his activities.

Number 12 is Stadukhin's deposition before the Yakutsk authorities about the reports of an island with walruses near the mouth of the Kolyma River and of the Pogycha River rich in sables. Number 13 contains the instructions issued to him by these authorities to look for the island and river. Number 14 reports his delay en route to the Kolyma. His report of his voyage in the summer of 1649 (no. 15), the most important of the group, gives us most of the information we have about his voyage, as well as information about the fate of two of the four koches from the expedition of 1648 that were lost during the early stage of the voyage. Why Müller did not elect to include this detail in his account is not clear. The next document (no. 16), in the form of excerpts from a petition by promyshlennik Ivan Kazanets, confirms Stadukhin's report and furnishes a few additional details. The last document of the group (no. 17), the report of Seliverstov, does not appear to have been included in Müller's portfolios, but it is reproduced here in excerpted form because it is the report to which Dezhnev refers as containing false information about him and a false claim to discovery of the sandspit at the entrance to Anadyr´ Bay.

Document 12

26 April 1647. Testimony of service-man Mikhail Stadukhin about the Kolyma, Chyukhcha, and Pogycha rivers, the natives living along them, and the unexplored island in the Arctic Ocean near the mouth of the Kolyma River.

On the 26th day of April of the year 155 [1647] service-man Mikhalka
Stadukhin, who arrived at the Yukutsk ostrog on the 23rd day of
November of the year 154 [1645] from the Kolyma River with the
sovereign's tribute collection, before the arrival of voyevoda Vasiliy
Nikitich Pushkin and associates, under questioning stated to voyevodas
Vasiliy Nikitich Pushkin and Kiril Osipovich Suponev and d'yak Petr
Stenshin in the main office at the Yakutsk ostrog:

He was on the Kolyma River for 2 years for the sovereign's tribute
collection. The Kolyma River is big; it is like the Lena River; it goes
to the sea. Also it and the Lena are under the same winds, from the
east and from the north. Along the Kolyma River live Kolyma natives
of their own tribe; there are many reindeer and walking-sedentary
people[1] with their own language. In the vicinity of that Kolyma there
is a nearby river, Chyukhcha by name, and this Chyukhcha River
empties into the sea through its own mouth, with its emergence on
this side of the Kolyma River.

Along this Chyukhcha River live natives of their own tribe, called
Chyukhchi, like the Samayads, reindeer and sedentary. They had a
woman, a Kolyma captive named Kaliba. This woman lived among
these Chyukhchi for 3 years. She told him that there is an island which
is on the left side when going in boats by sea to the Kolyma River.
This island begins to come into sight in the ocean from the mainland
on the left hand going from the Lena, from Svyatoy Nos, to the Yana,
and from the Yana to the Sobach'ya, the same as the Indigirka; and in
going from the Indigirka to the Kolyma River that island is much in
sight, and snowy mountains, avalanches, and streams are all known.
The promyshlenniks guess that this mountainous island, a belt in the
sea, is entirely one, that it goes from Pomor'ye, from the city of
Arkhangel'sk,[2] from Mezen' to Novaya Zemlya, and that it is all one
island from opposite the mouths of the Yenisey, Taz, and Lena and
is called Novaya Zemlya. In the winter the Chyukhchi on this side of
the Kolyma cross on reindeer to that island in one day from that river,
from their dwellings. They kill the sea walrus on that island and bring
back the walrus heads with all the teeth, and they offer prayers in their
own fashion to these walrus heads. He [Stadukhin] said that he had not
seen the walrus tusks among them, but promyshlenniks told him that
they had seen the walrus tusks among the Chyukhchi; the ends of their

[1] Vladimir G. Bogoraz (*The Chukchee* [Leiden and New York, 1904–9], p. 681) refers
to them as 'maritime Chukchee'.
[2] This phrase is omitted in the version published in *DAI* and *RM*.

reindeer sleighs are all one walrus tusk. There are no sables among these Chyukhchi because they live on the tundra near the ocean, but there are very good dark sables all along the Kolyma.

From the Kolyma to that river which is beyond the Kolyma, called the Pogycha – they go to it from the Kolyma in three days-and-nights or more during sailing weather. It is a large sable river with many natives along it. They have their own language.

Vtorko Gavrilov [alone] of all the service-[men] remains on the Kolyma River now...If the sovereign will order many of his sovereign's service-men sent to those rivers, there will be a big collection of tribute on those rivers, and there will be great profit for the sovereign's treasury. Now and in the future there is to be expected a big collection of tribute. The sables are all good [and] dark and are native animals. All the foxes are red or polar. There are no other animals besides these on these rivers because the place is very cold. The service-men and promyshlenniks live on these rivers and always eat fish because these rivers [have] fish and the fish are of many kinds.

On the verso of *list* 240: Ivashko Mikhaylov affixed his signature to this statement in place of Mikhail Stadukhin by his order.

TsGADA, YaPI, *stolbets* 611, *list* 240.

Original published in *ORZPM*, pp. 221–2; *RM*, pp. 59–60; *Russkaya tikhookeanskaya epopeya*, pp. 73–4. Copy published in *DAI*, Tom III, pp. 99–100.

Document 13

5 July 1647. Except from the instructions of Yakutsk voyevoda Vasiliy Pushkin to Mikhail Stadukhin regarding a journey to the Pogycha River and the search for walrus tusks on the island opposite that river.

Instructions to service-man Mikhalko Stadukhin and companions on the 5th day of July of the year 7155 [1647] in accordance with the ukaz of the sovereign tsar and grand prince of all Rus', Aleksey Mikhaylovich, and the order of voyevodas Vasiliy Nikitich Pushkin and Kiril Osipovich Suponov and d'yak Petr Stenshin:

He is to go on the sovereign's service on the sovereign's boats from Yakutsk ostrog down the Lena River to the mouth of the Lena River, where it empties into the sea; and along the sea to the Kovyma River and from the Kovyma River to the new Pogycha River for the collection of tribute and *pominki*[1] of the sovereign tsar and grand prince

[1] Furs as gifts by the natives to the Russians over and above the tribute (Fisher, 1943, pp. 49, 60).

of all Rus´, Aleksey Mikhaylovich, for the search for and subjection of the new Pogycha non-tribute paying natives under the exalted hand of the sovereign tsar...[Here follows a repetition of Stadukhin's testimony as given in document 12 preceding.]

Mikhalko Stadukhin and service-men are to go from the Yakutsk ostrog on service in the sovereign's boats via the Lena River, going out from the Lena River onto the sea, by sea to the Kovyma River, and from the Kovyma River by sea to that new Pogycha River for the collection of the sovereign's tribute and the subjection of the new non-tribute paying natives under the sovereign tsar's exalted hand, not delaying anywhere or for an hour. Upon arrival at the new Pogycha River among those Pogycha natives a zimov´ye is to be built with a stockade in whatever place is the most suitable, wherever that may be. He is to reinforce the fortification around that zimov´ye with every sort of defence.

Mikhalko is to order the service-men to investigate and to question the promyshlenniks about that island, Novaya Zemlya, that is in the sea opposite the Pogycha River, whether there are sea walruses on that island. If there are, whether the natives go to that island in the winter to hunt those animals and whether they kill those sea walruses. Mikhalko is to send [men] to those natives and to summon them under the sovereign tsar's exalted hand and with persuasion to take good 'best' men from them as hostages, as many as suitable. He is to order them to pay tribute with walrus tusks, large and medium-sized, and in the absence of walrus tusks to take walrus skins with fat; to take good large and medium-sized ones; he is not to take tusks less than a pound in weight.[1] He is to take the walrus tusks from them according to local practice, according to the people, as much as one can pay and to record it accordingly by name.

If promyshlenniks begin to hunt for walruses on that island, however many of them may be hunting, take from these men walrus tusks for the sovereign's ten per cent tax. If anyone on the island has the head of the animal itself and it has two very large good tusks, or two heads with four tusks to a pud or three or four heads with eight tusks to a pud, collect all the tusks of such walruses for the sovereign, recording and evaluating them, and send them to the Yakutsk ostrog. He is to give the promyshlenniks money from the sovereign's treasury and the various customs receipts that will have been collected. If no money should have been collected into the sovereign's treasury, he is

[1] For the desiderata in walrus tusks and other related matters see Spasskiy, 1821, pp. 20–2.

to write about it. He is to send the walrus tusks to voyevoda Vasiliy Nikitich Pushkin and associates at the Yakutsk ostrog. He is to give the traders and promyshlenniks money for the walrus tusks from the sovereign's treasury according to value, not delaying [payment] until the Yakutsk ostrog.

For interpreting among the Pogycha natives Mikhalko is to take from boyar-son Vasiliy Vlas'yev on the Kolyma, from the local Kolyma Yukagirs who are with the service-men, whoever is reputable and available. Mikhalko is to have personal jurisdiction over the sovereign's collection of tribute and pominki in sables and all kinds of furs. If he finds and declares walrus tusks, he and the service-men are ordered to collect them and to strive without fail.

AAN, *fond* 21, *kniga* 30, *no.* 138. Copy.
Published in: *RM*, pp. 64–6.

Document 14

After 4 October 1647. Excerpt from a report of Mikhail Stadukhin about a delay en route to the Pogycha River.

Service-man Mikhalko Stadukhin and his companions make obeisance to voyevodas Vasiliy Nikitich, Kiril Osipovich, [and] Petr Grigor'yevich of the sovereign tsar and grand prince of all Rus', Aleksey Mikhaylovich, at the Lena portage [*sic*].

In the past year 155 [1647] in accordance with the edict of the soverign tsar and grand prince of all Rus', Aleksey Mikhaylovich, and your voyevodal orders we, Mikhalko Stadukhin and companions, were sent on the sovereign's service to the new river Pogycha, the same as the Anandyr' River. In God's anger the winds were heavy while sailing down the Lena River and did not allow us into the ocean quickly, and at sea the winds were frightening, and we are wintering at the tribute zimov'ye on the Yana River.

To save time I went with a few men on sleds across the portage to the Indigirka. I left the remaining men to come by sea in the koch. These were given to us from the sovereign's sailing equipment in the sovereign's treasury: an anchor and anchor rope; the anchor rope became worn out. If God's mercy had not hastened to us – promyshlenniks came upon [us] at sea, and they gave us rope and an anchor. If it were not for the promyshlenniks, we would have been wrecked at sea. I made obeisance to the sovereign tsar and grand prince of all Rus', Aleksey Mikhaylovich, and submitted a petition at the tribute zimov'ye on the Yana River to service-man Koz'ma Loshakov, that there was sailing equipment in the sovereign's treasury at the tribute zimov'ye on the Yana River, an anchor and rope that were too old. Koz'ma Loshakov gave us an iron anchor of a pud and a half and a seventeen-sazhen piece of sail rope. These were our reserves; they were expended while wintering on the Yanga. As we moved on, we borrowed from the promyshlenniks at high local prices. Help [us], Vasiliy Nikitich, Kirilo Osipovich, Petr Grigor'yevich. Do not forget our labour...

AAN, *fond* 21, *kniga* 30, *no.* 115. Copy.
Published in: *RM*, p. 67.

Document 15

7 September, or later, 1649. Report of Lena service-man Mikhail Stadukhin from the Kolyma River to the voyevodas at Yakutsk ostrog regarding his voyage eastward from the Kolyma River.

Service-man Mikhalko Stadukhin and companions make obeisance to voyevodas Vasiliy Nikitich, Kiril Osipovich, and Petr Grigor'yevich, at Yakutsk.

In the past year 157 [1648–9] I, Mikhalko Stadukhin, journeyed by sea from the Kovyma River to the new river Pogycha in koches. We went by sea from the Kovyma River for seven days-and-nights with sails unslackened, but we did not reach the river. I took some captives, native Koryaks, who lived on the coast near the sea. Under questioning...they stated: 'We do not know of any river nearby because a mountainous cliff lies close to the sea. We do not know where the mountain ends.' Certain service-men and traders, Yerasimko Ankidinov, Semeyka Dezhnev, with ninety men, set out for that river in the year 156 [1648] in seven koches, and the captives said this about them: 'Two koches were wrecked at sea, and our people killed them. The rest of the men lived at the edge of the sea, but we do not know whether they are alive or not.' On the basis of the natives' reports we dared not go on by sea lest the service-men die uselessly. We returned to the Kovyma River on the 7th day of September in the year 158 [1649].

There are a great many walruses and walrus tusks. If it pleases the sovereign to order service-men sent with grain supplies to that sea [of] a great many walruses, the sovereign's profits will be much. Yushka Seliverstov[1] knows all about the walruses, the walrus tusks, and sea route. Maritime matters are Yushka's business. I, Mikhalko, sent Yushka from the Kovyma River to the Lena ostrog with the sovereign's treasury, with the walrus tusks, and ordered him to appear at the main office with the sovereign's treasury, with the walrus tusks – two heads with four tusks, 29 pounds in weight, as well as half a pud of Spasskiy bone,[2] four tusks weighing half a pud, an axe, and two fragments. The sovereign's treasury of fish tooth bones has a seal and labels.

It was made known to me, Mikhalko, that there is a river nearby across the mountains. I went by sled from the Kovyma River in great need. I approached the trader Mikhaylo Bayev about supplies and equipment and about a loan. He, Mikhaylo, went with us and supported us in the sovereign's service with grain supplies and other kinds of equipment. We obtained a pud of flour from him for eight roubles.

The service-men who left Yakutsk without the sovereign's order and without your voyevodal release, Vaska Bugor and companions – these service-men made their obeisance to the sovereign tsar and grand prince of all Rus', Aleksey Mikhaylovich, and presented a petition to me, Mikhalko, to participate in the sovereign's service with me, Mikhalko, on the new river. I accepted them and sent their petitions to you with this report.

AAN, *fond* 21, *kniga* 30, *no*. 162. Copy.
Published in: *RM*, pp. 116–17.

Document 16

1655. Excerpts from a petition to tsar Aleksey Mikhaylovich by promyshlennik Ivan Fedorov Kazanets about his service on the Lena, Kolyma, and Anadyr' rivers with Mikhail Stadukhin and Semen Dezhnev.

Your sovereign's orphan, promyshlennik Ivashko Fedorov Kazanets, makes obeisance to the sovereign tsar and grand prince of all Rus', Aleksey Mikhaylovich. In the past year 155 [1648], sovereign, service-man Mikhaylo Stadukhin was sent from the Lena ostrog on your sovereign's service to the new transmontane rivers beyond the Kovyma River in search of new non-tribute paying people, and salaried

---

[1] Though he was a service-man, Belov identifies him in one place as a promyshlennik (*RM*, p. 117, note 2).
[2] Evidently walrus tusks donated by the promyshlenniks and cossacks to the Spasskiy monastery in Yakutsk (*RM*, p. 117, note 3).

service-men, ten men altogether, were sent with him. There was no one to serve with these service-men in your sovereign's distant service on the new rivers, that is, in the populous places on those rivers. I, your orphan, made obeisance to you, sovereign, and submitted a petition on the Lena River to service-man Mikhaylo Stadukhin to serve with him, Mikhaylo, for two years in your sovereign's service, without your sovereign's grain and money salary, with my own gun and powder, risking my poor head in great debt. I went with him, Mikhaylo, at sea. I, your orphan, spent the winter on the Yana River. I incurred a heavy debt in grain supply and fishing equipment, salmon and other nets...

To save time, the winter having passed, service-man Mikhaylo Stadukhin went in the spring by sled from the Yana River to the Indigirka River. He took me, your orphan, along for your sovereign's clerical duties. I, your orphan, bought grain supplies, skis, a sled, dogs, dog food, and I went into debt, risking my poor head with heavy obligations. I crossed over to the Indigirka River. Travel by the sled route from the Yana River to the Indigirka River [took] seven weeks. Having arrived on the Indigirka River, we built a koch. I, your orphan, went with him, Mikhaylo, by sea to the Kovyma River. I, your orphan, spent the winter with him, Mikhaylo, on the Kovyma River. I bought grain supplies, flour at five roubles or more a pud, and I went on your sovereign's service to the non-tribute paying Chukhoch'i...

After wintering on the Kovyma River, service-man Mikhaylo Stadukhin went by sea in a koch to the new rivers and took me, your orphan, with him for clerical duties. We went by sea from the Kovyma River sailing for seven days-and-nights, never slackening sail, but did not reach the river. Service-man Mikhaylo Stadukhin sent me, your orphan, with service-man Yvan Baranov on a trip for informants. I, your slave, went along the coast for two days-and-nights, and we reached two yurts of Koryak natives... We took captives and brought them to Mikhaylo Stadukhin. In the questioning... the captives told Mikhaylo: 'We do not know of any rivers near or far.' Mikhaylo, the service-men, and promyshlenniks had no grain supplies and could not catch fish because mountains lay near the sea. Service-man Mikhaylo Stadukhin, not wanting the service-men and promyshlenniks to freeze to death, returned by sea to the Kovyma River. We arrived [back] on the Kovyma River, [where] I spent the winter with Mikhail. I bought grain supplies and fishing equipment at very great cost, binding my poor head in great debt.

Service-man Mikhaylo Stadukhin went with sleds from the Kovyma

River to the new rivers across the mountains, and he took me, your orphan, with him for your sovereign's various clerical matters. I incurred a heavy debt for an outlay of grain supplies, fishing equipment, sleds, skis, dogs, and several other items. I, your orphan, crossed over to the new river Anandyr´ with Mikhaylo. I travelled for seven weeks from the Kovyma River to the Anandyr´ River by the sled route, along the tundra and across the mountains in violent winds. By the fate of God's whispering I did not see half of the world of God. In your sovereign's varied [and] considerable sled service on foot I became lame.

Service-man Mikhaylo Stadukhin, sovereign, went from the Anandyr´ River to the Penzhina River. Seeing that I was poor, lame, and in debt, he released me on the Anandyr´ River. From these places on the Anandyr´ River I, your orphan, am serving with service-man Semen Dezhnev of Yakutsk ostrog, as of this date in every sort of your sovereign tsar's service. While in your sovereign's service I will buy salmon nets at thirty roubles, a skein of twine for five roubles, an arshin of canvas for salmon nets for two roubles, a pound of powder for six roubles, and a pound of lead for one rouble. I, your orphan, searched at sea with Semen Dezhnev for your sovereign's rich and valuable treasury – fish tooth bone. During the many years in your sovereign's service I became poor and greatly in debt. I wander from court to court without your sovereign's grain and money salary.

Merciful sovereign tsar and grand prince of all Rus´, Aleksey Mikhaylovich, grant me, your poor orphan, for my service and many activities while in your sovereign's service your sovereign tsar's salary, which Christ the Lord will acknowledge to you, righteous sovereign, so that I, your orphan, shall not perish at last and so that I, your orphan, hereafter will not leave your sovereign's service. Sovereign tsar, have mercy; grant [this].

AAN, *fond* 21, *kniga* 31, *no.* 67. Copy.
Published in: *RM*, pp. 245–7.

Document 17

Not later than 1 September 1654. Excerpts from the report of Yakutsk service-man Yuriy Seliverstov on the Anadyr´ River to Yakutsk voyevoda Ivan Akinfeyev about his trip to the Anadyr´ River and his activities there and relations with Semen Dezhnev and others.

Service-man volunteer Yushko Seliverstov makes obeisance to stol´nik and voyevoda Ivan Pavlovich Akinfeyev and d´yak Osip Stepanov of

Yakutsk ostrog, [officials] of sovereign tsar and grand prince of all Rus´, Aleksey Mikhaylovich, at Yakutsk ostrog.

According to instructions under the Lena seal and signed by the d´yak I, Yushko, was sent from the Yakutsk ostrog down the Lena River and by sea beyond the Kolyma River to the Anadyr´ and Chendon.[1] I pledged returns for the great sovereign's treasury, to give fifty puds [1,800 pounds] of walrus tusks. By the sovereign's order I, Yusko, was directed to summon with kindness and without cruelty the non-tribute paying native peoples on the Anadyr´ and Chendon rivers, the Khodyntsy, Anauls, and Koryaks, for the purpose of the sovereign's tribute, to be in irredeemable slavery. I, Yushko, went in the spring with thirty-two service-men volunteers from the Kovyma River across the mountains by way of the mountain sled route. We, Yushko and service-men volunteers, travelled for many weeks across the mountains. I, Yushko, arrived on the new Anadyr´ River. Our supplies were strained. We, Yusko [sic], went down the Anadyr´ for many days in hunger...

I, Yushko, and the volunteers reached the Russians in the zimov´yes. Service-men and promyshlenniks lived in the zimov´yes [and] two commandants had been chosen from them, Semen Ivanov Dezhnev and Nikita Semenov. The names of the service-men and promyshlenniks: trader Onisim Martem´yanov and service-men Pavel Vasil´yev Kokoulin, Ortemey Fedotov Soldat, Fedot Yemel´yanov Vetoshka, Ivan Yakovlev´, Dmitriy Vasil´yev, promyshlenniks Vasiliy Yermolayev Bugor the younger, [and] twenty-five men, but not Semen Motora, who was killed. Semen Dezhnev and Nikita were selected in Motora's place, and they serve in accordance with the order to Semen Motora. I, Yushko, undertook to tell them, Semen and Nikita, the sovereign's orders, that I, Yushko, was ordered to be in command and to collect the sovereign's ten per cent tax. Semen Dezhnev and Nikita Semenov, as well as Onisim Kostromin, live on these rivers self-determining and self-empowered...

Semen [and the others] trade among themselves in all kinds of goods and do not pay the sovereign's ten per cent and transaction taxes. In the past year 160 [1652] Semen Dezhnev, Nikita Semenov, Onasim Kostromin, Vasiliy Yermolayev, and companions went to the sea, to the sandspit. They gathered 102 or more puds [3,632 pounds] of walrus tusks, seven tusks to a pud, and eighty puds [2,880 pounds] or more

---

[1] The Gizhiga River according to Belov (1955, p. 41) and Polevoy (1964b, p. 229); the Penzhina according to Dolgikh (1960, p. 409).

of small tusks and fragments. In the present year 162 [1654] service-men Semen Dezhnev, Nikita Semenov, and Onasim Kostromin went to sea from the Anadyr' River in koches to collect at sea dead tusks [i.e., from dead animals] the walrus tusks. I, Yushko, set about telling him: 'You, Semen, go to sea to take over all the dead tusks as your own property and do not pay the sovereign's ten per cent tax from that collection. I, Yushko, have pledged big returns for the sovereign, to deposit fifty puds of walrus tusks in the treasury. Where will I, Yushko get these tusks? Having had hopes for the dead tusks, I pledged a profit for the sovereign.' They, Semen Dezhnev and his men, do not listen to me and have collected all the dead tusks around the Anadyr' Bay. There is no place for me, Yushko, to gather the tusks inasmuch as I was praised on the Lena before Dmitriyavich Fronzbekov and d'yak Osip Stepanov [the non-sequitur, sic]. In the present year 162 [1654] I, Yushko, and service-men volunteers went down the Anadyr' River to the sea for walrus tusks. Thirty-one service-men volunteers went with me in two koches. Instructions to Mikhalko Stadukhin were sent with me, but he, Mikhalko, was not on the Anadyr' River; he had gone on. In the instructions Mikhalko was ordered to send Motora and his men and Onasim Kostromin to the Lena River from the Anadyr' River, but Stadukhin had gone on to other rivers...

I, Yushko, on my own initiative set about speaking to Nikita and Onasim Kostromin: 'Pay attention to the instructions that order you sent to the Yakutsk ostrog.' But they, Nikita Semenov and Onasim Kostromin, did not heed your sovereign's order...

There was written in Mikhail's instructions: It is ordered to tell the fugitives Vas'ka Bugor and companions that they are ordered to serve the sovereign with Mikhail. I, Yushko, read the order aloud, and Vas'ka Bugor, the fugitive, and Yevseyko Pavlov, hearing such commissioned word from the sovereign, began serving the sovereign together with me, Yushko. Also promyshlennik Yushko Trofimov serves the sovereign with me...

On the verso: The year 163 [1654-5].

AN, LOII, YaA, *karton* 13, *stolbets* 7, *sstav* 6-13.

Published in: *RM*, no. 35, pp. 119-22.

Note. A second and quite similar report by Seliverstov to the voyevoda at Yakutsk, written after 30 March 1655, was published in *DAI*, Tom IV, pp. 9-12, from the copy taken by Müller. This later one says somewhat less about the journey to and arrival on the Anadyr' and more about his charges against Dezhnev, Semenov, and their friends: that they tried to exclude him from walrus hunting, struck him physically, vilified voyevoda Frantsbekov at Yakutsk, refused to recognize his authority inherited from Stadukhin. In these complaints one can read jealousy of Dezhnev and an effort to discredit him with the authorities at Yakutsk in the hope of superseding Dezhnev and Semenov in command on the Anadyr'.

★　★　★

For part of his 1758 account Müller depended upon oral information rather than firsthand documentary reports, the part relating to the fate of Fedot Alekseyev and his companions. The Kamchadals were his ultimate source of information, but since he did not go to Kamchatka during his ten-year tour of Siberia, his information had to come from those who had been there. He does not name his informants, but they appear to have been in Yakutsk. In 1737 he incorporated the information he had gathered about Kamchatka in a memorandum which was intended to guide Stepan P. Krasheninnikov, one of three, and the most capable of the three, students who accompanied Müller and Gmelin in Siberia, in his researches in Kamchatka. Müller had expected to include Kamchatka in his travels, but unforeseen developments forestalled him. Instead Krasheninnikov was sent by himself to conduct the expedition's investigation of that peninsula. Müller's memorandum was later published, in 1774, as a supplementary article titled 'Geographie und Verfassung Kamtschatka aus verschiedenen schriftlichen und mündlichen Nachrichten gesammelt zu Jakuzk, 1737' in Georg W. Steller's *Beschreibung von dem Lande Kamtschatka...*[1] In the memorandum Müller devoted a paragraph (p. 5) to the appearance of the Russians in Kamchatka before its conquest in 1698–9. It reflects an early stage of knowledge of the Russians in pre-conquest Kamchatka. It is given here.

Document 18

Müller's remarks in 1737 on the Fedotov legend.

Fourteen and a half versts from there a little river, the Nikul, otherwise known as the Feodochita, falls from the same [i.e., southeastern] side into the Kamchatka, which is noteworthy because of the first Russian inhabitants of the land, who, as history tells us, emerging from the

---

[1] Full title is *Beschreibung von dem Lande Kamtschatka dessen Einwohnern, deren Sitten, Nahmen, Lebensart und verschiedenen Gewohnheiten* (edited by J. S. B. [Jean Benoit Scherer]; Frankfurt and Leipzig).

mouth of the Lena River, arrived in Kamchatka, having been tossed about by a storm, a considerable number of years before the actual conquest of the land of Kamchatka, and they settled down at the mouth of this little river, which retained the Russian name from the highest-born among them.

★ ★ ★

From Krasheninnikov's three years of arduous life and travel and observation in Kamchatka came his classic description of that land, first published in 1755 and republished in a modern edition in 1949.[1] It is he who presents the most detailed statement of the Fedot Alekseyev tradition in the 18th century. Krasheninnikov in fact wrote two statements, an earlier and shorter one, not published until 1949 (document 19),[2] and the later and longer one found in his *Description of Kamchatka* (document 20).

Document 19

Krasheninnikov's preliminary version of the legend about Fedot Alekseyev.

Prior to the conquest of the Kamchatka land promyshlennik Fedot, commander of a koch, and 17 promyshlenniks were the first in this land, having gone from the mouth of the Lena River with another promyshlennik named Foma in 7 koches. Two of these koches arrived at the mouth of the Anadyr´River under the command of promyshlennik Foma, and they settled in the Anadyrskiy ostrog, which then had only recently been established. A third koch, which carried Fedot, arrived at the mouth of the Kamchatka, having sailed around the Chukotskiy promontory,[3] and he proceeded up that river to a small river, Ikolka [Nikul], which comes in from the right side and is 50[4] versts below the Upper ostrog. It is now called the Fedotovshchina. The rest of the four koches disappeared without a trace.

Fedot and his companions passed the winter at the mouth of the aforesaid Ikolka River, having built a zimov´ye.[5] In the spring he sailed in the same koch out of the mouth of the Kamchatka River into the sea, and, sailing around the Kuril 'spade' [Cape Lopatka], went along the Penzhina Sea [Sea of Okhotsk] to the Paren´ River where he and

[1] *Opisaniye Kamchatki* (St Petersburg; modern edition, Moscow).
[2] 1949, p. 740. This in turn Krasheninnikov wrote in two versions; the one not reproduced here is on p. 479.
[3] This detail is omitted in the other version of this preliminary account.
[4] 100 in the other version.   [5] Omitted in the other version.

his companions spent the winter. That winter he was killed by his brother over a slave, and then the Koryaks killed all the rest of them...

AAN, *fond* 21, *opis'* 5, *no.* 60, *list* 32.

Published in 'O zavoyevanii kamchatskoy zemlitsy, o byvshikh v rasnyye vremena ot inozemtsov ismenakh i o buntakh sluzhivykh lyudey' in Krasheninnikov, 1949, p. 740.

Document 20

Krasheninnikov's published account of the legend about Fedot Alekseyev.

With the extension of Russian power in the north and the founding of settlements along the most important rivers which empty into the Icy Sea, from the Lena River eastward to the Anadyr', increasing effort was constantly made to learn about the lands beyond the Anadyr' and to bring the heathen living there under subjection. Because of this it was reiterated to every commandant that he should seek by every means to obtain information as to which people lived where and in what numbers, what kind of weapons they had, what sort of wealth, and the like. Thus Kamchatka could not have been unknown at the time when several Koryaks of the Penzhina and Olyutora seas were subjected to fur tribute from the Anadyr', for as Kamchatka neighbours the local people [i.e., the Kamchadals] were known to them, even more so to the reindeer Koryaks, who often nomadized in Kamchatka itself. But I do not have sufficient evidence about who was the first Russian in Kamchatka. According to oral information this was ascribed to a certain trader, Fedot Alekseyev, whose name, Fedotovshchina, was given to the little river Nikul, which empties into the Kamchatka. Supposedly he went by the Icy Sea from the mouth of the Kolyma River in seven koches; supposedly he was separated from the other koches in a storm and carried to Kamchatka where he wintered with his koch. In another summer, rounding the Kuril 'spade', he reached the Tigil' River by way of the Penzhina Sea. They were killed by the local Koryaks in the winter. They themselves provided the reason for this killing when one of them killed another, for the Koryaks, who had considered them to be immortal because of their firearms, seeing that they could die, did not want such fearsome guests among them. The information about his sea route from the Kovyma River is supported by the report of service-man Semen Dezhnev, for Dezhnev declares that their journey was unfortunate. Trader Fedot Alekseyev was carried away from him by a storm without news. It carried him [Dezhnev] at sea for a long while and later threw him ashore on the forward end beyond the Anadyr' River. But there is some doubt in the discussion of his [Fedot Alekseyev's] stay in Kamchatka that the Nikul River was named the Fedotovshchina after his name, for in his same report of 7162 [1654—*sic*] it is stated that Dezhnev went on a trip near the sea, and he took from the Koryaks the Yakut woman of the late Alekseyev, who told him that Fedot and one of the service-men died from scurvy; others were killed by them. A few men were left, and they fled stark naked in lodki, where it is not known. Concerning the zimov'yes built on the Nikul River the Kamchadals confirm that they were built by Russians and that their ruins have been seen down to our times.

But this difference in information appears to be averted perhaps if it is assumed that Fedot and his companions did not die on the Tigil', but between the Anadyr' and Olyutora; for it would not then be contrary to the information when we surmise that he wintered on the Kamchatka with his koch and sailed around Lopatka to the Tigil' River, that from there he went back toward the Anadyr' either by sea or overland along the Olyutora coast and died on the way. His other companions were either killed or disappeared without a trace, wanting to escape being killed. But be this as it may, this expedition was a small one and not of great importance because nothing of value followed from it, not only in regard to the interests of the state, but not even in regard to very reliable information about Kamchatka. For, as indicated above, no survivors from the expedition appeared. On this account the expedition of cossack pyatidesyatnik Volodomir Atlasov can be considered as the first expedition into Kamchatka.

Krasheninnikov, 1949, pp. 473–5. Another, less literal, translation into English is in Stepan P. Krasheninnikov, *Exploration of Kamchatka, 1735–1741* (translated with notes and introduction by E. A. P. Crownhart-Vaughan; Portland, Oregon; 1972), pp. 299–300.

CHAPTER 4

OTHER SOURCES

In the last chapter we grouped together documents used by Müller. In this chapter we reproduce other documents and sources bearing on Dezhnev and his voyage. With one exception there is no indication that Müller used them even if he knew of them.

At the end of the last century the archivist Ogloblin, as we noted in chapter 1, uncovered in the archives of the Siberian Department four petitions submitted by Dezhnev to the authorities between July 1662 and February 1665. The transfer after World War II of the 17th-century archives of Yakutsk to the Central State Archive of Historical Documents in Moscow was followed by the uncovering of the originals of certain documents in Müller's Portfolios, as we have seen, and by the discovery of other documents related not only to Dezhnev's career, but to Russian maritime activity in northeastern Siberia. Both the archivist Orlova and the scholar Belov took advantage of the availability and ordering of the documents in these archives to publish compilations of documents selected from them. Several of the documents in this chapter have been taken from these compilations. Polevoy explored the collection from the Yakutsk archives and has turned up two documents which have enabled him to make significant revisions of a couple of matters in the traditional account of the voyage. The last selection presented here is not, however, derived from these archives, for it is a reprinting of a section from another published work. The order of presentation here, as in the preceding chapter, is chronological since the treatment in the following chapters is largely chronological.

Our first document (no. 21) is one from which we learn that Dezhnev was married to a Yakut woman. The second (no. 22) is a travel document or passport[1] from the Yakutsk customs office showing the goods which Fedot Alekseyev carried with him on his journey to the Olenek River. This travel document gives us a picture of the capital outlay that Alekseyev had in Siberia, both in number and kinds of goods

---

[1] A travel document or passport (*proyezzhaya gramota*) was required of all travellers in Siberia, government or private, in order to be cleared from one customs house or barrier to another (Lantzeff, 1943, p. 14). It listed all goods carried and the duty paid on them.

and equipment. Document 23 was found by Polevoy, a petition from Stadukhin, Dmitriy Yarilo, Dezhnev, and others, whose contents led him to conclude that the first Russian outpost established on the Kolyma was Sredne-Kolymsk, not Nizhne-Kolymsk, and the year of founding to be 1643, not 1644. It is a valuable and clarifying discovery. Document 24 is a deposition taken in Yakutsk in 1644 from several cossacks who reported hearing from natives of rivers to the east of the Kolyma where silver ore and furs were to be found. These rumours were preliminary to reports about the Pogycha River. The next document (no. 25) is a declaration of goods at the Yakutsk customs office of the two merchant's agents in whose boat Dezhnev made the voyage. It has the same usefulness as the travel document issued to Fedot Alekseyev. Document 26 contains excerpts from the instructions issued by the voyevoda at Yakutsk to commandant Vasiliy Vlas'yev and sworn-man Kiril Kotkin, sent to the Kolyma to relieve Gavrilov, the commandant who despatched Dezhnev on the voyage. It contains a helpful description of the Kolyma region, its geography, inhabitants, and tribute potential, and lists many of the service-men there. This document provides mainly background information.

Document 21

No later than 17 August 1641. Petition of Yeniseysk cossack Semen Ivanovich Dezhnev to tsar Mikhail Fedorovich about the care of his wife.

Your slave, Yeniseysk cossack Sen'ka Ivanov Dezhnev, makes obeisance to the sovereign tsar and grand prince of all Rus', Mikhail Fedorovich.

Merciful sovereign tsar and grand prince of all Rus', Mikhail Fedorovich, please allow me, your slave, sovereign, to keep for myself the provisioning of my little captive, my Yakol'skaya wife named Abakayada Sichyu, over the winter. I leave a cow and a calf to the Yakut Manyukuya of Borogonskaya volost'. Sovereign, be merciful, please.

On the verso: Recorded in the book, the 17th day of August of the year 149 [1641].

AN LOII, YaA, *karton* 3, *stolbets* 19, *sstav* 1.

Published in: Belov, 1948, Appendix, p. 132; *RM*, p. 103.

Document 22

6 July 1642. Travel document carried by Fedot Alekseyev en route to the Olenek River via the Lena River, issued by the Yakutsk customs office.

The year 150 [1642], the 6th day of July. A list of grain supplies, working equipment, and Russian goods from the customs house of customs head Druzhina Trubnikov [issued] to Fedot Olekseyev Kolmogorets, agent of Oleksey Usov, merchant of the Moscow gostinaya sotnya, which he will take with him down the Lena River to the nearby Olenek River for fishing and sable hunting:

700 puds [12 ½ tons] of rye flour	[700 r.[1]
[2 puds (72 pounds) of tin][1]	20 r.
4 puds of green copper in kettles	40 r.
20 pounds of small and large blue beads	12 r.
10 pounds of glass beads	6 r.
100 arshins [78 yards] of white woollen cloth	30 r.
50 small bells with tassels[2]	5 r.
350 sazhens [273 yards] of fishing net [1 sazhen = 28 inches]	70 r.
20 *skoloty podoshevnyye* [meaning not known]	30 r.
25 sable snare-nets	25 r.
60 axes	60 r.
2 puds [72 pounds] of fishing line	12 r.
100 arshins of medium and heavy canvas	15 r.]

His grain supplies, working equipment, and Russian goods have a Lena customs value of 1,025 r. Customs and departure duties were [not] collected at the customs house in the Lena ostrog from his grain supplies, working equipment, and Russian goods because when he returns from sable hunting, the sovereign's ten per cent taxes will be collected from him in sable pelts.

His nephew, Fedotkov Omel'ka Stepanov, is going with him. With him are going his employees (pokruchenniks): Nikita Prokop'yev, Tren'ka Yevseyev, Ortyushka [Ondryushka] Fedorov, Levka Semenov, Luchka Alimpiyev Urusko Oleksandrov, Timoshka Ignat'yev, Fil'ka Aleksandrov, Nasonka Kozim, Osipko Nikiforov, Tren'ka Nazarov, Kirilko Ivanov, Fed'ka Ivanov, Chyudinko Martynov, Ivashko Osipov, Mit'ka Vetchanin, Panfilko Ivanov, Ivashko Osipov [*sic*] Mironko Ivanov, Bogdashko Onisimov, Timoshka Myasin, Mishka Shabakov, Nikita Fedorov.

[1] Prices and bracketed item supplied from a list submitted to the customs office by Fedot Alekseyev (*ORZPM*, p. 169).   [2] Bakhrushin, 1951, p. 86.

Self-employed hunters (svoyeuzhiniks) [using] the same grain supplies and working equipment are going with him: Ostashka Kudrin, Mit'ka Yakovlev, Maksimko Larionov, Yushko Nikitin, Vas'ka Fedotov.

A departure tax of 1 altyn each was collected from Fedotka, his nephew, employees, and the self-employed hunters; and in the present year 150 [1641–2] 8 altyns, 2 dengas, were collected from Tren'ka Yevseyev, Ostashka Kudrin, Mitka Yakovlev, Maksim Larionov, and Yushka Nikitin on the Vilyuy, and from Fedotka, from his nephew, and from employees in full in the customs house in the Lena ostrog.

Customs head Druzhina Trubnikov affixed the seal of the Siberian government of the great river Lena to this list of the sovereign tsar and grand prince of all Rus', Mikhail Fedorovich.

TsGADA, YaPI, *stolbets* 13, *listy* 162–3.
Published in: *RM*, pp. 104–5.
The list which Fedot Alekseyev submitted the same day to the customs head and on which this list is based appears in *ORZPM*, pp. 169–70 (YaPI, *stolbets* 2147 [46], *listy* 70–1).

Document 23

After 1 March 1644. Petition for payment of salary for service on the Kolyma River and the establishment of an outpost there by Mikhail Stadukhin, Dmitriy Mikhaylov Yerilo, Semen Dezhnev, and twenty others.

Your sovereign's slaves, Lena service-men Mishka Stadukhin, Mit'ka Mikhaylov Yarilo, Ftorko Gavrilov, Onisimko Ivanov, Grishka Fofanov, Zav'yalko Sidorov, Semeyka Dezhnev, Makarko Tveryakov, Mishka Savin Konoval, Mokeyko Ignat'yev, Sergeyko Ortem'yev; and Tomsk service-man Romashka Ivanov Nemchin, Ivashko Belyana, Semeyka Motora; Yeniseysk service-man Pospelko Koz'min, Krasnoyarsk service-man Borisko Prokov'yev; and your sovereign's orphans promyshlenniks Ivashko Gavrilov Kulkin, Sysoyko Vasil'yev, Ul'yanko Karpov, Ivashko Pavlov, Ofon'ko Yakimov, Ivashko Soburov, Fed'ka Fedorov make obeisance to the sovereign tsar and grand prince of all Rus', Mikhail Fedorovich.

On the 8th day of July in the past year 151 [1643] we, your sovereign's slaves and orphans, met at sea, and we service-men and promyshlenniks, Mishka Stadukhin and his men and Mit'ka Mikhaylov Yerilo and his men joined together as one in order for us, your sovereign's slaves, to carry out the various services for your sovereign [and] to go together as one to the new river Kovyma to new non-tribute paying people, to the reindeer and walking-sedentary people, to call them to your sovereign's bounty and to request tribute from them.

When we, your sovereign's slaves, arrived at the new river Kovyma before the non-tribute paying reindeer people [and their] chiefs Panteli and Koralyu on the 15th day of July, and when we, your sovereign's slaves, set about calling these chiefs to your bounty and telling them about your sovereign's majesty so that those chiefs themselves and their tribesmen would pay tribute, and so that these natives would be under the sovereign's exalted hand in eternal slavery, these non-tribute paying reindeer natives, the chiefs Panteli and Koralyu and their tribesmen, resisted and did not listen or submit and did not give tribute for themselves or tribesmen and began to fight with us service-men. There was a big gathering of them. We, your sovereign's slaves and orphans, fought with these natives all day until evening. The chiefs Panteli and Karalyu [sic] said to us: 'Why do you request tribute from us? This land is ours and we rule over it, and we will not let you ashore.' Those reindeer people followed us, your sovereign's slaves, in boats (lotki) for three days away from their living areas. They did not allow us, your sovereign's slaves, ashore for there were very many of them. We fought with them in strugi.[1] In that fighting service-man Ramashka Nemchin killed a leading tribesman; Makarko Tveryakov killed a man; Borisko Prokov'yev was wounded in the right hand; Ivashka Soburov was wounded.

We, your slaves and orphans, went on up the Kovyma River to the walking–sedentary people. On the 25th day of July we, your sovereign's slaves and orphans, came to the walking sedentary people, to chief Olay. We, your sovereign's orphans, began to call this chief to your sovereign's bounty with all his family and tribesmen, and we began to ask from him, sovereign, the sovereign's tribute. That chief Alay and his brothers and tribesmen went into a stockade and resisted and did not obey. 'We will not give tribute to your sovereign', he said, 'because this land is ours and these people are mine.' We, your sovereign's slaves and orphans, begging God's mercy, began to take action against them and to move toward the stockade. [We] laid siege to chief Olay, his brothers, and tribesmen in the stockade. By God's mercy and your sovereign's good fortune chief Olay came out of the stockade. Olay, his brothers, and tribesmen moved to an opening. At

---

[1] Ordinarily flat-bottomed river boats propelled by oars or sails. It is not clear whether in this case the word refers to small boats carried on the koches and used here to engage the natives at close quarters or not. The boat in which Yerilo and his men sailed from the Alazeya was a koch (ORZPM, p. 143), as presumably was Stadukhin's.

that opening Lena service-man Semeyka Dezhnev killed one of his blood brothers, and service-man Mit'ka Mikhaylov, Ftorko Gavrilov, Grishka Fofanov, Onisimko Ivanov drove off Olay's son, a 'best' man, and captured him alive. Olay and his men went to the rescue of his son. Promyshlennik Ivashko Kuklin killed Olay's uncle; Sergeyko Ortem'yev was wounded in the knee of the right leg; Sysoyka Vasil'yev was wounded in the right thigh; Ofon'ka [Yakimov] Chyukchey[1] was wounded in the waist on the left side; Pospelko Koz'min killed a tribesman; Ivashko Belyana killed a man; Moleyko Ignat'yev was wounded in the right hand; Ivashko Pavlov killed a man.

After that attack, as we, your slaves and orphans, advanced toward Olay's stockade on the 30th day of July, chief Olay came to us, your sovereign's slaves, and began speaking: 'Do not kill my son, and I will hunt the sovereign's tribute and pay tribute every year.' We, your sovereign's slaves, erected an ostrozhek in Olay's living area. Olay's son sat as a hostage. On the 28th day of January of the present year 152 [1644] Olay and his brothers and tribesmen came and gave tribute to the great sovereign from himself and his tribesmen. We, your sovereign's slaves, set about telling chief Olay about your sovereign's majesty and your sovereign's beneficent word so that Olay, his brothers, and tribesmen would be pacified and obedient and under your sovereign's exalted hand in perpetual slavery and that he would call on other chiefs [to submit]. We, your sovereign's slaves, gave Olay the sovereign's award, and Olay accepted the sovereign's gift honourably, and he listened to our words, to what we, your sovereign's slaves, said about your sovereign's majesty.

Olay went up the Kovyma to the 'best' chiefs, to Necha and to Necha's brother Kalyana. On the 28th day of February Alay and these upriver chiefs, Necha and his brother Kalyana, came to us, your sovereign's slaves, at the ostrozhek. Upon arrival Necha and his brother Kalyana started berating us, your sovereign's slaves, and to rail against us with all sorts of abusive language. Necha and his brother said to us, your sovereign's slaves: 'Why have you come to our land and built an ostrog without asking our permission?' We, your sovereign's slaves, spoke to Necha and his brother Kalyana about your sovereign's majesty and requested tribute from them. Necha and his brother Kalyana spoke to us: 'What kind of tribute from us to you? We own the land here. We will not only not pay tribute to you, we will not give you water from the Kovyma to drink or trees for firewood. We do not wish to

[1] He was a Chukcha (Boris P. Polevoy, 'Nakhodka chelobit'ya pervootkryvateley Kolymy', *Ekonomika, upravleniye i kul'tura Sibiri XVI–XIX vv.* [Novosibirsk, 1966], p. 290).

become slaves in our own land.' We, your sovereign's slaves, asking God's mercy, [came] out of the ostrozhek to fight with Necha and his brother Kalyana, and by God's mercy and the sovereign's good fortune Semeyka Motora killed a man in that fight, and promyshlennik Yl'yanko Karpov killed a man, and the service-men and promyshlenniks captured Necha's blood brother; service-men Mishka Stadukhin and Mishka Konoval and promyshlennik Fedka Fedorov captured Necha's blood brother alive. In that combat service-man Zaval'ka Sidorov was wounded in the chest; before that Mishka Stadukhin was wounded by Necha's brother Kalyana; and Mishka Konoval was wounded in the leg. On the 1st day of March after the fight Necha came and gave twenty sables as tribute and started speaking to us, your sovereign's slaves: 'Do not kill my brother Kalyana and I will pay the great sovereign tribute every year without stopping from all my brothers and tribesman. Hereafter I will work honestly and zealously for the great sovereign, and I will call the other chiefs to the sovereign's gifts and tribute.'

Merciful sovereign tsar and grand prince of all Rus', Mikhail Fedorovich, reward us, your sovereign's slaves, in our service, sovereign tsar, with whatever you command. Have mercy, sovereign tsar, please.

Signed by Dmitriy Mikhaylo [and] Vtoroy Gavrilov for twelve service-men and promyshlenniks (including M. Stadukhin), and by Ivan Gavrilov Kulkin for eight service-men and promyshlenniks.

TsGADA, YaPI, *opis'* 3, 1645–6, *delo* 25, *listy* 1–3.

Published in: Polevoy, 1966, pp. 287–9.

Document 24

29 September 1644. Excerpt from the depositions in the main office at Yatutsk of cossacks Lavrentiy Grigor'yev, Ivan Yerastov, Tret'yako Alekseyev, and others regarding the Kolyma and Neloga rivers and the tribes inhabiting the neighbouring regions.

On the 29th day of September of the year 153 [1644] service-man Lavrushka Grigor'yev stated under questioning: Service-man Grishko Kisel' brought to him in the year 151 [1643–4] instructions under the sovereign's Lena seal from stol'nik and voyevoda Petr Petrovich Golovin, and those instructions were sent to service-man Mit'ka Mikhaylo Yarilo.[1] He, Mit'ka, was ordered to find out about silver ores

---

[1] This refers to the instructions issued to him under the name Dmitriy Zyryan, a name by which he was also known, and preserved now in LOII (YaA, *kniga* 4, *sstavy* 20, 42–3 [Belov in *RM*, p. 46, note 1]).

and to question the natives closely against the statements of a Yukagir shaman, whom Yeleska Buza had brought with him, as to what river it is where there is silver ore and how far it is from the Indigirka River.

Lavrushka reported that in accordance with the instructions he, Lavrushka, questioned the native chief [and] shaman Porocha and his wife about the silver ore, whether there is any silver ore near that river, whether it is close to the Indigirka River and how far. The Kovyma chief said to Lavrushka under questioning: 'There is the Neloga River beyond the Kovyma, [and] it empties into the sea through its own mouth. On the Nel'ga River close to the sea there is silver ore in a mountain, in a cliff. Walking natives live at a certain place in earthen yurts near that mountain. The clan has its own language, not Yukagir. They call themselves Natki. These people take white "bead-stuff" from the river, and they have much of this bead-stuff.'[1] The Chyundon River[2] went from the upper reaches of the Neloga River. The Chyundon River empties into the Kovyma River near the sea. Yukagir people live along that Sun[p'ya] River. On the upper part of that river there live a people [who are] a clan of their own; they have tattooed faces. 'The Natty', they say, 'come to the tattooed faces from the Neloga River, from the silver ores, to trade in the upper part of that Chyundon River, and they fight with them for awhile. The Neloga people sell silver and bead-stuff to the tattooed faces. The tattooed faces sell reindeer and knives. The Neloga people have much silver and bead-stuff.'

Lavrushka showed the shaman white bead-stuff and beads. The shaman said: 'The bead-stuff on the Neloga River is not like that; it is better than the Russian bead-stuff and beads.' The shaman says that he has seen that bead-stuff of theirs and his wife saw it. According to the shaman's remarks he thinks the bead-stuff to be pearl.

Lavrushka asked the Yukagir hostage, chief Shenkod'ye, a shaman, about the Neloga River, without the Kovyma hostage Porochi's [being present]. Under questioning the shaman Shenkod'ye confirmed the remarks of the Kovyma chief-shaman about the Neloga River and silver ore word for word. The Tungus woman U[zber]chik, who is an interpreter on the Yndigirka River, translated these remarks...

[1] *Odekuy* in Russian, which means a kind of blue bead. What it refers to here is not clear, but evidently such beads were made from it, so I have coined the word 'bead-stuff' as a translation of it. Bakhrushin (1951, p. 89) defines it as a kind of bead made from crystal. In this document the word seems to apply to the material from which the beads were made, so the term 'bead-stuff' seems applicable.

[2] The Anyuy River according to Belov (*RM*, p. 47, note 3).

TsGADA, YaPI, *stolbets* 43, *listy* 28–9.
Published in: *ORZPM*, pp. 125–6; *RM*, pp. 44–5, with a few slight variations.

Document 25

27 June 1646. Declaration of goods of Afanasiy Andreyev and Bezson Astaf'yev, agents of merchant Afanasiy Fedotov Gusel'nikov, at the Yakutsk customs house, on their departure for the Indigirka, Kolyma, and other rivers.

The 27th day of June of the year 154 [1646]. Declaration in the customs house for the head of the customs house and barriers, Pervyy Osipov Usachev, and [his] associates, of Ofonasiy Fedotov, brother of Vasiliy Fedotov Gusel'nikov, Moscow merchant of the gostinaya sotnya, that he, Ofonosiy, is sending from the Yakutsk ostrog down the Lena River and by sea to the Indigirka, Kolyma, and other nearby rivers for sable hunting and trade with his agents Ofon'ka Andreyev and Bezson Ostof'yev his, Ofonosiy's employees Ivashko Nesterov Okruchzhenin [Okruzhenik?], Petrushka Kozmin Usolets, Yelfimko Merkur'yev, Fomka Semenov, Romashko Ivanov Mezenets, Borisko Ivashko Ustyuzhanin, Kirilko Lavrent'yev Cherdinets,[1] [taken] from his travel document and from the travel document of Vasiliy's agent Ivashko Yakovlev Chirka.

There go with them grain supplies, Russian goods, and equipment for sable hunting:

200 puds [3·6 tons] of rye flour	160 r.
100 skeins of fishing line	100 r.
71 cups	35 r.
72 blouses with Yaroslav stitching and binding, one golden	46 r., 16 altyns, 4 dengas[2]
5 red hides	15 r.
16 snowshoe boots	13 r.
95 woollen mittens [pairs?]	45 r.
5 mukluks	1 r.
200 arshins [155 yards] of course grey cloth	60 r.
28 small bells with tassels	2 r., 26 a., 4 d.
13 loadstones in bone	5 r.

[1] Belov (1949, p. 462), citing what seems to be the same document, but carrying a different archival designation, presents a list which excludes Ivashko Nesterov Okruchzhenin and includes one Aleksey Melent'yev Vychugzhanin and Ivan Semenov Zyryan.

[2] 200 dengas = 1 r.; 6 dengas = 1 altyn; 2 dengas = 1 kopeck; $33\frac{1}{3}$ altyns = 1 r.; 1 poltin = 50 kopecks or $\frac{1}{2}$ r.

400 copper buttons	26 a., 4 d.
Half pound of sublimate of mercury	1 r.
6 guns, 3 rifles, 3 smoothbores	20 r.
2 gun locks	2 r.
25 pounds of *tsylibukhi* [meaning undetermined]	10 r.
14 pounds of pepper	7 r.
15 metal bars	3 r.
52 axes	26 r.
30 pounds of powder	34 r.
A pud and one-eighth [40·5 pounds] of copper in kettles	23 r.
120 elkskin strips	10 r.
120 deerskin strips	12 r.
200 arshins of fine linen	10 r.
20 sheepskin caftans	31 r.
6 blankets	18 r.
5 puds [180 pounds] of wax candles	60 r.
6 crowbars	3 r.
5 small frying pans	1 r., 1 poltina
450 sazhens [1,050 yards] of fishing net	90 r.
480 arshins [373 yards] of sail canvas	24 r.
	[Total 871½ r., 7 a.]

Foreman Afonos'yev Aleshka Maslov of Vychegda and employee
Ivashka Semenov went with him. With them were grain supplies of

40 puds [1,440 pounds] of rye flour	32 r.
40 elkskin strips	10 r.
26 deerskin strips	2 r., 20 a.
40 skeins of fishing line	40 r.
80 sazhens [187 yards] of net thread	16 r.
100 arshins [78 yards] of medium linen	8 r.
5 Yaroslav blouses	3 r.
20 woollen mittens	10 r.
20 cups	10 r.
2 red hides	6 r.
6 mukluks	1 r.
15 arshins [11·7 yards] of coarse grey cloth	4 r. and a poltin
15 arshins of white cloth	4 r.
6 axes	3 r.
5,000 blue beads	2 r. and a poltin
2 crowbars	1 r.
3 red snowshoe boots	2 r. and a poltin
6 bezmens [15 pounds] of wax candles	4 r.

2 gun locks	12 r.
2 pounds of powder	1 r., 26 a., 2 d.
20 pounds of copper in kettles	6 r.
2 small frying pans	20 a.
A rawhide	2 r.
	[Total 18½ r., 2 d.]

TsGADA, YaPI, *stolbets* 2087, *listy* 13–17.
Published in: *ORZPM*, pp. 209–10; *RM*, pp. 107–9.

Document 26

5 July 1647. Excerpts from the instructions of Yakutsk voyevoda Vasiliy Nikitich Pushkin to boyar-son Vasiliy Vlas'yev and sworn-man Kiril Kotkin about travelling to the Kolyma River and their duties there.

On the 5th day of July of the year 7155 [1647] in accordance with the ukaz of the sovereign tsar and grand prince of all Rus', Aleksey Mikhaylovich, and the order of voyevodas Vasiliy Nikitich Pushkin and Kiril Osipovich Suponev and d'yak Petr Stenshin of the Yakutsk ostrog instructions [are issued] to boyar-son Vasiliy Vlas'yev and sworn-man trader Kirilka Yur'yev Kotkin and [other] sworn-men.

He is to go with service-men on the sovereign's service from the Yakutsk ostrog down the Lena to the mouth of the Lena River, where it empties into the sea, and by sea to the Kovyma River, to the ostrozhek where service-man Mikhalko Stadukhin and service-men established a zimov'ye with fortification for the collection of tribute and pominki of the sovereign tsar and grand prince of all Rus', Aleksey Mikhaylovich, and for searching out and bringing new Kolyma non-tribute paying natives under the sovereign's exalted hand.

On the 30th day of September of the past year 154 [1645] service-man Mikhalko Stadukhin and Vtorko Gavrilov and companions wrote from the Kovyma to the Yakutsk ostrog to former stol'nik and voyevoda Petr Golovin and associates,[1] and in their report it was written that the Kovyma River is big and wide and that there are many natives and sables on the Kovyma River; that the natives on the Kovyma River are sedentary; in the winter and summer they stay in one place, walkers; but the reindeer people – they wander from place to place, to the lakes.

In the present year 155 [1647] service-man Mikhalko Stadukhin

[1] This report has not been found in the files of the Yakutsk main office (Belov in *RM*, p. 63, note 3). Moreover, at the end of September 1645 Stadukhin was near or at Zhigansk on his way back to Yakutsk, not on the Kolyma.

stated under questioning in the main office at the Yakutsk ostrog: He was on the Kolyma River for two years for the collection of the sovereign's tribute... [Here follows Stadukhin's deposition as recorded in document 12.]

The service-men on the Kovyma with Vtorko [Gavrilov and] the hostages are Sergeyko Artem'yev, Semeyko Dezhnev, Mishka Savin Konoval, Makarko Tveryakov, Semeyka Ivanov Motora, Pashko Levont'yev, Mikhalko Semenov, Pospelko Kuz'min, and Lena service-man Gerasim Ankudinov, who petitioned to serve with them. They have no grain supplies; and no casting nets, lines, or stationary nets have been sent from Yakutsk. There is great need. There is nothing to catch fish with and to feed the hostages.

There are many non-tribute paying natives, reindeer and walking, up along the Kovyma River and nearby rivers. The Kovyma is a big river, bigger than the Indigirka, smaller than the Lena. It is not known how far up [it goes], whether its upper part is far away. Small tributary rivers empty into the Kovyma [with] fish since they come from lakes. Down below there is a tributary river from the right side sailing downstream, the Anoya [Anyuy], and at the mouth of the Anoya River a new tribute zimov'ye was established. According to the testimony of the hostages the Onoya flows from a lake far away [Lake Ilirney]. Many reindeer natives live along the upper part of that river and in the vicinity of the lake from which it emerges. At the mouth of the Onoya there are three hundred or more reindeer men. They do not give the sovereign's tribute. Beyond the ridge of the mountains is the big river Kovycha, where the forest is small, many reindeer people live, and there are sables. The food on the Kovyma is fish, and swimming reindeer live [there] and many moose. Goods suitable for the natives are small axes, knives, and canes and Yakutsk shield-piercing clubs, and small pots and iron arrows...

Boyar-son Vasiliy Vlas'yev and service-men and sworn-man are to go from the Yakutsk ostrog on the sovereign's service in government boats by way of the Lena River, and emerging from the Lena River into the sea [to go] by sea to the Kovyma River for collection of the sovereign's tribute and the bringing of new non-tribute paying natives under the sovereign's exalted hand, delaying not an hour on the way. Having arrived at that ostrog on the Kolyma where service-man Vtorko Gavrilov and companions are now, Vasiliy is to take over from Vtorko Gavrilov the hostages listed... [There follow to the end of the document several pages of detailed instructions regarding the collection of tribute, care of the hostages, and a host of other administrative tasks and matters, including exploration of the island with walruses.]

TsGADA, YaPI, *stolbets* 611, *listy* 263–82.
Published in: *ORZPM*, pp. 233–46 (some parts omitted). A short portion in *RM*, pp. 61–3. This latter version is taken from a Müller copy in AAN, *fond* 21, *kniga* 30, *no.* 139. It has several minor differences in wording and a major insertion of a passage (p. 62) purporting to report a communication from customs sworn-man Petr Novoselov on the Kolyma dated 15 June 1647, less than a month before these instructions were issued. No explanation is given as to how the report could have reached Yakutsk in three weeks' time.

★ ★ ★

The next five documents (nos. 27–31) are of Dezhnev's authorship though not actually written by him. The first is a petition discovered by Polevoy, which Dezhnev submitted to Gavrilov in the spring of 1648 in order to be free to participate in the voyage. The other four are the petitions brought to light by Ogloblin. Only the first, the one submitted in July 1662 at Yakutsk and then sent to Moscow, contains significant information about the voyage. The other three, submitted in Moscow, repeat some of the information. They are included as much for the fact that they were authored by Dezhnev as for the information they contain. The last of the four mentions his nephew, whom he wants to take to Siberia with him. It is perhaps relevant too to be able to see what the documents do not include.

Document 27

After 12 May 1648.[1] Dezhnev's petition to commandant Gavrilov admitting non-compliance with an order to testify about a charge against him filed by Mikhail Glazun.

I, Semeyka Ivanov Dezhnev, your sovereign's slave, make obeisance to the sovereign tsar [and] grand prince of all Rus´, Mikhail Fedorovich. In the present year 156 [1647–8], sovereign, Krasnoyarsk service-man Mikhaylo Semenov [Glazun] petitioned Vtoroy Gavrilov on the Kovyma River regarding violence against his captive. I, your slave Semeyko, did not respond before service-man Vtoroy Gavrilov in this

---

[1] Though not dated, this document followed an earlier one dated 12 May 1648 and modifies a position Dezhnev took in the earlier document (Boris P. Polevoy, 'Novoe o nachale istoricheskogo plavaniya S. I. Dezhneva 1648 g.', *Izvestiya Vostochno-sibirskogo otdela Geograficheskogo obshchestva SSSR* (Irkutsk), Tom LXIII (1965c), pp. 53–4.

[matter], but said that I would not answer before him, that I would answer this [charge] in the Lena [ostrog] before the voyevodas. I was guilty in this matter in that I, your sovereign's slave, did not answer the petition before service-man Vtoroy Gavrilov. Merciful sovereign tsar [and] grand prince of all Rus', Mikhail Fedorovich, please, sovereign, order me, your slave, not to cause trouble with any kind of action or inaction or in any way to go astray hereafter. I am your slave in this matter and submit a guilty petition. Tsar, sovereign, have mercy, please.

TsGADA, YaPI without further identification.
Published in: Polevoy 1965c, p. 54.

Document 28

July 1662. Dezhnev's petition submitted to the voyevodas at Yakutsk.

Your slave, Semeyka Dezhnev, service-man from the great river Lena, from the Yakutsk ostrog, makes obeisance to the sovereign tsar and grand prince Aleksey Mikhaylovich, autocrat of Great and Little and White Russia. In the year 146 [1637–8], great sovereign, I, your slave, was sent from the Yeniseysk ostrog to the Yakutsk ostrog with boyar-son Petr Beketov and service-men to collect your sovereign's tribute, and I, your slave, went with Petr Beketov. In the past year 147 [1638–9] I, your slave, carried out all kinds of duties at the Yakutsk ostrog for your sovereign with boyar-son Parfen Khodyrev and service-men. In the presence of Parfen Khodyrev chief Sakhey of the Kangalaskiy tribe killed two service-men, Fedotko Shivrin and Yelfin Zipunok, and after killing these men Sakheyko fled from his village to distant parts, to the Orgutskaya volost'. Service-man Ivan Metlekh was sent to this volost' to collect your sovereign's tribute, and Sakhay's son Tolgoyko killed Ivan Metlekh. Parfen Khodyrev sent me, your slave, to this same Orgutskaya volost'. for the collection of your sovereign's tribute, and I took 140 sables from chief Sakhey, his children, and kinsmen, and from other Orgutskiye Yakuts.

In the fall of the past year 149 [1640], great sovereign, secretary-chief (*pismyanoy golova*)[1] Vasiliy Poyarkov sent me, your slave, with service-man Dmitrey Mikhaylov [Zyryan] and companions on horse-back from the Yakutsk ostrog to the Yana River by way of the winter

[1] Correctly *pismennyy golova*, literally 'writing head', i.e., a military officer who could keep records and attend to the correspondence of the office (Lantzeff, 1943, p. 54).

route across the mountains to collect your sovereign's tribute. For your service, I, your slave bought two horses, paying 85 roubles, and clothing, boots, and various service equipment, buying them at the Yakutsk ostrog from the traders and promyshlenniks at high prices. My outlay cost me more than 100 roubles. We, your slaves, took 340 sables and two brown foxes from the Yakuts on the Yana River as your sovereign's tribute.

Dmitrey Mikhaylov sent me, your slave Semeyka, and three others with the sables, with your sovereign's tribute, to the Yakutsk ostrog, to stol´nik and voyevoda Petr Petrovich Golovin and associates. I and my companions, while en route to the Yakutsk ostrog, were met by forty or more Lamut Tunguses who started a fight with us. They shot at us with bows, and we fired at them with guns. I, your slave, killed [some of] their 'best' men in that fight, and we wounded many other Tunguses. During that fight the Lamuts wounded me in the knee of the left leg with an arrow. Arriving at the Yakutsk ostrog, I turned your sovereign's tribute treasury of 340 sables over to stol´nik and voyevoda Petr Golovin and associates in the main office.

In the past year 150 [1641–2], great sovereign, stol´nik and voyevoda Petr Golovin and associates sent me, your slave, from the Yakutsk ostrog to the Oyemokon River[1] with Mikhail Stadukhin and 14 men to collect your sovereign's tribute, without your sovereign's money and grain salary, and on our own horses, two to a horse. We, your slaves, bought horses at high prices, as well as clothing, boots, and all the service equipment, which cost us, your slaves, 150 roubles. On the Oyemokon we took your sovereign's tribute from the Tungus chief Chona and his brothers and kinsmen, and from [other] Yakuts with an increase over the previous [collection]. About a hundred and five or more non-tribute paying Lamut Tunguses gathered and shot up our horses and started a fight with us, your slaves. We, your slaves, fought with them, firing our guns, while the tribute-paying Tunguses and

---

[1] Also spelled Omokon, Yemekon, Yemokon, and by Belov (1955, p. 36), Oymekon, but most commonly Yemokon. No river in Siberia carries any of these names today. There are a settlement and a plateau in the region west of the upper Indigirka River called Oymyakon, and the river appears to be a western tributary of the Indigirka in that area. Under the name Omokon it is described as being the same as the Sobach'ya River (ORZPM, p. 141), a name by which the Indigirka was also known, indicating that it was a part of that river system. Elsewhere in this document 28 Dezhnev states that he and his companions 'sailed...from the upper Oyemokon River to the Indigirka and down the Indigirka to the sea'. This identification of the Yemokon with the Indigirka is clarified in volume 2 of the Geografichesko-statisticheskiy slovar´ rossiyskoy imperii (compiled by Petr P. Semenov–Tyan Shanskiy; St Petersburg, 1865), page 337, where it is explained that the Indigirka is formed by the confluence of the two rivers Kuydusun and Omekon.

Yakuts stood with us and shot at them their bows. By God's mercy and your sovereign's good fortune we, your slaves, killed ten Lamut Tunguses in that fight and wounded many others. In that fight the Lamut Tunguses wounded me in the elbow of the right arm with an arrow, and with another arrow they wounded me in the thigh of the right leg. In that fight the Tunguses killed our tribute paying chief Uday as well as tribesman Tyusyuk and many other tribute-paying men, and wounded many others and devastated them completely. We, your slaves, sent your sovereign's tribute treasury of sables from the Oyemokon River to the Yakutsk ostrog on our remaining horses with service-men Denis Yerilo and Ivan Kislo.

After inquiring from the Lamut Tungus tribute payer Chona where we, your slaves, Mikhail Stadukhin and companions, might look for new non-tribute paying people and increase the tribute collection for you, great sovereign, we built a koch and sailed, thirteen men in all, from the upper Oyemokon River to the Indigirka and down the Indigirka to the sea.

On the basis of a report of the natives I, your slave, went with Roman Nemchin to service-man Dmitrey Mikhaylov [Zyryan] and his men for consultation so that we, your slaves, might join with Dmitrey in your sovereign's service to increase the collection of tribute and bring under your exalted hand natives not yet subjugated or compliant. Dmitrey and I, your slave, having found Alazeya Yukagirs not paying tribute, seized as a hostage Toyta, son of chief Mantsit. His capture led to a fight with the Yukagirs, and I, your slave, was wounded in the left shoulder by an arrow.

When I was on the Kovyma River, I, your slave, found the Oymok Yukagirs on an expedition with Dmitrey and Mikhail Stadukhin and service-men. In the capturing of hostages there was a fight with the Oymoks, and in that capture I killed the brother of 'best' man Allay, and we took Allay's son Kenit as a hostage. They shot me, your slave, clear through the left hand at the wrist with an iron-tipped arrow. Having Kenit as a hostage, we collected your sovereign's tribute from his tribe for three years.

Dmitrey Mikhaylov and Mikhail Stadukhin together with their men went by sea in a koch with your sovereign's tribute treasury of sables to the Yakutsk ostrog while I remained behind at the ostrozhek on the Kovyma River with service-man Vtoroy Gavrilov and his men, thirteen altogether, for your sovereign's tribute collection. The Yukagir natives, seeing us, your slaves, to be so few, assembled five hundred or more. They advanced against the ostrozhek and besieged us and wounded many; they wounded me, Semeyka, in the head with an iron-tipped arrow. Many natives forced their way into the outpost. By God's mercy and your sovereign's great good fortune we killed the traitor Allayko with a spear in a hand-to-hand fight, and we killed many other Yukagirs with him and wounded many more. Fearing for their lives, they fled from the ostrozhek.

Dmitrey Mikhaylov and Mikhail Stadukhin and their men, while on the way to the Yakutsk ostrog, met at sea sworn-man Petr Novoselov and traders and promyshlenniks. Petr Novoselov brought instructions to service-man Dmitrey Mikhaylov from stol'nik and voyevoda Petr Golovin and associates at the Yakutsk ostrog, ordering Dmitrey to be in command until your sovereign's [further] order on the Kovyma River [and] on the newly discovered rivers, the Indigirka, Alazeya, and Sobach'ya.[1] Dmitrey, together with sworn-man Petr Novoselov and ourselves, your slaves, were ordered to search all out for new rivers, to make a profit for you, great sovereign, to bring natives anew under your tsarist exalted hand, and to seek tribute from them.

The commissioned Dmitrey Mikhaylov and sworn-man Petr Novoselov worked for you, sovereign, with great zeal. He sent us, your slaves, to natives not yet compliant or tributary, who did not serve you, great sovereign, and did not pay your sovereign's tribute. We, your slaves, went on your sovereign's service against non-tribute paying natives; we spared not our heads, we shed out blood, and we accepted every kind of privation. We collected your sovereign's tribute from the non-tribute paying people with great zeal. Commissioned man Dmitrey Mikhaylov and sworn-man Petr Novoselov sent us, your slaves, with thirty or more traders and promyshlenniks, to fight your sovereign's traitors, the Yukagirs, who were drawing near in an attack against the ostrozhek. We, your slaves, captured the Yukagir Alivin, son of Cherm, as a hostage, and in that capture the Yukagirs wounded me in the muscle of the left arm.

Subsequently traders and promyshlenniks made their obeisance to you, great sovereign, and submitted a petition to sworn-man Petr Novoselov on the Kovyma River[2] to send the traders and promyshlen-

---

[1] As another name for the Indigirka River (p. 75 above; *ORZPM*, p. 214) it would be a second reference in the same statement to that river. Was there another Sobach'ya River in the Kolyma basin as Polevoy suggests? (Chapter 7, p. 24 and note 32.)

[2] It must have been Gavrilov to whom the petition was presented, as was done the year before. Novoselov left the Kolyma on 15 June 1647 (*ORZPM*, p. 252). After fourteen years

niks, Fedot Alekseyev and companions, to the new Anandyr´ River and other nearby rivers in search of new non-tribute paying people where profit in tribute collection could be made for you, great sovereign. The traders and promyshlenniks petitioned that I, your slave, should go with them for your sovereign's tribute collection, for the purpose of searching for new non-tribute paying people, and for your sovereign's business in general.

I, your slave, went with these traders and promyshlenniks by sea, ninety men in six [sic] koches. Having passed the mouth of the Anandyr´, by God's judgment all our koches were wrecked by the sea, and the traders and promyshlenniks were drowned from shipwreck at sea or were killed on the tundra by natives, and others died from hunger. Altogether sixty-four men perished.

I, your slave, was left with twenty-four men from all these companions of mine, and twelve of these companions [following] a winter route on snowshoes and sleds failed to reach the Anandyr´ because of frost, hunger, and want. Twelve men disappeared without a trace on the road. With twelve men altogether I, your slave, dragged myself to the Anandyr´ River, and not wishing to die of starvation, went with these companions on an expedition to the non-tribute paying Kanauls and Khodyntsy. By God's mercy and your tsarist good fortune we took as hostages two men from the Anaul tribe, Kolupayko and Negovo; and from the Khodynskiy tribe Chokchoy; and two Chuvanskiye men, Leonta and Podonets. While capturing Podonets he cut me, your slave Semeyko, on the chest with a knife. With these hostages in hand we collected your sovereign's tribute of 30 sables from their brothers and kinsmen.

Afterwards for several years by your good fortune, great sovereign, we took as hostages from the Khodynskiy tribe Oblyaka, Ondryushka, Aldybeyko, Akineyko, Panilko, Chinchildayko, and Petrushka. For these hostages, as well as their brothers and kinsmen, we collected no small amount of your sovereign's tribute from their tribesman in this present year 170 [1661–2]. In coming years your sovereign's tribute will be collected on the Anandyr´ and other nearby rivers with an increase each year over the previous year. We looked around for fish tooth bone [walrus tusks], and every year volunteer service-men promyshlenniks hunted walruses for fish tooth bone. In the past year 167 [1658–9], great

did Dezhnev confuse the cirumstances of the petition of 1647 with those of the petition of 1648? He submitted another petition in the latter year, in May (document 27), and he submitted it to Gavrilov.

sovereign, by your sovereign's order boyar-son Kurbat Ivanov of the Yakutsk ostrog and service-men took over from me, your slave, the ostrozhek and hostages on the Anandyr´ River.

I, your slave, having begun at the Yeniseysk ostrog, performed your sovereign's service of every sort and collected your sovereign's tribute on the great river Lena and on the other distant adjacent rivers in new areas, on the Yana, Oyemokon, Indigirka, Kovyma, and Anandyr´ rivers, with my own resources [and] without your sovereign's salary in money and grain. While performing these services for you, sovereign, these many years I suffered all kinds of want and destitution, ate larch and pine bark, and accepted filth for twenty-one years.

Merciful sovereign, tsar and grand prince Aleksey Mikhaylovich, autocrat of all Great and Little and White Russia, grant me, your slave, your sovereign's salary in money and grain for the years past; and for my blood and wounds and many ordeals grant me, your slave, sovereign, additional salary, how much God will make known to you! Oh sovereign, order stol´nik and voyevoda Ivan Fedorovich Golenishchev-Kutuzov Bol´shoy to accept this my petition and send it with a report to you, great sovereign, at Moscow. Tsar and sovereign, have mercy!

TsGADA, Sibirskiy Prikaz, *stolbets* 768, *listy* 2–7.
Published in: Ogloblin, 1890, pp. 54–8; Samoylov, 1945, pp. 141–7.

Document 29

23 September 1664. Dezhnev's petition submitted to the Siberian Department in Moscow.

Service-man Sen´ka Dezhnev, your slave, of Yakutsk ostrog on the great river Lena makes his obeisance to the sovereign tsar [and grand prince Aleksey Mikhaylovich],[1] autocrat [of all Great, Little, and White Russia].[1]

I, your slave, served your father of blessed memory on the Yana, Indigirka, Alazeya, and Kolyma rivers with service-men and commanders Dmitrey Mikhaylov and Mikhail Stadukhin, and they made a great profit in the collection of tribute for your sovereign's treasury. I went by sea from the Kolyma River to look for new rivers, and I found the new river Anandyr´ in addition to previous rivers. While on the new river in your great sovereign's service I built a zimov´ye and

---

[1] Omitted by Ogloblin.

an ostrog. I took hostages on that river and collected for you, great sovereign, tribute and the ten per cent tax, 279 sables and sable backs, 284 sable bellies, 15 puds 36 funts [574 pounds] of walrus tusks. I, your slave, and companions on the Anandyr' pay our respects to you, great sovereign, with two walrus tusks 32 funts [29 pounds] in weight as a gift. The sable tribute and tusks from the Anandyr' River will go to you, great sovereign, on this date.

I, your slave, supported myself on your great sovereign's service on the new rivers with my own money and my own equipment, and I, your slave, was not given any of your sovereign's salary in money, grain, and salt from the year 151 [1642–3] to the year 170 [1661–2]. In the past year 170, great sovereign, your stol'nik and voyevoda, Ivan Bol'shoy Golenishchev-Kutuzov at Yakutsk, paid me, your slave, your sovereign's salt salary from the year 151 [1642–3] to the year 170 from your great sovereign's salt treasury, but I, Sen'ka, was not paid your sovereign's money and grain salary because of the shortage of money and grain in past years. A statement about my service to you, great sovereign, was written from the Yakutsk ostrog. While on that service for you, great sovereign, supporting myself and serving you, great sovereign, for a long time without your sovereign tsar's salary, taking natives as hostages, I risked my head, was severely wounded, shed my blood, suffered great cold and hunger, and all but died from starvation. While on that service and as a result of shipwreck I became impoverished and incurred heavy unpaid debts, and was finally ruined by these debts.

Merciful sovereign tsar [and grand prince Aleksey Mikhaylovich],[1] autocrat [of all Great, Little, and White Russia],[1] grant me, your slave, for my service to you, great sovereign, for equipment, for taking hostages, for wounds and blood, for shipwreck, for all the necessary suffering, your great sovereign's grain and money salary for the years 151 [1642–3] to 170 [1661–2] as my service payment in full so that I, your slave, will not be in debt servitude, on the verge of bankruptcy, and leave your sovereign's service, and finally perish! Tsar, sovereign, have mercy, please.

TsGADA, Sibirskiy Prikaz, *stolbets* 768, *listy* 10–11.
Published in: Ogloblin, 1890, pp. 58–9; Samoylov, 1945, pp. 147–8.

[1] Omitted by Ogloblin.

Document 30

13 February 1665. Petition submitted by Dezhnev to the Siberian
Department in Moscow.

Your slave, service-man Sen'ka Dezhnev of the Yakutsk ostrog on the
great Lena River, makes his obeisance to the sovereign tsar [and grand
prince Aleksey Mikhaylovich],[1] autocrat [of all Great, Little, and White
Russia].[1]

I, your slave, served your father [of blessed memory][1] and you in
Siberia, at Tobol'sk, at Yeniseysk, and on the great river Lena and other
rivers for twenty years as a surrogate ataman. I shed my blood and
received many wounds, took hostages and collected tribute anew for
you, great sovereign, for the hostages, and searched for and gathered
walrus tusks. My service for you, great sovereign, is known and
recorded in the Siberian Department. Merciful tsar [and grand prince
Aleksey Mikaylovich],[1] autocrat [of all Great, Little, and White
Russia],[1] reward me for my service, my blood and wounds, and for
profit in tribute. Order me, sovereign, promoted to sotnik in your great
sovereign's service at the Yakutsk ostrog, or however the Lord God
tells you about me. Order sovereign, three hundred puds [5·4 tons] of
grain supplies purchased at the Lena portage for my use during all the
years. Have mercy, sovereign tsar, please.

TsGADA, Sibirskiy Prikaz, *stolbets* 762, *list* 1.
Published in: Ogloblin, 1890, pp. 59–60; Samoylov, 1945, p. 148.

Document 31

25 February 1665. Petition submitted by Dezhnev to the Siberian
Department in Moscow.

Sen'ka Dezhnev makes his obeisance to the sovereign tsar [and grand
prince Aleksey Mikhaylovich],[1] autocrat [of all Great, Little, and White
Russia].[1]

In the present year 173 [1664–5], sovereign, I, your slave, have spent
time in the Yakutsk ostrog on your service, great sovereign, in
accordance with your order, great sovereign. My nephew, Ivashko
Ivanov, lives in Great Ustyug neither 'tax-obligated' nor a townsman;
he moves from court to court with his wife Tat'yanka, daughter of
Grigor'yev. Merciful sovereign tsar [and grand prince Aleksey

[1] Omitted by Ogloblin.

Mikhaylovich],[1] autocrat [of all Great, Little, and White Russia],[1] please order me, your slave, sovereign, to take my nephew and his wife Tat'yanka with me to Siberia, to the Yakutsk ostrog, and order that a travel permit for this be issued to me. Tsar, sovereign, have mercy, please.

TsGADA, Sibirskiy Prikaz, *stolbets* 762, *list* 10.
Published in: Ogloblin, 1890, p. 60; Samoylov, 1945, p. 149.

★ ★ ★

Document 32 is a petition in 1681 of a number of promyshlenniks to Yakutsk to be allowed to return there. Several of them claim to have come to the Anadyr´ with Dezhnev, though he is not named in the petition and was no longer there (in fact he was dead), and were still engaged in state service. From the petition we learn the names of several of Dezhnev's associates on the Anadyr´. Document 33 is the testimony of one Petr Popov, sent from Anadyrsk in 1711 in a futile attempt to persuade the Chukchi on the Chukotskiy Peninsula to submit to Russian rule. The document was found in Müller's Portfolios in the last century, and he included it in his account of 1758, though not in connection with Dezhnev's voyage. Its utility for us is the information it contains which helps modern scholars to identify Dezhnev's 'great rocky nos'. For that reason it is placed here rather than in the preceding chapter. The last document, if it may be termed such, is a long discussion by Captain James King in the official account of Cook's voyage into the north Pacific in 1778–9 explaining why the two men concluded that East Cape was Dezhnev's rocky nos. Reproduced many times since first publication of the official account, it is included here for the convenience of both editor and reader.

Document 32

No later than 9 August 1681. Petition of promyshlenniks to tsar Fedor Alekseyevich about their obligatory duties at Anadyrsk with a request for release from them and permission to go to Yakutsk.

Your orphans, promyshlenniks Kiryushka Stefanov, Petrushka Ani-kiyev Shchukin, Mishka Malafeyev, Vas'ka Alekseyev, Lar'ka Loginov, Panko Lavrent'yev, Fomka Semena, Ivashka Savin Prikol, Pron'ka Yerofiyev, Yakun'ka Ignat'yev, Nekhoroshko Grigor'yev, Savka Va-

---

[1] Omitted by Ogloblin.

sil'yev, Ivashko Fomin, Vas'ka Fomin, Nekhoroshko Panfilov, Yefimko Kirilov,[1] Ivashko Grigor'yev, Pashko Leont'yev, Maksimka Semenov, Yakun'ka Afonas'yev make obeisance to the sovereign tsar and grand prince Fedor Alekseyevich, autocrat of all Great, Little and White Russia.

In past years, great sovereign, we your orphans arrived on the Anadyr' River at the time when there were no hostages of your great sovereign on the Anadyr' River, and there were no officials on that river before us. When the officials first arrived on the Anadyr' River in compliance with your great sovereign's order, they started having us, your orphans, go on expeditions. We, your orphans, served you, great sovereign, under the officials with water and grass [i.e., at their own expense]. The officials did not release us, your orphans, from the Anadyr' River because of the shortage of men. We, your orphans, were guards of your great sovereign's treasury and hostages, and unlike the service-men we paid taxes and dues and provided food for the hostages. As a result we, your orphans, were impoverished and finally ruined and our wives and children bondaged in eternal servitude. In past years we have paid quitrent (*obrok*) and given the fifth denga to you, great sovereign.

Merciful sovereign tsar and grand prince Fedor Alekseyevich, autocrat of all Great, Little, and White Russia, please order us, your orphans, great sovereign, freed from guard duty in the Anadyrskiy ostrozhek and release us, your orphans, from the Anadyrskiy ostrozhek and order, great sovereign, this our petition sent under dispatch to the Yakutsk ostrog. Please, tsar, have mercy.

On the verso: Ivashko Ankudinov affixes his signature to this petition in place of promyshlenniks Pron'ka Yarofeyev, Savka Vasil'yev, Fomka Semenov, Ivashko Fomin, Panfilka Lavrent'yev,[2] Nekhoroshka Panfilov by their request. Yefimko Kirilov affixes his signature to this petition of his father [*sic*] Kirilka Stefanov, of Morozko Malafeyev,[3] Druzhinka Alekseyev, Yakovka Ofonos'yev, Oleshka Melent'yev, Petrushka Shchukin by their order, and for himself.

AAN, LOII, YaA, *karton 32, stolbets 14, sstav 15.*

Published in: *RM*, pp. 164–5.

---

[1] Belov (*RM*, p. 165, note 2) takes him to be Yelfimko Merkur'yev, the employee of Andreyev and Astaf'yev, but that Merkur'yev was killed in 1652–3 (p. 62 above).
[2] A Panfilko Lavrent'yev returned to the Kolyma in 1655 (p. 70 above)—the same man?
[3] Same as Mishka Malafayev?

Document 33

2 September 1711. Deposition of Yakutsk service-man Petr Popov, sent to the Chukotskaya land for the gathering of information about the local inhabitants and summoning them to payment of tribute.

On the 2nd day of September of the year [1]711 Yakutsk service-man Petr Il'in son of Popov, Anadyrsk promyshlennik Yegor Vasil'yev Toldin, and newly baptized Yukagir Ivan Vasil'yev son of Tereshkin stated in the judicial chamber at Anadyrskiy ostrog before the commandant, cossack pyatidesyatnik Matvey Shrevykin [the following]:

On the 13th day of January in the present year [1]711, in accordance with the ukaz of the great sovereign and the memorandum of the previous commandant of the Anadyrskiy ostrog, Fedor Kotkovskiy, Petr and his companions were ordered to go from the Anadyrskiy ostrog down the Anadyr´ River and to collect tribute for the great sovereign's treasury from the river Chyukchi, from Nokon and kinsmen, 5 men, who paid tribute into the great sovereign's treasury at the Anadyrskiy ostrog in the past year [1]710. Petr and his companions were ordered to go from the mouth of the Anadyr´ River to the Nos and to visit the unpacified Chyukchi, and, having reached them, to summon them under the exalted autocratic hand of his tsarist majesty with kindness and consideration so that the Chyukchi will pay into the great sovereign's treasury tribute in sables, various kinds of foxes, and walrus tusks, and to request hostages from them. Petr and his companions were ordered to find out for certain what genuine oath these Chyukchi use in binding agreement among themselves according to their religion, what kind of places they live in, in the mountains or by the sea, [whether they are] reindeer or walking; what they live on, and whether they know of any islands in the sea off that Nos. If they know of any islands, these peninsular Chyukchi are to be asked about them. Are there any people and animals on these islands, and what kind of wealth do they have? Having observed and inquired about everything, Petr is ordered to write it down precisely in a book and to draft a map of that Chyukotskaya land and to deliver that map over his own signature in the judicial chamber at the Anadyrskiy ostrog.

In accordance with the above written ukaz and memorandum of the great sovereign Petr and his associates, the interpreters Yegor Toldin [and] Ivan Tereshkin, went from the mouth of the Anadyr´ River to the Nos, and beyond the ocean bay they visited the unpacified

Chyukchi and summoned them into eternal payment of tribute under the exalted autocratic hand of his tsarist majesty with the utmost zeal. The unpacified Chyukchi told Petr and his companions: Before now Russians came to these Chyukchi by sea, and at that time these Chyukchi did not pay any tribute to the Russians, and they will not pay now or give their sons as hostages.

Petr and his associates arrived on the Anadyr´ River from that Nos on the 28th day of July of the present year [1]711, and with [the help of] cossacks Mikhaylo Shchypunov and comrades they collected tribute for the present year [1]711 for the great sovereign's treasury from Pokon and kinsmen, 5 men, at the rate of one red fox per man; and again they summoned the river Chyukcha Kapochil, Nokanov's brother, into eternal tribute payment under the autocratic hand of his tsarist majesty; and that Chyukcha arrived at the Anadyrskiy ostrog with Petr and associates with the tribute payment.

In accordance with their religion the Chyukchi give an oath in binding agreement among themselves by a hand toward the sun.

The reindeer Chyukchi on the Nos live in the mountains because they move their reindeer herds about from place to place. The walking Chyukchi live in earthern huts (*yurty*) on both sides of the Nos along the sea near the sandspits where the walruses pass the time. The reindeer and walking Chyukchi maintain themselves by hunting wild reindeer, ocean whales, walruses, sturgeon, seals, roots, and grasses in the mountains and along the rivers.

Opposite that Anadyrskoy Nos, from both sides, the Kolymskoye and Anadyrskoye seas, there is, they say, an island, and peninsular Chyukchi Makachkin and tribesmen spoke to Petr and his companions with assurance about that island: There are 'toothed' people on that island. Their beliefs, other customs, and language are not those of the Chyukchi. Especially in old times and at present [relations] between the peninsular Chyukchi and these island people are warlike; they fight each other. [Sometimes] the island people get the better of it, and the Chyukchi the same. Petr and his companions saw about 10 of these island men among the Chyukchi taken as prisoners. These people have teeth in addition to their natural ones. In the summer the crossing from the Nos to that island is made in one day in baydars with paddles, and in the winter the crossing is made easily in one day on reindeers. There is every kind of animal on that island: sables, martens, and all sorts of foxes [including] polar foxes, wolves, ermines, polar bears, and sea beavers. They keep large herds of reindeer. They eat marine animals, berries, roots, and grasses. There are various kinds of trees on that island: cedar, pine, spruce, fir, and larch. Petr and his companions saw those kinds of wood from the island among the Chyukchi in their baydars, kayaks, and yurts. The island peoples live in the same way as the Chyukchi: they have no leaders.

On the Nos there are no other animals than red foxes and wolves, and they are few in number because there is no place for animals to live on the Nos; there are no forests. According to an estimate of the leading peninsular reindeer and walking Chyukchi men there are 2,000 or more besides the Anadyr' River [Chyukchi], and there are 50 or more of the river men.

Makachkin and the island people, estimating the number who were captives of the Chyukchi, told Petr and his companions that there are three times their number among the Chyukchi. Makachkin said that he has been on that island on expeditions over many years. The Chyukchi call that island 'the big land'.

The route from the Anadyrskiy ostrog to the Nos itself by reindeer directly overland and across the Belaya River to Matkol' by reindeer trail is 10 weeks or more if there are no blizzards. The peak called Matkol' by the Chyukchi is near a big bay, in the vicinity of its middle inlet.

Imperial Academy of Sciences, Müller's Portfolios, Yakutskaya *kniga, akt* no. 39. Its current archival location is not specified.

Published in: *Pamyatniki sibirskoy istorii* (2 vol., St Petersburg, 1882–5), Tom I, pp. 456–9.

Document 34

Captain James King's discussion of East Cape and Dezhnev's great rocky nos.

Having now passed Beering's Straits, and taken our final leave of the North East coast of Asia, it may not be improper, on this occasion, to state the grounds on which we have ventured to adopt two general conclusions respecting its extent, in opposition to the opinions of Mr. Muller. The first, that the promontory named East Cape is actually the Easternmost point of that quarter of the globe; or, in other words, that no part of the continent extends in longitude beyond 190° 22' East: the second, that the latitude of the North Easternmost extremity falls to the Southward of 70° North. With respect to the former, if such land exist, it must necessarily be to the North of latitude 69°, where the discoveries made in the present voyage terminate; and, therefore, the probable direction of the coast, beyond this point, is the question I shall endeavour, in the first place, to investigate.

As the Russian is the only nation that has hitherto navigated these seas, all our information respecting the situation of the coast to the Northward of Cape North, must necessarily be derived from the charts and journals of the persons who have been employed, at various times, in ascertaining the limits of that empire; and these are, for the most part, so imperfect, so confused, and contradictory, that it is not easy to form any distinct idea of their pretended, much less to collect the amount of their real discoveries. It is on this account, that the extent and form of the peninsula, inhabited by Tschutski, still remain a point, on which the Russian geographers are much divided. Mr. Muller, in his map, published in the year 1754, supposes this country to extend toward the North East, to the 75° of latitude, and in longitude 190° East of Greenwich, and to terminate in a round Cape, which he calls Tschukotskoi Noss. To the Southward of this Cape he conceives the coast to form a bay to the Westward, bounded in latitude 68° 18′, by Serdze Kamen, the Northernmost point seen by Beering in his expedition in the year 1728. The map, published by the academy of St. Petersburg, in the year 1776,[1] gives the whole peninsula intirely a new form, placing its North Easternmost extremity in the latitude 73°, longitude 178° 30′. The Easternmost point in latitude 65° 30′, longitude 189° 30′. All other maps we saw, both printed and in manuscript, vary between these two, apparently more according to the fancy of the compiler, than on any grounds of more accurate information. The only point in which there is a general coincidence, without any considerable variation, is the position of East Cape in latitude 66°. The form of the coast, both the South and North of this Cape, in the map of the academy, is exceedingly erroneous, and may be totally disregarded. In that of Mr. Muller, the coast to the Northward bears a considerable resemblence to our survey, as far as the latter extends, except that it does not trend sufficiently to the Westward; receding only about 5° of longitude, between the latitude of 66° and 69°; whereas, in reality it recedes nearly ten. Between the latitude of 69° and 74°, he makes the coast bend round to the North and North East, and to form a considerable promontory. On what authority, now remains to be examined.

Mr. Coxe, whose accurate researches into this subject give his

---

[1] It was published in 1774 (James R. Masterson and Helen Brower, editors, *Bering's successors, 1745–80* [Seattle, 1948], p. 6, note 2).

opinion great weight, is persuaded that the extremity of the *Noss* in question, was never passed but by Deshneff and his party, who sailed from the river Kovyma in the year 1648, and are supposed to have got around it into the Anadyr. As the account of this expedition, the substance of which the reader will find in Mr. Coxe's Account of Russian Discoveries, contains no geographical delineation of the coast along which they sailed, its position must be conjectured from incidental circumstances; and from these it appears very manifest, that the Tschukotskoi Noss of Deshneff is no other than the promontory called, by Captain Cook, the East Cape. Speaking of the *Noss*, he says, "One might sail from the isthmus[1] to the river Anadyr, with a fair wind, in three days and three nights." This exactly coincides with the situation of the East Cape, which is about one hundred and twenty leagues from the mouth of the Anadyr; and as there is no other isthmus to the Northward between that and the latitude of 69°, it is obvious that, by this description, he must intend either the Cape in question, or some other to the Southward of it. In another place he says, "Over against the isthmus[1] there are two islands in the sea, upon which were seen people of the Tschutski nation, through whose lips were run pieces of the teeth of the sea-horse." This again perfectly agrees with the two islands situated to the South East of the East Cape. We saw no inhabitants on them; but it is not at all improbable, that a party of the Americans, from the opposite continent, whom this description accurately suits, might, at that time, have been accidentally there; and whom it was natural enough for him to mistake for a tribe of the Tschutski.

These two circumstances are of so striking and unequivocal a nature, that they appear to me conclusive on the point of Tschutskoi Noss, notwithstanding there are others of a more doubtful kind, which we have from the same authority, and which now remain to be considered. "To go," says Deshneff in another account, "from the Kovyma, to the Anadyr, a great promontory must be doubled, which stretches very far into the sea;" and afterward, "this promontory stretches between North and North East." It was probably from the expressions

---

[1] Dezhnev did not, we know, call his nos an isthmus, nor does Coxe when he reports Dezhnev's description of it. He calls it a promontory (1780, pp. 315, 317; 1787, pp. 254, 255, 423). King must have picked up this designation from the English translation of Müller's account in his *Nachrichten von Seereisen* (1761, pp. v, vi). Müller uses the term *die Landecke* (1758a, pp. 9, 10), which the Russian translator renders as *nos* (1758b, Tom VII, pp. 11, 12) and Golder as cape (1914, p. 271), and as I have done. It might also be translated as 'continental corner'. The English translator evidently mistook the word for *die Landenge* or isthmus.

contained in these passages, that Mr. Muller was induced to give the country of the Tschutski the form we find in his map; but had he been acquainted with the situation of the East Cape, as ascertained by Captain Cook, and the remarkable coincidence between it and their promontory or isthmus (for it must be observed, that Deshneff appears to be all along speaking of the same thing), in the circumstances already mentioned, I am confident, he would not have thought those expressions, merely by themselves, of sufficient weight to warrant him in extending the North Eastern extremity of Asia, either so far to the North or to the opinion we have adopted, if we suppose Deshneff to have taken these bearings from the small bight which lies to the Westward of the Cape.

The deposition of the Cossac Popoff, taken at the Anadirskoi *ostrog*, in the year 1711, seems to have been the next authority on which Mr. Muller has proceeded; and beside these two, I am not acquainted with any other. This Cossac, together with several others, was sent by land to demand tribute from the independent Tschutski tribes, who live about the Noss. The first circumstance, in the account of this journey, that can lead to the situation of Tschukotskoi Noss, is the distance from Anadirsk; and this is stated to be ten weeks journey, with loaded rein-deer; on which account it is added, their day's journey was but very small. It is impossible to conclude much from so vague an account; but, as the distance between the East Cape and the *ostrog* is upward of two hundred leagues [1,110 km] in a straight line, and therefore may be supposed to allow twelve or fifteen miles a day; its situation cannot be reckoned incompatible with Popoff's calculation. The next circumstance mentioned in this deposition is, that their route lay by the foot of a rock called Matkol, situated at the bottom of a great gulf. This gulf Muller supposes to be the bay he had laid down between latitude 66° and 72°; and accordingly places the rock Matkol in the center of it; but it appears equally probably, even if we had not so many reasons to doubt the existence of that bay, that it might be some part of the gulf of Anadir, which they would undoubtedly touch upon in their road from the *ostrog* to the East Cape.

But what seems to put this matter beyond all dispute, and to prove that the Cape visited by Popoff cannot be to the Northward of 69° latitude, is that part of his deposition, which I have already quoted, relative to the island lying off the Noss, from whence the opposite continent might be seen. For as the two continents, in latitude 69°, have diverged so far as to be more than three hundred miles distant, it is highly improbable, that the Asiatic coast should again trend in such a manner to the Eastward, as to come nearly within sight of the Coast of America.

If these arguments should be deemed conclusive against the existence of the peninsula of the Tschutski, as laid down by Muller, it will follow, that the East Cape is the Tschukotskoi Noss of the more early Russian navigators; and consequently, that the undescribed coast, from the latitude of 69° to the mouth of the river Kovyma, must uniformly trend more or less to the Westward. As an additional proof of this, it may be remarked, that the Tschukotskoi Noss is always represented as dividing the sea of Kovyma from that of Anadir, which could not be the case, if any considerable cape had projected to the North East in the higher latitudes. Thus, in the depositions taken at Anadirsk, it is related, "that opposite the Noss, on both sides, as well in the sea of Kovyma, as in that of Anadir, an island is said to be seen at a great distance, which the Tschutski call a large country; and say, that people dwell there who have large teeth put in their mouths, that project through their cheeks." Then follows a description of these people and their country, exactly corresponding with our accounts of the opposite continent.

Cook and King, 1784, Vol. III, pp. 262–7.

CHAPTER 5

DEZHNEV'S PRE-VOYAGE YEARS: NORTH RUSSIA TO THE KOLYMA

The first specific bit of information which we have about the life of Semen Ivanov Dezhnev before his voyage in 1648 is the fact that in the course of his state service he transferred from Yeniseysk to Yakutsk in 1638. His life before that year is largely a matter of conjecture. We do not know when he was born or where. We know very little about his family and its social status. We do not know where he grew up or what he did before he entered state service. We do not know when he entered state service or why he chose to go to Siberia. The most that we can expect are a few informed guesses.

From the modicum of information available it is reasonable to conclude that Dezhnev came from the northern part of European Russia, from the area adjacent to the lower Northern Dvina River and the White Sea, which is part of the region known as Pomor'ye, the maritime region of European Russia along the White Sea and Arctic Ocean. From this area and the river cities and towns of northern Russia came a disproportionate number of the emigrants to Siberia. Here the process of peasant bondage, which had tied so many peasants to the land by the middle of the 17th century, operated only to a limited degree. This was due in considerable measure to the harsh climate and an insufficiently fertile soil, incapable of a cericulture that could support both a landowning and a dependent cultivating class. The peasants remained relatively free, making their living as artisans or traders or as individual petty entrepreneurs or promyshlenniks, exploiting natural resources such as fur-bearing animals, fish, salt, minerals, etc. In this region were found many men without fixed domicile, not yet tied by the state to a permanent taxpaying category like the peasants and townsmen (*posadskiye lyudi*). Such men were called *gulyashchiye lyudi*, that is, itinerants or migrants. They moved from place to place finding employment where they could for as long as they could or would.[1] For these men, as well as the promyshlenniks and traders, Siberia promised much and drew many there.

[1] Lantzeff, 1943, pp. 59, 141, note 123.

From two or three bits of information gleaned from the sources it appears probable that Dezhnev's home community was the town of Pinega, situated on the river of the same name, an eastern tributary of the Northern Dvina near its mouth. It was not far from Kholmogory, somewhat upriver on the Northern Dvina, and from Arkhangel'sk near the river's mouth. Even so these bits of information relate more to a nephew of Dezhnev than directly to himself.

On 25 February 1665 Dezhnev submitted a petition to the Siberian Department in Moscow asking that his nephew Ivashko (Ivan) Ivanov and wife be permitted to accompany him back to Yakutsk (document 31). The nephew is identified as living in Ustyug the Great, as not subject to the tax on peasants (*tyaglo*), as not a member of the town corporation (*ni v posade*), as moving from one peasant court or household to another. In other words he was a free man, a migrant worker. Ogloblin concluded from this information that the nephew lived in Ustyug and that accordingly Dezhnev came from that city too.[1] But it is more likely that the nephew happened to be living in Ustyug only at the time of the petition, having moved there from somewhere else. Search of the records of the administrative district in which Ustyug lay reveals no Dezhnevs living there.[2]

Belov is persuaded that Dezhnev came from Pinega. In the land register for the Kholmogory *uyezd* of 1710 it is noted that in a village near Pinega Dezhnevs are listed as holders of land and a court or household. One Ivan Ivanov Dezhnev in particular appears as a holder of land and a court who had left 'a long time ago' to work for money. In the customs records of Pustozerskiy ostrog near the mouth of the Pechora River Ivan Ivanov Dezhnev is mentioned as having advertised himself as being available to work for hire. Belov assumes that this Ivanov is the same nephew for whom forty-eight years earlier our Dezhnev sought permission to accompany him to Siberia. On the strength of this assumption he concludes that Dezhnev came from a poor peasant family in the Pinega maritime area. He believes his conclusion to be reinforced by finding in several of the petitions Dezhnev authored certain words, the names of implements and materials, that were peculiar to the area of Pinega and nearby Mezen'. Belov also believes that since there were few men in the White Sea maritime region who did not have some connection with the sea, Dezhnev must have gained seafaring experience before leaving for

---

[1] 1890, p. 38.
[2] Belov, 1955, p. 32.

Siberia.[1] Belov's conclusions can be neither proved nor disproved in the absence of more evidence, but in light of what we do know about Dezhnev they are not unreasonable.

We can surmise that Dezhnev, like his nephew after him, lacked the resources to make it as a peasant on the land and so became a migrant, seeking whatever employment was available. That mode of life being uncertain, we can believe that the greater certainty of state employment attracted him to it. One can believe too that the spirit of adventure and the opportunities for personal gain in frontier Siberia motivated his entering state service; and one suspects from his pressing ever eastward during his Siberian years that he shared the restlessness that impelled many others to Siberia in the years of its conquest.

When he entered government service and went to Siberia are other unknowns about Dezhnev. We do know in 1630 some 500 free migrants in Tot´ma, Ustyug, Vologda, Sol´vychegodsk, and other places in northern Russia were selected for service in Tobol´sk, the main administrative centre of Siberia. In the fall of that year 150 of these men, mostly from Ustyug, passed through Verkhotur´ye in the Urals, the main point of entry into Siberia, en route to Tobol´sk. Very possibly Dezhnev was in that group. If so, then from Tobol´sk he was later transferred to Yeniseysk, on the upper Yenisey River, whence in 1638 he moved to Yakutsk.[2]

The Russians first penetrated the Lena River basin in the late 1620s. Service-men from Yeniseysk moved into the upper part of the basin and men from Mangazeya on the Tazovskaya Bay into the lower part. Soon rival exploring parties from Tomsk and Tobol´sk entered the basin in pursuit of the gain to be found in that region. The Russian advance led to the establishment of several outposts in the basin, including Yakutsk in 1632, which by virtue of its strategic location relative to the major tributaries, east and west, became the most important outpost in the basin. The damage to the Russians and to the natives resulting from the clashes between rival parties of service-men led the central authorities in Moscow to raise Yakutsk in 1638 to the rank of a major administrative outpost with its own voyevodas and geographical jurisdiction and to declare the area off limits to the service-men from other administrative centres in Siberia. Thereafter the advance farther east and the exploitation of far eastern Siberia, especially the northeast, was directed from Yakutsk.[3]

[1] 1955, pp. 32–3; *RM*, p. 89.   [2] Belov, 1955, p. 33.
[3] Sergey V. Bakhrushin, *Nauchnyye trudy* (Moscow), Tom III (1955), p. 152.

The first voyevodas to be appointed from Yakutsk were Petr Petrovich Golovin and Matvey Bogdanovich Glebov. They were instructed to assemble 395 service-men from various towns in Siberia, including Yeniseysk, and to proceed with them to Yakutsk.[1] Because of transportation and other problems the voyevodal entourage did not reach Yakutsk until 1640. During the interval between appointment and arrival the local commandant at Yakutsk, Parfen Khodyrev, continued in charge. After his removal in May 1640 on charges of bribery, illegal trade, and other abuses, he was succeeded by Ivan Galkin, who then served under the new voyevodas. It is doubtful that all 395 service-men were transferred to Yakutsk together or at once. We do not know definitely that Dezhnev was one of them, though it is highly possible that he was. He himself states that he moved to Yakutsk in 1638, probably in the late winter or spring, for customs records preserved in the Siberian Department mention a commercial transaction involving Dezhnev at Yakutsk dated 12 June 1638.[2]

Dezhnev tells us in his 1662 petition (document 28) that he was sent to Yakutsk 'to collect the sovereign's tribute' and that is what he spent the next three years at Yakutsk doing. Petitions in the Yakutsk archives from several service-men collectively about service in the Yakutsk jurisdiction include Dezhnev's name, but no dates of service are mentioned. We do have more information about three missions in which he took part, two of which he mentions in his petition of 1662. In August 1640 he was sent to the Tata and Amga rivers to pacify two feuding tribes of Bataruskiye Yakuts. His return after an absence of only thirteen days suggests that he handled his assignment expeditiously. That such a task should have been given to him indicates unusual qualities in him, for the role of peacemaker between quarrelling natives was not usually assigned to the ordinary cossack or service-man. In the fall of that year he was to collect tribute from rebellious Kangalarskiye Yakuts, who attacked, unsuccessfully, the Yakutsk ostrog itself. After being driven off some of the rebellious chiefs submitted and paid tribute, but others, particularly one Sakhey Otnakov, refused. Two service-men sent to gain his submission Sakhey killed, and a third one sent on the same errand suffered the same fate. The task was then given to Dezhnev by Parfen Khodyrev. In his petition of 1662 he reports the results, though not the manner or means by which he accomplished them: '...I took 140 sables from chief Sakhey, his children and

[1] George V. Lantzeff and Richard A. Pierce, *Eastward to empire* (Montreal and London, 1973), p. 139.   [2] Belov, 1955, p. 33.

kinsmen and from other... Yakuts.' Upon returning to Yakutsk he was sent with ataman Dmitriy Mikhaylov Zyryan overland on horseback to the Yana River, the next major river east of the Lena, to collect tribute. This river, as well as the Indigirka River, the next major river beyond that, had been discovered by Russian cossacks from Yeniseysk and Krasnoyarsk, who reported that the rivers went to the sea, had many tributaries, many sables, and many reindeer and sedentary natives.[1] Zyryan's party collected from the Yukagirs of the area 340 sables and two black foxes (their pelts were even more prized than the sables'). In the spring of 1641 Zyryan sent Dezhnev and three other service-men back to Yakutsk with the 'sable treasury'. A group of forty or more Tunguses attempted to waylay the small party, but Dezhnev and his three companions managed to fight them off – though Dezhnev suffered a leg wound – and to bring the treasury safely to Yakutsk. Zyryan, whom we encounter again, chose to remain in the region to collect more tribute. He and the other ten men proceeded to the Indigirka zimov'ye where he took charge.[2]

Up to this point in his career Dezhnev had demonstrated much zeal and enterprise in his service for the state, and a potential for leadership. Unlike, however, the man under whom he was next to serve, Mikhail Vasil'yev Stadukhin, he had not been given a top field command. Stadukhin stood in well with the new voyevoda, Golovin. He was the nephew of a major Moscow merchant, Vasiliy Gusel'nikov, and, like Dezhnev, is thought to have come from Pinega. With close family ties to the upper merchantry of the Muscovite state he became a man, so Belov argues,[3] whom Golovin thought it advisable to cultivate and favour. Such connections placed Stadukhin in the upper echelons of cossackdom. Dezhnev, on the other hand came from a lower level. There are other contrasts between these two men, who later became rivals. Stadukhin was arrogant, ambitious, maybe avaricious, and ready to step on or exploit weaker or defenceless men, Russian or native, not above robbery or pillage. It is not accidental that those who served under him on the Yemokon and Kolyma Rivers became his enemies, whereas with Dezhnev one finds few complaints against him and no charges of serious abuse of authority. As much as one can determine from the rather stereotyped reports and petitions, he appears to have been free of venality and arrogance, to have got along well with his fellow service-men, and to have gained the respect of his superiors in command. It is to be noted that while on the Anadyr´ River he shared

[1] Belov, 1955, pp. 34–5.   [2] Belov, 1955, p. 36.   [3] 1955, pp. 36–7.

joint command with Semen Motora and subsequently with Nikita Semenov without apparent friction. It is one of the happier episodes of history that ability and enterprise with a measure of luck were to bring the 'good guy' fame and honour, even if belatedly, and relegate the 'bad guy' to the background.

It is relevant at this point to note a complaint that Dezhnev was to repeat more than once: the cost to him of state service. It frequently happened that the service-men had to provide their own equipment and food supplies. They were entitled to a 'salary' while on state service consisting of salt, flour, powder and lead for the firearms which established the Russians' superiority over the natives. Other goods and money were on occasion provided. But sometimes the local supply of such items was insufficient, for a variety of reasons. They had to be transported long distances from Russia or western Siberia. Some local officials were not above selling state supplies for their own gain. As a consequence service-men often went long periods of time without adequate salary and had to petition for reimbursement. Thus it was not an unusual complaint when service-men pointed out what they had had to spend to equip themselves for state service, as does Dezhnev in his petition of 1662 where he notes that for his participation in the expedition to the Yana River he had had to purchase among other items two horses, costing 85 roubles, and clothing, boots, and various pieces of equipment bought from traders and promyshlenniks at a cost of 15 roubles. Altogether he paid out 150 roubles (document 28), which for that time was a lot of money, particularly for a man of such limited resources as Dezhnev appears to have been. Such equipment and provisions were not used exclusively, however, in state service; the service-men often engaged in gainful activities for themselves on such expeditions.[1]

Returning from the Yana River, Dezhnev was assigned in August 1641 to serve under Stadukhin with fourteen other men on the Yemokon River, a recently discovered western tributary of the Indigirka River.[2] This assignment, though Dezhnev could not know it then, marks the beginning of a twenty-year absence from Yakutsk in which he moved eastward to the Indigirka River, then to the Kolyma, whence he departed on his historic voyage to the Anadyr´ where he remained for the next twelve years before returning to

---

[1] It appears that Dezhnev was allowed to keep 36 sables he had acquired while serving on the Yana instead of being required to sell them to the state at lower than market prices, this to help reimburse him for the expenses he had incurred (*ORZPM*, pp. 17, 119).

[2] *ORZPM*, p. 141.

Yakutsk. His impending departure became the occasion for his submission of a short petition (document 21) from which we learn that he had a wife, contrary to a long-held belief that he was a bachelor. His wife was a native Yakut named Abakayada Sichyu. From this union came a son Lyubima. In his petition he requests permission to turn the care of his wife over to a Yakut named Manyakuya along with a cow for assistance in her support. He also arranged before departure to have her baptized into the Orthodox faith, which changed her status from that of a native to something more akin to that of a Russian.[1]

The Yemokon basin to which Stadukhin's contingent was ordered was one of the coldest places in the world; winter temperatures reach −60 °C (−78 °F) or lower. Few natives were attracted to the area: some Tunguses from the Moma River, an eastern tributary of the Indigirka, and upper Okhota River and some Yakuts from the Aldan River only temporarily.[2] The contingent spent the fall and winter there, collecting tribute from the Tunguses and Yakuts. But in April events took an unfortunate turn. In a night attack Okhota Tunguses killed the Russians' horses and a few Yakut allies in an unsuccessful effort to free one of their chiefs who earlier had been captured by the Russians. With the retreat of the Tunguses back to the Okhota River and a scarcity of animals and fish on the Yemokon River it became pointless to remain there, and Stadukhin did not want to return to Yakutsk virtually empty-handed. Learning from a Yakut of the big Moma River, a river with 'many people', he decided to go there.[3]

In the spring of 1642 the Russians built a koch and sailed to the mouth of the Indigirka. Here they found a large number of cossacks and promyshlenniks, including Zyryan (who at this point appears in the documents with a second appellation, Mit'ka Yerilo or Yarilo) and his men.[4] In the summer Zyryan had led a party of fifteen service-men and promyshlenniks in two koches down the Indigirka River to the sea in search of new lands. Advancing eastward along the coast, they came to the mouth of the Alazeya River, which lies in between the Indigirka and the Kolyma. After a fight with 300 natives the party moved upstream to the forested area and there built a zimov'ye. From the Yukagir natives Zyryan learned that a large river, the Kolyma, lay three days' journey by reindeer to the east, where there were many people, sables, and fish, a region not yet visited by the Russians. Zyryan

[1] Belov, 1955, pp. 37–8, citing YaA, karton 3, stolbets 19, sstavy 1–6.
[2] Belov, 1955, p. 36.
[3] Belov, 1955, p. 38; ORZPM, pp. 120, 121, 492.   [4] ORZPM, p. 143.

was loath, however, to risk his small contingent among so many hostile natives by seizing hostages or pushing again to the east. At this point Stadukhin and his party, which included Dezhnev, arrived at the zimov'ye, having also set out by koch for the east shortly after Zyryan. As rivals the two leaders were not friendly, so Dezhnev was entrusted with the task of inviting Zyryan and his men to join Stadukhin's party, which he succeeded in persuading Zyryan to do. At the end of June or the beginning of July 1643 the combined groups went down the river to the sea and turned eastward.[1] Sometime after July 8 the Russians reached the mouth of the Kolyma and began to sail up that river. On July 15 they encountered hostile reindeer natives (this is reminiscent of the Russians' experience on the Alazeya), nomadic Chukchi or maybe Chuvantsy.[2] The Russians called on them to submit and pay tribute, but the natives refused and prevented the Russians from landing. After a day of fighting they were forced to continue upriver, the natives following them in boats and on shore for three days. Ten days later, on July 25, the Russians came to a Yukagir village of an Omok tribe, whose chieftain was Alay. He and his people also refused to submit and pay tribute, but unlike the reindeer natives they were unable to repel the Russian attack even though they retreated into a protective stockade. In five days of intermittent fighting Dezhnev killed one of the brothers of the chief and captured one of his sons, who became a hostage. These and other casualties led the natives to capitulate and accept the Russians' demands. The Russians then proceeded to erect an ostrozhek 'with a stockade' on their land (document 23). Thus two years after leaving Yakutsk, Dezhnev found himself on the Kolyma River where he was to remain for the next five years.

During these five years Dezhnev functioned much as he had at Yakutsk, that is, participating in the collection of tribute from the natives and the subjection of natives still outside Russian authority, as well as engaging in fur trapping and trade on his own. Meanwhile, the two commanders, Stadukhin and Zyryan-Yerilo, set off in the summer of 1645 by sea with a large sable treasury for Yakutsk. En route they met sworn-man Petr Novoselov, who carried orders to Zyryan

---

[1] Belov, 1955, pp. 40–1; 1973, p. 66. Stadukhin's petition after 1 March 1644 (document 23) presents a different version of the union of the two groups: the two parties met at sea on 8 July 1643 and joined forces so as to carry out the sovereign's various services and to go to the Kolyma River. Belov bases his account on the report of Fedor Chyukchev, a member of Zyryan's party, who was sent back to Yakutsk with the sable treasury and submitted a report there (*ORZPM*, p. 143).   [2] Dolgikh, 1960, pp. 549–50.

from the new voyevodas at Yakutsk, Vasiliy N. Pushkin and Kiril O. Suponov, to undertake a search for the Neloga River (the Chaun River?) and the silver ore reported to be found there (document 24).[1] Zyryan accordingly returned to the Kolyma as the commandant of the ostrozhek. When he died early in 1646,[2] he was succeeded by Vtoroy Gavrilov, an original member of Stadukhin's party on the Yemokon, who, like Dezhnev, remained on the Kolyma.[3] Meanwhile, Stadukhin continued on, reaching Zhigansk on the lower Lena River in the fall. The navigation season having ended, he went on by dog sled and arrived in Yakutsk in late November.[4] There he remained until July 1647 when he was ordered again to the east to find the Pogycha River and an island nearby where reportedly walrus tusks could be obtained (document 13).

We have traced Dezhnev's career to his arrival on the Kolyma River, but we have said nothing as to where he was stationed on that river. To be sure, Dezhnev participated in the establishment of the first Russian outpost there, but it was not given a name that would identify it as one of the three outposts built on the river. Nizhne-Kolymsk, Sredne-Kolymsk, and Verkhne-Kolymsk were names that did not come into use until later. When one goes through the documents reproduced here, one finds that references to a specific place on the Kolyma River are the exception. The writers of reports, petitions, and instructions were content simply to refer to the Kolyma (or Kovyma) River even though from the context it appears that a particular place on the river was meant, usually the main outpost. In his reports and petitions Dezhnev states in several places that he went 'to the Kovyma' or 'from' it, or that he was 'on the Kovyma River' (documents 8, 9 [p. 52], 10 [pp. 56, 57, 58], 27, 28 [p. 104]). The petitions and reports of those associated with him on the Kolyma such as Stadukhin and Gavrilov, and the instructions from the voyevodas at Yakutsk follow the same wording (documents 3, 4, 11–13, 15, 16). Yet in each case it becomes evident that the writer had in mind a particular place on the river, not the river in general. For examples: In the instructions to Vlas'yev and Kotkin in 1647 (document 26) they are told to go to the Kolyma River, to the fortified zimov'ye established by Stadukhin. In the next sentence the instructions report that Stadukhin and Gavrilov wrote, not from the zimov'ye, but 'from the Kovyma'. In that same year Gavrilov reports that Isay Ignat'yev and

[1] RM, p. 46, note 2; cf. ORZPM, pp. 122–3. [2] Belov, 1955, p. 53.
[3] ORZPM, pp. 119–20. [4] Belov in RM, p. 61, note 1.

his men 'returned to us on the Kolyma River' and further on that 'Fedot Alekseyev and companions [came] to us in the main office' (document 3). In May 1648 Dezhnev stated in a petition that Gavrilov was petitioned 'on the Kovyma River' (document 27), presumably at his headquarters. In some instances the writer makes a more restricted reference: 'the Kovymskiy ostrozhek' (documents 3, 5, 6); 'the Kovymskiy ostrog' (document 5); 'the ostrozhek' built by Stadukhin or 'that ostrog on the Kolyma where service-man Vtorko Gavrilov and companions are now' (document 26); 'the tribute zimov'ye on the Kolyma River' (document 10, p. 58); 'the ostrozhek on the Kovyma' (document 28, p. 104).[1] But none of these designations clearly attaches itself to any of the three outposts. In only three cases are there found in these documents identifying designations of outposts. In 1647 in their instructions to Vlas'yev and Kotkin the Yakutsk voyevodas refer to a new tribute zimov'ye 'at the mouth of the Anoya [Anyuy] River' (document 27), and in a petition the next year Ivan Baranov mentions 'the lower tribute zimov'ye on the Kovyma River' (document 7). In 1655 Yemel'yan Vetoshka wrote that in 1648 petitions were presented 'on the Kolyma River at the mouth of the Anyuy River' (document 11). Still, one does not learn from these documents that the two designations just mentioned refer to the same outpost. Elsewhere in his petitions he mentions 'zimov'yes'; that is, there were more than one, but he does not locate them. Thus the questions of where the chief administrative outpost on the Kolyma was located and from what place Dezhnev's two voyages set forth are left up in the air.

The answer given to these questions by most writers has been Nizhne-Kolymsk. This answer appears to have originated with Müller and remained unchallenged for want of a close reading of his accounts, as well as of other relevant documents as they became available. To be sure, these documents do not answer the question, but in the absence in them of any mention of a main – or any – outpost by name they do raise it. With one exception Müller followed the practice found in the documents and referred to the Kolyma River, not to a given outpost. But in that exception he mentions in his account in 1758 an ostrog built on the lower Kolyma River in 1644 by Stadukhin and his companions: 'In 1644 Mikhaylo Stadukhin, a cossack from Yakutsk, had built the lower ostrog on the Kolyma with several of his

---

[1] From these several examples it can be seen that at least in eastern Siberia no clearcut distinction was maintained in the designations applied to the three kinds of outposts, except that a major settlement like Yakutsk was never called an ostrozhek or zimov'ye.

companions' (document 2, p. 35). Characteristically he provides no source for this statement (is it document 23, the report of Stadukhin and others?). Evidently he assumed that because the Russians made their first contact with the Kolyma by sea, at its mouth, they built their first outpost near that mouth before moving up the river. Meanwhile, nowhere else does he identify a specific settlement on the Kolyma River, not even in connection with the organization and departure of the two expeditions of 1647 and 1648. He says simply that they departed 'from the Kolyma River'. Thus it was from Müller, not the documents, that later writers got the notion that Nizhne-Kolymsk was the first Russian settlement on the Kolyma and that from the outset it was the administrative centre of that river basin. The persistence of these conclusions appears to be another instance in which an alleged fact becomes so well entrenched in the literature and people's mind that the signs that could have alerted them to a different conclusion are passed over unnoticed.

The present site of Nizhne-Kolymsk, incidentally, is not necessarily its original site. A few scholars have placed the first site at different locations and in a different year. I. Shklovskiy, writing in 1892, placed it 80 versts (50 miles) farther down the river on the Stadukhinskiy channel.[1] Belov placed it there too, but claims that it was moved to the present site a year later. He also moved the date of founding back one year to 1643,[2] as did Vladimir I. Ogorodnikov.[3] Dmitriy I. Lebedev located the original site of the outpost about 20 km from the present one, but found it difficult to determine whether 1643 or 1644 was the year of founding.[4]

To the question, which was the first Russian settlement on the Kolyma, a new answer has been given, first by the ethnographer Boris O. Dolgikh, without elaboration,[5] and then by Polevoy, who bases his answer on new archival material.[6] Their answer is that the original ostrozhek built by Stadukhin, Zyryan, and the others, including Dezhnev, was not at Nizhne-Kolymsk, but at Sredne-Kolymsk, some 600 km (375 miles)[7] up the river from its mouth. Polevoy gives the

[1] Boris P. Polevoy, 'O mestopolozhenii pervogo russkogo poseleniya na Kolyme', *Doklady Instituta geografii Sibiri i dal'nego vostoka* (Irkutsk), 1962a, no. 2, p. 66, citing *Zapiski vostochno-sibirskago otdeleniya Imperatorskago russkago geograficheskago obshchestva*, Tom II, p. 96.

[2] *RM*, pp. 262, 320–1; Belov, 1955, pp. 41, 43; 1956, p. 153.

[3] Dmitriy M. Lebedev, *Geografiya v Rossii XVII veka (do-petrovskoy epokhi)* (Moscow and Leningrad, 1949), p. 53, citing Vladimir I. Ogorodnikov, *Pokoreniye yukagirskoy zemli* (Chita, 1922); Polevoy, 1966b, p. 285.   [4] 1949, p. 53; Polevoy, 1966b, p. 286.

[5] 1960, p. 410.   [6] 1962a, pp. 66–75.

[7] My estimate. Belov estimates the distance at 650 km (p. 134 this chapter).

year of founding as 1643, not 1644, and carries his answer further by stating that it was the main administrative outpost and residence of the commandants during the first decade of Russian occupation of that basin. Nizhne-Kolymsk and Verkhne-Kolymsk were founded a couple of years later, and Nizhne-Kolymsk did not become the main administrative outpost until more than a decade had passed. Polevoy also contends that it was at Sredne-Kolymsk that Dezhnev's voyage had its origins and from which the Russian flotilla of koches departed in 1648.

The starting point for Polevoy's case is the petition presented sometime after 1 March 1644 by Stadukhin, Zyryan, Dezhnev, and others to the Yakutsk authorities (document 23) in which the initial conquest and establishment of 'the ostrozhek with a stockade' are narrated, a document Polevoy uncovered in the archives.[1] These events we have already related, so now we ask, how do they support Polevoy's case?

First, he notes that Petr Novoselov tells us[2] that in the 1640s the Russians covered the 140 km (90 miles) from the mouth of the Kolyma to Nizhne-Kolymsk by towpath in three days. This, we may observe, is nearly 50 km a day, and if during the long Arctic summer days the Russians moved their boats the whole twenty-four hours of the day, they made an average speed of about 2 km (a mile and a quarter) an hour. Stadukhin's party, on the other hand, went upstream by sail and should have been able to sail as fast as, if not faster than, by towing. Sailing upstream, Polevoy argues, presented few difficulties. He quotes S. V. Obruchev to the effect that the stretch of the Kolyma below Sredne-Kolymsk 'is noted for a slow current and strong winds'.[3] Stadukhin himself reports elsewhere that the Kolyma and Lena are 'under the same winds, from the east and from the north' (document 12). In sailing upstream one proceeds south to a point just east of Nizhne-Kolymsk where the direction of the river's course becomes east–west; about 130 km (80 miles) to the west the river bends to the left and the direction becomes southwest–northeast. On such a course northerly and easterly winds should have facilitated sailing against the current.

The petition states that on July 15 the Russians encountered reindeer

---

[1] In another document, his report of 1659, Stadukhin again asserts his role in the founding of the ostrozhek: '...I went by sea to the Kovyma River, and I established a tribute zimov'ye with a stockade on the Kovyma River...' (RM, p. 262).

[2] Polevoy does not say where.

[3] Kolymsko-indigirskiy kray (Leningrad, 1931), p. 9, cited by Polevoy, 1962a, p. 68.

natives, who fought them off and forced them to continue upriver where on July 25 they came upon a village of sedentary natives. We are not told where the Russians met the reindeer natives, but it seems likely that it was near the site of the later Nizhne-Kolymsk, near the mouth of the Anyuy River. In the instructions issued to Vasiliy Vlas'yev and Kiril Kotkin in July 1647 at Yakutsk, prior to their departure for the Kolyma to take command there, they were informed that reindeer natives nomadized along the Anyuy, some 300 or more of them at the mouth of the Anyuy (document 26). If we take 50 km a day as the ordinary minimum distance covered when moving upriver with following winds, in ten days the Russians should have been able to sail the 450 km (280 miles) between the site of Nizhne-Kolymsk and the site of Sredne-Kolymsk. Even if we accept the counter contention by Belov that the Russians encountered the reindeer natives near the mouth of the Kolyma rather than near the mouth of the Anyuy, in ten days they should have passed well beyond the site of Nizhne-Kolymsk.

Further evidence that a settlement upriver from Nizhne-Kolymsk was established sometime before it is to be found in the above-mentioned instructions to Vlas'yev and Kotkin. In them it is stated: '*Down below* there is a tributary from the right side sailing *downstream*, the Anoya [Anyuy], and at the mouth of the Anoya River a new tribute zimov'ye was established' (emphasis added). Still more evidence comes from the tribute collection records maintained by Novoselov in 1646–7 (i.e., from 1 September 1646 to 31 August 1647).[1] Polevoy asserts that they leave no doubt that they were kept at the ostrozhek built by Stadukhin and Zyryan. First, they contain detailed information about tribute collected there from Alay's son Kinita, from Kalyana, and from various kinsmen of Kalyana, Alivin, and Alay, the Yukagir natives mentioned in the petition as living in the region where the ostrozhek was founded. Records uncovered by Dolgikh in the archives of the Siberian Department show again the identification of the upriver Yukagirs with Stadukhin's ostrozhek. Tribute was still being paid there by Kalyana, Alivin, and Alay, and their kinsmen in 1651 and 1659.[2] Second, Novoselov's record books, at the end, list the tribute collected at the lower and upper zimov'yes, thus identifying Stadukhin's ostrozhek as the middle one. Third, in these record books is an entry: 'The collection of Gerasim Ankudinov, Makarka Tveryakov, and companions in the present year 155 [1646–7] down the Kovyma at the mouth of the

---

[1] Polevoy, 1962a, p. 68, citing YaPI, *opis'* 4, *kniga* 177.
[2] 1960, p. 416.

Anyuy...'[1] It is hard to escape the conclusion that Nizhne-Kolymsk, the lower tribute zimov'ye, was found below Stadukhin's 'ostrozhek with a stockade'. At the same time this information suggests that Nizhne-Kolymsk was in existence by the end of 1646, founded perhaps as early as the fall of 1645, if Ivan Baranov's testimony that he served 'at the lower tribute zimov'ye on the Kolyma River' in the years 154 (1645–6) and 155 (1646–7) (document 7) is accepted.

For Polevoy's other contention, that Sredne-Kolymsk was the administrative centre for the Kolyma basin and remained so for more than a decade, one finds support in the fact that Novoselov appears to have maintained his records of customs and tribute collection at the middle zimov'ye or ostrozhek. Other strong evidence is found in the previously mentioned instructions of the Yakutsk voyevodas to Vasiliy Vlas'yev and Kiril Kotkin. The two men – Vlas'yev as commandant and Kotkin as sworn-man – are ordered to go 'to the Kovyma River to the ostrozhek where Mikhalko Stadukhin and service-men established a zimov'ye with fortification', which we have identified as the outpost on the middle Kolyma, and there to assume command of 'that ostrog where Vtorko Gavrilov and companions are now' and 'to take over the hostages' (document 26).[2] What is particularly revealing about these instructions is the fact that about four-fifths of them (the part not translated and reproduced here) are given over to detailed instructions regarding the provisioning of service-men, the search for new lands, the care of hostages, the collection of tribute and customs duties, the transportation of the receipts to Yakutsk, and many other matters.[3] Such detailed instructions were not issued by the voyevodas at Yakutsk to the agents in charge of outlying zimov'yes, but to commandants of the major outposts, who in turn passed on such parts of them as were appropriate to the subordinate outposts. These instructions also assigned jurisdiction to Vlas'yev and Kotkin over the area of the upper Kolyma and the rivers adjacent to it.[4]

Vlas'yev and Kotkin reached the Kolymskiy ostrozhek in August 1648, by way of the ocean route.[5] Not long thereafter Vlas'yev made a trip to the upper zimov'ye, which may have been founded by Motora.[6] Later, according to a report in 1650 Motora, then stationed at the lower tribute zimov'ye, turned over there the customs receipts and tribute to Vlas'yev who, Motora says, 'arrived from the Kovyma

[1] Polevoy, 1962a, p. 68.   [2] Polevoy, 1962a, p. 69.
[3] ORZPM, pp. 236–51.   [4] ORZPM, p. 236.
[5] Polevoy, 1962a, p. 69, citing LOII, YaA, karton 12, stolbets 1, list 3.
[6] Polevoy, 1962a, p. 69, citing YaPI, opis' 4, kniga 177.

River...at the lower tribute zimov'ye' to announce the tsar's awards to the men there and to arrest Vasiliy Bugor and his men, the fugitive cossacks.[1] In 1650 service-man Timofey Buldakov was sent from Yakutsk to relieve Vlas'yev. In March 1651 he reported that 'on arriving on the Kovyma River at the middle tribute zimov'ye I took over the tribute zimov'ye, hostages, and the sovereign's treasury...'.[2] Similarly in June 1652 his successor, Ivan Rebrov, was ordered to go 'to the Kovyma, to the ostrozhek where Mikhail Stadukhin and service-men established a zimov'ye with fortification', to 'that ostrog where Timoshka Buldakov and service-men are now, to take over from Timoshka Buldakov the hostages...and the sovereign's service-men in the upper, middle, and lower zimov'yes...'.[3] Rebrov arrived at 'the middle tribute zimov'ye' in late November 1652 and there assumed command as directed.[4] Among the hostages whom he took over were the sons of the tribal leaders whom Stadukhin had encountered in 1643. Rebrov reported a food shortage that threatened the welfare of the hostages, a primary responsibility of the commandant. He attempted to relieve it by sending men to the upper and lower zimov'yes to purchase provisions from the promyshlenniks there.[5] All these items of information tell us that as late as 1652 the outpost on the middle Kolyma was still the residence of the commandant and the administrative centre for the Kolyma basin.

This new interpretation of the priority of Sredne-Kolymsk over Nizhne-Kolymsk is challenged by Belov, the only scholar to respond in print to Polevoy's thesis. He insists that Nizhne-Kolymsk was the site of Stadukhin's ostrozhek and the first Russian outpost on the Kolyma.[6] He advances two arguments against Polevoy's thesis. First, the nomad camp of Alay's tribe was not, he contends, necessarily found on the middle Kolyma since the Yukagirs customarily nomadized closer to the ocean in the summer where they carried on trade with the Chukchi. He goes on to say that according to Stadukhin's reports (he does not say which ones) he and his men established a new zimov'ye on the lower Kolyma upon arriving at that river. Sredne-Kolymsk was established later, in 1645–6, by Petr Novoselov. Second, Belov does not accept the postulated speed of the Russians' koches moving

[1] *ORZPM*, pp. 260–1. Attention should be called to this curious wording: Vlas'yev 'arrived *from* the Kovyma River...at the lower tribute zimov'ye' (emphasis added). Since the lower zimov'ye was on the Kolyma River, 'Kovyma River' must refer to the main outpost, in keeping with the practice we noticed above.
[2] *DAI*, Tom III, p. 283.   [3] *DAI*, Tom III, p. 350.
[4] *RM*, p. 225.   [5] *RM*, p. 227.
[6] 1973, p. 214, note 77.

upstream. To cover the 650 km (400 miles), which he calculates the distance from the mouth of the Kolyma to Sredne-Kolymsk to be, called for a speed not matched by any known example of that time. He writes that Polevoy equates (he does not say where) the distance from the mouth of the Kolyma to Sredne-Kolymsk to that from the mouth of the Alazeya to the mouth of the Kolyma, when actually the latter distance is half that of the former and required fourteen, not twelve, days to cover.[1] If the speed on the river was the same as that on the ocean, the Russians could have covered only 270 km (180 miles) in twelve days, and that would not have been enough for them to have reached the site of Sredne-Kolymsk.

Belov characterizes Polevoy's arguments as unconvincing. But his counter-arguments are equally unconvincing. First, Belov makes Alay's tribe nomadic and has them nomadizing in the summer. Yet the report of Stadukhin and the others in 1644 states specifically that they were sedentary, that they were 'walking' natives (document 23). Novoselov found these Yukagirs on the middle Kolyma in 1646–7; the Siberian Department records for 1651 and 1659 place them there too. Moreover, in the 1647 instructions to Vlas'yev and Kotkin (document 26) it is unequivocally stated: '...the natives on the Kovyma River are sedentary; in the winter and *summer* [emphasis added] they stay in one place, walkers (*peshiye*); but the reindeer people – they wander from place to place and to the lakes'. Belov quotes this same statement to support his characterizing Alay's tribe as nomadic, but he does so by omitting a key section in the middle so that it reads: 'The natives on the Kovyma River...[are] reindeer people...' *et seq.* Thus he completely alters the meaning of the part relating to Alay's tribe.

Second, even if we accept Belov's description of Alay's tribe as nomadic, in the absence of explicit information about where the Russians met the reindeer natives, there is just as much justification for placing them within feasible sailing distance of the Nizhne-Kolymsk site, as Polevoy does, as for placing them nearer the ocean, as Belov does. Belov's contention cuts both ways and so proves nothing. Meanwhile, nowhere in his article does Polevoy equate the distance from the mouth of the Kolyma to Sredne-Kolymsk to that between the mouths of the Alazeya and Kolyma rivers. Actually the latter distance is two-thirds, not half, that of the former. And when he writes that to have covered 650 km in twelve days calls for a speed unmatched in those days, he overlooks that in the same study he posits a distance

[1] The report of Stadukhin and the others (document 23) says ten days, July 15–25.

of 1,400–1,750 km covered in *seven* days by Stadukhin in 1649, as we shall see in chapter 8.

Finally, in all three versions of his study on Dezhnev, Belov states that Stadukhin, returning to the Kolyma in 1648, and Vlas'yev, going there as the new commandant, arrived at *Sredne*-Kolymsk.[1] It is unfortunate that Belov chose not to examine the rest of Polevoy's evidence. Even if the reindeer natives had not forced the Russians to establish their first outpost a considerable distance up the Kolyma River, there were good reasons for the Russians' doing so. In the 17th century new settlements in Siberia usually arose where the greatest aggregate of furs could be expected – the most fur-bearing animals, the most natives, the most promyshlenniks (one of ten of their furs was taken by the state). Good water routes were also a consideration. The middle Kolyma flows through a forested area whereas the lower Kolyma passes through the thinner forest adjacent to the tundra and through the tundra itself. Good sables abounded in the former region along with arctic foxes; far fewer sables were found in the latter. Too, the Yukagirs near Sredne-Kolymsk were sedentary and easier to bring under control than were the nomadic Chukchi and Koryaks near Nizhne-Kolymsk. Sredne-Kolymsk was the head of navigation for ocean-going koches and about equidistant from Verkhne-Kolymsk and Nizhne-Kolymsk. It was on the main overland route from the upper Indigirka and Alazeya. It is to be remarked that the zimov'ye which Yerilo-Zyryan established first on the Alazeya River was in the upper, not lower, reaches of that river. Control over the whole Kolyma basin was facilitated by Sredne-Kolymsk's middle position.

But Sredne-Kolymsk had some disadvantages as well.[2] Food supply was one of them. The local resources of fish were inadequate and importing them was difficult. Some hostages starved to death. In 1650 the land route to the Anadyr' was discovered. Thereafter more and more promyshlenniks and traders passed through Nizhne-Kolymsk to the Anyuy, Omolon (a major eastern tributary of the Kolyma), and Anadyr' rivers, by-passing Sredne-Kolymsk. Revenue collections at Sredne-Kolymsk dropped. The decision to try to impose tribute on the Chukchi led to strengthening the fortification of the lower zimov'ye, raising it to the condition of an ostrozhek, and to commandant Konstantin Dunay's decision to move his official residence there in 1655. Continuing conflict with the Chukchi forced the Russians to maintain the fortification, and it came to be thought of as the main ostrozhek.

[1] 1948, p. 73; 1955, p. 61; 1973; p. 79.   [2] Polevoy, 1962a, pp. 73–4.

This primacy in subsequent years and the absence of clear evidence to the contrary concealed the fact that Nizhne-Kolymsk was not the first Russian outpost on the Kolyma or the main one in the early years of the Russian occupation. Both the new evidence and the old point to Sredne-Kolymsk as the main Kolyma outpost in the period of Dezhnev's voyage.

CHAPTER 6

THE GATHERING FORCES

The discovery of the Kolyma River, accompanied by reports of many natives and an abundance of sables, especially the highly valued darker ones, drew a large number of promyshlenniks and traders to this new river along with the service-men sent from Yakutsk.[1] It soon became one of the most active areas in the Yakutsk jurisdiction. In 1647 the customs office at Yakutsk issued passports or travel documents to 404 men headed for the Indigirka and Kolyma Rivers. On the Kolyma itself that same year local customs officials collected head taxes from 396 men, while 1,653 sables valued at 3,760 r. were collected from Russians as the ten per cent first-fruits tax. In succeeding years the proceeds from this tax were the highest of any area under the authority of Yakutsk.[2]

At the same time the standard pattern of the conquest of Siberia, whereby occupation of one region brought reports of other regions ripe for exploitation and further probing by service-men and promyshlenniks, occurred on the Kolyma. From the natives the Russians heard reports of other rivers lying east of the Kolyma with many natives and many sables; also walrus ivory and silver. That such reports were sometimes garbled or exaggerated was, of course, no deterrent; rather, they were an incentive. One of the first reports was that heard in Yakutsk in 1642 from three Yukagir hostages brought there by Yelisey Buza. They told of a Neloga (or Neroga) River near the Indigirka. They described it as a separate river with its own mouth, above which at a short distance was a mountain with silver ore and not far beyond that a village of a tribe called Nattyla.[3] Two years later one Lavrentiy Grigor'yev, sent to the Indigirka to have these reports investigated, returned with information corroborating much of the report, adding a report of 'bead-stuff' to be found in the river and placing the river east, not west, of the Kolyma, as well as correcting the tribal name

---

[1] E.g., document 24; also *ORZPM*, p. 128.

[2] Belov, 1955, p. 52. He mentions (p. 53) that an annual market was held in August on the Kolyma (Polevoy places it at Sredne-Kolymsk – see p. 156 below) where traders from the Lena and promyshlenniks from the forests met for trade.

[3] *DAI*, Tom II, p. 262; *RM*, p. 41; N. N. Stepanov, 'Pervyye russkiye svedeniya ob Amure i gol'dakh', *Sovetskaya etnografiya*, 1950, No. 1, p. 178.

to Natty (document 24).[1] Ivan Yerastov, another service-man on the Indigirka, conveyed the same information to Yakutsk.[2]

About the same time that Grigor´yev and Yerastov were reporting in Yakutsk the Russians on the Kolyma learned of a river east of them with a different name, the Pogycha.[3] Stadukhin carried this information to Yakutsk on his return there in the autumn of 1645. To reach the Pogycha, he said, was a journey of three days-and-nights. It was a 'large sable river' with many natives, who had their own language (document 12). Stadukhin also brought back information about an island in the sea northwest of the Kolyma where walruses were to be found.

Stadukhin's report was borne out by other service-men. Reporting to Moscow in the summer of 1646, the Yakutsk voyevodas Pushkin and Suponev wrote:

Ivashko Yerastov and his companions, forty men, stated under questioning that they have now learned of a new land. Emerging from the mouth of the Lena, one goes to the right side by sea towards the east beyond the Yana, beyond the Sobach´ya [Indigirka], beyond the Olozeyka, beyond the Kovyma rivers to the new river Pogycha. Into that river flow other tributary rivers. Many natives of various tribes, non-tribute-paying people, live on the Pogycha and the other nearby rivers, and they pay no tribute to anyone anywhere. Before this date, sovereign, no Russians have been on the river.

They have the very best dark sables...[4]

Yerastov picked up this information probably on the Indigirka no later than 1645.[5]

The news about the Pogycha River aroused much interest in Yakutsk. Sometime in 1646 Yerastov and forty service-men asked

[1] The kernel of substance behind the report of the Neloga River in its two versions appears, according to Belov (1955, p. 54; 1973, p. 79), to have been the Chaun River, which empties into the Chaunskaya Bay some 375 km east of the mouth of the Kolyma River; or, according to N. N. Stepanov (1950, pp. 179–82), with whom Dolgikh agrees (1960, p. 389, note 119), the more distant Amur River, near which lived tribes called Gol´dy which were also known as Natty. The Gol´dy, Stepanov suggests, probably acquired silver items from China and Mongolia through trade, but did not mine or refine silver ore itself. Migrating reindeer Yukagirs could have been the transmitter of this information, which they passed on to the Russians in order to induce them to move on or join them against the Koryaks. Cf. pp. 139–40 below.

[2] ORZPM, p. 127.

[3] In document 26 another river beyond the mountains is mentioned and is referred to as the Kovycha. Belov (1955, p. 54) takes this to be another name for the Pogycha, but Polevoy thinks otherwise (see p. 141, note 1, this chapter, below).

[4] ORZPM, p. 215.

[5] Boris P. Polevoy, 'O "Pogyche"-Pokhache', Voprosy geografii Kamchatki, 1970c, Vypusk 6, p. 83; N. N. Ogloblin, 'Vostochnosibirskiye polyarnyye morekhody XVII veka', Zhurnal Ministerstva narodnago prosveshcheniya, Chast' CCCXXXXVI, May 1903, otdel 2, pp. 56–57; Belov, 1949, p. 459.

voyevoda Pushkin for salary grants in money and grain for two years and for permission to go to the Pogycha. Pushkin was unwilling, however, to grant permission without authorization from Moscow.[1] A shortage of supplies and equipment in the local treasury for two koches may have contributed to his unwillingness.[2] This refusal caused great discontent among the service-men, who were determined to go to the Pogycha. When instead Pushkin finally put his man Stadukhin in charge of an expedition to the river and Stadukhin replaced more experienced men from Yerstov's group with his own men, the discontent escalated into open rebellion led by two popular cossacks, Vasiliy Bugor and Stepan Borisov, whose arrest and flogging were ordered. About fifty service-men, including Bugor and Borisov, and promyshlenniks defied the voyevodas and, seizing boats from traders, headed for the 'rivers beyond the mountains', avowedly to make a profit for the tsar, but also for themselves.[3]

Lest the rebels reach the Pogycha first, Pushkin sent Vasiliy Vlas´yev, assigned to replace Gavrilov as commandant at Sredne-Kolymsk, to overtake the rebels and send them back to Yakutsk, which he was unable to do. At the same time Pushkin expedited preparation for Stadukhin's expedition to the Pogycha, issuing orders to him on 5 July 1647 to return to the Kolyma to look for the Pogycha as well as the island with walruses, which the orders placed opposite the Pogycha (document 13). Thus three groups departed down the Lena and headed eastward, two ultimately for the Pogycha and one for Sredne-Kolymsk. All three came together at the mouth of the Yana where 'great and terrible winds' barred further progress. The next summer all three arrived at Sredne-Kolymsk only to learn that others had got a headstart on them to the Pogycha.[4]

The documents do not explicitly identify the Neloga-Neroga River as the Pogycha or explain the replacement of the former by the latter

[1] *ORZPM*, pp. 215–6, 217; Ogloblin, 1903, pp. 56–7.
[2] *ORZPM*, pp. 145, 212.
[3] Belov, 1955, p. 59–60; 1973, pp. 85–7.
[4] Belov, 1955, p. 61; 1973, p. 87. He states (1949, p. 460) that fugitive cossacks joined Stadukhin's party. He also mentions briefly that on 4 June 1648 one Ivan Dmitriyev Sinitsyn, agent of the merchant Gryagin, and promyshlennik Grigoriy Afanas´yev Ustyu-zhanin obtained travel documents for the Pogycha River and set out the next day. With them sailed 121 traders and promyshlenniks, carrying flour and goods valued at 10,947 r., a large sum for those days (citing TsGADA, Yakutskoye oblastnoye upravleniye, *stolbets* 9). En route they learned of the departure of Alekseyev and Dezhnev for the Anadyr´. What happened to this large group Belov does not say. Sinitsyn was on the Kolyma in 1650, and in the late 1650's he served on the Anadyr´ as a sworn-man customs agent (*ORZPM*, pp. 263, 324, 402). Though this episode is evidence of the great interest in the Pogycha at Yakutsk, Belov omits it from both his 1955 and 1973 studies of the voyage.

in the reports of the service-men, but the location of the Pogycha as three days-and-nights from the Kolyma suggests that the two rivers were at first thought to be the same. Pushkin's orders to Stadukhin, which placed the walrus island opposite the mouth of the Pogycha whereas Stadukhin had placed it a bit northwest of the Kolyma, points to a similar understanding. This coincidence of location seems, however, to have been shortlived and is only one aspect of a confusing picture. From this point on the names Neloga and Neroga are no longer mentioned in the documents, and it was the Pogycha River that excited the Russians' imagination. It also acquired a new identification. Reporting to Yakutsk about being held up by bad weather at the Yana, Stadukhin identified the Pogycha as also the Anadyr´ River – 'the new river Pogycha, the same as the Anadyr´ River' – but without explanation as to his source of information or whether the Pogycha-Anadyr´ was three days-and-nights distant from the Kolyma or was in the vicinity of the real Anadyr´ (document 14). Stadukhin's report about his later voyage from the Kolyma in search of the Pogycha indicates that he still thought it emptied into the Arctic Ocean (document 15). Yerastov's information points to the same belief. Nevertheless, we learn little from the documents as to its supposed location other than that it was 'beyond the Kovyma'.

What lay behind the reports about the Pogycha River with its many natives and sables is uncertain. Belov thinks that in effect it was the Neloga-Neroga River under a different name and stemmed from the existence of the Chaun River; but where the name Pogycha came from he does not say.[1] Vladimir G. Bogoraz,[2] Lev S. Berg,[3] and Sergey F. Bakhrushin[4] on the other hand, all remark on the similarity of 'Pogycha' to 'Pokhach', the name of a river that flows into the Bering Sea west of Cape Olyutorskiy. Bogoraz[5] notes that 'the darkest and longest-haired sables' were found on the Pokhach. If the Pokhach was in fact the basis of the reports about the Pogycha, one then has to explain how a river flowing into the Pacific Ocean at a distance of some 1,100 km (700 miles) from the Kolyma was transformed into a river flowing into the Arctic only three days-and-nights' sailing from the Kolyma. How did the Yukagirs of the Kolyma know of a river in what is now the northern part of the Kamchatka oblast´? Polevoy suggests an answer.[6]

[1] 1955, p. 54; 1973, pp. 79–80. [2] 1904–9, p. 683, note 5.
[3] Berg, 1946, p. 39, note 3. [4] Bakhrushin, 1955, Tom III, pp. 128–9.
[5] 1904–9, p. 683, note 5. [6] In his 1970c.

He writes that from a time before the advent of the Russians on the Kolyma, the reindeer Yukagirs of the Indigirka and Kolyma journeyed eastward to the distant Penzhina, Paren´, and upper Gizhiga rivers, which lie north of the Kamchatka Peninsula in a region sometimes visited by Koryaks. It was here that they acquired many of the sables they paid as tribute on the Kolyma and Indigirka rivers. Here they heard of the Pokhach, which they were unable to visit because their way was blocked by the Koryaks, a people second only to the Chukchi in their warlike qualities. In telling the Russians about the river the Yukagirs probably hoped that the Russians would be induced to leave the upper Indigirka and Kolyma and that they would also gain in their visitors a strong ally against the Koryaks. But how the Russians came to interpret this information about the Pokhach-Pogycha so as to place it near the Kolyma is not known. Language may have been more of a barrier to accurate understanding than we realize.[1]

As in Yakutsk, so on the Kolyma River, there was a great desire to find the Pogycha River. The first move in that direction of which there is record was the short voyage to the east in the summer of 1646 by Isay Ignat´yev Mezenets and eight other promyshlenniks (document 3). Emerging from the mouth of the Kolyma, they sailed for two days-and-nights and reached a bay on whose shore they encountered natives whom they took to be Chukchi.[2] In the absence of an interpreter communication was difficult and distrust considerable. There followed the dumb trade episode described by Müller. While the natives stood aside, the Russians placed goods on shore and retreated to their boat. The natives came forward, selected the items they wanted and left items of their own in exchange, then retreated. The items they left included several made from walrus tusks. The Russians evidently concluded from this that walruses were to be found in the vicinity. The information that valuable walrus ivory could be found along this Arctic coast could only have heightened the tension about finding the rivers east of the Kolyma. As to the site of the exchange between natives and Russians, Belov believes it to have been on Chaunskaya Bay, which is 350 to 400 km east of the Kolyma, a distance that could have been covered in two days of round-the-clock sailing.[3]

[1] A similar explanation is advanced for the report about the Kovycha River in document 26. Near Cape Olyutorskiy and not far from the Pokhach River there was the Kovacha River (Polevoy, 1970c, p. 85).

[2] Vrangel (1840, p. xxiii) thought that this bay might be an inlet on Chaunskaya Bay opposite Rautan Island where there is one such as Ignat´yev describes, surrounded by steep rocks.　　　　　　　　　　　　　[3] 1949, p. 459; 1955, p. 57.

The next move was the aborted first voyage of Alekseyev and Dezhnev. We know rather little about it. Most of what we do know comes from a few statements by Gavrilov and Dezhnev (documents 3, 4, 8). The initiative for its organization came from Alekseyev.[1] The appelation 'Kholmogorets' sometimes applied to him, identifies him as a resident of Kholmogory, the port on the Northern Dvina River near the White Sea. He is also referred to as the son of Popov, though usually he went by Fedot or Alekseyev or both names. A trader by occupation, he was employed as an agent by Aleksey Usov. He was sent to Siberia by Usov in 1639 together with another agent, Luka Siverov.[2] They went to Tyumen, Tobol'sk, and Tomsk, and then the two men arrived in Yeniseysk in June 1641. They carried on little trade in western Siberia, expecting to cash in on the much higher prices for goods in eastern Siberia. In Yeniseysk they applied for and received a passport to Yakutsk, which they reached a year later.[3] In Yakutsk the two agents found that the agents for other metropolitan merchants were already well entrenched, so they decided to go elsewhere. Alekseyev proposed that they go to the Olenek, a river paralleling the Lena to the west and emptying into the Arctic; but Siverov would go no farther than Zhigansk on the lower Lena, so the two parted company after dividing men and goods. Eleven men went with Siverov, 29 with Alekseyev, including his nephew (document 22).[4] It was common then for more than one group, as well as individual self-employed traders and service-men going or coming from outposts, to travel together for the sake of security. Often such a caravan or flotilla would be accompanied by service-men to provide protection, to subject new natives officially to Russian authority, and to collect tribute. Also a sworn-man might be sent along as a customs agent to collect duties on the traded goods and the first-fruits tax of ten per cent. The expedition to the Olenek was a large one, some one hundred men, with service-man Ivan Rebrov in charge. Alekseyev took a large quantity of goods with him (document 22). Two years later, however, this undertaking went sour. In 1644 the Tunguses of the Olenek attacked the Russians there and either killed them or drove them out, in Alekseyev's case with substantial loss.[5] Hoping to recover his losses,

---

[1] Here I follow Belov's reconstruction of Alekseyev's activities in his 1949, pp. 461–2; 1955, pp. 62–4; and 1973, pp. 95–9.

[2] *ORZPM*, pp. 192–3. [3] *RM*, pp. 99–101.

[4] Also *ORZPM*, pp. 169, 173–4. The names of the men are listed here and in document 22. The number may have been 28 for the name Ivashko Osipov appears twice.

[5] Belov, 1973, p. 97.

he turned east, passing to the Yana, then to the Indigirka and Alazeya, and finally the Kolyma River. But here, as on the Lena, he found the competition to be stiff, and so again he sought a greener pasture, turning once more to the east, to the 'new lands', to the Pogycha River.

His party now consisted of twelve men besides himself. So great, however, was the interest in going to the Pogycha that he had no difficulty in finding nearly forty others, mostly self-employed promyshlenniks, to form an expedition to the new river in search of walrus tusks and sables. As before, he wanted a representative of the state to accompany the expedition, so he requested Gavrilov to appoint one. It was Dezhnev who volunteered for the job in a petition to Gavrilov, in which he promised to collect seven forties (280) of sables for the sovereign, a large number and a considerable risk, for failure could bring confiscation of goods and imprisonment. Gavrilov accepted the offer: 'We sent Semeyka Dezhnev with the trader Fedot Alekseyev for that profit and to look for other new rivers and wherever the sovereign's profit might be made. We gave them instructions that wherever they found people not paying tribute, they were to take hostages, collect tribute from them and bring them under the sovereign's exalted hand...' (document 3). Thus it was that in June 1647 Alekseyev and Dezhnev and some fifty others set forth in four koches down the Kolyma River for the new river Anadyr'.[1]

It has hitherto been assumed that the expedition was organized at and departed from Nizhne-Kolymsk, in the belief that it was at that time the main outpost on the Kolyma. But nowhere in the documents is either Nizhne-Kolymsk or Sredne-Kolymsk specified as the place of organization or departure. In light of the discussion in the preceding chapter regarding the status of each of the two settlements, one is led to conclude that Sredne-Kolymsk, not Nizhne-Kolymsk, was the place. This conclusion is supported by the fact that by implication Pushkin, the voyevoda at Yakutsk (document 26), and Dezhnev himself, explicitly (document 28) place him at the 'ostrozhek on the Kovyma River' in 1645, and by the fact that Gavrilov's report on the voyage of Ignat'yev and the departure of Alekseyev and Dezhnev for the Anadyr' was written from the 'Kovyma ostrozhek'. Nizhne-Kolymsk had yet to be referred to as an ostrozhek. Meanwhile, it should be noted that at this stage of development toward the historic voyage the leading role belonged to Alekseyev, though once the expedition got under way,

[1] Belov, 1949, p. 460–1; 1955, p. 64; 1973, 98–9.

Dezhnev as representative of the state may have been regarded as the official leader and Alekseyev as second in command.

The expedition was destined not to go far. Gavrilov, reporting in June 1648, states laconically that 'Semeyka did not reach the new river. He returned from the sea and spent the winter on the Kovyma River' (document 4). Several years later Dezhnev said the same thing: 'I was sent on your sovereign's service to the new river Anandyr' by the great sea-ocean, but that year the ice did not permit it. I...returned to the Kovyma River and spent the winter there' (document 8). In view of the fact that during that summer Stadukhin, Vlas'yev, and Bugor with their respective parties were blocked from further progress to the east at the mouth of the Yana River, one surmises that the summer of 1647 was a poor one for Arctic eastward navigation, always precarious at best. The 'great and terrible winds' came from the north and east, making sailing eastward in the kind of boats then used virtually impossible and blowing the pack ice close to shore, greatly narrowing or closing off the navigable channels.[1]

Meanwhile, in 1647 there arrived on the Kolyma River a party of ten men made up of promyshlenniks, both self-employed and employees, led by two traders, Afanasiy Andreyev Vorona and Bezson (or Andrey) Astaf'yev. These two were agents of the Moscow merchant and member of the gostinaya sotnya, Vasiliy Gusel'nikov. Gusel'nikov's operations in Siberia were greater than those of Usov. In the period 1641–9 his agents presented at the Lena customs house goods worth more than 15,000 roubles, a large sum for those days (about 250,000 gold roubles in the 19th century). As many as 200 traders and promyshlenniks were engaged in his business operations. Andreyev and Astaf'yev brought with them 1,073 roubles' worth of goods, including thirteen 'loadstones in bone', a kind of primitive compass.[2] It would be in their koch that Dezhnev and his men would sail the next summer.[3]

In that same year another individual arrived on the Kolyma who would participate in the voyages the following year, at the head of a

[1] In his petition submitted in the summer of 1648 (document 7) the service-man Ivan Baranov states that in 1647 he had learned of the new river Anadyr' and set out by sea for it only to encounter 'impassable ice'. He does not say with whom he went, whether he was a leader or member of a group, or whether he was officially authorized to do so. It seems most likely that he went with Alekseyev and Dezhnev on their aborted voyage. He does corroborate the presence of impenetrable ice.   [2] *ORZPM*, p. 210.

[3] Belov, 1949, pp. 460, 462; 1955, pp. 65–6; 1973, pp. 99–101. He writes (1949, p. 462) that Afanasiy Andreyev Vorona participated in the first expedition to the Kolyma with Stadukhin and Zyryan, returning to Yakutsk in 1645, presumably with Stadukhin. However, the 1644 petition of Stadukhin, Zyryan and others (document 23) contains no mention of Andreyev.

group of his own. This is Gerasim Ankudinov.[1] Not much is known about him. He arrived on the Lena in the first party of cossacks and served at Yakutsk for several years. In 1641 he was sent with Vasiliy Vlas'yev to Ust-Yansk, the zimov'ye at the mouth of the Yana River. Later, learning of rich sable rivers farther east, the two men left Ust-Yansk without authorization and headed east. En route they attacked and robbed traders and promyshlenniks. Vlas'yev was caught and returned under guard to Yakutsk, but Ankudinov escaped capture and, assembling a number of followers, reached the Kolyma in 1647.[2] He did not participate in the aborted voyage to the Anadyr', perhaps because he did not control the participating parties and was unwilling to subordinate himself to another leader. He and the men he drew to himself, to judge from the complaints lodged against them, were a source of much trouble to traders, promyshlenniks, and service-men alike.[3]

Thus it was that by the year 1647 the men who became the principals in assembling personnel and in promoting the expedition to the Anadyr' had arrived on the Kolyma, at the ostrozhek founded by Stadukhin. Three of them, Alekseyev, Andreyev, and Astaf'yev, were agents of wealthy Moscow merchants, with the resources to gather around them traders and promyshlenniks who were either their employees or independent petty enterprisers in need of transportation and protection. The other two, Dezhnev and Ankudinov, were service-men: the one requested by the agents to serve as the state's representative, the other a fugitive or outlaw self-assigned to the expedition. The one characteristic all of them had in common, both serv ce-men and private enterprisers, was the desire to profit from the reputed wealth of the Anadyr'. The state would have to be cut in for its large share, but there was still room for individual gain. As in so much European discovery it was the prospect of great economic gain that lured these men into geographical exploration with its high risks and excessive hardships.

[1] Though usually spelled 'Ankudinov', Yefimov (1950, p. 59) says that it should be 'Ankidinov'.
[2] Belov in *RM*, p. 63, note 6; 1949, pp. 462–3.
[3] Belov, 1949, pp. 462–3; 1955, pp. 66–7; 1973, pp. 101–2.

CHAPTER 7

THE PARTICIPANTS

The failure of the attempt in the summer of 1647 left many of the participants undaunted, not the least of whom was Fedot Alekseyev. It was he evidently who initiated the second attempt to reach the Anadyr´ by sea. Some of those who had taken part in the aborted voyage did not participate in the second, but their number was more than offset by other men anxious to seek their fortunes on the new river. As a result the second voyage numbered ninety individuals sailing in seven koches.

Since Alekseyev did not survive to provide a record of the organizing of the expedition and his part in it, one turns to Dezhnev, the surviving leader. Unfortunately what he tells us about its beginnings is meager and in one detail confusing. Reviewing the episode in his petition of 1662, Dezhnev says that a petition was submitted to Petr Novoselov, the sworn-man on the Kolyma, to send 'traders and promyshlenniks, Fedot Alekseyev and companions', to the Anadyr´ River and that 'the traders and promyshlenniks petition that... [I] should go with them...' (document 28). This is the confusing detail, for in a communication written at Zhigansk on the lower Lena River to the voyevodas at Yakutsk Novoselov reports that he arrived there on 9 September 1647 with the sable treasury, having left the Kolyma ostrozhek on June 15 that same summer.[1] Two explanations come to mind. In relating the event fourteen years later Dezhnev confused the petition for his services presented in 1647 with that presented in 1648;

---

[1] *ORZPM*, p. 252. Novoselov left the Kolyma River so as to transport the sable treasury to Yakutsk. His successor on the Kolyma was Tret´yak Ivanov Zaborets. Novoselov mentions meeting Vlas´yev, Gavrilov's replacement, at the lower outpost on the Lena on August 13.

His success in reaching Zhigansk in the summer of 1647, + ⁄ing left the Kolyma on June 15, is in striking contrast to the failure of Dezhnev and Alekseyev to get much beyond the mouth of the Kolyma although they too started down the Kolyma in June (document 3). Information to explain these contrasting results is not at hand. Dezhnev does not report where the impassable ice was encountered and when the party turned back, so it is conceivable that it managed to get as far as Cape Shelagskiy, where so many of the subsequent attempts to sail east were blocked, before having to turn back. Thus it may have been that the area around the mouth of the Kolyma was sufficiently open to navigation for Novoselov to have made it into the less ice-plagued waters west of the Kolyma and thence to the Lena. Too, if the winds were predominantly from the east and north as Stadukhin reported, they would favour Novoselov on a westbound course and hamper Dezhnev on an eastbound one.

or he could have dictated or the scribe written 'Novoselov' instead of 'Gavrilov' by mistake. One inclines to the first explanation when, as we shall see, we encounter other and similar errors of recollection in that petition of 1662.[1] In any case we are left without certainty as to which year's petition Dezhnev is referring to. His reporting, we might observe, leaves some doubts about certain sequences of events and the lengths of time between the events.

If the petition to go to the Anadyr´ was in fact submitted to Novoselov in 1647 rather than to Gavrilov, the commandant on the Kolyma, this was done presumably because customs clearance was required for the goods and supplies to be taken on the voyage. Whether the request to have Dezhnev accompany them was part of the same petition or the subject of another one submitted to Gavrilov is not clear from Dezhnev's wording. Gavrilov reported in 1648 (document 4) that Dezhnev petitioned him to go the Anadyr´, promising 285 sables, and that he sent Dezhnev to the Anadyr´, issuing instructions to him as well as to Alekseyev. He also provided gifts for the natives. In his report of 1655 (document 9) Dezhnev states that 'in the past year 156 [1648] on the 20th day of June, I, Semeyka, was sent from the Kovyma River to the new river Anadyr´...'. This is the extent of the information provided by Dezhnev about the onset of the voyage. To fill in the picture we have to go to other evidence, much of it indirect and incomplete. This is exemplified when we try to establish the membership of the expedition.

The make-up of the expedition cannot be reconstructed completely. No one document discusses or describes it extensively or in detail. Those who did say anything about it did so briefly, like Dezhnev and Gavrilov, or in passing, like Stadukhin. The information about it, in other words, is fragmentary. The only scholar who has attempted to establish the membership of the expedition, its groups and their numbers, is Belov.[2] First stated in his article of 1949 and revised in the second and third editions of his monograph on the expedition, Belov's reconstruction is this: The ninety persons constituted four groups. The first was that of Fedot Alekseyev and comprised twenty-nine men, whose number and names Belov draws from the travel document issued to Alekseyev in Yakutsk on the eve of his departure for the Olenek River on 6 July 1642 (document 22). The second was that of Aleksey Andreyev and Bezson Astaf´yev and consisted of ten men, most of them

[1] See p. 105, note 2; this chapter, p. 153; and p. 186, note 3.
[2] 1949, pp. 461–4; 1955, 64–70; 1973, 95–105.

from north Russian towns, whose number and names Belov drew also from customs records, from the list prepared at Yakutsk before leaving for the Indigirka and Kolyma rivers (document 25). The third group was that led by Dezhnev himself and consisted of eighteen men besides himself, all but two of them evidently unattached promyshlenniks whom he equipped, in part at least, from his own resources and who functioned after reaching the Anadyr´ as service-men but without salary.[1] Belov bases this grouping on a petition submitted by twenty promyshlenniks at Anadyrsk in 1681 in which they state that they served on the Anadyr´ when there were no hostages or officials there, that is, from the first appearance of the Russians, before an officially authorized commandant arrived (document 32).[2] The fourth group was officially not a part of the expedition. That was the detachment led by Gerasim Ankudinov. Unsuccessful in his bid to be appointed the state's representative in place of Dezhnev, he and his followers decided to go along without authorization. The entire group numbered thirty according to Dezhnev (document 6), most of them being promyshlenniks.[3]

Upon close scrutiny of Belov's reconstruction, however, some flaws and inconsistencies emerge. First, in respect to Alekseyev's group, Belov draws his figure of twenty-nine members from the customs release which was six years old at the time of departure of the expedition. This ignores one possibility and one certainty. Did that number remain constant over the six years in the face of the action of the Tungus in driving the Russians out of the Olenek basin? Were there no deaths, no defections during the six years? Meanwhile, only twelve men went with Alekseyev on the first attempted voyage in 1647 (document 3). Did the rest of the twenty-nine remain on the Kolyma? If so, did the reluctant seventeen become acquiescent a year later? Or was Alekseyev able to recruit replacements, the number becoming coincidentally twenty-nine again? Belov states only that Alekseyev increased his detachment to twenty-nine,[4] but cites no other source of information so that we are forced to conclude that his figure is unsubstantiated, and we do not really know the size of his group, only that he led one.

[1] 1955, p. 69; 1973, p. 105. Belov notes several transactions by Dezhnev involving the purchase and sale of furs and loaning money in the years 1646–8, from which Dezhnev accumulated modest savings (*ORZPM*, pp. 493, 495). On the other hand, Dezhnev pleaded 'great need' as his reason for going hunting on the Kolyma in the winter of 1647–8 (Polevoy, 1965c, p. 53).

[2] 1955, pp. 69–70; 1973, p. 105; *RM*, pp. 165–6. Two of the twenty men listed, Yelfimko Kirilov Merkur'yev and Fomka Semenov Permyak, were members of Andreyev's and Astaf'yev's party, so it is the remaining eighteen whom Belov sees as constituting Dezhnev's party (*RM*, pp. 165, note 2).

[3] Belov, 1955, p. 104.   [4] Belov, 1955, pp. 64–5.

HAKLUYT SOCIETY

The President and Council of the Society are pleased to announce that nine volumes (Second Series Volume 148, 152-159) are in an advanced state at press. During 1981 and 1982 these volumes will be mailed to members. However, the pace at which these volumes progress is irregular and consequently it is probable that some of these volumes will appear out of Second Series number sequence. The Annual Report and News Bulletin will inform members which volumes have been distributed, and members are requested to check these statements before writing to claim missing volumes.

June, 1981.

The figure of ten as the number of men in Andreyev's and Astaf'yev's party Belov derived from the names mentioned in the customs declaration (document 25). Actually twelve names appear there, but Belov does not list two of them in his 1949 article.[1] One of them, that of a third agent of Gusel'nikov, Ivashko Yakovlev Chirka, is probably justifiably excluded, for his name does not appear again in the relevant documents. The name of the other Belov later does include in his list in the 1955 edition of his *Semen Dezhnev*, but offsets it by omitting the name of one of those listed in his earlier article, and he confuses the matter a bit by writing that Andreyev's party consisted of nine men.[2] He must have used 'nine' as the number of Andreyev's employees and thereby demoted Astaf'yev to that rank. Be it ten, eleven, or twelve, however, the number is not likely to have changed much in the two years since making the declaration. The group did not suffer the kind of disaster that Alekseyev's did on the Olenek River in 1644 and as a small group was more likely to have remained together over the shorter period of time.

The accuracy of the figure of thirty for Ankudinov's party is not open to serious question for it is one given at the time of departure by a man in the position to know, namely Dezhnev himself. On the other hand, Belov's claim that the contingent led by Dezhnev numbered eighteen cannot be readily verified. Of the twenty petitioners listed in the petition of 1681 Foma Semenov Permyak was an employee of Andreyev and Astaf'yev. Belov took Yefimko Kirilov to be Yelfimko Merkur'yev, another of their employees, and so he reduced the number to eighteen.[3] But Merkur'yev died in 1652–3. The number then becomes nineteen. Even so the figure is not final. How many of those in the koch in which Dezhnev travelled were at the time of its wrecking Ankudinov's men, transferred to it after the wreck of his koch on the great rocky nos, and so could have been among the survivors who carried out service on the Anadyr'? Belov himself affirms that some of Ankudinov's men were taken into Dezhnev's koch and served with him on the Anadyr'.[4] Further, even though the petition reads as though all twenty promyshlenniks had served on the Anadyr' from the beginning of the Russian occupation, not all twenty could have arrived

[1] Page 462. [2] Page 66.

[3] *RM*, p. 165 note 2. In his 1949 article (p. 463) Belov reduced the number to seventeen after saying that twenty men went with Dezhnev, on the strength of the belief that one Aleksey Melent'yev is listed in both the 1681 petition (document 32) and the 1646 customs record. On the other hand, in the list of twenty appear the names of Ivashka Fomin and Vas'ka Fomin. Are these two men or the same one? That would keep the number at seventeen.   [4] 1955, p. 68.

there with Dezhnev, for he tells us that of the twenty-four men besides himself who survived the shipwreck twelve (or nine)[1] disappeared, leaving another twelve (or fifteen) to continue on with Dezhnev. We have to conclude that only some of the twenty petitioners arrived on the Anadyr′ with Dezhnev and so may be considered as members of his original contingent. Moreover, it defies experience to conclude that all twenty petitioners had remained there thirty-three years. Some may have, yet Dezhnev reported in 1655 the killing of service-men and promyshlenniks and the departure of promyshlenniks with Stadukhin.[2] He himself left the Anadyr′ in 1660 and died in 1672. Belov's figure thus turns out to be wrong, and we are left with the realization that the size and members of Alekseyev's and Dezhnev's respective groups are not established. Our efforts in this matter are further rendered ineffectual by the fact that there were three other koches. When we subtract the ten men of Andreyev's and Astaf′yev's party and the thirty with Ankudinov, we are left with a balance of fifty to be divided among five boats, and of the occupants of three of them we know nothing. Actually the number of men on the expedition is 89, not 90, for Alekseyev's Yakut concubine has to be included in the latter figure, a calculation confirmed by Dezhnev's statements that altogether 64 men perished on the voyage and that he and 24 others were thrown ashore in the wrecking of his koch (documents 9 and 28).

One aspect of the membership of the expedition that has received little attention is the very small number of service-men who participated in it. We know of only two by name, Dezhnev and Ankudinov. If there were others, they are not mentioned in the documents and must have been in Ankudinov's group. There could not have been many in any case for there were few service-men on the Kolyma after Stadukhin's return to Yakutsk in 1645. In the instructions issued to Gavrilov's successor, Vasiliy Vlas′yev, and sworn-man Kiril Kotkin, by the voyevoda at Yakutsk in July 1647 the service-men on the Kolyma serving with Gavrilov are listed, and they number nine, including Dezhnev and Ankudinov (document 26). Semen Motora is a third, and we know that he reached the Anadyr′ River by the overland route in 1650. Whether any of the remaining six joined Dezhnev is not known, but it is doubtful that Gavrilov would have let any of them accompany Dezhnev for they were needed to guard and maintain the hostages and collect the tribute. The only names mentioned by Dezhnev in his reports

---

[1] See the discussion on p. 186 below of the number who survived.
[2] Page 62 above.

on the voyage (documents 9 and 10), with one exception, are those of traders and promyshlenniks; the exception is Ankudinov. It is significant too that in reporting the voyage in his petition of 1662 (document 28) Dezhnev remarks that 'traders and promyshlenniks' petitioned that he should go with them and later that 'traders and promyshlenniks' were drowned or killed on the tundra by the natives. There is no mention of service-men. Baranov in his petition of 1648 (document 7) states that 'promyshlenniks who serve...on the Kovyma River' went to the new Anadyr´ River. We may conclude that the personnel of the expedition was drawn overwhelmingly from promyshlenniks and traders. This preponderance of promyshlenniks over service-men continued for some time on the Anadyr´, as documents 10, 11 and 32 attest.

As with the sizes of the four groups, so with the distribution of the 89 men among the seven koches — we cannot be certain about it. Ninety individuals and seven koches average out just under thirteen occupants to a koch, which is not to say that the koches were of uniform size and carrying capacity. Three of the koches are to be associated with specific individuals, Ankudinov, Alekseyev, and Dezhnev or Andreyev and Astaf´yev. It is to be presumed that Alekseyev owned his, having the resources to build or buy one. Ankudinov states in his petition (document 5) that he would provide his own boat. Whether the one in which Dezhnev travelled was owned by him or by Gusel´nikov's two agents is open to dispute. Dezhnev tells us that after the disappearance of the twelve men who went up the river after reaching the Anadyr´ he turned over the possessions of Andreyev and Astaf´yev to Yelfimko Merkur´yev, one of their employees, and he mentions another of their employees, Fomka Semenov, as among the twenty-five survivors of the wrecking of the koch (document 9). These remarks seem to indicate Andreyev and Astaf´yev as owners of the koch. That Dezhnev's own resources at that time were low, he having spent the winter in efforts to restore them, and that he joined the expedition no earlier than six weeks prior to departure point also to this conclusion. The small size of the two agents' party could well have left room for Dezhnev and others of his group. Since Andreyev and Astaf´yev had the primitive compasses, it would be appropriate for the leader to go in a boat equipped to lead the way. There is no evidence to show that Gavrilov as commandant provided Dezhnev with a government koch, as sometimes was done for service-men on an official mission. If indeed it was the koch of Andreyev and Astaf´yev in which Dezhnev journeyed all the way to the Anadyr´ region, then that fact and the wording of Dezhnev's statement about turning over their possessions to Merkur´yev indicate that the two agents were among the twelve who disappeared.

Ogloblin, on the other hand, was of the opinion that Dezhnev made the voyage in his own koch.[1] He first cites that part of Dezhnev's petition of 1662 (document 28) in which Dezhnev states that he financed his service from the Yana River to the Anadyr´ with his own means, without any reimbursement from the state. Then Ogloblin goes on to say:

we know that he was interested in the commercial side of the expedition...'I supported myself...', writes Dezhnev in his second petition in 1664, 'on your great sovereign's service on the new rivers with my own money and my own resources...' That 'the resources' referred not only to Dezhnev's equipment on the voyage, but to something greater (the furnishing of a koch, the hiring of employees for hunting, etc.) the following passage from the petition speaks: Dezhnev affirmed that 'as a result of shipwreck I became impoverished and incurred heavy unpaid debts'. (Document 29.)

For some reason or other Ogloblin does not quote the first part of the sentence last quoted. It reads: 'While on that service [from 1642 to 1662] and as a result...' Thus it was not the shipwreck alone that impoverished him, but the years of accumulated unreimbursed service. One should bear in mind that in both of the petitions cited Dezhnev was speaking of two decades of service from which his losses and debts derived, not just of the voyage to the Anadyr´. His other petitions bear witness that being in debt was a not uncommon condition for him (e.g. document 8).

Belov's position on the question is ambivalent and inconclusive. In his 1949 article[2] he states that Dezhnev went in the koch of the two agents, but in notes in his documentary collection, *Russkiye morekhody* (1952), he mentions 'Dezhnev's koch' in such a way as to imply ownership of it, though he cites no sources for such a conclusion.[3] He also states that part of the goods of the two agents were brought to the Anadyr´ in 'Dezhnev's koch' and that the two men went on other boats.[4] These contradictory positions perhaps explain why in the two later revisions of his study on the voyage he backs away from such statements and says merely that the two agents attached themselves to Dezhnev's group, adding material strength in the form of experienced seamen and navigation instruments.[5] He continues to claim however,

[1] 1890, p. 20. [2] Page 462. [3] Page 109, note 2; p. 162, note 2.
[4] *RM*, p. 109, note 2. [5] 1955, p. 65; 1973, p. 101.

that Dezhnev equipped in part at least the men who went with him, though no mention is made of a koch as part of the equipment.[1] Thus, despite modern research the question of ownership of the koch which carried Dezhnev to the Anadyr´ is given the uneasy answer that more likely it belonged to Andreyev and Astaf´yev than to Dezhnev.

Earlier we presumed that Alekseyev owned his koch and noted that Ankudinov promised to provide one of his own. Given Alekseyev's leading role in organizing the expedition, there is no reason to doubt that he owned the koch in which he sailed. Ankudinov's promise to provide his own koch does suggest that he owned the one in which he sailed, as does Dezhnev's reference to it as Ankudinov's when mentioning its being wrecked on the great rocky nos. Yet one cannot but wonder how he acquired the resources to buy or build a koch that would carry thirty men. Did he seize it from promyshlenniks or traders? Did he join with some of the promyshlenniks in his party to acquire or construct it? Or was it actually owned by some of the members of his party, and his telling Gavrilov that he would provide his own koch was simply to let Gavrilov know that he did not expect the state to provide him with one? The most that can be said is that it was privately owned; and the same has to be said about the remaining koches given the almost total promyshlennik–trader composition of the expedition.

We have said that the expedition consisted of seven koches and based our conjectures on that number. There is, however, testimony that says the number is six, and it comes from Dezhnev himself. In his petition of 1662 (document 28) he states: 'I, your slave, went with these traders and promyshlenniks by sea, ninety men in six koches.' Indeed this is the only place where Dezhnev specifies the number of koches. In light of this assertion Ogloblin, who discovered the petition and first published it, adopted six as the number of vessels. He attributed the number 'seven' to Müller, who, he argued, had difficulty differentiating the old Slavic character for '6' from that for '7', which closely resemble each other.[2] However, Müller does not indicate his source for the number 'seven', so we do not know whether it appeared in his source as the word for 'seven' (sem') or the Cyrillic character for '7' (actually a letter).[3]

---

[1] 1955, p. 70; 1973, p. 105. [2] 1890, p. 21, note 1.

[3] In his article of 1737 (and repeated in the 1742 version of it) Müller specified three koches, Dezhnev's and 'the two koches of service-man Gerasim Ankudinov and the trader Fedot Alekseyev' (document 1). No other koches are mentioned. On his map of 1754 and 1758 he shows the 'Track of 3 Russian Ships in 1648 one of which arrived in

Sergey V. Bakhrushin in this century followed Ogloblin.[1] Belov advances a different explanation of the discrepancy.[2] Dezhnev, in his opinion, did not regard Ankudinov and his men as legitimate members of the expedition, as men for whom he was responsible. On the contrary, they were outlaws and interlopers, coming along without authorization; and he continued to hold this view even though he took several of Ankudinov's men into his boat after the latter's koch was wrecked on the great rocky promontory. Fourteen years later, when claiming in Moscow compensation for his achievements, he believed he should not rightfully have to share with his competitor the honour of having discovered 'the new land'. This is a plausible explanation, but it has one weakness: why did Dezhnev specify ninety men in six koches instead of sixty?

In the published documents the information that there were seven koches is found only in Stadukhin's report to Yakutsk after returning from his unsuccessful attempt in 1649 to reach the Pogycha River by sea (document 15). He states explicitly that Ankudinov and Dezhnev with ninety men set out for that river in 1648 'in seven koches'. Belov asserts that contemporaries and associates of Dezhnev mention seven vessels and that in Yakutsk seven was the figure given, as it was in numerous service records, but he cites no documents to corroborate his statement. He states further that he has found no documents of the 17th century mentioning six koches.[3] Most recent writers have followed Müller rather than Ogloblin in this matter. It is, of course, possible that after fourteen years Dezhnev's memory played him false or even that his amanuensis made a slip of the pen. Perhaps here one should follow the rule of historical evidence that in the case of two conflicting items of evidence, other things being equal, one takes the statement of the document closer in time to the event in question.[4]

The large number in Ankudinov's detachment and possibly in Alekseyev's, if carried in only two koches, means that the number of

Kamtschatka'. Where or how he derived this figure he does not say, but it seems most likely that he adopted it because only three koches are mentioned by Dezhnev in his report. Müller did not know of Dezhnev's petition of 1662 in which he specifies six koches, and he does not mention Stadukhin's report of 1649 in which he mentions seven koches, so it may well have been that at the time of writing his article Müller had not read that report. By 1758 he had read it and so specifies seven koches in his later account, though he left the figure '3' on his map. Krasheninnikov (document 20) puts the number at seven.

[1] 1955, Tom III, pp. 129, 153, note 33, 209.
[2] 1955, pp. 74–5.   [3] 1955, p. 75.
[4] If Dezhnev's assertion of 90 men in six koches is correct and if, as Belov opines, Dezhnev regarded Ankudinov's party of thirty men as outside his jurisdiction, then one has to revise the total number of participants upward to 120 or 121.

men in each of the vanished four would average many fewer than thirteen, so few in fact as to lead to the conclusion that they were small vessels, which might explain their prior disappearance. On the other hand, some of Alekseyev's and Ankudinov's men may have split off to travel in one or more of the four koches. This may well have happened when we recall that after the wreck of Ankudinov's koch the boats of Dezhnev and Alekseyev were able to accomodate his party (document 10), and this in turn suggests that Alekseyev's party was smaller than 29 to begin with. But be it all as it might have been, these matters remain speculative, an unsatisfactory substitute for absent facts.

In the case of two of the parties, those of Alekseyev and of Andreyev and Astaf´yev, we have a record of the kinds of supplies, equipment, and articles of trade taken with them, in the form of the travel document of the former (document 22) and customs list of the latter (document 25) drawn up at the time of their departure from Yakutsk in 1642 and 1646 respectively. The main item of food was the staple, rye flour. Pepper was also taken. The Russians depended heavily on fish as another food staple, so we find fishing net and lines listed. Frying pans and kettles are the cooking utensils listed. Articles of clothing were blouses of several kinds, kaftans, mittens, and ski boots. Cloth was an item in large amount, both coarse wool and fine linen. Not surprisingly a coarse linen or canvas for sails is shown in large quantity. A few firearms (*pishchali* – arquebuses and muskets?) and powder, on which the Russians' superiority over the natives depended, appear on the customs list. A large number of beads, glass and the much demanded 'blue beads', are included, along with little bells with tassels, which were used to signal when a sable had been trapped in a net,[1] and copper buttons, which were intended for trade with the natives. Cups were another article presumably for trade. Of particular interest are the thirteen 'loadstones in bone' that appear on the list of Andreyev and Astaf´yev. Crowbars,[2] used to knock holes through the ice for fishing and to pry the ice away from the sides of boats, leather, for the repairing of boots and shoes, and wax candles are the remaining items. Whether the listed items were intended wholly for trade, with the Russian service-men and promyshlenniks, as well as the natives, in exchange for sables and other furs, or were for use by the members of the two groups is not clear. But for us their significance is that they substantiate the nature of the expedition as expressed in the preceding chapter: an economic enterprise for the acquisition of wealth by both the state and

[1] Bakhrushin, 1951, p. 86. [2] Bakhrushin, 1951, p. 87.

individual participants. Geographical exploration was the means to that end, as it was in the case of so many geographical discoveries before and after Dezhnev's time.

As with the aborted voyage of 1647, so with the voyage of 1648: the question arises, where was it organized and from what point did it depart? And again the documents are not explicit on these points. Traditionally the locale of the provenance of the second voyage has been thought to be Nizhne-Kolymsk, but on the basis of circumstantial evidence one has to conclude that in this case too it was Sredne-Kolymsk. Such evidence, however, does not come this time from Gavrilov. The commandant does not say, when reporting the start of the voyage, where he was writing from; he says only that he released Dezhnev 'to the new river Anadyr' from the Kovyma River' (document 4). Evidence does come from Ankudinov's petition to Gavrilov to replace Dezhnev as the state's representative. He asks to be sent 'from the Kovymskiy ostrog' and says that a list of his men is posted in the 'main office in the Kovymskiy ostrozhek' (document 5). Likewise Dezhnev in his petition countering Ankudinov's states that he had earlier submitted a petition 'in the Kovymskiy ostrozhek' (document 6). Novoselov, we learned earlier, reported that he left for Yakutsk 'from the Kovymskiy ostrozhek on the Kovyma River'. We have argued in chapter 5 that in these years the terms 'ostrog' and 'ostrozhek' applied to Sredne-Kolymsk, not to Nizhne-Kolymsk, which was still termed the 'lower tribute zimov'ye' (document 7). A zimov'ye, it may be added, did not ordinarily include and was not considered as housing a main office.

From a much later source comes support for this conclusion. In a manuscript written in 1742 by Yakov Lindenau, a translator for the Second Kamchatka Expedition, there is this passage:

According to the words of those Chukchi there comes through the Russians reliable information that supposedly some seventy or more years ago Russian merchants in twelve kochs [departed from] the middle Kolymskoye zimov'ye, where formerly there was a market for trade by the latter, who went [on the voyage] and who were separated one from the other by severe ocean weather. Some sailed to Kamchatka and others arrived at that island which is called the Big Land.[1]

Scholars agree that this passage relates to the voyage of Dezhnev despite the discrepancy of twelve instead of seven koches.[2] Confirmation that

[1] Aleksandr I. Andreyev, 'Zametki po istoricheskoy geografii Sibiri XVI–XVII vv.', *Izvestiya VGO*, Tom LXXII (1940), Vypusk 2, p. 156.
[2] Berg, 1946, p. 51; Aleksey V. Yefimov, *Iz istorii russkikh ekspeditsiy na tikhom okeane...*(Moscow, 1948), p. 146; 1950, pp. 155–6.

the first market on the Kolyma was at Sredne-Kolymsk was found by Polevoy in a later 17th-century document which noted that 'from the market to the upper and lower Kolymskiye zimov'yes [was] a trip of three days by dog sled'.[1] To be sure, the inaccuracies in this passage reduce its credibility, and standing alone it is not firm proof; but where it coincides with other evidence, it is a reinforcing datum.

On the other hand, not all the men who joined the expedition came from Sredne-Kolymsk. The service-man Ivan Baranov, who did not go on the expedition, remarks in a petition to Yakutsk after its departure that 'the promyshlenniks who serve...on the Kovyma River, by virtue of petitions at the tribute zimov'yes, went from the Kovyma River to the new Anandyr' River, and others went to Russia', leaving 'no one at these tribute zimov'yes, sovereign, to perform your sovereign's services because there are few service-men' (document 7). The departure of 89 men for the Anadyr' must indeed have greatly depleted the manpower on the Kolyma River.[2]

Information of recent discovery serves to put Dezhnev too in Sredne-Kolymsk at the onset of the voyage. This information, presented by Polevoy, is contained in two petitions submitted by Dezhnev in the months before the voyage and discovered not long ago in the Soviet central archives.[3] Dezhnev returned evidently to Nizhne-Kolymsk after the unsuccessful voyage of 1647. There on 11 November 1647 he loaned money to a cossack named Mikhail Semenov Glazun and took from him as security a young Yukagir girl named Kichiga. But she left him and returned to Glazun. When Dezhnev demanded her return, Glazun refused him. Not long thereafter Gavrilov, the commandant, visited Nizhne-Kolymsk, and Dezhnev chose the moment to file a complaint against Glazun. In it he explained that 'he was going up the Kolyma because of his great needs', that is, to hunt or acquire sables.[4] The best hunting grounds were upriver, not around Nizhne-Kolymsk. This brought him in time to Sredne-Kolymsk. We know from another statement of his, in 1654 (document 8), as well as from one by Gavrilov in 1648 (document 4) that Dezhnev spent the winter on the Kolyma. His move up the river is corroborated in a petition presented at Sredne-Kolymsk in early March 1648 by service-

[1] 1965c, p. 56, citing YaPI, opis' 3, 1700, no. 32, listy 2–3.
[2] Baranov's information gives rise to the possibility that parts of the expedition may have assembled at Nizhne-Kolymsk and Verkhne-Kolymsk in addition to Sredne-Kolymsk, all seven koches coming together at Nizhne-Kolymsk. Novoselov, when reporting from Zhigansk, explains the absence of any service men accompanying him because of the shortage of them on the Kolyma (ORZPM, p. 252).
[3] Polevoy, 1956c, pp. 51–6.
[4] Polevoy, 1965c, p. 52, citing YaPI, opis 3, 1648, no. 3.

man Parfen Yevseyev in which he mentions that a certain Sidor Ivanov for 15 roubles 'gave Dezhnev in the forest on the Sobach'ya some sables he had caught.[1] In the 17th century Sobach'ya was another name for the Indigirka, and the best route from it to the Kolyma was by way of the upper Alazeya River to Sredne-Kolymsk.[2] It is possible that the Sobach'ya mentioned was not the Indigirka, but another river of that same name in the Kolyma basin.[3]

It was only after returning to Sredne-Kolymsk and after meeting with Glazun that Gavrilov took up Dezhnev's complaint. Meanwhile, Glazun filed a cross-complaint, claiming that Dezhnev himself was the cause of Kichiga's returning to him. On 12 May 1648 Gavrilov summoned Dezhnev, who was then in Sredne-Kolymsk, to a confrontation with Glazun, but both Glazun and Dezhnev, according to an official document, refused to submit to trial locally and stated that they would take up their case in Yakutsk before the voyevodas.[4] It thus appears that as late as 12 May 1648 Dezhnev was planning to return to Yakutsk and so was not involved in the organizing of the second voyage and that he was unaware that his participation would be requested again. But when it was, Dezhnev changed his mind about not wanting to stand trial at Sredne-Kolymsk and retracted his refusal to testify. In order to gain Gavrilov's approval to participate he submitted a statement in which he confessed the error of his stand (document 27). Only then did Gavrilov consent to Dezhnev's going to the Anadyr'.[5]

Our information is not explicit on the matter, but it would appear that the lead in organizing the second expedition to the Anadyr' was taken by Fedot Alekseyev. After all, he was the one who had initiated the organizing of the first and aborted voyage the summer before. Dezhnev names him as the leader of the traders and promyshlenniks who petitioned Novoselov to go to the Anadyr' (document 28), and Gavrilov gave him instructions about collecting the customs duties while on the Anadyr', a role second only to that of head of the expedition (document 4). No doubt Alekseyev found a ready response from Andreyev and Astaf'yev, who had not been involved in the first expedition, but who were interested in the possibilities for trade along

[1] *ORZPM*, p. 494.

[2] *ORZPM*, p. 143; Polevoy, 1962a, pp. 71, 72.

[3] Polevoy, 1965c, p. 53. He argues that the government rules of the time forbade Kolyma service-men from crossing over to another major river basin and that the service-men mentioned in another document related to the transaction were all Kolyma service-men (*ORZPM*, p. 495). See p. 105, note 1 above.

[4] Polevoy, 1965c, p. 53. [5] Polevoy, 1965c, p. 54.

the rivers near the Kolyma. That there were 89 men on the voyage demonstrates its popularity and acceptance.

When after the first voyagers' return efforts to organize a second began is not told us, but the fact that service-men, traders, and promyshlenniks in all three zimov'yes on the Kolyma petitioned to participate, according to Baranov, suggests that the organizing efforts got under way in the winter. It would take a while for the news of the organizing efforts to reach the other two outposts, for the petitioning of the authorities, and for them to respond. During most of this time Dezhnev must have been out hunting and thus unaware of the proposal to undertake another voyage to the Anadyr´. His return made him available, and so sometime in May or June, as he states in his petition of 1662, 'the traders and promyshlenniks petitioned that I...should go with them for your sovereign's tribute collection and for searching for new non-tribute people and for your sovereign's various affairs' (document 28).

Dezhnev was as eager to go on the second voyage as he had been on the first. He promised, if sent, to collect 285 sables for the tsar's treasury, five more than he had pledged the year before. With Dezhnev's 'confessions' in hand Gavrilov gave his consent and commissioned him as the person in charge (prikazchik) of the expedition, responsible for the search for non-tribute paying natives, for their subjection, for the taking and care of hostages, and for the collection of tribute. The attraction for a service-man like Dezhnev was not alone professional, the chance to command. It was also the opportunity to improve his own economic condition, to acquire furs and, as it turned out, walrus ivory, over and above those that he collected for the state.

Alekseyev, as we noted earlier, was appointed in effect second in command in that he was charged with the duties of sworn-man, of customs officer. As a merchant he could be drafted for that job, but not for that of commander, who had to be a service-man. His duties were mainly that of collecting the first-fruits tax of ten per cent from the furs and other items of value obtained by the traders and promyshlenniks, as well as from the service-men who engaged in trading or trapping on the side as Dezhnev had done in the winter of 1647–8.

Dezhnev's appointment was challenged by Ankudinov, who was determined to go to the Anadyr´ River. To be put in charge would improve his own chances for gain. Accordingly he submitted a petition (document 5) to replace Dezhnev as commander, promising to obtain for the sovereign seventy more sables that Dezhnev had pledged. Here he erred, however, in thinking that Dezhnev had pledged 210 sables and that his promise of 280 outbid Dezhnev by a large margin. Dezhnev counter-attacked with another petition (document 6) in which he pledged 290 sables instead of the previous 285 (did he think it advisable to increase his margin over Ankudinov's bid from five to ten?), and he charged Ankudinov and his thirty followers with wanting to loot and pillage the traders and promyshlenniks and to despoil the natives. Such actions would frighten off many of those planning to go on the expedition and ultimately reduce the state's take. In light of Ankudinov's past behaviour and of Dezhnev's greater experience, it is not surprising that Gavrilov trusted Dezhnev more than his rival and denied Ankudinov's petition. It was then that he and his men decided to go along anyway. Whatever Ankudinov's ethics and past reprehensible behaviour, however, one has to recognize his determination, boldness, and physical courage. He had the qualities to survive on a rough frontier.

In light of the recent information uncovered by Polevoy we have to conclude that Dezhnev's role as leader was a late development, conferred upon him by authority rather than by direct involvement in the assembling of the expedition and a considerable investment of his own resources.[1] As late as May 12 he was intending to return to Yakutsk. Previously he had pled indigence and spent the winter seeking sables to restore his economic resources. On more than one occasion he pled economic need (documents 8, 9, 28). He was not, evidently, a money-maker. Müller was correct at the outset when he wrote that it was Alekseyev and others who initiated the enterprise, that Dezhnev was a later joiner. There is, one might add, another aspect of the role of leader which was to descend on Dezhnev: he survived to reach the Anadyr´ and later to return to Yakutsk, there to tell about his experiences. Alekseyev, Andreyev, Astaf´yev, and Ankudinov did not. So Dezhnev emerges more conspicuously as the leader.

[1] Cf. Belov, 1973, pp. 201–2.

CHAPTER 8

THE VOYAGE

The voyage got under way on June 20. In the light of Baranov's statement (document 7) that most of the men on the Kolyma had left either for the Anadyr' or for Russia (via the Lena River and Yakutsk), it is probable that vessels other than the seven koches departed from Sredne-Kolymsk that day for there was safety in numbers in the run down the river to the open sea. The end of the second or third week in June was a customary time of departure from Sredne-Kolymsk for those who wanted to be on hand at the mouth of the Kolyma when the ice broke up enough to permit ocean navigation. This most often occurred from the beginning to the middle of July, though it could happen as early as the first week of June and as late as late July.[1] The year before Novoselov had left on June 15. For want of any statements to the contrary one is left with the assumption that the Anadyr'-bound flotilla emerged from the mouth of the Kolyma some time in early July.[2]

We know almost nothing about the particulars of the seven koches which embarked upon the long voyage. What was the size of any or all seven, how were they rigged and equipped, what were their speed and sailing characteristics, how much service had they seen, were they new? These are questions customarily asked when treating voyages of discovery. But in this case the documents are silent on such matters. Thus we are left mainly with describing koches in general, or more particularly, those found on the Lena River and the Arctic coast east of it.

The Russian koch was a special kind of vessel well suited by its hull form to navigating the ice-filled water of the Arctic Ocean and superior

[1] Berg, 1946, p. 37; Polevoy, 1965 d, p. 55. These dates, it must be remembered, are according to the Julian calendar, ten days behind the western calendar in the 17th century. By the latter calendar the date of departure is June 30.
[2] Polevoy takes Golder to task for questioning the departure date of June 20 (1965 c, p. 55). In this instance Polevoy is wrong; he seems to have misread Golder's remarks. Golder does not question the departure date. Rather, he claims that it would have taken a month to reach the mouth of the river and that in the part of the navigation season remaining after July 20 there would not have been enough time to reach the Anadyr' River, and that, of course, is a different matter. Berg makes the same mistake (1946, p. 37).

in that environment to the deep-sea vessels that the Dutch, English, and others brought into the Russian Arctic in their efforts to find a passage to the far east.[1] The hull form of the koch was a Russian contribution to marine architecture, developed since the 15th century by those mariners living on the Arctic seaboard of northern Russia between the White Sea and Yamal Peninsula, the maritime region known to the Russians as Pomor'ye. One Soviet student of Russian vessels and shipbuilding considers it the first special type of vessel for navigating in icy waters.[2] This particular contribution and its superiority in this respect over western vessels should not be surprising when one calls to mind the fact that the only people living in the Arctic region and possessing a technology more advanced than and resources superior to those of the aborigines were the Russians. Even so, the aborigines also developed a kind of boat that met their needs and was well suited to the Arctic maritime environment, a skin and frame boat that was light and manoeuvrable and moved easily amidst the ice floes. The distinctive characteristics of the seagoing koch were its relative lightness compared to deep-sea craft, its manoeuvrability, its shallow draft, and its flat-bottomed hull with curved sides, which led the Dutch observer of Russia, Nicholaas C. Witsen, to describe it as a 'round boat'.[3] These characteristics enabled it to avoid collisions with the ice or to ride up on it if trapped by the ice, to negotiate leads or polynias (open water channels through the ice), and to be towed across shoals. Western vessels had flatter sides, angled rather than rounded at the chines,[4] were heavier timbered, deeper in draught, with a single skin of planking, and less manoeuvrable, and so more vulnerable to the ice, to colliding with and being damaged by it. The koch was much better able to thread the waters between the shore and pack ice, or if caught by the ice, to ride it out on drift ice without damage.[5] It was the koch that became the principal Russian vessel used in sailing the waters off the northeastern Arctic coast of Siberia, a region to which, we have noted, many Pomor'yan Russians were drawn.

[1] I am indebted to Commander David W. Waters, former deputy director of the National Maritime Museum at Greenwich, for his critical review of this section on the koch and for the improvements he suggested.

[2] Petr A. Ryabchikov, *Morskiye suda: istoriya razvitiya i sovremennyye tipy sudov* (2nd edition; Moscow, 1959), p. 59.

[3] *Noord en oost Tartaryen*...(3rd edition; Amsterdam, 1785), p. 686; Vladimir Yu. Vize, 'Novyye svedeniya o russkom arkticheskom moreplavanii v XVII veke', *Letopis' severa*, Tom I (1949), p. 86.

[4] Chine is the line between the bottom and side of the hull.

[5] Mikhail I. Belov, 'Arkticheskiye plavaniya i ustroystvo russkikh morskikh sudov v XVII veka', *Istoricheskiy pamyatnik russkogo arkticheskogo moreplavaniya XVII veka*...(Leningrad and Moscow, 1951), pp. 65–6; 1956, pp. 204–5.

Until lately not much was known about the koch. Earlier writers like Johann E. Fischer, the contemporary of Müller who wrote a history of Siberia drawn from the latter's account,[1] N. P. Zagoskin, the student of pre-Petrine Russian vessels,[2] V. G. Bogoraz, the noted anthropologist and student of the Chukchi,[3] and even more recently the contemporary scholar Vladimir Yu. Vize, student of the Russo-Siberian Arctic,[4] viewed it as a less than rugged, rather primitive boat held together by willow roots and thongs, and of limited use and life. The Siberian koch was thought to be less well built than the Pomor'yan for, presumably, it had to rely on local materials for its construction, which did not include iron. It was propelled mainly by oars, assisted by a single mast with a deerhide sail, and carried a wooden anchor to, which a rock was attached. It was flat-bottomed without a keel, its planking and framing bound together with roots and leather thongs, reinforced with wooden trenails or pegs, more flexible than rigid. It was good for only three or four voyages and might be thought of as one perhaps better suited to river travel than one to which life and property might be entrusted in an ice-strewn sea.[5]

Of late, however, Belov has uncovered documents in the Soviet archives from which he has assembled a description of the koch, especially as built and used in northeastern Siberia in the 17th century, a description that reveals it as a more substantial and durable vessel than has been thought, capable of coping rather successfully with the hazards of Arctic navigation.[6] To be sure, the more primitive boats such as Fischer and the others describe no doubt did exist and were used, perhaps more in western than eastern Siberia, but that they were the only kind and were typical of koches in general, or of those used between the Lena and Kolyma rivers, now seems unlikely.

The construction of the koches in Siberia was most highly developed in the Yakutsk jurisdiction. Most of the boat builders and navigators were from Pomor'ye. They brought their experience and skills with them and adapted the koch to the conditions of the Siberian Arctic Ocean.[7]

The koches used on the Lena and the rivers of northeastern Siberia

[1] *Sibirskaya istoriya* (St Petersburg, 1774), p. 373 and note 41, as cited by Belov, 1956, pp. 203–4.
[2] *Russkiye vodnyye puti i sudovoye delo v dopetrovskoy Rossii* (Kazan', 1910), pp. 460–2.
[3] 1904–9, p. 687.
[4] *Morya sovetskoy Arktiki; ocherki po istorii issledovaniya* (3rd edition; Leningrad, 1948a), pp. 41, note 1, 42.
[5] Belov, 1951, pp. 64, 72; 1956, p. 203; Ryabchikov, p. 58.
[6] 1949, pp. 464–5; 1951, pp. 63–80; 1956, pp. 203–12.
[7] Belov, 1951, pp. 64–5.

as well as along the Arctic coast between those rivers were somewhat larger and sturdier in construction than those in Pomor'ye and on the rivers of western Siberia and the Obskaya and Tazovskaya bays. Those built by the merchants were usually made stronger and were better equipped than those put out by the government yards. The koches reached as many as sixty feet in length and were up to twenty feet in width, with a draft of five or six feet. Light dry pine or larch were the preferred wood for construction.[1] Since they did not have to be hauled along portages and the rivers were deep enough, they could be built with keels and a rigid frame like the western ships.[2] Vertical stem and stern posts and a skeleton of branching ribs were all firmly attached to a keel and well braced with crossbeams to provide a strong and rigid framework. This was covered by a skin of edge-to-edge planking, doubled to increase resistance to pressure and blows from the ice. The crossbeams also supported the deck. The hull was caulked with hemp and payed with tar. Raised flooring on the bottom of the hold helped to keep the cargo clear of bilge water. In cross section the hull resembled an oval cut in half lengthwise. It was this shape and the strong construction, combined with the shallow draft and relative lightness of the koch, that made it unusually manoeuvrable in confined waters and enabled it to rise upward in response to sideways pressure from the ice and to ride over it. Proof of this is that relatively few koches were lost by damage from the ice alone. Fastening was made with wooden trenails as well as iron nails, spikes, and bolts. On the deck were one or two cabins, occupied by the commander and his assistant. Crew members and passengers had to find places in the hold.[3]

The koch had only one mast, with a canvas sail. It is relevant to note that both Alekseyev's party and that of Andreyev and Astaf'yev listed canvas among their goods. The surface area of the sail was as large as 100–110 square metres. Oddly enough, though the documents contain information about the size of the sail, they say nothing about its shape, or about the manner in which it was bent to the yard, whether as a square sail or a spritsail or other type; but it seems certain from descriptions of the craft's sailing power that the sail was square rigged. It was made of panels of sail cloth, the lengths of which were often recorded, but not their widths. The wording in certain sources suggests that it consisted of two panels.[4]

[1] Belov, 1951, p. 76; 1956, pp. 208–9.
[2] Ryabchikov, p. 59.
[3] Belov, 1951, pp. 73–4, 77. Ryabchikov accepts more of the earlier ideas about the koch than does Belov.   [4] Belov, 1951, p. 78; 1956, pp. 210–11.

Fig. 1   Koch – side view, taken from drawing by N. D. Travin (Belov, 1951, p. 75).

The koches carried anchors made of iron when available; if not, then wooden anchors with heavy rocks attached were used. As the most essential pieces of ground tackle, three or four anchors were often carried in reserve.[1] Other equipment included a capstan or windlass, sometimes a wind-driven pump, and a karbas or two (a rowed boat like a dory). The karbas was used for going ashore, fishing, laying out the anchor, and towing the koch across shoals or off or out of the ice.[2] Little or nothing appears in the documents about the rudder of the koch. Drawings and models which reconstruct the koch show, however, a very shallow rudder (since the koch rode high in the water) hinged to the sternpost and turned by a long tiller.[3] It is not to be presumed that all koches in northeastern Siberia matched this description in all

[1] Belov, 1951, p. 66.
[2] Belov, 1951, pp. 74, 77, 79. As a type of boat the karbas varied in size and purpose. The largest of them were oar and sail boats 5 m to 8 m in length and could carry up to 2,000 puds (33 tons). Smaller ones were used to carry one or two passengers and six oarsmen. The karbases carried on koches were no doubt of a small size, used for fishing and catching sea animals and carying them to shore or onto the ice. (Aleksandr Podvysotskiy, *Slovar' oblastnogo arkhangel' skago narechiya* [St Petersburg, 1885], p. 63; S. V. Mikhaylov, 'Drevnerusskoye sudostroyeniye na Severe', *Letopis' Severa* [Moscow and Leningrad], Tom 1 [1949], p. 104.)
[3] Belov, 1951, p. 75; Ryabchikov, p. 58.

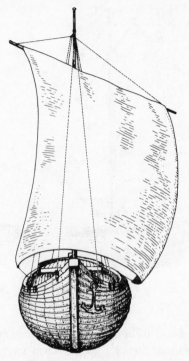

Fig. 2   Koch – front view, taken from drawing by N. D. Travin (Belov, 1951, p. 73).

details, but one can conclude that the koches here were of sophisticated design and construction for their time and place.

The pilot or helmsman, the *vozh* or commander, was responsible for the physical condition of the vessel and the fate of the crew. It was customary in koches carrying cossacks for the oldest mariner among them to be named commander or pilot. The size of the crew varied between six and twelve, sometimes maybe as many as fifteen, depending on the size of the koch, while the number of occupants carried could be as high as 35 or 40; and the weight of the cargo ranged from a few tonnes to as many as 45.[1]

Regarding any navigation instruments which may have been used on the 1648 voyage we have only one clue, the thirteen primitive

---

[1] Belov cites cases of 950, 1,090, and 1,600 puds or 17, 19·6, and 28·8 tons respectively (1951, p. 76; 1956, p. 209).

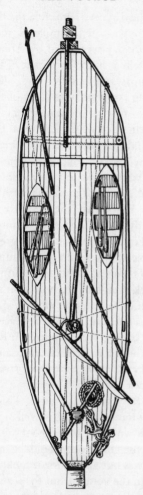

Fig. 3   Koch – overhead view, taken from drawing by N. D. Travin
(Belov, 1951, p. 75).

compasses appearing in the 1646 customs list of Andreyev and Astaf'yev
(document 25). These compasses were pieces of loadstone in a setting
of bone.[1] Some, but probably not all, of them two years later had been
sold or exchanged for furs. What other navigation instruments might
been carried we can only guess; certainly a sounding lead and line. It
is known from archaeological discoveries on Faddeya Island and the

[1] Belov, 1949, p. 465.

shore of Sims Bay of the Taymyr Peninsula that in the second decade of the 17th century copper-cased compasses and compass sun-dials mounted in mammoth ivory were used by Arctic navigators, which confirms what Witsen tells us in the latter part of the century that these navigators used the compass and sounding lead.[1] There our information ends. Presumably sailing continually in sight of the coast made more advanced instruments of navigation unnecessary.

Perhaps the main deficiency of the koch was that it was limited to sailing before the wind, the characteristic of a square-sailed vessel with a shallow draught. It required a following wind, for what it gained in riding lightly on the water or against the ice, it lost in sideways water pressure against the hull, essential to sailing with the wind before the beam. Though Belov states that the Yakutsk documents do not mention oars,[2] other writers do.[3] Indeed, oars must have been necessary in narrow polynias and essential to making progress with unfavourable winds, and unfavourable winds were not uncommon, especially when proceeding eastward. If the weather became stormy and the seas rough, the Russians had to seek refuge by anchoring in some cove or mouth of a river where they set up a shelter on shore (stanishche). This occurred most commonly when a north wind pushed the ice pack close to shore.[4]

As the best way of coping with the ice the Russians chose 'to go along the shore' even though it often entailed sailing longer distances. With the breakup of the ice at the mouths of rivers or along the coast they would enter the sea and follow a course parallel to the shore as the way opened with the retreat of the ice. This meant not crossing the open water at the mouths of bays, as well as waiting for the pack ice or ice floes to be blown away from the shore. However, if the ice floes were not too dense, the koch could be manoeuvred through them. This procedure was not all loss for it took advantage of the fact that the ice could screen the vessels from the seaward side, from more turbulent seas where in the event of a sudden storm too often disaster lurked.[5] It may be noted, however, that occasionally the Russians ventured into the open sea; but the practice generally was to sail close to shore, one similar to that used by the Siberian natives in their skin-and-frame boats propelled by paddles. There is little or no reason

[1] V. V. Danilevskiy, 'Russkiye navigatsionnyye pribory pervoy chetverti XVII veka', Istoricheskiy pamyatnik russkogo arkticheskogo moreplavaniya XVII veka (Moscow and Leningrad, 1951), pp. 53–8; Witsen, 1785, p. 667; Vize, 1949, pp. 81, 82.
[2] 1951, p. 80.   [3] E.g. Ryabchikov, p. 58.
[4] Ryabchikov, p. 59. Cf. the quotation from Strahlenberg, p. 269 below.
[5] Belov, 1973, p. 108.

to doubt that it was used by the Dezhnev–Alekseyev–Ankudinov expedition in the summer of 1648.

In Dezhnev's time nothing like a ship's journal or log book was kept by Siberian boatmen. Whether, and how, they calculated distances along the coast are matters of little or no information. The same is true of latitude and longitude. It was not until Peter's time that astronomically determined points were established on the Russian mainland. Thus we have few records from which the speed of koches can be learned. We have to depend on those reports in which the starting and terminal points are specified and the elapsed time indicated. Elapsed time was most often stated in Arctic navigation in 24-hour days. Since the Arctic navigation season included the period of long days with little or no darkness, round-the-clock sailing was feasible along the coasts. On the other hand, reports of voyages often failed to mention whether any stops were made or how closely the contours of the coastline were followed with the result that our calculations of speed produce only approximate answers at best. With these qualifications in mind we turn to some cases drawn from the documents by Belov.[1]

In 1647 Petr Novoselov and others on a voyage from the Kolyma to the Lena covered the stretch from the mouth of the Alazeya to the easternmost channel of the Indigirka, a distance of 60 km, in five hours. Twelve km an hour is at the rate of $6\frac{1}{2}$ knots. Another voyage that same summer covered the 500 km from the Indigirka to the Kolyma in three 24-hour periods, which averages out as 167 km per day at a rate of 3·8 knots. In 1649 a party of traders went from the Kolyma to the Alazeya, 410 km, in three days-and-nights, for a daily distance of 137 km and a rate of 3 knots.[2] Still another voyage in that summer covered the 850 km from the Indigirka River to the Yana in four days, thus averaging 212 km a day and making its average speed 8·8 km per hour or 4·76 knots, which is faster than appears usual. Yet in the following year five koches made it from Svyatoy Nos to Khromskaya Bay (between the Yana and Indigirka rivers), a distance of 250 km, in one day for an average speed of 12 km per hour or 5·6 knots. In 1676 a voyage from the mouth of the Lena covered a distance of 400 km, in three 24-hour periods, which works out as 133 km a day at 3 knots.[3]

Belov cites a couple of other voyages whose speed was noticeably

[1] 1956, p. 212.

[2] Belov gives the distance as 475 km, but if it is 60 km from the Indigirka to the Alazeya and 500 km from the Indigirka to the Kolyma, it has to be fewer than 475 km from the Alazeya to the Kolyma. By my measurements on the map the distance is 410 km.

[3] Belov, 1951, pp. 68–9; 1956, p. 212.

less. In 1651 Yuriy Seliverstov sailed from Yakutsk down the Lena River to Svyatoy Nos, a journey of 2000 km, in 29 days. This averages 69 km a day, or 2·9 km an hour, a rate of $1\frac{1}{2}$ knots. In 1654 a voyage from the Kolyma to Yakutsk (3000 km) took 43 days, thus averaging 70 km a day, for a speed of 1·57 knots.[1] These examples bear out normal experience that the longer the distance, the lower the average speed. The highest speed, $6\frac{1}{2}$ knots, was attained over a 60-km stretch; the lowest over 2000- and 3000-km distances, fewer than two knots. Over the intermediate distances three to five knots seem not uncommon. By way of comparison Belov tells us that English vessels in 1711 sailing from London to Arkhangel'sk through seas less strewn with ice than the Arctic averaged 2·2 and 2·7 knots, and Dutch vessels averaged even fewer.[2]

Although a considerable amount of new information has been turned up relating to the expedition of Dezhnev and Alekseyev since Müller's time, most of it relates to the antecedent events, the participants, its point of origin, and its initiation. Little, on the other hand, has been added to what we know about the voyage itself. There is still a dearth of information about it.

About the first stage of the voyage, from Sredne-Kolymsk to the mouth of the Kolyma River, we are certain of little more than the starting date, 20 June 1648. How long it took to reach the mouth and whether ice there delayed the voyagers we do not know. More, but not much more, is known about the next stage, the Arctic Ocean stage from the mouth of the Kolyma River to the eastern face of the Chukotskiy Peninsula. The single most obvious aspect of this stage is the survival of three of the koches, those carrying Dezhnev, Alekseyev, and Ankudinov, and the disappearance of the other four. Actually we do not know whether Ankudinov's koch was wrecked before it reached the end of the great rocky nos or succeeded in passing through the Bering Strait. In any case it appears to have made it through most of the Arctic segment of the voyage. In view of the failure of eight attempts between 1649 and 1787 to traverse this route, because of impassable ice in seven of the attempts,[3] and of no successes until 1878–9, the survival of the three koches appears remarkable. Like Müller we have to conclude that the ice conditions during that summer of 1648 were uncommonly favourable. Dezhnev tells us as much in the report which he and Semenov made in 1655 (document 10, p. 62). In 1653

---

[1] Belov, 1951, p. 69.   [2] 1956, p. 212.
[3] Stadukhin turned back in 1649 because of a shortage of provisions (document 15).

the two men built a koch with the intention of transporting the treasury furs back to Yakutsk by the same route along which Dezhnev had reached the Anadyr'.[1] They abandoned the proposed trip for lack of adequate boat equipment and from taking to heart the natives' warning that 'not every year is the ice carried from the shore out to sea'. In our time Belov has uncovered evidence pointing to unusually favourable ice conditions in the Arctic that summer. One Yakov Semenov declared that in sailing from the Kheta River to the Anabar River (along the Khatanga Bay and Laptev Sea east of the Taymyr Peninsula) he encountered no ice in the sea. The koches of Ivan Belyan and Lyubim Leon'yev travelled freely from the Alazeya River to the Lena; and service-man Stepan Ivanov and a party of traders made an unbroken voyage from the Kolyma River to Zhigansk on the lower Lena, a distance of 2,700 km, a distance greater than that from the Kolyma to the Anadyr'.[2] Even so four, maybe five, of the seven starting koches in 1648 were wrecked along the Arctic coast. Was it superior seamanship, sturdier boats or just luck that accounts for the survival of the remaining two?

Meanwhile, there is other evidence that the voyage was far from an easy or swift one. If we allow that the flotilla of koches set forth from the mouth of the Kolyma by the end of the first week of July, a time within the normal breaking up of the ice there, then some seventy days elapsed between that time and September 20 when the Russians engaged in a fight with the Chukchi somewhere on the Chukotskiy Peninsula. If the fight occurred on or near the eastern tip of the peninsula, as it has usually been supposed, the distance covered was betwen 1,350 and 1,450 km, as we shall see later. That is an average of 19–21 km per 24-hour day. These figures suggest that a considerable amount of time must have been spent in places of shelter awaiting favourable weather and winds. We do not know, on the other hand, to what extent the expedition followed the shoreline of Chaunskaya and Kolyuchinskaya bays, those two deep indentations in what is otherwise a quite regular coastline. In looking for the mouth of a large river they presumably would have had to ascertain whether or not it emptied into a large bay instead of the open sea. Too, the men may

---

[1] It is not clear whether the two men built one or two koches at this time. Their report says that they obtained timbers so as to go by sea to Yakutsk. Later in the report they say that they turned over two koches to Seliverstov in 1654 (document 10, p. 63), but do not say when they were built. This statement evidently led Müller first to say that Dezhnev and Semenov built two koches in 1653 (document 1); but in his 1758 account he says that they built only one (document 2), and he does not mention the two given to Seliverstov.   [2] 1955, p. 75; RM, p. 331.

have had to spend time fishing to maintain their food supply, and surely they must have had to look for fresh water. We know of two occasions of fighting with the natives, so there could have been others. The success of Dezhnev and twenty-four men in reaching the region of the Anadyr´ should not disguise the fact that the voyage was arduous and costly as the loss finally of all the boats and 64 of the 89 men attest.

What happened to the four koches which disappeared? Müller did not know. The beginnings of an answer came with Ogloblin's discovery of Dezhnev's four petitions in the archives of the Siberian Department in Moscow. His petition of 1662 (document 28) contains a clue to their fate. Some more information was revealed in the report of Stadukhin to the Yakutsk authorities after his return from the voyage of 1649 (document 15). It tells us explicitly what happened to two of the koches.

Stadukhin, it will be recalled, left Yakutsk in 1647 with orders to search for the new Pogycha River. He and the Yakutsk authorities knew nothing of what was being done on the Kolyma River to the same end. He got no farther than the Yana River that summer and arrived in Sredne-Kolymsk in 1648 too late to push on that year from the Kolyma River by sea. In July 1649 with thirty men he set sail for the Pogycha, now also known as the Anadyr´, in two koches, one of which was soon wrecked at sea.[1] In his report to Yakutsk in September he writes: 'We went by sea from the Kolyma River for seven days-and-nights with sails unslackened, but we did not reach the river' (document 15). Putting ashore, he sent the promyshlennik Ivan Kazanets, who was serving as his clerk, and service-man Ivan Baranov to find native informants. Travelling along the coast for two days-and-nights, they came upon two Koryak encampments. They captured a few of the natives and brought them back to Stadukhin (document 16). Under questioning they told the Russians: 'We do not know of any river nearby because a mountainous cliff (kamen' utes) lies close to the sea. We do not know where the mountain ends.' Stadukhin then mentions in his report that 'certain service-men and traders, Yeresimko Ankidinov, Semeyka Dezhnev, with ninety men, set out for that river in the year 156 [1648] in seven koches...'. From the natives the

---

[1] Belov, 1955, p. 84; 1973, p. 111, citing TsGADA, YaA, karton 13, stolbets 7, When in July the expedition started is not known. The information comes not from Stadukhin, but from the report by Vetoshka and others in 1655 from Anadyrsk (document 11). The report as published is taken from Müller's copy, and the day of the month is missing, indicated by dots of ellipsis. Regarding Stadukhin's loss of a second koch see p. 176, note 3 below.

Russians learned that 'two koches were wrecked at sea, and our people killed them. The rest of the men lived at the edge of the sea, but we do not know whether they are alive or not.'

It seems probable from what Dezhnev tells us in his petition of 1662 that the other two unaccounted-for koches suffered the same fate. In a confusingly worded passage he states: 'I, your slave, went with these traders and promyshlenniks by sea, ninety men in six koches. Having passed the mouth of the Anandyr´, by God's judgment all our koches were wrecked by the sea, and the traders and promyshlenniks were drowned from shipwreck at sea or were killed on the tundra by natives, and others died from hunger. Altogether sixty-four men perished.' If this passage is taken literally, Dezhnev is saying that the wrecking of all the koches occurred after passing the mouth of the Anadyr´. Yet he mentions men killed on the tundra and elsewhere reports the loss of Ankudinov's koch on the great rocky nos; and we have just learned from Stadukhin that at least two koches were lost before Ankudinov lost his.[1] Therefore, the phrase 'Having passed the mouth of the Anadyr´' has to be taken to mean 'by the time the mouth of the Anandyr´ had been passed' all or most of these things had happened. So interpreted, the sentence 'the traders and promyshlenniks were drowned from shipwreck at sea or were killed on the tundra by natives...' becomes consistent with Stadukhin's information and no doubt explains what happened to the other two missing koches and their occupants.[2]

It would add to our knowledge of the Arctic stage of the voyage if we could determine from the information provided by Stadukhin and Kazanets where approximately the Russians' contact with the Koryaks occurred and thus where the two koches were lost and their occupants killed. The two reports provide these items of information: (1) After leaving the Kolyma River, the Russians sailed for seven days-and-nights with sails unslackened. (2) Kazanets and Baranov continued on, by foot we assume, for two days-and-nights before encountering natives whom they took to be Koryaks and from whom they seized informants. From these informants they learned (3) that the former knew of no river thereabouts because a mountainous cliff lay

---

[1] Is Dezhnev here too excluding Ankudinov from his calculations, as Belov argues? If so, Dezhnev still includes Ankudinov's men in his totals.

[2] One of the perils confronting Arctic mariners is mentioned by Dezhnev when reporting his proposal of a voyage back to Yakutsk (document 10, p. 62). He says: 'I, Semeyka, and my men know that the ocean is big and eddies near the land strong, and we dared not go without good boat equipment, without a good sail and anchor.'

close to the sea and they did not know where it ended;[1] and (4) that it was along their coastal habitat that the two koches were wrecked and the men killed. Evidently at this point in the voyage of 1648 favourable weather had deserted the Russians. Not only were two of the koches wrecked, but the rest of the Russians lived for awhile at the edge of the sea.

On the basis of this information two Soviet scholars have attempted to place the locale of the Koryaks and the loss of the two koches. One is the ethnographer Boris O. Dolgikh, who in his study of the native tribes of Siberia in the 17th century turns to the accounts of Stadukhin and Kazanets in an effort to place the location of the Koryaks. He thinks the Russians may have mistaken Chukchi for Koryaks because of the similarity of their two languages. But more pertinent in placing these Koryaks is his reasoning that if Isay Ignat´yev reached Chaunskaya Bay in 1646 after two days-and-nights of sailing, Stadukhin must have gone much farther east in 1649 in seven days-and-nights. Dolgikh 'assumes' that he reached a point between capes Billingsa and Shmidta (Ryrkapiy).[2] He does not elaborate on the reasons for this assumption.

The other Soviet scholar is Belov, who has made much the greater effort to establish the locale of this episode, though his conclusions have changed over the years. In his article of 1949 he places it near Cape Shelagskiy at the northeast corner of Chaunskaya Bay, near a settlement of Shelagi, a branch of Chukchi (actually Eskimos) whom the Russians called Koryaks in distinction from Chukchi living nearby.[3] In the second edition of his *Semen Dezhnev* he first says that Stadukhin was turned back by ice at Cape Shelagskiy,[4] but farther on he narrates the voyage as it has been narrated here and in documents 15 and 16, and he explains that Stadukhin turned back because he did not want his men to die of starvation.[5] Then came Dolgikh's observation regarding the discrepancy between the two days-and-nights of sailing by Ignat´yev to reach Chaunskaya Bay, which Belov accepted,[6] and the seven days-and-nights by Stadukhin to reach Cape Shelagskiy. This and some new evidence he unearthed in 1972 led Belov markedly to revise his view on the site of the loss of the two boats.

He places the site much farther east, near Kolyuchinskaya Bay. Beginning with the assumption that Stadukhin's koch could make 200 to 250 km in a 24-hour day (4·5 to 5·6 knots), Belov calculated that in seven such days of continuous sailing Stadukhin's party travelled

---

[1] Müller describes it as rocky and steep (document 1). [2] 1960, p. 550 and note 822.
[3] 1949, p. 466. [4] 1955, p. 75.
[5] 1955, p. 84. [6] 1955, p. 57

1,400 to 1,750 km from the mouth of the Kolyma River, a distance which would place its stopping point somewhat west of Kolyuchinskaya Bay, in an area where contact with the Koryaks could occur. He disagrees with Dolgikh's siting of the farthermost point of advance between capes Billingsa and Shmidta.[1]

Belov finds confirmation of his calculations on a map which he examined in Paris in 1972 in the archive of the depot of maps and charts of the navy.[2] The map, he writes, was drawn by Petr Meller (or Miller), probably before 1719. Meller was the son of a Dutch mid-17th century merchant immigrant and became a prosperous merchant and industrialist in the time of Peter the Great, with a great interest in and knowledge of the geography of Russia. In fact in 1719 Peter sent him on an expedition to explore the Obskaya Bay and Tazovskaya Bay.[3] His map is of northern Asia. Its most conspicuous feature is a large, very elongated island, Novaya Zemlya, 'a belt in the sea', extending from west of the Lena River to a point a bit east of the tip of the Chukotskiy Peninsula. Belov is persuaded that the map reflects the understanding of Stadukhin, Dezhnev, and others on the Kolyma about this Novaya Zemlya, especially of Stadukhin whose testimony at Yakutsk in April 1647 (document 12) describes such 'a belt in the sea'. Moreover, Belov notes that on 1 March 1659, after ten years of journeying along the Arctic coast, of travel via the Anyuy to the Anadyr´ and from there to the Penzhina River and other regions to the south, he sent 'books and a sketch map (chertezh) of the land and rivers' with the sable treasury to Yakutsk.[4] Belov is convinced that Stadukhin's map showed this Novaya Zemlya and contained other information that only he could have known and that this map came into the hands of Meller. Only Stadukhin could have known: (1) the exact location of the Koryaks on the north coast of Chukotka since he was the first and only Russian visitor there for the next century and a half;[5] (2) the farthest extremity of the Chukotskiy Peninsula, in the form of a rocky cape – a mountainous cliff – which extend to the east and whose end the Koryaks said they did not know; (3) the island opposite the Chukoch'ya River as an integral part of the Novaya Zemlya. These features, including the phrase 'a rocky belt in the sea', are all found on Meller's map and nowhere else.[6]

[1] 1973, p. 112.

[2] 1973, p. 84; Albert Isnard, 'Joseph-Nicolas Delisle, sa biographe et sa collection de cartes géographiques à la Bibliothèque nationale', Bulletin de la section de géographie du Comité des travaux historiques et scientifiques, Tome III (1916), pp. 59, 139, 142.

[3] Fisher, 1977, p. 11.   [4] DAI, Vol. IV, p. 122.

[5] On this point how could Belov overlook Dezhnev, who had stopped in this Koryak territory the summer before?   [6] 1973, pp. 94–5.

Persuaded that Stadukhin is the source of the information on Meller's map, at least as far as the Arctic region is concerned, Belov turns to it to fix the position of Stadukhin's contact with the Koryaks and that of the loss of the two koches. On the Meller map, Belov reports, the distance from the Kolyma to the eastern end of the Chukotskiy Peninsula is relatively correct. According to the distance scale on the map, expressed in versts, that distance is 1,600 versts or 2,400 km (2,330 km when measured on modern maps).[1] Kolyuchinskaya Bay is shown at the 1,900- to 2,000-km point, and the Koryak region west of it at the 1,800-km mark. Thus, Belov concludes, the episode in question occurred 400 to 500 km west of the end of the Chukotskiy Peninsula.[2]

Belov's data and conclusions are open to question. First, if Stadukhin could sail for seven days-and-nights without striking his sail and approach Kolyuchinskaya Bay, then the weather conditions must have been unusually favourable along the coast east of the Kolyma, as favourable or more favourable than those of the summer before. Dezhnev and company presumably took seventy days after leaving the Kolyma to reach the point where on September 20 the fight with the Chukchi on the great rocky nos took place. This suggests that Belov overestimates the speed of Stadukhin's koch during the seven days-and-nights. To make 200 to 250 km a day calls for an average speed of 4·5 to 5·6 knots. In light of the examples given earlier in this chapter that seems too high, especially to be maintained steadily over a seven-day period.[3]

[1] The verst of the 17th century was 700 sazhens or 1·49 km as against the 500 sazhens or 1·06 km it became in the time of Peter the Great (Vladimir Dal', *Tolkovyy slovar' zhivogo velikorusskago yazyka, sub nomine*).
[2] 1973, pp. 112–13. He does not state whether the shoreline distances of Chaunskaya and Kolyuchinskaya bays are included in the 2,400-km figure.
[3] Martin Sauer, who accompanied Commodore Joseph Billings on his expedition in the north Pacific, reports that he learned in 1791 from the Chukchi at the eastern end of the Chukotskiy Peninsula that they sometimes travelled by sea from the eastern end to Chaunskaya Bay, a distance of about 1,000 km, in fifteen days, sleeping on shore at night. This is 66 km or 41 miles a day. Whether this bit of information provides a meaningful comparison is hard to say. The Chukchi baydars were probably more manoeuvrable and moved more readily through shallow waters and polynias, but the speeds attainable with paddles must have been significantly less than those with a sail. (*An account of a geographical and astronomical expedition to the northern parts of Russia*...[London, 1802], p. 253.)
Stadukhin's account raises some interesting questions that probably cannot be answered, though if they could, the answers would help fix the place of his farthest advance. He states that his seven-day voyage by sea began at the Kolyma River. Two days were spent by Kazanets and Baranov in finding the Koryaks. Another two days presumably were spent in returning to the Russians' camp, and how long a time intervened between the Koryaks' arrival at and departure from Stadukhin's camp we do not know. From the beginning of the seven days to the departure of the Koryaks probably took two weeks, maybe more. Vetoshka says that the voyage got under way in July (document 11), but because of the

Second, doubt arises about Belov's claims that Meller had access to Stadukhin's sketch map of 1659 and that on Meller's map is shown the exact place where Stadukhin's men encountered the Koryaks. One is left, however, without the means of checking Belov's claims because he does not tell us in what form that information appears on the map, whether as an inscription explicitly stating the fact of the meeting or only a notation that the Koryaks lived along the coast west of Kolyuchinskaya Bay, and the map is reproduced in his book on such a small scale as to be almost worthless for purposes of corroboration.[1] Further, Meller's map places the western limit of Novaya Zemlya west of the Lena River and extends it beyond the end of the Chukotskiy Peninsula, whereas Stadukhin's description of it in his statement of April 1647 (document 12) places its western limit opposite Arkhangel'sk as Mezen' in Pomor'ye and extends it only to a point opposite the Pogycha River, then thought to be about three days-and-nights' sailing beyond the Kolyma. Too, Belov claims that on Meller's map the farthest extremity of the Chukotskiy Peninsula takes the form of a mountainous cape (*kamen' utes*), information provided by the Koryaks. But Stadukhin reports them as stating that the mountainous cliff along the shore extended beyond their area and that they did not know its end.[2] If the natives did not know, then how did Stadukhin know how much farther the coast along which he had been sailing stretched and whether the mountainous cliff extended all the way to the end of the peninsula, unless he learned of it from Dezhnev and his men? One is led to ask just how much of his information Meller obtained from Stadukhin's report and sketch map and how much from other and later sources. After all, sixty years elapsed between the delivery of Stadukhin's map

defect in the document mentioned in note 1, p. 172 above we do not know when in July, presumably early in the month when the ice breaks up. We can expect that Stadukhin would have wanted to start for the Pogycha as soon as possible. He returned to the Kolyma on September 7, to Sredne-Kolymsk we may assume. A reasonable estimate of the elapsed time for the voyage and events relating to the Koryaks is eight weeks, from early July to early September. What did his party do for six of those eight weeks? It is reported that early in the voyage he lost one of his two koches (document 2; also Belov, 1973, p. 112; 111 (citing YaA, *karton* 13, *stolbets* 7); Vrangel', 1840, p. xxiv), so he must have encountered some rough weather. He also collected some walrus tusks and furs. Did such collection occur on the outgoing or the return trip? Seven days-and-nights of unbroken sailing seem to preclude any stops, but by the time the party reached Koryak territory its provisions had been so reduced as to make Stadukhin unwilling to risk going any further. The pieces of the puzzle do not fit well.

[1] Map is in his 1973, opposite p. 152.
[2] It was the prospect of this barrier that helped persuade Stadukhin to turn back. He was short of provisions, and the coastal mountains with their promise of rocks in the sea and the absence of rivers (the Koryaks knew of none) precluded fishing as a source of food (document 16; see also document 1).

at Yakutsk and the drafting of Meller's map. In that time much speculation occurred over the geography of the northern part of Siberia. A considerable number of sketch maps with differing conceptions were drawn, and they found their way to Yakutsk, Tobol'sk, and Moscow.[1] In short, Meller's map does not provide conclusive support for placing the contact between Russians and Koryaks and the loss of the two koches just west of the Kolyuchinskaya Bay.[2]

Third, Belov's estimates of the distance and speed of Stadukhin's voyage are too high. He evidently takes the distance of 2,400 km between the Kolyma and eastern tip of the Chukotskiy Peninsula from the distance scale on Meller's map. According to the best information I can find the distance is no more than 1,370 km (850 miles).[3] Given this shorter distance, on the basis of 200 to 250 km average daily distance covered, at an average speed of $4\frac{1}{2}$ to 5 knots, as claimed by Belov, Stadukhin should have reached the eastern face of the Chukotskiy Peninsula. This reinforces our earlier suggestion that Belov's estimate

[1] For a short discussion of the cartography of northeastern Siberia in the latter 17th and early 18th centuries see Fisher, 1977, pp. 25–52. See also chapter 10 below, pp. X: 00–00.

[2] Indeed, Polevoy provides other information as to the inapplicability of Meller's map to this question. In letters of 26 February and 22 July 1980 he writes that Meller's map is his only in the sense that at one time he owned it, not that he made it. It appears to be the third map of Siberia made by Strahlenberg, in 1718, one which he was forced to sell. He subsequently found that it contained significant inaccuracies. It came into the possession of Meller, who presented it to Peter the Great in 1721 (Mariya G. Novlyanskaya, *Filip Iogann Stralenberg*...[Moscow, 1966], pp. 43–4, 66; Fisher, 1977, p. 66). The conclusion that the map which Belov calls Meller's map is Strahlenberg's third map is reached from the fact that on both maps the name 'Yedso' is mistakenly given as an alternate name for Kamchatka. This mistaken designation appears on Strahlenberg's map of 1718, after Strahlenberg had talked with the Japanese castaway Sanima in Tobol'sk during the latter's stop there en route from Kamchatka to St Petersburg. (Strahlenberg, 1730, pp. 31, 438; Boris P. Polevoy, 'O karte "Kamchadali" I. B. Gomana', *Izvestiya AN SSSR, seriya geograficheskaya*, 1970a, Vypusk 6, pp. 102–3.) Polevoy is of the opinion that the map Belov saw in Paris is most likely the original, sent there by Joseph N. Delisle, who surreptitiously made copies of many maps during his stay in Russia and spirited them out of the country to Paris. Polevoy also writes that the Stadukhin map which Belov sees as a source for Meller's map shows only his route of travel after leaving the Anadyr' in 1651 (see p. 242) and nowhere shows the Arctic Ocean or seaboard. Thus Polevoy by one route and I by another arrive at much the same conclusion: the so-called Meller map is not viable evidence for determining where Stadukhin stopped and turned back on his 1649 voyage. his 1649 voyage.

[3] As measured on Operational Navigation Charts C-7 and C-8 (scale 1:1,000,000) of the Defense Mapping Agency, Aerospace Center, St. Louis, Missouri. On the basis of the distances set forth in *Arctic pilot* (6th edition), vol. I, pp. 487–9, 493–4, and in *Bering Sea and Strait pilot* (4th edition), p. 551, both issued by the Hydrographic Department of the Admiralty (London, 1959 and 1966) the total distance is somewhat less, 700 nautical miles or 1,300 km. A letter from the Navy Oceanography Division of the United States Navy in Washington 12 July 1978 gives the same distance, a figure derived from the American Geographical Society's 1975 Map of the Arctic Region. These distances, as are the others used in connection with the voyages of Dezhnev and Stadukhin, are the direct navigational distances between two points. They do not allow for the convolutions of the shoreline or for such bays as Chaunskaya, Kolyuchinskaya, and Kresta, unless otherwise noted.

of the speed of Stadukhin's koch is too high. Since Stadukhin's and Kazanets' reports tell us nothing about the speed of their voyage, we have to seek a clue elsewhere.

One perhaps can be found in the voyage of Ignat'yev in 1646 to what Belov and others believe was Chaunskaya Bay, the bay where the episode of dumb trade occurred (document 3). The distance from the mouth of the Kolyma River to the western entrance to the bay is approximately 200 km. To have learned that it was a bay and to have reached a place south of the entrance on the western shore where natives would be found his party must have gone at least another 50 km (the northern half of the western shore is backed by marshes).[1] Thus the total distance for the one-way trip is 250 km or 125 km per 24-hour period for an average speed of 2·8 knots. At such an average speed Stadukhin's party would have covered 875 km in seven days-and-nights, and that places his stopping places about 75 km east of Cape Shmidta. When the distance travelled by Baranov and Kazanets to the Koryak encampment, at the most probably 50 km, is added, one has placed the location we are trying to determine at a point about a third of the way from Cape Shmidta to Kolyuchinskaya Bay or 360 km from Uelen at the northeast corner of the Chukotskiy Peninsula. This is compatible with Belov's placement of the site of the Koryaks and loss of the koches. By overestimating both the distance and speed of the koch he may have offset one error with another and so have been right for the wrong reason. On the other hand, if Stadukhin followed the practice of sailing along the shore and followed the perimeter of Chaunskaya Bay for a distance of 300 km, our calculations and estimates have to be changed. The terminal point would then be between Cape Billingsa and Cape Shmidta, which is where Dolgikh puts it.

With what certainty can we fix the locale of the contact with the Koryaks and the loss of the two koches from this discussion of the distance travelled by Stadukhin's party? A distance of about 900 km is compatible with the area inhabited by Koryaks. The location of shoreline mountains, however, turns out to be disconcertingly incompatible. According to the topographic maps showing the coastline from the Kolyma River to Uelen, as well as the description of the shoreline between these two points contained in the *Sailing Directions* published by the United States Hydrographic Office and the *Pilot* volumes

---

[1] Vrangel' (1840, p. xxiii) states that there is in Chaunskaya Bay a bay enclosed by steep rocks, which could have been the place where the exchange of goods took place. He places it opposite Rautan Island south of the entrance to Chaunskaya Bay, a distance of about 275 km from the Kolyma.

published by the British Admiralty (both drawn from Russian sources) no shoreline mountains are to be found between capes Billingsa and Shmidta or east or west of this sector for a considerable distance. Coastal plains and lagoons characterize this part of the coast. A 100-km stretch of mountainous coast is found immediately east of Cape Shelagskiy, and another such stretch begins 50 km northwest of Uelen and extends for another 50 km in that direction. According to Belov the Russians should have passed well beyond the first mountainous stretch in seven days-and-nights of continuous sailing, but not even Belov claims that they advanced within 100 km of the end of the Chukotskiy Peninsula. We are left consequently with a clouded conclusion about where the two koches met with disaster in the summer of 1648.

There is a third possible answer, one provided by Ferdinand P. Vrangel', admiral in the imperial navy and chief manager of the Russian-American Company at Novo-Arkhangel'sk from 1830 to 1835. While still a lieutenant he commanded an expedition which surveyed the Arctic coast from the Kolyma River to Kolyuchinskaya Bay from the land side in the years 1820–3, to close the gap in scientific information about the Arctic coast between Cape Shelagskiy and Cape Shmidta, the westernmost point reached by Captain Cook in 1778. In the appendix to his published account in English of the expedition he traces the exploration of this area. He writes this about Stadukhin's voyage of 1649:

He then continued to sail in an easterly direction for seven days, without finding the mouth of any important river, nor was he able on landing, to obtain any information on the subject from the natives... The steep and rocky character of the coast, according to Stadukhin, made it impossible to fish; so as the ship's stores were nearly exhausted, he was obliged to turn back, without having obtained the object of his voyage. From the time occupied, it is probable that Stadukhin and his companions must have been beyond Cape Chelagskoi. This is also borne out by his description of the coast, which in the vicinity of the cape, consists of rocks and cliffs projecting to a considerable distance into the sea.[1]

Vrangel's conclusion accords with the topographical evidence we have mentioned, but varies markedly from the estimates of distances travelled made by Dolgikh, Belov and, tentatively, by myself. If we accept Vrangel's conclusion, we have to change several of the assumptions on which the conclusions of the three of us rest. Certainly one has to assume a lower average rate of speed than 2·8 knots. If that

[1] 1840, pp. xxiv–xxv.

is so, then the bay reached by Ignat'yev probably was not Chaunskaya Bay, but some bay west of it. In the case of Stadukhin's voyage circumnavigating Chaunskaya Bay in conformance with the practice of sailing along the shore would account for two or three of the seven days. To have done this appears reasonable in light of the fact that Stadukhin was looking for the mouth of the Pogycha–Anadyr' River, believed to be three days-and-nights' sailing to the east. But would a favourable wind that kept the sail unslackened have prevailed as the koch's course changed direction by 180° in following the shore of the bay? In any case Dolgikh's and Belov's conclusions presume unusually favourable conditions of wind and ice. Further, Ignat'yev found Chukchi, Stadukhin Koryaks. Dolgikh is persuaded that Ignat'yev and his men encountered Chuvantsy, then unknown to the Russians. Had these natives been Chukchi, only whole tusks of marine animals would have been found among them, not the items made from such tusks as were exchanged with the Russians. The natives met by Stadukhin's party could have been Chukchi or Eskimos, but the evidence on this point is not firm.[1]

In this dichotomy in the evidence what choice does one make? Vrangel's choice rests on unchanging physical evidence and explicit statement of the natives that mountains lined the coast along and beyond their habitat, how far they did not know. Stadukhin accepted their statement to the extent of turning back in the face of the difficulties which this rocky coast posed for his men's survival. This is hard evidence and points to the stretch of coast from Cape Shelagskiy 100 km to the east. The main problem in this choice is the seven days-and-nights of continuous sailing.[2] Would it not have carried Stadukhin beyond the 100-km stretch of rocky coast? On the other hand, the evidence adduced by Dolgikh, Belov, and myself is conjectural and based on assumptions as to speed of sailing and sailing conditions. It is soft evidence. One is therefore led to the conclusion that on the basis of the available evidence and knowledge of the coast as depicted on maps Vrangel's judgement is to be accepted over those of Dolgikh and Belov. The objections to Vrangel's conclusion are more easily explained away than the fact of the rocky coast ignored in

---

[1] Dolgikh, p. 550. Not knowing whether the natives Stadukhin and Kazanets called Koryaks were sedentary or nomadic further complicates our speculations.

[2] Unless in stating that 'he went by sea from the Kolyma River' Stadukhin meant by 'Kolyma River' Sredne-Kolymsk, which, as we saw in chapter 5, could be meant, the river being substituted for the outpost. Then part of the seven days was spent in travel down the river. But still, Stadukhin says that he went by sea from the river.

Dolgikh's explanation and placed in Belov's where a rocky coast does not exist. It would appear that Belov's judgement in 1949 is closer to the actuality than he later thought.

About the third and final stage of the voyage, from the eastern face of the Chukotskiy Peninsula to the wrecking of the two remaining koches south of the Anadyr´ River, we know the most, though it is far from as much as we would like. Two islands inhabited by natives wearing labrets were seen; a fight with the Chukchi occurred on September 20; at the beginning of October a storm blew up that separated the two koches and sent them separately to destruction on the shore south of the Anadyr´ River. The wrecking of Ankudinov's koch could have occurred during this stage too. Dezhnev and his men spent ten weeks finding their way to the Anadyr´, which they reached down near the sea. Then followed the disappearance of nearly half of the men, the building of boats and trip up to the river to the country of the Anauls, the imposition of tribute on them, and the building of a zimov´ye. With these developments the original objective of the voyage was achieved.

Though Dezhnev tells us more about what happened during this stage of the voyage than about the others, we are still left with a number of unanswered questions: (1) Where did the fight with the Chukchi occur? (2) Where did the wrecking of Dezhnev's koch take place? (3) Did in fact Alekseyev, Ankudinov, and their men reach Kamchatka? (4) What is the identity of the great rocky promontory and of the two islands on which the labret-wearing natives lived? Answers to these questions have been given, with what satisfaction we shall see.

We have virtually no information that enables us more than to guess where the fight with the Chukchi took place on September 20. The fact that it occurred late in the navigation season suggests that it took place somewhere on the south coast of the Chukotskiy Peninsula, on the shores of the Gulf of Anadyr. Belov, on the other hand, believes that he can pinpoint the place quite closely. He finds a clue in an episode that occurred some twelve years later. In the summer of 1660 Kurbat Ivanov, Dezhnev's successor at Anadyrsk as commandant, embarked on a voyage with 22 men which carried them along the coast north and east of the Anadyr´ to a 'big bay', probably Kresta Bay just east of where the southern coast of the Chukotskiy Peninsula turns south, and thence eastward along that coast to another bay near which they found their objective, a rookery or sandspit frequented by walruses, where they hoped to find dead walruses from which to obtain their ivory tusks ('fish tooth bone'). Ivanov had learned of this sandspit from the Chukcha woman of Fomka Semenov Permyak, one of the members of the party of Andreyev and Astaf'yev and one of the survivors in Dezhnev's party who helped him found the zimov'ye at Anadyrsk.[1] Upon reaching the sandspit the Russians found that she had described it and its environs quite accurately, so much so, Belov argues, as to lead to the conclusion that she had lived near there before her capture. From this Belov further surmises that she was captured by Semenov in the fight with the Chukchi, and so he concludes that the fight took place near her home area. The bay where Ivanov's party stopped Belov believes to be Provideniya Bay, which borders the west side of Cape Chukotskiy, the southeast corner of the Chukotskiy Peninsula. By seizing the wife of a local Chukcha Ivanov and his men coerced the man into leading them to the sandspit, evidently not far away. Belov finds evidence persuasive to him that it was part of Cape Chukotskiy. He points out that on Remezov's map of Kamchatka, 1712–14 (Map 1),[2] there appears a cape at the southeast corner of the Chukotskiy Peninsula on which there is the inscription 'Chukchi rookery' (*Chukoch'ya korga*), and on the Anadyrskaya map (Map 3), better known as L'vov's map, there also appears a cape at the southeast corner on which appears the inscription 'rookery' (korga).[3] The source for these inscriptions, Belov claims, is Kurbat Ivanov, and the reason for its designation as Chukotskiy is that a Chukcha woman first described it and a Chukcha man led the Russians to it.[4] From such evidence and conjectures Belov concludes that the fight with the Chukchi took place on that cape.[5]

Belov's argument appears plausible and perhaps convincing, especially in placing the walrus rookery on or near Cape Chukotskiy. But there is one weak spot, and that is his assumption that Fomka Semenov

[1] RM, pp. 268–70; ORZPM, pp. 405–6.

[2] *Atlas geograficheskikh otkrytiy v Sibiri i v severo-zapadnoy Amerike XVII–XVIII vv.* (edited by Aleksey V. Yefimov; Moscow, 1964), map no. 48. Here it is called the Remezov-Atlasov map of Kamchatka and is believed to have been made in 1701 from information in the reports of Vladimir Atlasov, the conqueror of Kamchatka. Polevoy ('Semen Remezov i Vladimir Atlasov [k utocheniyu datirovki rannykh chertezhey Kamchatki]', *Izvestiya ANSSSR, seriya geograficheskaya* [Moscow], 1965 b, Vypusk 6, pp. 95–6) and Leonid A. Gol'denberg (*Semen Ul'yanovich Remezov: Sibirskiy kartograf i geograf, 1642–posle 1720 gg.* [Moscow, 1965], pp. 189, 193) think otherwise. See Fisher, 1977, p. 38, note 24.

[3] *Atlas*, map no. 55 and p. 39. See Fisher, 1977, p. 45, note 42, for a discussion of its provenance and date.

[4] When Ivanov's party reached the sandspit, they found no walruses; the animals had abandoned it, and only a few carcasses, but no tusks, were left.

[5] 1949, pp. 466, 470; 1973, pp. 121–2.

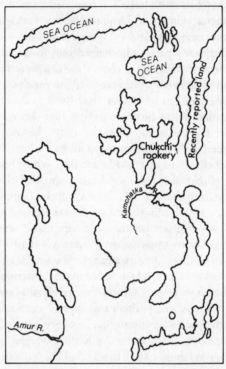

Map 1   Remezov's map of Kamchatka, 1712–14 (*Atlas*, no. 48)

captured the Chukcha woman in the fight with the Chukchi on
September 20. If he did, it means that she travelled with him after the
fight, through the storm at sea and the ten-week march to the Anadyr´.
But whereas Dezhnev's report of 1655 and petition of 1662 imply the
presence of Alekseyev's woman on the expedition, in them there is
not even a hint of the presence of Semenov's Chukcha woman. In stating
in his 1662 petition that 64 men perished in the expedition and in stating
in that petition and his earlier report that his party of 25, including himself,
survived the voyage, he accounts for 89 men. The ninetieth person has
to be the Yakut woman, about whose survival he learned in 1654
(document 9). We have no evidence of this sort for Semenov's woman,
and we first learn of her in a report written in 1661. Hence, one has
to ask, whether Semenov acquired her in the fight with the Chukchi
or after he reached the Anadyr´ and had established himself at Anadyrsk.
He was a promyshlennik whose hunting could have taken him far into

regions where there were Chukchi; or he could have acquired her from Chukchi who visited Anadyrsk to trade.[1] The information which she furnished, too, could as well have been secondhand, not firsthand. Moreover, under what circumstances could a Russian have captured a native woman in the first encounter between the Russians and the local Chukchi, which evidently was a draw at best for the Russians, and have kept her, or have been allowed to keep her by his companions? One has to conclude that Belov's thesis of Cape Chukotskiy as the place of the fight with the Chukchi is not demonstrated by his line of reasoning, and we still do not know where the fight occurred.

It may further be noted that from their profiles and the descriptions of them in the *Sailing Directions* of the United States Hydrographic Office Cape Chaplina rather than Cape Chukotskiy appears the more suitable for a walrus rookery.[2] It consists of a triangular sandspit enclosing a freshwater lagoon whereas Cape Chukotskiy has a rocky shore. If the walrus preference was for sandspits such as the rookery at the entrance to Anadyr´ Bay, then the bay and cape visited by Ivanov could just as well have been Cape Chaplina and nearby Tkachen Bay. But these are conjectures. They respond to doubts, but do not provide assured answers to our questions.

Some time after the fight with the Chukchi the two Russian groups put to sea again. Several days later a storm blew up and after October 1 Dezhnev's koch was carried out of sight of Alekseyev's, whose party was never seen again, and Dezhnev's found itself tossed about at the mercy of the sea. It was finally thrown ashore and wrecked, but where Dezhnev did not know except that it was 'on the forward end beyond the Onandyr´'. He tells us that there were twenty-five of them in the koch and that 'cold and hungry, naked and barefoot', they proceeded thereafter by land and by routes they could not recall, reaching the lower Anadyr´ after ten weeks.

Here they faced the problem of finding food. They 'could catch no fish; there was no forest'. So the party divided and went separate ways. Twelve of the men, Dezhnev says, went up the river. After twenty days, during which they found neither food nor people, nor traces of them, they turned back. Within three days' travel of Dezhnev's camp they stopped for the night despite the urging of Fomka Semenov to

[1] Polevoy wrote me (November 1974) that Semenov's woman was captured in the 1650's.
[2] *Sailing directions for the east coast of Siberia: Mys Otto Shmidta to Sakhalinskiy zaliv (Sakhalin gulf)* (2nd edition; Washington, 1952), pp. 46–7, 74.

keep going. He and two other men continued on to Dezhnev's camp.[1] When members of the relief party arrived at the stopping place, the nine who had remained behind had disappeared without a trace. The following spring, having constructed boats, probably from driftwood, the survivors went up the Anadyr´ and at or near the present-day Markovo established a zimov´ye.

Dezhnev's reports present confusing statements as to the number of survivors. He states in two places that twelve men went up the river in search of food (documents 9 and 28). He later states that there were only twelve men and himself left when the survivors went upriver next spring (document 10 [p. 58]). Yet Fomka Semenov and two others from the first twelve returned to Dezhnev's camp, and we already have learned that Fomka survived to participate in Ivanov's expedition. It would seem that only nine men disappeared in the search for food. There were twenty-five men in the party when the koch was wrecked. Nine disappeared.[2] Thus we have to conclude, as does Belov, that fifteen besides Dezhnev, not twelve, as he reports, survived to establish the outpost that became Anadyrsk. Otherwise Dezhnev either reported the number who went in search of food incorrectly, or three men died over the winter, and he gives no hint of that.[3]

Dezhnev's wording implies that the wrecking of their koch left him and his men with little more than the shirts on their backs. This does not appear, however, quite to have been the case. His remarks about later developments indicate that the men salvaged some of their possessions from the wreck. On the occasion when Dezhnev sent a rescue party to the falterers who had searched in vain for food, he sent with it an old blanket and his last pallet. The men of that beleaguered group dug pits in the snow. This presumably called for some kind of tools, though they may have improvised with what could be found on the spot. Elsewhere (document 28) Dezhnev says that the men who went in search of food used sleds and snowshoes. Most likely they were made from materials at hand, yet such manufacture implies the possession of at least a few tools. The building of boats the following spring likewise implies tools, particularly axes and knives. Finally,

---

[1] A tenth one may have disappeared or died. In his narrative of this episode (document 9) Dezhnev says that Fomka Semenov Permyak tried to persuade his faltering companions to continue on to camp, but that only Sidorko Yemel´yanov and Ivashko Zyryanin went with him. Fomka and Sidorko, Dezhnev reports, reached camp, but he says nothing more about Zyryanin. Did he finally falter too and disappear?

[2] 1955, p. 82; 1973, p. 123.

[3] In his petition of 1662 Dezhnev gives a different version. He states that the twelve failed to reach the Anadyr´ in the first place, (document 28, p. 106).

Dezhnev explicitly mentions the possessions of Andreyev and Astaf´yev, evidently two of the men who disappeared near Dezhnev's camp, possessions which he turned over to their employee, Yelfimko Merkur´yev. Despite the difficulties in obtaining food the fact remains that at least half of those thrown ashore in October managed to survive the harsh winter. It is hard to believe that they could have been completely without tools and equipment.

This conclusion appears valid in light of Belov's statement that the officials at Yakutsk furnished each detachment of service-men with a set of tools, which made it possible to construct boats in the course of a journey. The tools included augers, chisels, adzes, gimlets, draw-knives, saws, and axes.[1] This is not to say that the Yakutsk or Kolyma authorities had so equipped Dezhnev's koch (we have seen that it was a private, not a government koch), only that those travelling in koches carried such tools. Given the number of boats wrecked or damaged as the Russians moved about Siberia and along the Arctic and Pacific coasts, such tools would at times have meant the difference between life and death. Preserving them must have been a top priority.

Where was Dezhnev's koch wrecked? He states only that the wrecking occurred 'on the forward end beyond the Onandyr´'. This is scarcely more than what he tells us about the place of the fight with the Chukchi, and so again we have to attempt an educated guess. Wherever it was, the Russians found themselves throughout their ordeal in uninhabited country. Müller advanced the view that the 'forward end' was Cape Olyutorskiy, some 700 km (430 miles) south of the mouth of the Anadyr´ in a straight line, choosing this cape perhaps because it took Dezhnev and his men ten weeks to reach the river (document 2). Since Müller's time a majority of scholars, both Russian and Soviet, have gone along with this view.[2] But more recently it has been challenged by B. P. Kuskov, a Soviet scholar.[3]

Kuskov argues that the Russians could not have advanced along a straight-line route from Cape Olyutorskiy to the Anadyr´ because so much of the intervening country is mountainous. The route would have had to be a winding one, with the result that for every kilometre of straight-line advance additional ones would have had to be traversed. This would have been true if the route followed the shore for the coast is broken by many bays and lagoons and numerous shoreline cliffs stand

---

[1] 1952, p. 72.
[2] E.g. Müller, document 2; Belov, 1949, p. 466; 1973, p. 123.
[3] 'Byl li Fedot Popov na reke Kamchatke?', *Voprosy geografii Kamchatki*, Vypusk 4 (1966), pp. 94–100.

in the way. Thus two factors have to be taken into account: How many kilometres a day could the Russians walk and how many kilometres of actual travel on an average were required to advance one kilometre in a straight line toward the Anadyr'? The best we can do is to set up some reasonable assumptions and proceed from them.

The promyshlenniks' endurance was great, and the urgency of survival must have spurred them on. But, as Dezhnev writes, they were 'cold and hungry, naked and barefoot', and evidently they remained hungry for most of the trip, and were still hungry upon arrival at the Anadyr' as the departure of half of the men up the river in search of food testifies. They built sleds presumably to carry such provisions and goods as they had managed to salvage from the wreck.[1] Dragging them took energy and made for a slowed pace. October, November, and December are the months of frequent snowstorms and frosts in that part of the world, which could have interfered with travel. The men no doubt followed more than one false trail and had to backtrack out of dead ends. Dezhnev gives no evidence of guidance from natives who elsewhere often aided the Russians in finding their way through country new and strange to them. Also, time must have been taken out to hunt for food or fish in rivers or streams.[2] In the light of considerations such as these Kuskov estimates that in the ten weeks their straight-line advance was about 350 km (215 miles), at the most 400 (250 miles). This distance puts the place of shipwreck near Cape Navarin. It may be added that Cape Navarin is the easternmost of the capes south of the Anadyr'. Is this what Dezhnev had in mind in specifying 'the forward end'?

How valid is Kuskov's conclusion? An answer does not emerge clearly and remain irrefutable. If we accept his conclusion that the starting point of the journey was Cape Navarin, we accept the corollary conclusion that the average daily advance in a straight line was 5 to 5·7 km (3 to 3·5 miles). Our appraisal of Kuskov's conclusion is hampered, however, by the fact that we do not know whether the Russians in the latter part of their journey followed a route along the floodplain of the lower Velikaya Osnovaya River, which empties into the Onemen estuary just below the mouth of the Anadyr'. If so, the level character of the floodplain may have made for more direct and rapid progress in this part of the journey, but many streams and lakes,

[1] Dezhnev mentions the use of sled and snowshoes in his petition of 1662 (document 28), but not in his report of 1655 (document 9).
[2] Müller makes the same assumption (document 1).

as well as marshes on both sides of the river may also have presented difficulties. Probably these opposing factors cancel each other out if indeed the Russians followed this route. We are left then to estimate how far they can be expected to have advanced in a straight line in seventy days. If the ratio of actual travel to straight-line advance was three to one – and given the nature of the terrain it may well have been – they would have had to walk an average of 15 to 17 km (9 to 10·5 miles) a day to advance the 5 to 5·7 km a day necessary to go from Cape Navarin to the Anadyr´ in seventy days. In view of the men's physical conditions, the encumbrances to travel, and their ignorance of the country, these distances probably mark the upper limit of their capacity. If the daily distance walked was less, it may have been offset by a lower ratio of kilometres walked for each kilometre of advance toward the Anadyr´. But the variables are so many that further speculation seems futile.

An alternate approach is to apply our figures to Cape Olyutorskiy and see whether the result seems reasonable. To advance 700 km in a direct line in seventy days – all of the sector between the cape and Cape Navarin in mountainous terrain – calls for an average of 10 km a day of such forward advance. To achieve that under the three-to-one ratio means 30 km a day of walking; a two-to-one ratio means 20 km a day. Both of these distances seem beyond the Russians' capacity. Thus Cape Olyutorskiy appears ruled out as the site of the terminus of the voyage and Cape Navarin the more plausible one.

Another alternative is to take account of the statement of Petr I. Popov, who was sent from Anadyrsk to the Anadyrskoy Nos in 1711.[1] In his report (document 33) he writes that it took ten weeks to travel from Anadyrsk to the Matkol peak (Mt Bol'shoy Matachingay) north of Kresta Bay, a direct-line distance of fewer than 500 km, using reindeer sleds over a known route and in the absence of blizzards. The shorter distance of 350–400 km from Cape Navarin to the Anadyr´ could easily be offset by the factors of no reindeer travel and no knowledge of the route. Again it appears that Kuskov's reasoning is sound.

Kuskov, it needs to be noted, believes that Dezhnev and his men followed a route close to the shore, an opinion shared by A. Zelenin at the end of the last century and indicated by the archivist Lavrentsova.[2] To have gone across the mountains in the late fall and winter, Kuskov

[1] See chapter 9, pp. 223, 230–1.
[2] 1898, pp. 2184, 2191; *RAE*, p. 130, note 10.

contends, would have been madness. A route close to the shore would have given them a point of reference and would have promised more in the way of food and hunting or finding sea animals cast ashore. Such a route, he adds, could not, however, have been traversed from Cape Olyutorskiy in seventy days. The Russians would have had to travel nearly 1,000 km (620 miles) for an average of 15 km (9 miles) a day under retarding conditions, which included many bays and lagoons and shoreline cliffs. This is a reasonable conclusion so far as Cape Olyutorskiy is concerned, but doubt is cast on Kuskov's notion that Dezhnev and his men followed a coastal route by Dezhnev's assertion that 'we went by land [uphill?] by what routes we do not know' (document 9). The mountains, like the coast, could provide fresh food, as well as fresh water and the means of shelter; and would not sleds be as easily drawn over the snow in the mountains as along a shoreline route? Most important, would not Dezhnev have mentioned such a route and reference point as readily known and recalled as the coast? Would he have not known the route?

Dezhnev and his companions survived their ordeal to tell their contemporaries and us what happened to them, however meagrely. Fedot Alekseyev, Gerasim Ankudinov, and their companions did not. Two versions have come down to us as to what happened to them.

One of the versions is that found in Dezhnev's report of 1655 (document 9). In a brief passage near the end he states: 'In the past year 162 [1653–4] I went on an expedition near the sea, and I captured Fedot Alekseyev's Yakut woman from the Koryaks.[1] This woman said that Fedot Alekseyev and service-man Gerasim died from scurvy and some companions were killed. A few remained, who fled in lodki with only their souls, I do not know where.' Thus we learn that death was the fate of Alekseyev, Ankudinov, and others; flight of the rest. But we are not told where these events happened or who the natives were.

The Yakut woman, as a woman and a native, was spared. From Dezhnev's statement that he captured her from the Koryaks we may conclude that the natives who did the Russians in were likewise Koryaks. That conclusion in turn points to the region south of the Anadyr', which was Koryak territory. In their joint report of 1655

[1] In his 1737 article Müller presents details about Dezhnev's capture of the Yakut woman that Dezhnev himself does not report. Upon the approach of the Russians the native men fled with their best wives, leaving the other women and slaves behind. He reports the woman as saying that Alekseyev's koch was wrecked nearby. Where he learned these details he does not say. Did he pick them up from oral reports in Yakutsk or are they touches of his own embellishment? The latter does not seem in character for him.

(document 10, p. 65) Dezhnev and Semenov tell us that in 1654 the Russians 'went to the sandspit against the Koryaks because they live not far from the sandspit'. This helps to identify the locale of the Koryaks with whom the Yakut woman was living and so is an indication of where Alekseyev's koch was wrecked. The facts that the sandspit visited by Dezhnev is on the south side of the entrance to Anadyr´ Bay and that the south side of the lower Anadyr´ came to be known as the 'Koryak side' in distinction from the northern 'Russian side'[1] further identify the locale. Thus it appears that the site of the wrecking of Alekseyev's koch and the area where the fate of himself and his associates was meted out is closer to the mouth of the Anadyr´ than is the place where Dezhnev's koch was thrown ashore. Kuskov suggests that whereas Dezhnev and his men found themselves in uninhabited country, the other party encountered natives.[2] Over what period of time these fatal developments occurred is not known. Alekseyev's and Ankudinov's scurvy must have taken several weeks to run its course, and the lodki in which those not killed fled were not built overnight. So at least several weeks must have elapsed. On the other hand, unless their scurvy developed long after arriving in Koryak country, the scurvy victims must not have lasted out the winter. Probably only after the Russians had been considerably weakened did the natives risk attack.

Müller presents this version in both of his accounts (document 1 and 2), drawing his information from Dezhnev's reports,[3] but he adds an epilogue to explain what might have happened to the Russians who fled the Koryaks' murderous intent. When Vladimir V. Atlasov, the conqueror of Kamchatka in 1697–9, came to that peninsula, so Müller writes in both accounts, he heard from the Kamchadals (Itelmans) a story common among them that 'a certain Fedotov, who probably was Fedot Alekseyev's son, and some of his comrades lived among them and married their Kamchadal women' (document 2, p. 38). The Kamchadals further explained that the Russians built dwellings at the mouth of the little Nikul River, a southern tributary of the Kamchatka River, remains of which could be seen at the time of the conquest. Thereafter the Nikul River was known as the Fedoticha (or Fedotov-

[1] Polevoy, 1962a, p. 151; 1965a, p. 108.
[2] 1966, p. 95. This reasoning would have to be re-examined if it should turn out that the Koryak natives from whom Dezhnev captured the Yakut woman were nomadic, not sedentary.
[3] Though in his 1737 account Müller reports the Yakut woman as saying that 'Fedot's boat was wrecked nearby', he omits the statement in his 1758 account – because it was not found in Dezhnev's report?

shchina or Fedotovka). They were first regarded by the natives as gods and therefore untouchable until they fell to quarrelling and drew blood. Thereafter some of them crossed over to the Penzhina Sea (Sea of Okhotsk), but all were finally killed by the Kamchadals or Koryaks. Shorn of several of the details just recounted and reduced to a group of Russians, this tale was so reported sixteen years later by Müller in his 'Geographie und Verfassung von Kamtschatka' (document 20).

The story has a crucial defect when applied to Fedot Alekseyev; he had no son with him on the expedition. A nephew, Yemel'yan Stefanov (document 22),[1] yes, but not a son. It is possible that the 'Fedotov's son'[2] was another Fedot's son, even perhaps the one in Alekseyev's party, Vas'ka Fedotov, who is listed in the 1642 travel document issued to Alekseyev (document 22). If he continued with Alekseyev to the end and succeeded in fleeing from the Koryaks, then one has to ask how he and the other fugitives managed to sail the 1,200 km to the Kamchatka River 'with only their souls'. On the other hand, in view of the fact that it is now pretty certain that Russians penetrated deep into Kamchatka in the mid-17th century,[3] another possibility is that there was a Fedot's son among them. But once again we find ourselves able only to suggest answers, not provide them.

Writing at about the same time as Müller, Stepan P. Krasheninnikov, in his description of Kamchatka, reported a similar story, though it differed in one important respect (document 20). In a discussion of who was the first Russian in Kamchatka he writes that according to oral information the first Russian was

a certain trader Fedot Alekseyev whose name, Fedotovshchina, was given to the little river Nikul, which empties into the Kamchatka. Allegedly he went by the Icy Sea from the mouth of the Kolyma in seven koches; allegedly he was separated from the other koches in a storm and carried to Kamchatka, where he wintered with his koch. In another summer, rounding the Kuril 'spade' [Cape Lopatka], he reached the Tigil' River by way of the Penzhina Sea. They were killed by local Koryaks in the winter.

The Koryaks considered them immortal because of their firearms, but freed of this illusion when one Russian killed another, the Koryaks

---

[1] *ORZPM*, pp. 170–1; Belov, 1949, p. 461.

[2] Actually this is a redundancy for Fedotov means 'Fedot's son'. See Aleksey V. Yefimov's discussion of Russian usage in personal names in *ORZPM*, pp. 20–1, note.

[3] Boris P. Polevoy, 'Zabytyy pokhod I. M. Rubetsa na Kamchatku v 60-kh gg. XVII veka', *Izvestiya AN SSSR, seriya geograficheskaya* (Moscow), 1964a, Vypusk 4, pp. 131, 133; 'K istorii formirovaniya geograficheskikh predstavleniy o severo-vostochnoy okonechosti Azii v XVII v.', *Sibirskiy geograficheskiy sbornik Instituta geografii Sibiri i dal'nego vostoka Sibirskogo otdeleniya AN SSSR*, Vypusk 3 (1964c), pp. 232–5.

turned on them and killed them all in order to rid themselves of such fearsome guests. Krasheninnikov then goes on to note Dezhnev's information about Alekseyev's death and to question that the Nikul River was named after him. He also states that the Kamchadals confirmed the building of the zimov'yes on the Nikul River where remains were still to be seen. In an earlier version, unpublished until 1949, Krasheninnikov specified the Nikul River as the place where Fedot Alekseyev spent the winter (document 19).

Unlike Müller Krasheninnikov places Fedot Alekseyev himself in Kamchatka, and it was with him that the tradition of Alekseyev in Kamchatka began. Others have continued it with variations in some details. Spasskiy in 1821 told essentially the same story as Krasheninnikov without disclosing his sources.[1] Since World War II L. S. Berg,[2] A. V. Yefimov,[3] and V. Yu. Vize,[4] have espoused it. But it is I. I. Ogryzko who has gone the farthest in adopting the thesis. He undertakes to establish Alekseyev as the first Russian discoverer of Kamchatka, as well as of the northern Kuril Islands.[5] Most important for his purpose is the map of 1726 of Ivan Kozyrevskiy, who first went to Kamchatka in 1700. This map was published by S. I. Baskin in 1949. On it Kozyrevskiy wrote many notations. The one for the river Fedotovshchina reads: 'There were two zimov'yes. In past years there were the men on the Kamchatka from Yakutsk [who came] by sea in koches. In our years two koches took tribute from the old men. They said they know the zimov'yes even today.'[6] For Ogryzko this is conclusive evidence that Alekseyev was on the Kamchatka River. The conviction persists accordingly that Alekseyev and his followers were carried to Kamchatka by the storm and met their end near the Tigil' River, about halfway up the western side of the peninsula. It is a thesis that bears examination, and Kuskov has made it.[7]

It is to be doubted that the storm which blew Dezhnev's koch ashore somewhere in the vicinity of Cape Navarin blew Alekseyev's 1,000 to

---

[1] Kuskov 1966, p. 97.   [2] 1946, p. 47.

[3] 1948, p. 146; 1950, p. 61.

[4] *Russkiye polyarnyye morekhody iz promyshlennykh, torgovykh i sluzhilykh lyudey XVII–XIX vv. Biograficheskiy slovar'* (Moscow and Leningrad, 1948 b), p. 16.

[5] 'Ekspeditsiya Semena Dezhneva i otkrytiye Kamchatki', *Vestnik Leningradskogo universiteta*, 1948, No. 12, pp. 36–47; 'Otkrytiye kuril'skikh ostrovov', *Yazyki i istoriya narodnostey severa SSSR* (Leningrad, 1953), pp. 167–207.

[6] Semen I. Baskin, 'Bol'shoy chertezh kamchadal'skoy zemli', *Izvestiya VGO*, Tom cxxxi (1949), p. 231; Ogryzko, 1948, p. 43; 1959, p. 43; 1953, pp. 169–70; N. N. Stepanov, 'Stepan Petrovich Krasheninnikov i yego trud "Opisaniye zemli Kamchatki"' in Krasheninnikov, 1949, p. 15. Each of the three scholars punctuates the notation differently.

[7] 1966.

1,200 km farther south near the mouth of the Kamchatka River. Would that much distance separate the landings of the two craft? Ogryzko says that the two were separated in the open sea,[1] but were they? The two parties were looking for the mouth of the Anadyr´ River. Under that circumstance one would expect them to be sailing within sight of land and thus could expect the beaching of the two boats to occur at no great distance from each other. If they were in the open sea when the storm hit them, then, a greater disparity between landing places might be expected. To be sure, we can be more certain of a coastal course as against the open sea than we can of where a violent storm would carry two helpless koches.

Ogryzko is persuaded that the 'Fedotovshchina' that appears on Kozyrevskiy's map refers to Fedot Alekseyev. But Kozyrevskiy does not say that. In 1726 the names of the participants in the voyage were still not known. The discovery of Dezhnev's reports was still ten years in the future. For all Kozyrevskiy knew the Fedot or Fedotov referred to was someone else. In fact, Ogryzko provides a basis for thinking that it was. It is his opinion that Kozyrevskiy made the connection between the name of the river, Fedotovshchina, and Fedot Alekseyev in a manner analogous to the assignment of the name 'Kozyrevskaya' to a tributary of the Kamchatka River where his father Petr had placed the natives under tribute.[2] In like fashion Fedot's presence on the Nikul River gave rise to its becoming known as the Fedotovshchina. The flaw in this argument is that the 'Fedotov' in Fedotovshchina is a patronymic, not a surname as in Kozyrevskaya, and means the 'son of Fedot'; and so it fits in much better with Müller's version than with Ogryzko's, which had Fedot Alekseyev as the first Russian in Kamchatka. Further, it is overlooked that Kozyrevskiy's notation specified *two* koches as collecting tribute from the old men. Whence came the second koch?

For the sake of argument Kuskov concedes that it might have been possible for Alekseyev to have reached the Kamchatka River. Then he asks, Could Alekseyev have wintered on the Nikul River? In answer he first asks, When did Alekseyev reach the Kamchatka River? His and Dezhnev's koches became separated sometime after October 1. Under favourable conditions a koch could make the 1,500 km from the Anadyr´ to the Kamchatka in ten days. But since a storm marked at least the first ten days of the voyage, it could have taken several days more than ten. Alekseyev most likely reached the Kamchatka in the

---

[1] 1953, p. 169.   [2] 1953, p. 170.

last third of October, when its lower course drops below freezing. Yet despite a favourable wintering location not far from the mouth of the Kamchatka Alekseyev and the others decided to go upriver some 300 km and there set themselves up for the winter. Why was presumably valuable time used in this fashion?

A second question: Could they have made it up the river in time? In the region of the Klyuchkaya River, some 100 km upriver, it freezes in early November and still earlier farther up. Unless the winter there of 1648 was unusually mild, it is doubtful that Alekseyev's koch could have reached the Nikul River.

A third question: How long did the two zimov'yes last? Kozyrevskiy, Müller, and Krasheninnikov all affirm that the Kamchadals knew the two structures in their time; at least from the ruins. Would not the Russians have been in a hurry to construct winter shelters, and therefore would they have built them solidly enough to last for sixty or seventy years when it was their intention to remain there only over the winter? They are purported next spring to have returned down the Kamchatka River and sailed around the peninsula and up its west coast.

What was the probable age of the Kamchadals who said that they sat as hostages, and is their age compatible with the years 1648–9 when these events are claimed to have happened? If they had been in their twenties at the middle of the 17th century, an age younger than that of most hostages, they would have been in their seventies at the beginning of the 18th century. Did Kamchadals have that long a life span?

It is possible, Kuskov argues, for any one of these conditions to have existed alone, unconnected with the rest, but for all of them to have combined to produce the result claimed by Ogryzko and others is highly improbable. We are asked to believe that (1) the storm carried Dezhnev to Cape Navarin and Alekseyev to the Kamchatka estuary; that (2) instead of hurrying to build winter shelters the Russians ascended the Kamchatka River for 300 km; that (3) the freezing of the Kamchatka River came late that year; that (4) the rapid construction of two zimov'yes was so good that they lasted nearly sixty or seventy years; that (5) Alekseyev abandoned such solid zimov'yes, a new river, and hostages not to return to the Anadyr', but to sail south; and that (6) despite Russian custom the river on which he wintered was not called Alekseyev, his patronymic, or Popov, a sobriquet by which he was sometimes known, but by the patronymic of his given name, Fedot. To this list of improbables may be added the consideration that as a merchant commissioned as a customs agent Alekseyev was authorized to collect customs duties, but not tribute from the natives; nor was he authorized to take hostages. It was to exercise these last two functions that Dezhnev had been sent with Alekseyev and the others. In this connection one is prompted to ask where was Ankudinov during this time? He had been taken into Alekseyev's koch after the wrecking of his own. Was he lost at sea? As a service-man he was empowered to collect tribute and take hostages. It would not have been in the nature of the man to yield authority to Alekseyev. And in the view of Alekseyev's wound from the fight with the Chukchi might not Ankudinov's chances for survival have been the greater? In face of all these forceful arguments the burden of proof rests on Ogryzko and those of like mind. It is to be remarked that Belov, with whom we disagree on a number of matters, is not one of them.[1]

Greater force is given to Kuskov's arguments by virtue of the fact that an alternate explanation of the fate of Alekseyev and Ankudinov exists, one without troublesome questions to be answered, one quite in keeping with the nature and hazards of the enterprise upon which they embarked, and that explanation is, of course, the one reported by Dezhnev as told to him by Alekseyev's Yakut woman. Meanwhile, if the Fedotov legend has a rational explanation, it most likely will be found in the reports of visits by Russians to Kamchatka long before Luka Morozko (1665–6) and Vladimir Atlasov. The upriver location of the two zimov'yes, their solid and enduring construction, and the more likely age of the hostages fit in much better with the reports of Russians on the Kamchatka in the 1660s, having come there overland.[2]

[1] 1973, p. 122, but cf. 1949, p. 464.
[2] Cf. Polevoy, 1964b and 1964c. In view of the fact that Krasheninnikov's account of the Fedotov tradition constitutes its basic and most detailed explication, which Kozyrevskiy's notation, in Ogryzko's opinion, confirmed, it should be observed that Krasheninnikov did not present it unquestioningly. Like Herodotus he reported what he heard, noting that it was oral tradition and qualifying it with the adverb 'supposedly'. Too, he noted that there was doubt that the Nikul River was named Fedotovshchina after Alekseyev. He also recognized the account of the Yakut woman and tried to reconcile the two accounts by suggesting that Alekseyev and his companions did not die on the Tigil' River, but somewhere along the Olyutora coast while trying to reach the Anadyr'. The fact that he wrote an earlier account (document 19) of the Fedotov episode, which contained errors regarding the voyage before the storm, and revised it into the form in which it was published, is indicative of his effort to get at the truth. Too, that he wrote more than one version suggests that the Fedotov legend circulated in more than one form.

CHAPTER 9

THE GREAT ROCKY NOS

The identity of the great rocky nos has been, and should be, a matter of major concern to both sceptics and believers regarding Dezhnev's voyage. If it can be shown that there exists somewhere on the Arctic coast, as against the Bering Strait, a promontory with the features ascribed to the great rocky nos by Dezhnev, such as Cape Shelagskiy, one can contend that after reaching that cape he and Alekseyev did not round the Chukotskiy Peninsula, but crossed it instead and resumed the voyage along its southern coast (Slovtsov) or stumbled onto the Anadyr' River (Golder), never seeing the Bering Strait. If not, then that contention disintegrates. For the proponents of the voyage, following Müller, it is necessary to establish the nos at the northeastern corner of Asia so as to demonstrate that by rounding it, through the Bering Strait, the two men went all the way be sea, thereby proving the separation of Asia and America. Meanwhile, it is ironic that of the several phases and aspects of the voyage Dezhnev provides the most details about the great rocky nos, yet it is about its identity that there has been the most debate and disagreement.

Five promontories have found advocates, beginning with Müller. But before examining the cases for the five we need to note the characteristics of the nos as described by Dezhnev and his associates. Most of the characteristics are given in Dezhnev's report of 1655 (document 9), in the following passage, which is taken from Müller's copy of the report since it was the only one available until the last two decades and thus the one used by scholars until recently:

In going by sea from the Kovyma River to the Anadyr' River there is a nos. It extends far into the sea, but it is not the nos which lies off the Chukoch'ya River.[1] Mikhaylo Stadukhin did not reach this nos. Opposite this nos are two

[1] It has been generally believed that this nos is Cape Shelagskiy and that the Chukoch'ya River is the one about 45 km west of the Kolyma River. However, according to Polevoy, Lavrentsova doubts that this Chukoch'ya River is the one Dezhnev alludes to, for it is too far west of Cape Shelagskiy. Polevoy thinks that it was one of the left tributaries of the Anadyr', the present Tanyurer River, from whose upper reaches the Chukotskiy range of mountains extends northwest, culminating in Cape Shelagskiy. If one views the land between the Arctic Ocean on the north (right) and Chaunskaya Bay on the west (left) as a peninsula ending at Cape Shelagskiy, then it too extends 'far into the sea' (1965a, pp. 109–10).

islands, and Chukchi live on them They have carved teeth, [in] holes in the lips, [made from] fish tooth bone. This nos lies between north and northeast, and on the Russian side there is a landmark: a little river emerges. The Chukchi set up a camp (*stanov'ye*) there, which consists of towers of whalebones. The nos turns around (*krugom*) [and] under (*podleglo*) toward the Onandyr' River. A good run from the nos to the Onandyr' is three days-and-nights and no more. To go from the coast to the river is no farther (*nedaleye*) for the Anandyr' empties into a bay.[1]

In the report of the same year submitted by him and Nikita Semenov (document 10, p. 63) some of the foregoing details are repeated and a few added:

[Yur'ye] did not reach the great rocky nos. That nos extends very far into the sea, and a great many Chukchi live on it. On the islands opposite the nos live people called 'toothed' becaused they pierce the lip with 2 teeth [made from] large bones. This is not the first sacred nos from the Kolyma. We, Semeyka and companions, know this great nos because the boat of Gerasim Ankudinov and his men was wrecked on it, and we took the shipwrecked men into our boats. We saw the 'toothed' people on an island (*na ostrovu*). The Anandyr' River and sandspit are far from that nos...

The petition of Fedor Yemel'yan Vetoshka and associates (document 11) also mentions the nos, repeating some of the details of the other two: the extension of the nos into the sea, the many people on it, the islands – which they knew – with many people – which they saw – and the great distance of the nos and islands from the Anadyr' River.

From these descriptions ten features may be set down by which to identify the nos: It was big and rocky or mountainous, extended far into the sea, lay between north and northeast, and turned around and under toward the Anadyr' River. At the same time it was far from that river, though in a good run one could sail from the nos to the river in three days-and-nights. Opposite the nos were two islands inhabited by Chukchi, who wore 'fish tooth bone' or labrets of walrus ivory through the flesh near the mouth. On 'the Russian side' of the nos there was a small river, which emptied into the sea, and on this river Dezhnev and his men saw a Chukchi camp of towers made from whalebones. Finally, 'a great many Chukchi' lived on this nos.[2]

Müller was the first to try to identify the great rocky nos. He was faced with the problem of the pioneer, of not having much information to work with. His was not the advantage available to the modern

[1] *DAI*, Tom IV, p. 26.   [2] *DAI*, Tom IV, pp. 15, 21, 26.

scholar of carefully plotted maps which make this task largely that of finding the nos which best fits the characteristics specified by Dezhnev. Müller had to start from scratch, to conceptualize it first of all. The state of Russian, and thus western, knowledge of Chukotka, the area east of the Kolyma River and north of the Gulf of Anadyr´, in Müller's time was mixed at best. Several maps of the northeastern corner of Siberia had been made in the later 17th and early 18th centuries.[1] Most of them were holographic, the so-called sketch maps (*chertezhi*), without grids or scientifically determined base points. They were based on the reports of men like Yerastov, Dezhnev, and Stadukhin, who reported where they had been or what they had seen or learned from the natives. Aside from Dezhnev only Isay Ignat´yev, the two Stadukhins, and Kurbat Ivanov had firsthand knowledge of the coastline of Chukotka, mostly of the northwestern portions. Some information on the interior of the Chukotskiy Peninsula had been communicated by Petr Popov, a service-man sent from Anadyrsk by land in 1711 to the peninsular Chukchi to invite their submission to Russian authority, in a report that same year.[2] Even so, much of what was shown on the maps of this area was speculative and conjectural, so typical of the era of learning the world's geography.

Most of the maps depict Chukotka as unconnected with any large land mass other than Asia, as washed by oceans on three sides, perhaps reflecting some dissemination of knowledge of Dezhnev's voyage. On several of these maps Chukotka is shown as having two peninsulas of good size.[3] The one which particularly commands our attention is one named Shalatskoy or Shelaginskoy Nos on some of the maps. It extends to the north or northeast and is situated between the Kolyma River and the second and more easterly peninsula. Todays's Cape Shelagskiy is most likely the fact behind this imaginary peninsula. No one besides Dezhnev and maybe the two Stadukhins had passed east of Cape Shelagskiy, and that cape was believed to be difficult to circumnavigate or even impassable because of ice.[4] The other peninsula was south of the first one and extended eastward. It was called the Anadyrskoy Nos. The ocean between them formed a bay or large bight. How many of these maps Müller knew he does not say. He mentions three, two in such a way as to indicate clearly that they influenced his concept of the great rocky nos.

[1] For some of them see chapter 10, maps 10–18.
[2] *PSI*, Tom I, pp. 456–9.
[3] E.g. Fisher, 1977, pp. 29–31, 42–3 and figures nos. 6, 12, 16–18, 25.
[4] For a more extended discussion of this promontory see Fisher, 1977, pp. 42–7.

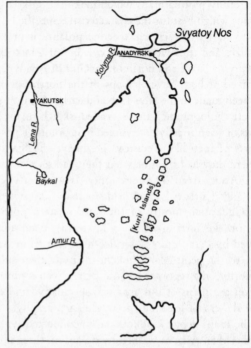

Map 2   Shestakov's map of Eastern Siberia (Grekov, 1960, p. 47)

The first, the one least influential, is that presented in St Petersburg in 1725 by Afanasiy F. Shestakov, a cossack leader from eastern Siberia (Map 2). Though it depicts a disproportionately small and only generally contoured Chukotka, on the northern side is to be noted a northward stretching peninsula. Müller says that he trusted this map only when corroborated by other evidence.[1] The second is the Anadyrskaya or so-called L'vov map (Map 3), which, Müller informs us, he obtained from a retired service-man, Ivan L'vov, in Yakutsk.[2] That Müller gave it much credence is indicated by his singling it out for particular attention and description in his 1758 account and by the fact that he took it back with him to St Petersburg. On it appear two peninsulas. The larger of the two is a broad-based peninsula extending

[1] 1758a, pp. 49–50; 1758b, Tom VII, p. 119; 1761, p. xxi; Fisher, 1977, pp. 164–5. The most legible reproduction of this map is in Grekov, 1960, p. 47.

[2] *Atlas*, no. 55; Müller, 1758a, pp. 51–2; 1758b, Tom VII, pp. 195–6; 1761, p. xxii. Sergey Ye. Fel', historian of 18th-century Russian cartography, shows that L'vov could not have been the author of the map and that is should be called the Anadyrskaya map. It was made probably around 1700 (*Kartografiya Rossii XVIII veka* [Moscow, 1960]; Fisher, 1977, p. 45, note 32).

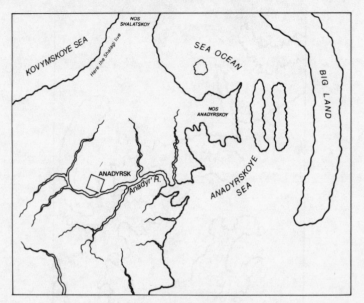

Map 3   Anadyrskaya map (*Atlas*, no. 55; Yefimov, 1950, p. 111; 1971, pp. 156–7)

far to the northeast and is cut off at the top by the edge of the map. It is labelled Shalatskoy Nos on the map, though Müller states that it is commonly called 'by us' Chukotskoy Nos. The other, to the south and facing east, reflects the modern Chukotskiy Peninsula. It is broad-faced with pointed capes at each corner, and though it is far from the Anadyr´ River, it is named Anadyrskoy Nos, Müller explains, from that river. In the open bay between the two peninsulas an unnamed island is shown.[1] The third map influencing Müller was made by Philipp Johann Tabbert von Strahlenberg, the Swedish prisoner of war who lived in Tobol´sk and moved around western Siberia. He composed one of the more knowledgeable maps of Siberia, which was published in his *Das nord und östliche Theil von Europa and Asia* in 1730 (Map 4). It portrays a narrow and elongated northward-extending peninsula east of the Kolyma River, labelled 'Noss Tszalatskoy', and an eastward extending one, called 'Noss Anadirskoy' and also marked 'Chukchi land'.[2]

[1] *Atlas*, map no. 55; Fisher, 1977, p. 46.
[2] *Atlas*, map no. 74; Müller, 1758a, pp. 281–2; 1758b, Tom VIII, p. 405; Fisher, 1977, pp. 46–7, 48.

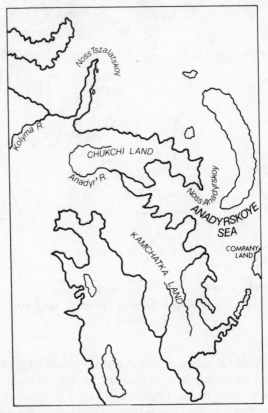

Map 4   Strahlenberg's map of Great Tartary, 1730 (detail) (*Atlas*, no. 74;
Strahlenberg, 1730, at end of volume)

Another influence on Müller must certainly have been that of Bering.
Elsewhere I have advanced the view that prior to departure on his first
voyage he had come to believe in the existence of the peninsula labelled
on the Anadyrskaya and Strahlenberg maps as the Shalatskoy Nos,
which Müller subsequently formulated as his Chukotskoy Nos. By
following its coast, as the instructions of Peter the Great seemed to order
him to do, he would be led north and east to America. He learned
otherwise in the course of that voyage.[1] He did not, however give up
the idea of the Shalatskoy Nos, only the idea that it might be an isthmus
or that it extended close to North America. The map drafted by the

---

[1] Fisher, 1977, chapter 4. Bering's objective was America, not a strait.

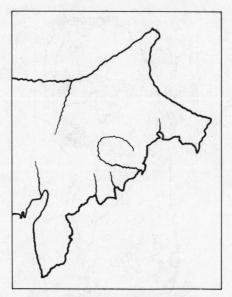

Map 5   Map of the First Kamchatka Expedition, 1729 (detail) (*Atlas*, no.
63; Berg, 1946, facing p. 88)

expedition (Map 5) shows the persistence of his idea.[1] On that map
there extends from the northern part of the Chukotskiy Peninsula
another peninsula pointing northeastward and shaped, in the words of
Karl von Baer, like 'a bull's horn'.[2] The French version labels it 'Cap
de Scheleginski',[3] whereas the Russian ethnographic version carries the
notation 'Shalagi nomadize [here]'. The eastern end of the Chukotskiy
Peninsula is square, and the southern corner is labelled 'Cap de
Tziokotskago' on the former and 'Ugol Chukotsko' (i.e. Chukotskiy
corner) on the latter.[4] Bering refers to the latter in his 'Report',
submitted to the Admiralty College on his return to St Petersburg in
March 1730,[5] and the name Cape Chukotskiy (in distinction from the
Chukotskiy Peninsula) has endured into modern times.[6] Prior to the

[1] *Atlas*, maps nos. 63–7 show it in four varied contexts. Also Fisher, 1977, pp. 86 and
89, figures nos. 26 and 29 respectively.
[2] *Peter's des Grossen Verdienste um die Erweiterung der geographischen Kenntnisse* (St.
Petersburg, 1872), p. 138.   [3] Fisher, 1977, p. 87, figure no. 27.
[4] *Atlas*, map no. 65; Fisher, 1977, p. 89, figure no. 29.
[5] Aleksandr S. Polonskiy, 'Pervaya kamchatskaya ekspeditsiya Beringa, 1725–29 goda',
Otechestvennyya zapiski (St Petersburg), [ser. 3], Tom LXXV (1851), otdel viii, p. 18.
[6] Some modern maps no longer identify it thus. The *Sailing directions for the east coast
of Siberia* of the U.S. Hydrographic Office, which does, describes it as 'a dark cape rising

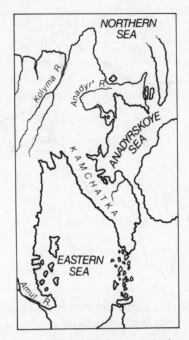

Map 6   Homann's map of Kamchatka, 1725 (*Atlas*, no. 58; Yefimov, 1950, p. 112; 1971, p. 171)

departure of Müller and Bering for Siberia in 1733 the two men discussed Bering's first voyage and matters related to it. As we noted in chapter 1, no doubt it was what Bering told Müller that alerted the latter to be on the lookout for evidence of the voyage from the Lena to Kamchatka 'fifty or sixty years ago'. So too must Müller have been persuaded to accept the concept of the mythical Shalatskoy Nos. We know from a map that he drew that Joseph Delisle, a member of the Imperial Academy of Sciences and adviser to the Admiralty College, accepted it.[1] If Delisle did, why not Müller?

No doubt, too, through Bering Müller must have become acquainted with the map of Kamchatka published in 1725 by Johann B. Homann, cartographer and map publisher in Nürnberg (Map 6). This map was

to a pointed ridge with a rounded hill at the end, off [whose] southern side are several high pointed rocks'. This is in contrast with Cape Chaplina to the east, which consists of a triangular sandspit surrounding a freshwater lake.

[1] *Atlas*, map no. 79; Fisher, 1977, p. 88; Golder, 1914, frontispiece; 1925, opposite p. 72.

made in Russia and was sent to Homann on the order of Peter the Great. It was this map on which, in all probability, Peter based his instructions to Bering in 1725. It shows the Chukotskiy Peninsula with reasonable accuracy, but more important it displays a northward-directed peninsula, broad at the base and tapering to a rounded tip, which extends from the north side of Chukotka into the Arctic.[1] Here is another version of the mythical Shalatskoy Nos.

There are two other possible, but unconfirmed, sources for Müller's concept of the great rocky nos. One of them is the report of Petr Popov, the cossack who visited the peninsular Chukchi in the summer of 1711 (document 33), a report which Captain James King thought Müller had used. Müller does reproduce Popov's report in a somewhat abridged and free translation when discussing the Chukchi,[2] but he gives no indication as to whether he drew from it any particular feature which he assigned to the nos. The second is Nicolaas C. Witsen, about whom more will be said in the next chapter. He published a map in 1687 which had considerable influence on European geographers. On it is reflected the concept of the mythical Shalatskoy Nos. But aside from one brief reference to Witsen in connection with Chukotka[3] Müller does not elsewhere mention him in his 1758 account.

Some time after uncovering Dezhnev's reports Müller drafted a map in rough form showing the northern part of Siberia from the Lena River to the mouth of the Anadyr´ (Map 7).[4] Perhaps the most conspicuous feature is a large mushroom-shaped peninsula, squat and round, in the upper right corner, connected with the mainland by a short narrow neck of land. It is labelled 'Tschukotzkoi Noss-Schelagi et Tschuktschi'. He carried this formulation over to his Academy Map of 1754 and 1758 (Map 8), which his Nachrichten von Seereisen was intended to accompany and explain.[5] On this map the head of the peninsula is less squat and more round and is roughly 325 km (200 miles) in diameter. In his 'Information about the Northern Sea Passage' of 1737 he names it 'the so-called Chukotskoy – the same as the Shelaginskoy or Shalatskoy – Nos' (document 1), and in his Nachrichten von Seereisen he calls attention to the fact that it differs from previous representations of the Chukotskoy Nos, particularly those in the Academy's atlas and on

[1] Fisher, 1977, pp. 64–5, 68–71.

[2] 1758a, pp. 56–60; 1758b, Tom VII, pp. 200–2; 1761, pp. xxiv–xxv.

[3] Johannes Keuning, 'Nicolaas Witsen as a cartographer', Imago mundi, vol. XI (1954), p. 99.

[4] Atlas, map no. 79; ORŽPM, map packet.

[5] Müller, 1761, frontispiece; L. Breitfuss, 'Early maps of northeastern Asia and the lands around the north Pacific', Imago mundi, Vol. III (1939), insert; Fisher, 1977, p. 100.

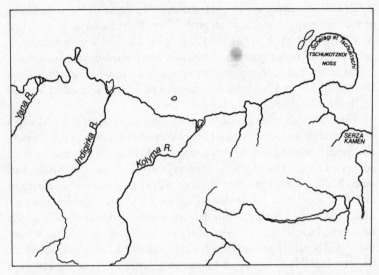

Map 7   Müller's preliminary map of Northeastern Siberia (detail)
(*ORZPM*, map packet)

Strahlenberg's map, on which it is much narrower.[1] From the Kolyma
River the coast runs eastward and then northeastward to this head. On
the eastern side the coast runs south from the head, then southeast to
form the northern coast of what the Anadyrskaya map calls the
Anadyrskoy Nos, but which Müller does not label.[2] The isthmus
connecting the head with the mainland is short, narrow in the north
and flaring broadly to the south. On the head appears the notation 'Land
of the Chukchi extent of which is not known', and for that reason
Müller outlines it with a broken line. It extends northeastward some
450 km (280 miles) almost to the 75th parallel, to a latitude about
600 km (375 miles) north of the latitude of the mouth of the Kolyma,
and east of the Anadyrskoy Nos, to 205° E. longitude.[3] This cartographic
depiction of the nos conforms with Müller's description of it in his 1737
article (document 1) where he states that it 'extended very far into the
sea in a northeasterly direction, then turned to the south. Opposite the
nos, maybe on the western side he [Dezhnev] saw two islands...'[4] As

[1] 1758a, pp. 279–80, 281; 1758b, Tom VIII, pp. 403, 404–5; 1761, p. 67; Belov, 1955,
p. 122.   [2] 1758a, pp. 118–19; 1758b, Tom VII, p. 394.
[3] These distances have been calculated on the basis of the map's grid.
[4] This depiction explains why in the 1737 article he says that Taras Stadukhin build new
boats on the 'eastern' instead of the southern side as one would expect when looking at
the Chukotskiy Peninsula on today's maps.

Map 8   Müller's Academy map, 1758 (detail) (Müller, 1761, frontispiece)

Müller depicts it the Chukotskoy Nos is the easternmost point of Asia.
On the earlier map two 'toothed' islands appear off the northwestern
coast of the head; they are omitted on the Academy map. On the other
hand, on the latter a broken line traces the 'track of 3 [sic] Russian ships
in 1648'.[1] The Anadyrskoy Nos is drawn as blunt-faced, but is not
named; only its northeastern corner carries a name, Serdtse Kamen´,
in the text as well as on the map.[2] On the map the track of Bering's
voyage of 1728 ends at this cape. The southeastern corner of the nos
is a sharply pointed cape, but is not named.

Müller, it is obvious, depended upon Dezhnev's reports for the shape
and features of the great rocky promontory, as well as its northeasterly
direction, for they differ from those on the Shestakov, Anadyrskiy, and
Strahlenberg maps. They constituted eyewitness evidence and as such
had priority over other sources. And so the 'Tschukotskoi Noss' on
Müller's maps is large (400 km or 250 miles in diameter), round (it turns
around and under), extends far into the sea (about 450 km or 280 miles),
points northeast (it lies between north and northeast) with two
'toothed' islands nearby (on the first version), and it is far from the

[1] See p. 153, note 3 above.
[2] 1758a, p. 118; 1758b, Tom VII, p. 394; 1761, p. 48; Grekov, 1960, p. 35; Fisher, 1977,
p. 99. For the location of Serdtse Kamen´ see this chapter, p. 211 below.

Anadyr′ (about 1,570 km or 970 miles).[1] Whether an unnamed river on the western approach is the little river on 'the Russian side' Müller does not say. It is probably too far west to qualify as such. The rocky character of the promontory, the natives with labrets, and the many Chukchi hardly lend themselves to depiction on other than a large scale map. Müller appears guilty of one discrepancy, one inherent in the evidence and perplexing to later investigators: the nos is not within sailing distance of three days-and-nights of the Anadyr′.[2] Still, where does one put the nos so that it is far from the Anadyr′ and at the same time within 72 hours' sailing time of that river? Are the two characteristics compatible? Is 72 hours' sailing time far? Müller provides no explanation of this dilemma nor indicates any awareness of it.

Meanwhile, in light of what appears to have been Müller's sources for his depiction of the northeast corner of Siberia we can understand why he shows two peninsulas where only one peninsula actually exists. But what is not clear is why he chose to identify Dezhnev's great rocky nos as the imaginary Shalatskoy Nos instead of the real Anadyrskoy Nos. Is there anything in the information provided by Dezhnev which helps to explain that choice? It is understandable why Müller preferred Dezhnev's information regarding the size, shape, and orientation of the great rocky nos over that in his sources: Dezhnev had been there, and no other Russian had. But Dezhnev does not mention two peninsulas, only one.

Dezhnev's information provides no explicit or conclusive answer, but it does suggest something by way of explanation. There is his statement that the nos lay between north and northeast. This would associate it more with the Shalatskoy Nos than with the Anadyrskoy Nos. Then there is the reference to the little river on the Russian side, which Müller took to mean the western side, the one from which the Russians approached the nos. Aside from mentioning the nos near the Chukoch′ya River Dezhnev mentions no other nos between the two rivers. Conceivably, then, the great rocky nos was the first nos east of the Chukoch′ya River, and that would make it the Shalatskoy Nos. In Müller's mistaken understanding of the northeastern corner the Anadyrskoy Nos had to be the second peninsula, and Dezhnev's failure

[1] These figures are based on the grid of Müller's map. From the mid-point on the eastern side of the Tschukotzkoi Noss to the southeast corner of the unnamed peninsula south of it is 10° of latitude or 1,000 km; from the corner to the mouth of the Anadyr′ is 10° of longitude, which along the 65th parallel is 470 km, for a total of 1,570 km.

[2] Polevoy, 1970b, p. 151.

to mention it could be attributed to his failure to say anything about the voyage between the point of the wrecking of Ankudinov's koch and the fight with the Chukchi on September 20. To put it another way, there is little or nothing in Dezhnev's information to contradict Müller's selection of the Shalatskiy promontory as Dezhnev's nos. Only Dezhnev's statement that one could sail from the nos to the Anadyr' in good weather in three days-and-nights might have given Müller pause in reaching his conclusion, but evidently it did not. And so he superimposed the great rocky nos on the Shalatskoy Nos, not knowing that he had chosen an imaginary peninsula instead of the real one.

The error of Müller's identification of the great rocky nos was revealed some two decades after the publication of the Academy map and accompanying text. It was done by the only truly convincing means possible, by exploration of the waters adjacent to Chukotka. Captain Cook and his successor in command, Captain Charles Clerke, explored the waters north and south of the Bering Strait in 1778-9. In August and September 1778 Cook's two vessels sailed through the Bering Strait into the Chukchi Sea and probed the pack ice north of Chukotka as far northwest as North Cape, now Cape Shmidta, at 69° N. latitude. Ice blocked farther northwestward advance. The following summer, after Cook's death in February 1779 in Hawaii, the expedition, now under the command of Clerke, again sailed through the Strait into the Arctic and searched as far north as 69° and 70° for an opening through the ice, mostly north of the Bering Strait between the longitude of Serdtse Kamen' and the American coast at Icy Cape.[1] On both occasions the Englishmen obtained a good view of the eastern face of the Chukotskiy Peninsula. In preparation for his task Cook had studied Müller's map and account of the Russian voyages, the modification of the map by Jacob Stählin von Storcksburg, secretary of the Russian Academy of Sciences, and his accompanying text, published in 1774 in English translation;[2] and Bering's account of his voyage of 1728 in the English paraphrasing in Volume II of the second edition of John Harris' *Navigantium atque Itinerantium Bibliotheca*, the addition of the editor, John Campbell.[3] Both Müller's and Stählin's maps were consulted frequently by Cook and his officers in the course of voyaging in the Bering and Chukchi seas. Stählin's map left Müller's Chukotskoy

---

[1] James Cook, *The journals of Captain James Cook on his voyages of discovery* (edited by J. C. Beaglehole; Cambridge, Eng.), Vol. III (1967), pp. 688-9.

[2] Masterson and Brower, 1948, p. 5; Beaglehole in Cook, 1967, p. lxii.

[3] (London, 1748), pp. 1018-22; see Fisher, 1977, p. 181.

Nos intact, but dropped it to 73° N. latitude, separated Chukotka from the westernmost bulge of North America by 15° of longitude, and placed a large island, which he called Alaschka, between them, twice as far from America as from Asia.[1]

Returning from the expedition's first excursion into the Chukchi Sea and along the northern coast of Chukotka, Cook wrote in his journal under the date of 2 September 1778 the following:

In the evening we passed the Eastern Cape... from which the Coast trends SW. It is the same point of land that we past on the 11 of last Month, thought then to be the East point of the island of Alaschka, but it is no other than the Eastern promontory of Asia and probably the proper Tchuktschi Noss. Though Mr. Muller in his Map of the Russian Discoverys, places the Tchuktschi Nos nearly in 75° of latitude and extends it some what to the Eastward of this Cape... it appears to me that he had no good Authority for so doing as will more fully appear from his account of the distance between the Nos and the River Anidar. But as I hope to visit these parts again I shall leave the descussion of this point untill then, and untill then I must conclude, as Behring did before me, this Promontory to be the Eastern point of Asia...

Cook then proceeds to a description of this promontory which, considering that he saw it only from the sea and did not set foot on it, is strikingly close to the modern description:

It is a Peninsula of considerable height, joined to a continent by a very low and to appearance narrow neck of land; it shew[s] a steep rocky cliff next the Sea and off the very point are some rocks like Spires. It is situated in the latitude of 66° 06′ N. longitude 190° 22′ East [169° 38′ W.], and is distant from Cape Prince of Wales on the American coast 13 leagues in the direction of N 53° W.[2] The land about this promontory is composed of hill and Valley, the first terminates at the Sea in Steep rocky points and the latter in low shores; the hills seem to be naked rocks, but the vallies had a greenish hue, but distitude of tree or shrub.[3]

[1] Beaglehole in Cook, 1967, pp. lxii–lxiv.

[2] Cook was off the true longitude by only 2′ to the east, but he underestimated the distance from Cape Prince of Wales. It is about 18 leagues or 55 miles.

[3] Cook, 1967, pp. 430–1. According to *Sailing directions for the east coast of Siberia* (p. 55 – Chg 2) the name Mys or Cape Dezhneva, which replaced East Cape as the name for the peninsula described by Cook, is applied to the central and easternmost headland on the peninsula, between Mys Peyek and Mys Uelen. In its common usage, however, Cape Dezhneva refers to the whole peninsula, not the smaller tip, and that is the usage followed in this study. Indeed the British pilot book. *Bering Sea and Strait pilot* (pp. 549–50) distinguishes between Poluostrov (peninsula) Dezhneva and Mys Dezhneva.

It may be pointed out that the dimensions of East Cape as calculated from the expedition's Chart of Norton Sound and Beering's Strait (chart LIII in James Cook and James King,

Some other of Cook's observations bear recording. As the expedition proceeded southeastward along the northern coast of Chukotka from North Cape, he observed on August 31 that

I was now well assured that this was the coast of the Tchuktschi, or the NE coast of Asia, and that thus far Captain Behring proceeded in 1728, that is to this head which Mr Muller says is called Serdze Kamen, on accou[n]t of a rock upon it in the shape of a heart; but I take Mr Mullers knowlidge of these parts to have been very imperfect. There are many elevaded rocks upon this Cape and possibly some may have the shape of a heart; it is a pretty lofty promontory with a steep rocky cliff facing the Sea and lies in the Latitude of 67° 63′ N, Longitude 187° 11′ E [172° 49′ W.].¹

The entries corrected two of Müller's errors. Cook found no evidence that Müller's Chukotskoy Nos extended northeastward; rather the northern coast of Chukotka ran northwest–southeast. Nor was Cape Serdtse Kamen´ situated as far east as Müller placed it, on the Bering Strait, essentially the site of East Cape. The true Serdtse Kamen´, with the supposedly heartshaped rock, is located at 66° 57′ N. latitude, 171° 43′ W. (188° 17′ E.) longitude, 135 km (85 miles) northwest of East Cape. On the other hand, Cook was not perfectly informed on this point either. His coordinates place Serdtse Kamen´ too far west and north, by one degree in each direction; and Bering did not see that cape. East Cape was the last bit of land he saw before his turn-around at 67° 18′ N. latitude, out of sight of land.² Even so, with Serdtse Kamen now more accurately located Cook was free to name the easternmost point of Asia East Cape.

A few days later, on September 4, while passing along the eastern face of the Chukotskiy Peninsula Cook recorded this in his journal:

A voyage to the Pacific ocean [London, 1784], Vol. II, between pp. 466 and 467) differ from those found on modern maps, specifically ONC C-8. The expedition's map shows the east–west distance of East Cape to be 36′ or about 27 km and the north–south distance across the isthmus to be 4½′ or 8·4 km. ONC C-8 shows the east–west distance of Cape Dezhneva to be between 20′ and 30′ or 15 to 23 km, depending on where one considers the isthmus to end and the mainland to begin. The trans-isthmus distance is 13 km. Thus the peninsula as East Cape is represented as more elongated and narrower than as Cape Dezhneva. This elongated depiction is repeated on the map of the Bering Sea in Mikhail D. Tebenkov's atlas of 1852 (*Atlas severozapadnykh beregov Ameriki ot beringova proliva do mysa Korrientes i ostrovov aleutskikh s prisovokupleniyem nekotorykh mest severovostochnago berega Azii* [St Petersburg, 1852], map no. 1), as shown on Map 10 (p. 253 below). See Kotzebue's description, p. 216 below. ¹ Cook, 1967, p. 429.

² Cook, 1967, p. 429, note 4; Fisher, 1977, pp. 82, 94; ONC C-8. It has recently been learned that Bering's vessel advanced a bit beyond 67° 18′, to 67° 24′ (A. A. Sopotsko, 'Vakhtennyye zhurnaly korablej V. I. Beringa', *Izvestiya VGO*, Tom CX (1978), Vypusk 2, p. 166.

At the same time the Southernmost point of the Main land bore 83° W distant 12 leagues, I take this to be the point which Capt. Behring calls the east Point of Suchotski or Cape Tchuktschi,[1] probably from some of that Nation coming off to him there. I make its latitude at be 64° 13' N.

In justice to Behring's Memory, I must say he has deleneated this Coast very well and fixed the latitude and longitude of the points better than could be expected from the Methods he had to go by. This judgement is not formed from Mr. Mullers accou[n]t of the Voyage or his Chart, but from the account of it in Harris's Collection of Voyages and a Map thereto annexed...which is both more circumstantial and accurate than that of Mr. Mullers.[2]

Cook did not, we know, return the next summer to continue the search for a northern passage or confirm his tentative conclusions regarding Müller's Chukotskoy Nos. After the return of the expedition to England in 1780 the Admiralty commissioned Captain James King to finish Cook's account of the voyage for publication, Cook's journal having ended one month before his death.[3] King, 'the intellectual of the voyage', had been second lieutenant on Cook's vessel, the *Resolution* and then advanced to first lieutenant following his death; after the death of Clerke he was named commander of the *Discovery*.[4] And so it fell to him to spell out the arguments refuting Müller's concept of the northeastern corner of Asia and supporting Cook's identification of Dezhnev's promontory, Müller's Tchukotskoi Noss, as East Cape, as the easternmost point of Asia (document 34).

The expedition's survey, so King's argument goes, revealed that no part of the Asiatic continent extends east of 192° 22' E. (167° 38' W.) longitude, and that 'the northeastern extremity' falls south of 70° N. latitude. Müllers' map places the northern limit of the Chukotskoy Nos just south of the 75th parallel and the eastern limit at the 205th meridian E. Where Müller's peninsula was supposed to be the expedition found only water and ice. To be sure, King notes, the expedition did not sail westward beyond North Cape, in latitude 69°, and it was unable to sail beyond 70° N. elsewhere, and so he concedes that there might be land north of these points which approached or joined America, as James Burney, then a lieutenant on the *Discovery*, was later to assert in 1818.[5] But King doubts it, for along the 69th parallel the two

---

[1] Bering did not use such terms. He called it the 'Chukotskiy corner' (*ugol chukotsko*) (Polonskiy, 1851, p. 18; Fisher, 1977, pp. 82, 95).
[2] Cook, 1967, p. 433. The map is that of the First Kamchatka Expedition in English translation.
[3] Beaglehole in Cook, 1967, pp. v, ccii.
[4] Beaglehole in Cook, 1967, pp. lxxvi, clxv; Cook, 1967, pp. 544, 1273.
[5] 1818, pp. 9–23; p. 13 above.

continents diverge so far as to be 300 miles apart and the Asiatic coast west of North Cape was not likely to trend eastward in sight of America. Rather, he was persuaded that the Asiatic coast continued to trend northwestward from 69° N. latitude.[1] The Chukotskoy Nos was always represented as separating the Kolymskoye Sea from the Anadyrskoye Sea, which could not be the case if a 'considerable cape' stretched to the northeast in the higher latitudes.

With Müller's Chukotskoy Nos eliminated, Dezhnev's great rocky nos had to be some other cape, and King's choice, like Cook's, was East Cape. Referring to the account of Dezhnev's voyage in Coxe's *Account of the Russian Discoveries between Russia and America*,[2] based on Müller and Dezhnev's report as translated by Simon Peter Pallas, King notes that the distance from East Cape to the mouth of the Anadyr´ was 120 leagues (666 km) and could be sailed in three day-and-nights in a fair wind. The 'North Easternmost extremity' could not be a cape north of East Cape, and it probably was not one south of it for none had two islands opposite it inhabited by people 'through whose lips run pieces of the teeth of the sea-horse'. For King these two circumstances were so 'striking and unequivocal' as to be 'conclusive' in establishing East Cape as the Chukotskoy Nos, as the great rocky nos. Dezhnev's description of the nos as stretching far into the sea and situated between north and northeast was not 'irreconcilable' with Cook's and King's opinion if Dezhnev were supposed 'to have taken these bearings from the small bight which lies to the Westward of the Cape'. It was this description, King claims, that induced Müller to give the country of the Chukchi the form he did, and 'the remarkable coincidence' between East Cape and 'their promontory or isthmus', the configurational conformity, further persuaded King that Dezhnev's nos is East Cape.[3] King concludes his argument by taking note of the deposition of Petr Popov (document 33) regarding the Chukchi, information which King thinks Müller seems to have used in formulating his concept of the Chukotskoy Nos. Popov's observation that it took ten weeks to travel from Anadyrsk to the nos and that there was a large island, 'the big land' whose inhabitants put large teeth through their cheeks, were consistent with the identification of East Cape as Dezhnev's nos.

[1] The Arctic coast of Chukotka runs northwest–southeast all the way from Cape Dezhneva to the 176th meridian E.

[2] 1780, pp. 315-16, note; 1787, pp. 253-5, note. Cook, of course, did not consult this work, it having been published after his death.

[3] Polevoy ('Soobshcheniye S. I. Dezhneva o "bol'shom kamennom nose" i proiskhozdeniye ego lozhnogo tolkovaniya', *Izvestiya AN SSSR, seriya geograficheskaya*, 1970b, Vypusk. 6, pp. 153, 154) stresses this point.

The effect of the findings of Cook's north Pacific expedition on the cartography of Chukotka has not commanded particular attention. Nevertheless it can be safely said that his findings effectively disposed of the myth of the Shalatskoy Nos, or Müller's Chukotskoy Nos. After all, Müller's conjecture had to give way to Cook's on-the-spot information. The effect is seen on several maps in the Soviet *Atlas of Geographical Discoveries in Siberia and Northwestern America* published in 1964, the most comprehensive published collection of Russian maps of the north Pacific.[1] One of the maps, no. 163, is a 'Copy of the map of the geographical voyage of Captain Cook, based on the London meridian'. Though the introductory remarks are in Russian, the map itself is in English, and the tracks of the voyage in the northern waters are plotted in great detail. Unfortunately the editor of the *Atlas*, Yefimov, says nothing about the provenance of the map – who made the copy and where, as well as how and where it reached Russia.[2] It could not have been too long after the return of the expedition to England, for accounts of the voyage began to be available in Russia as early as 1780.[3] The particular point of interest for us, of course, is that Müller's promontory is not on that map. Rather the Chukotskiy Peninsula is outlined in a configuration close to that of today. And in the *Atlas* there are some seven other maps of origin before 1800 on which the Chukotskiy Peninsula conforms closely to the outline of the peninsula on the 'Copy'.[4] Müller's promontory had vanished.

Its disappearance caused little comment. This is not surprising, for as a consequence of Cook's expedition and discoveries the Russian government became concerned over the security of the lands in the north Pacific discovered by its subjects and undertook measures to defend them. This focused attention on the Aleutian Islands and Alaska Peninsula. The appearance of British and later American merchantmen to trade with the natives added to the concern and led the government

[1] See chapter 8, note 0.

[2] In the spring of 1779 Captain Clerke turned over to the commandant of Kamchatka, Major Marcus Behm, Cook's journal, some maps, and other papers for delivery to the British ambassador at St Petersburg. One Mikhail Tatarinov at Irkutsk used the information in them to draft his own circumpolar map (John C. Beaglehole, *The life of James Cook* [Stanford, Calif., 1974], p. 160; in Cook, 1967, vol. III, p. cxlii; Svetlana G. Fedorova, 'Issledovatel'Chukotki i Alyaski kazachiy sotnik Ivan Kobeler', *Letopis' severa* [Moscow], Tom v [1971], p. 160). Though Tatarinov's map could hardly be the 'Copy' – the projection is different and he could not have known the track of the voyage for the rest of 1779 – it does indicate that the Russians learned of Cook's discoveries before the English did.

[3] Terence E. Armstrong, 'Cook's reputation in Russia', *Captain James Cook and his times* (Vancouver, B.C., 1979), p. 122.

[4] Nos. 162, 164, 174, 177, 181, 182, 185.

to focus on the southern limits of the Bering Sea. On the other hand, the northern coast of Chukotka had been revealed as an unpromising route between Europe and the Pacific. It held no attraction in the form of trade. Dezhnev's voyage and his great rocky nos no longer seemed relevant to the interests of most Russians and Europeans as they previously had. Also, it is at this point that Dezhnev's detractors – Robertson, Sarychev, and later Slovtsov – began to appear. A revival of sustained interest in the voyage and its questions was not to come until the last decade of the 19th century.

The matter of the identity of the great rocky nos came in for only intermittent attention during the next hundred years, with little searching analysis. Coxe, Burney, and Vrangel´ gave it the most attention. In his *A Comparative View of the Russian Discoveries with Those Made by Captains Cook and Clerke*, published in 1787, Coxe affirmed that the real 'Tschukotskoi Noss', which Müller had erroneously conjectured to lie above the 70th parallel, Cook called 'East Cape' and that Dezhnev 'doubled the Tschukotskoi Noss, or the East Cape of Cook'. Coxe's evidence was that of Cook and King.[1] Burney is also explicit: '...the Great Cape of the Tschuktzki...on which Ankudinov was wrecked, by its small distance from the River Anadir and also by the islands opposite to it, can be no other than the Cape in Bering's Strait, since named East Cape, on account of its being the most eastern land of Asia'.[2] Both men, contemporaries of Cook and indirectly and directly connected with his expedition, no doubt readily accepted the judgement of the great navigator and his lieutenant, King. Vrangel´, who explored the coast between Cape Shelagskiy and Kolyuchin Bay (where Müller had placed the base of his promontory) in 1822–3, accepted King's conclusion, for some of the latter's reasons: East Cape's direction relative to the mouth of the Anadyr´, the two islands opposite it, and the natives with the labrets.[3]

Between Cook's expedition and the voyage of Adolf E. Nordenskiöld a hundred years later four expeditions sailed into the Bering Sea, though only two of them passed through the strait. The accounts of three of these voyages pay almost no attention to East Cape. The Billings expedition went no farther north toward the Chukotskiy Peninsula than Lavrentiya Bay in its one foray in the summer of 1791. Martin Sauer's account of the voyage mentions neither the cape nor

[1] Pages 11–14; also in *Account of Russian discoveries* (3rd edition; London, 1787), supplement, pp. 423–6.
[2] *A chronological history of north-eastern voyages of discovery* (London, 1819), p. 68.
[3] 1840, p. xxvii.

Dezhnev;[1] Sarychev mentions Dezhnev, but only to reject his having circumnavigated East Cape, as noted in chapter 1.[2] Fedor P. Litke, who sailed to the Russian American colonies and the Aleutians in 1826-9, likewise went no farther north than Lavrentiya Bay, and he gives no attention to East Cape or Dezhnev.[3] Frederick W. Beechey, sent by the British Admiralty to rendezvous with Sir John Franklin in Kotzebue Sound after his descent of the Mackenzie River to the Arctic, sailed through the Bering Strait and back in the summer of 1826 and again in the summer of 1827, but on both occasions he sailed along the Alaskan coast east of the Diomede Islands. He does make one brief passing reference to East Cape, that 'in almost every direction [it] is so like an island'.[4]

It is only from the account of the fourth voyage, that of Otto von Kotzebue, that East Cape and Dezhnev get any attention. Kotzebue describes East Cape in as much detail as does Cook, but somewhat differently. It is worth quoting his description. In connection with his return from Kotzebue Sound he writes:

As it seemed to be the will of fate that we should visit East Cape, I steered thither and kept to the north side to be protected from the south wind [19 August 1816]. It consists of very high land, and in many places is covered with eternal ice, which appears to the navigator, at a small distance, to be only a narrow neck of land, which stretches far into the sea; that is probably the reason that Cook has drawn it in this form in his chart. But at the distance of five or six miles it appears as very low land which unites to the mountain, and deprives the promontory of the form of a tongue of land. At the extreme points of the Cape, in the low land, there is a conical mountain, which rises perpendicularly out of the sea, the summit of which has fallen in, and is open to the sea-side. The black rocks, which are confusedly fallen together, one of which quite in the form of a pyramid, is particularly distinguished, give to this place a frightful appearance...The low land to the W. forms a bend, on which we observed a number of subterraneous dwellings in the form of little round hills, about which were placed a number of whale ribs.[5]

On the 'Chart of Beering's Straits' at the end of Volume I Kotzebue shows East Cape as a kind of nubbin, short and stubby, unlike Cook's elongated headland. From Kotzebue's description one can understand

---

[1] 1802, ch. XVIII.   [2] Page 12, note 2 above.
[3] *Voyage autour du monde, 1826-1829* (Amsterdam and New York, 1971), Vol. II, chapter XI.
[4] 1831, Vol. I, pp. 246, 337-9; vol. II, pp. 532-45.
[5] *A voyage of discovery into the South sea and Beering's straits* (London, 1821b), Vol. I, pp. 243-4; *Entdeckungs-reise in die Sud-see und nach der Berings Strasse* (Weimer, 1821a), vol. III, p. 156.

why Cook and King were disposed to equate East Cape with Dezhnev's great rocky nos, though Kotzebue himself does not do so.

One who does make that equation is Adelbert von Chamisso, the naturalist on Kotzebue's expedition. In one work he mentions 'Ostcap (Cap Deshnew)', and in a second he gives 'Vostotschin-oi or Tschukutskoi-noss' as alternative names for East Cape; but farther on he specifies the 'projecting Tschukutskoi-noss (Anadirskoy-noss)' as bounding the north side of the Gulf of Anadyr'.[1] This would appear to identify the Tschukutskoi-noss as the Chukotskiy Peninsula and suggests Müller's concept of the promontory in scale, but not in location. Farther on in the second work he mentions Dezhnev's voyage and Burney's theory about an intervening isthmus, a theory which he rejects.[2]

The only other person before the last decade of the 19th century to see East Cape as Dezhnev's nos is Nordenskiöld, the Swedish geographer-explorer who navigated the entire Arctic coast of Eurasia in 1878–9. He says so in forthright terms. He writes: '...the easternmost promontory of Asia, East Cape, an unsuitable name, for which I have substituted on the map that of Cape Deschnev after the gallant Cossack who for the first time 230 years ago circumnavigated it'.[3]

Some accepted Cook's and King's identification; others appeared indifferent to it; still others challenged it. Slovtsov took the position that the Chukotskoy Nos could have been Cape Chukotskiy, not far from which is St Lawrence Island, whose configuration from a particular approach appears as two islands; or it could have been Cape Shelagskiy, 'to which Dezhnev's confused description could also apply'.[4] Slovtsov was persuaded, however, that the fight with the Chukchi occurred at Chaunskaya Bay or Cape Shelagskiy and that Dezhnev then crossed the Chukotskiy Peninsula to the Gulf of Anadyr' and never saw Bering Strait. Ogloblin, whose article in 1890 did so much to revive interest in Dezhnev's voyage, faced no such difficulty in naming Cape Chukotskiy as Dezhnev's promontory. Though it is difficult to believe that a scholar like Ogloblin would be confused by

---

[1] *Reise um die Welt* (Berlin, 1955), p. 132; 'Kamtschatka, the Aleutian Islands, and Beering's Straits' in Kotzbue, 1821b Vol. III, pp. 262, 263; 1821a, Vol. III, p. 156.
[2] In Kotzbue, 1821b, Vol. III, p. 266; 1821a, Vol. III, p. 157.
[3] *Voyage of the* Vega *round Asia and Europe* (London, 1881), Vol. II, p. 68. Map is at the end of Vol. II. Polevoy (1970b, p. 155) finds this to be the first time Dezhnev's name was applied to East Cape, but as we have just seen Chamisso so named it more than a half century earlier.　　　　　　　　　　[4] 1886, Vol. I, pp. 57–8.

the similarity of names, he seems to have taken Müller's Chukotskoy Nos to be the same as Bering's 'Chukotskiy ugol', later changed to Cape Chukotskiy. This meant that Ogloblin had to identify St Lawrence Island, for the same reason given by Slovtsov, or the islands Arakamchechen and Yttygran, which lie just east of the southern half of the face of the Chukotskiy Peninsula 55 to 75 km north of Cape Chukotskiy, as the two islands mentioned by Dezhnev.[1]

Despite Dezhnev's critics and the lack of interest of noted navigators of the Bering Sea, the identification of his nos first put forth by Cook and King became the prevailing one and was recognized by changing the name of East Cape to Cape Dezhneva (Mys Dezhneva) in 1898 on the 250th anniversary of his voyage, as noted in chapter 1. To what degree the renaming was a statement that Müller was right and Slovtsov was wrong, i.e. that Dezhnev sailed through the strait, and to what degree it was also an affirmation that East Cape was Dezhnev's nos is not clear. For Shokal'skiy, president of the Russian Geographical Society, upon whose initiative the change was made and who was the first Russian to agree in print with Cook and King, it was the latter,[2] a view shared by A. Zelenin.[3] Too, if one thought, as Ogloblin did, that Dezhnev's nos was Cape Chukotskiy, then one would expect that cape to have been so renamed. Meanwhile, the consensus about Dezhnev's voyage and the identity of his nos had become strong enough that Golder's denial of both just before World War I and his attempt to identify Cape Shelagskiy as the great rocky nos won few, if any, converts in Russia.[4] On the contrary it goaded certain Russian scholars into efforts to prove him wrong.

The most formidable case in support of the thesis of East Cape or Cape Dezhneva as the great rocky nos, the classic proof according to Belov, was provided by Lev S. Berg, the geographer-historian. In making his case he had in mind Slovtsov's and Golder's choice of Cape Shelagskiy as Dezhnev's nos and Ogloblin's choice of Cape Chukotskiy. Slovtsov had argued that the fight of the Russians with the Chukchi occurred at Chaunskaya Bay or near Cape Shelagskiy and that they then spent ten weeks of wandering in travel across the Chukotskiy Peninsula. He noted too that south of Cape Shelagskiy are two islands.[5] Berg points out that there are no islands opposite Cape Shelagskiy, though there are two, Big and Little Rautan, to the south inside Chaunskaya

[1] 1890, pp. 9, 10, 22, 23.
[2] Shokal'skiy, 1898, pp. 498, 500; Polevoy, 1970b, p. 155. See chapter 1, p. 213 above. above.   [3] 1898, p. 2181.
[4] To be discussed in the Epilogue below.   [5] 1886, Tom I, p. 58.

Bay. He notes further that Cape Dezhneva is the most prominent and highest peninsula on Dezhnev's route beyond Cape Shelagskiy.[1] Meanwhile, we may add that Slovtsov failed to deal with the remaining features by which Dezhnev identified his nos. Berg rejects Ogloblin's identification too. He notes Ogloblin's confusion in taking Müller's Chukotskoy Nos to be Bering's Chukotskiy corner.[2]

The identifying features to which Berg gives particular attention are the two islands opposite Dezhnev's nos and their labret-wearing inhabitants. For Berg these are the two Diomede Islands, which lie in Bering Strait midway between Cape Dezhneva and Cape Prince of Wales. He explains that the Chukchi were actually Eskimos, among whom the custom of labrets still existed. On first acquaintance Eskimos could be readily mistaken for Chukchi. Moving then to the stanov'ye in the form of towers made from whalebones, Berg contends that they were the framework of the semi-subterranean dwellings which the Chukchi made from the ribs and jawbones of the animal, a kind of structure no longer used. And there was a little river on the 'western side', as Berg designated the 'Russian side'. On the Arctic shore of Cape Dezhneva is the village of Uelen, some 5 km west of which there is a freshwater lagoon, the narrow passage into which could be mistaken for a small river; or it could be a river about 25 km west of the cape, discovered in 1912 and capable of taking vessels of medium size. Furthermore, in traversing the route from the Kolyma to the Anadyr' one makes a sharp change of direction at Cape Dezhneva, from southeast to southwest. This is what Dezhnev had in mind when he stated that the nos 'lay betwen north and northeast' and that it 'turned around [and] under toward the Onandyr' River'. At the same time Berg found no contradictions between Dezhnev's assertion on the one hand that one could sail from the nos to the Anadyr' in three days-and-nights in a good wind, a distance of 460 nautical miles,[3] and, on the other, his statement that the nos was far from the Anadyr'. He explains this by the fact that Dezhnev had in mind not the mouth of the Anadyr' River, but the entrance to Anadyr' Bay, 80 to 100 km from the mouth. In effect Berg adopted King's arguments and provided a more detailed

---

[1] 1946, p. 33.   [2] 1946, pp. 32, 33.

[3] 1946, p. 34. He does not specify whether the 460 miles are nautical or statute, but inasmuch as the source of his figure is a Russian pilot book (*Lotsiya beringova morya* [1909], p. 398) and he sets the terminus of the distance at the entrance to Anadyr' Bay (Cape Vasiliya and Cape Geka), making the distance from Cape Dezhneva 875 km or 470 nautical miles (my calculation), one concludes that they are nautical miles. Belov sets the distance at 800 km or 430 nautical miles ('Semen Dezhnev i amerikanskaya literatura', *Izvestiya VGO*, Tom LXXXIX [1957], Vypusk 5, p. 483; 1963, p. 445).

explication of this point of view. Two of Dezhnev's identifying features Berg failed to deal with, that the nos went far into the sea and that many Chukchi lived on it. Even so, by matching eight of the ten features with those of Cape Dezhneva and its geographical position relative to the Anadyr´ he seemed to have established beyond little doubt that the Cape Dezhneva of today is Dezhnev's great rocky nos.

Belov and Polevoy, however, do not agree with Berg's arguments in their entirety. Belov, who accepts Cape Dezhneva as the great rocky nos, finds it necessary to modify one of Berg's arguments, namely, that the 460 nautical miles from Cape Dezhneva to the entrance to Anadyr´ Bay could be covered in three days-and-nights. Belov does not think so and believes that Dezhnev had in mind Cape Chukotskiy, from which, he argues, a koch could be sailed in the 72-hour period.[1] To substantiate his claim that it was possible for a koch to sail from Cape Chukotskiy to the Anadyr´ in three days-and-nights he cites the return voyage of Kurbat Ivanov in 1660 from what Belov claims its Cape Chukotskiy. Meeting with a favourable wind, Ivanov and his men set sail on September 18 for the open sea, but soon a heavy storm arose, and three days were spent in riding it out and struggling to a place of shelter, where they spent two days. With the return of a favourable wind they resumed the voyage and reached the mouth of the Anadyr´ on the seventh day (v sed´moy den´).[2] The critical phrase here is 'on the seventh day'. Belov interprets it to mean on the seventh day from the beginning of the voyage and places the date of arrival at the mouth of the Anadyr´ at September 24. Consequently, if one subtracts the three days of the storm and two days in shelter, one is left with two days of sailing under favourable winds, and in effect two days-and-nights were sufficient to cover the distance.[3]

But Ivanov's words are open to a different interpretation: 'on the seventh day' could mean the seventh day after leaving the place of shelter. If that is true, Belov's illustration is destroyed. Too, in limiting the advance toward the Anadyr´ to the two full days of fair weather sailing Belov does not allow for the possibility that in the course of the storm the koch made progress toward the Anadyr´. At the same time one is compelled to ask why, if the distance from Cape Chukotskiy to the Anadyr´ could be covered in two full days, could not the distance

[1] 1955, p. 80; 'Novoye li eto slovo o plavanii S. I. Dezhneva? (po povodu stat'i B. P. Polevogo)', Izvestiya VGO, Tom xcv (1963), Vypusk 5, p. 445. On the basis of 460 nautical miles the average speed would have had to be 6·4 knots, an unlikely average.

[2] RM, p. 270; ORZPM, p. 406 incorrectly renders it v semoy den´.

[3] 1949, p. 471; 1955, p. 128; 1963, p. 445; 1973, pp. 121–2.

from Cape Dezhneva to Cape Chukotskiy, half that of the former, be covered in a third full day as Berg contends?

On a second point Belov finds himself forced to accept a change in one of Berg's arguments, the one concerning the identify of the stanov'ye. That change, however, is better discussed later in connection with the whalebone towers.

Polevoy's disagreement with Berg, and with Belov too, goes much further. In two articles, one published in 1962, the other in 1965,[1] he rejects Cape Dezhneva as the great rocky nos and contends instead that it is the whole Chukotskiy Peninsula. This conclusion in turn leads him to challenge several long accepted notions about the identifying features and the voyage itself.

He begins his argumentation with the meaning of the Russian word *nos*. Its literal meaning, 'nose', had derived meanings in the 17th century later supplanted by other terms. Then it meant both cape and peninsula. Although use of the modern word for cape, *mys*, is found in use on rare occasions in the 17th century,[2] the modern word for peninsula, *poluostrov* (a direct copying of the German *halbinsel*), did not emerge until the mid-18th century. Until then accordingly the word nos was applied to the Chukotskiy Peninsula.[3] Thus in using the word 'nos' Dezhnev does not differentiate between cape and peninsula. To find out which one he meant we have to examine what he tells us about the great rocky nos.

Dezhnev states that the nos 'lies between north and northeast'.[4] This clause has consistently been interpreted by investigators since Müller, including Berg and Belov, to mean that the long axis of the nos extended, or pointed between north and northeast,[5] Polevoy points out, however, that this characterization does not fit Cape Dezhneva; it points east. Its tip has a minor bend to the north, but it was hardly worth Dezhnev's mentioning. Polevoy's explanation starts from a

[1] 'Nakhodka podlinnykh dokumentov S. I. Dezhneva o yego istoricheskom pokhode 1648 g.', *Vestnik Leningradskogo gosudarstvennogo universiteta*, 1962b, Vypusk 6, pp. 145–52; 'O tochom tekste dvukh otpisok Semena Dezhneva 1655 goda', *Izvestiya AN SSSR, seriya geograficheskaya*, 1965a, Vypusk 2, pp. 101–11.

[2] E.g., *DAI*, Tom III, p. 325; *RAE*, p. 136.

[3] In this study I use 'cape' to refer to a lesser extension of land into the sea, like Cape Shelagskiy or Cape Dezhneva, whereas I use 'peninsula' to refer to a major extension such as Florida or Baja California, though I recognize that peninsula is applied to smaller, perhaps narrow, such landforms. When classification as either one or the other is uncertain or needs to be deferred, I use the Russian 'nos' or sometimes 'promontory'.

[4] '... *lezhit promezh siver na polunoshnik*'. These are old Pomor'yan terms for north and northeast in respect to both winds and directions. *Leto*, mentioned later, was the Pomor'yan term for south.   [5] Cf. Müller's map of 1758.

different premise. If one takes the mouth of the Anadyr´ River as one's base of viewing, a line drawn *north* will pass west of the Kresta Bay, the western limit of the Chukotskiy Peninsula. A line drawn to the *northeast* will pass close to the eastern end of the peninsula. This means of identification is consistent with the great extent of the nos mentioned by Dezhnev, and that extent characterizes it as a peninsula in the sense being used here. Polevoy remarks further that Yakutsk cossacks in the mid-18th century defined the position of other *nosy* in this manner.[1]

One of his most telling points derives from Lavrentsova's correction of one of the transcribing errors in Müller's copy of Dezhnev's first report of 1655. In that copy the sentence that reads 'The nos turns around (*krugom*) and under (*podleglo*) toward the Onandyr´ River' should read '...turns southward (*pod letom*) abruptly (*krutom*) toward the Onandyr´ River'. The copyist mistook 't' for 'g' in both instances. In the first he felt impelled to add 'm' to make a known word; in the second to add 'l' before 'o'. An abrupt turn to the south is an exact definition of the southern coast of the Chukotskiy Peninsula in relation to the location of the mouth of the Anadyr´ River. The nearest part of Dezhnev's nos must be sought directly north of the mouth of the Anadyr´. It is obvious that this information relates neither to Cape Chukotskiy nor to Cape Dezhneva, which turns west and from which the mouth of the Anadyr´ lies to the southwest, more west than south. The place where the Chukotskiy Peninsula turns sharply south is Kresta Bay, and the mouth of the Anadyr´ lies almost due south of it. Since Dezhnev's designation of 'between north and northeast' indicates a certain precision in stating compass directions, his directions can be trusted.[2]

This peninsular identification of Dezhnev's nos makes possible a clarification of two features which seem incompatible: his statements that one could sail in three days-and-nights from the nos to the Anadyr´ and that the nos was far from the Anadyr´ and the walrus rookery at the entrance to Anadyr´ Bay. Berg, as did those before him, took the three days-and-nights figure to apply to Cape Dezhneva, whose distance from the Anadyr´ he set at 460 miles. This distance, he claimed, could be covered in 72 hours with a favourable wind that would enable the koch to average six knots.[3] But, it now appears, what Dezhnev had in mind was the distance from the western boundary of the

---

[1] 1962b, p. 148; 1965a, p. 103.　　　　　　　　[2] 1962b, p. 149; 1965a, pp. 102–3.
[3] 1946, p. 34. At six knots the elapsed time would be somewhat more than 72 hours, 76·7.

Chukotskiy Peninsula in the vicinity of Kresta Bay. The distance from it through the Anadyr´ Bay and Onemen estuary to the Anadyr´ River is 280 km (173 miles), and it could be sailed in three full days (document 9). On the other hand, when Dezhnev states in his second report (document 10) that the Anadyr´ and sandspit are far from the nos, he had in mind its eastern end. The context for his remark is the 'toothed' people on the islands opposite the nos, mentioned in the preceding sentence. Dezhnev's two statements, one placing the nos fairly near, the other far from the Anadyr´, refer to two different parts of the peninsula, the western and eastern.

Another of Dezhnev's statements which, Polevoy claims, points to the Chukotskiy Peninsula rather than Cape Dezhneva is his remark that 'a great many Chukchi live on it'. Polevoy does not elaborate the point, but it may be noted that if Dezhnev's nos is limited to the cape as Cook and Kotzebue describe it, one has to doubt that it could support a great many Chukchi. Bering, Cook, and Kotzebue saw no inhabitants there (though Kotzebue saw several semi-underground dwellings), whereas Bering was visited by eight, later forty, natives at Cape Chukotskiy and Cook visited a Chukchi settlement at Lavrentiya Bay. This is not to say that no Chukchi lived on the cape; Uelen may have existed then. But given the very extensive character of the Chukchi economy, one has to question that Cape Dezhneva could have supported 'a great many Chukchi'. To find a great many one has to look beyond, and probably far beyond, the cape. This becomes more certain after examining Petr Popov's report of 1711.

In that year Popov, a service-man, was sent from Anadyrsk to the nos to persuade the Chukchi to accept Russian dominion. He failed in that objective, but he observed a good deal and brought back much information, submitted in a report dated 2 September 1711. Polevoy quotes these parts from it (document 33):

The reindeer Chukchi on the nos live in the mountains because they move their reindeer herds about from place to place. The 'walking' Chukchi live in earthen huts on both sides of the nos along the sea near the sandspits where walruses pass the time. The reindeer and 'walking' Chukchi support themselves by hunting wild reindeer, ocean whales, sturgeon, seals, roots, and grasses in the mountains and along the rivers...

...According to an estimate of the 'best' men there are about 2,000 or more peninsular reindeer and 'walking' Chukchi as well as the Anadyr´ River [Chukchi], and there are 50 or more river men...

The route to the Nos itself directly from the Anadyrskiy ostrog overland across the Belaya River to Matkol by reindeer trails on reindeer is ten weeks or more if there is no blizzard. The peak called Matkol by the Chukchi is adjacent to a large bay near its middle arm.

This description, according to Polevoy, is not of a single cape, but a peninsula with mountains, rivers, and capes on which live some 2,000 nomadic and sedentary natives. Matkol he identifies as Mt Bol'shoy Matachingay, the highest mountain on the peninsula (2625 m or 8600 feet) as does Berg.[1] It is near the northwestern shore of Kresta Bay. Today this area is regarded locally as marking the western limit of the Chukotskiy Peninsula.[2]

The correction of a second error in Müller's copy of Dezhnev's report bears on the identification of his nos. In Müller's copy Dezhnev specifies as one of the landmarks of his nos a Chukchi stanov'ye consisting of 'towers of whalebones'. It was on the basis of this settlement of towers that Berg identified the village of Uelen with its semi-undergound huts made from whalebones as the Chukchi stanov'ye. But it turns out that Dezhnev specified 'a tower' (bashnya), not 'towers' (bashni). Too, Berg overlooked Dezhnev's qualification that the stanov'ye was 'there' by a little river. Berg sees the river either as the entrance to a lagoon 5 km to the west or a small river 25 km to the west. Now that it develops that the stanov'ye consisted only of a single tower, one has to look elsewhere, Polevoy reasons, since Uelen has long been a multi-dwelling settlement. He adds that this conclusion disposes of the argument that Dezhnev could have mistaken the entrance to the lagoon west of Uelen for the little river. He was too experienced to make such a mistake.[3] Belov, in the face of this correction, advances the explanation that the tower was not a dwelling, but a kind of beacon for those navigating along the coast, the whitened whalebones showing up in the haze or light fog (on the order of the white slatted daymarks in use today).[4] But Polevoy rejects this explanation, insisting that the whalebone structure has been traditionally a form of Chukchi dwelling. The stanov'ye has to be found somewhere else along with the little river next to which it was built.

[1] 1946, p. 53, note 2.
[2] 1965a, p. 104. There are several references in the late 17th and early 18th centuries to the peninsula the Chukotskoy Nos. Polevoy has found some in documents still in the archives and unpublished (1965a, p. 105). Members of Bering's First Kamchatka Expedition mention it (Fisher, 1977, pp. 84, 118). And a note titled 'Chukchi' and found in Krasheninnikov's papers has this to say: 'The Chukchi live on a nos named Chukotskoy after them...' (1949, p. 737, citing AAN, razryad 1, opis' 13, no. 10, list 72 oborot). Elsewhere he writes that Fedot sailed around the 'Chukotskoy nos' (ibid. p. 740).
[3] 1962a, p. 149.   [4] 1963, p. 444; 1973, p. 118.

The tower and little river are connected with another identifying feature that Polevoy defines in a new way, 'the Russian side'. Berg and others have understood this to mean the western side of the nos, that is, of Cape Dezhneva, inasmuch as Dezhnev and the others approached the nos along the Arctic coast from the Russian territory to the west.[1] It was on this coast and to the west, they believed, that the little river emptied into the sea and where the camp was found.

Polevoy's view is that the Russian side is not some area adjacent to the Chukchi Sea in the Arctic or a synonym for the approach from the west, but the region lying west of Kresta Bay and extending south to the Anadyr´ Bay and lower Anadyr´ River, called 'the Russian side' in the 17th century by the Anadyr´ cossacks and promyshlenniks in differentiation from 'the Koryak side' south of the bay and lower river. Kurbat Ivanov in his report of 1660 puts the Russian side east of the Anadyr´ near 'a big bay', i.e., Kresta Bay.[2] Thus one has to look for these distinguishing marks of the nos in the vicinity of Kresta Bay.[3]

Finally, he expresses great doubt that the islands inhabited by labret-wearing Chukchi – actually Eskimos – are the two Diomede Islands. If Dezhnev's expedition visited Uelen and then went on to the Diomede Islands, it went east some 35 or 40 km, away from the coast, and this is unlikely for he and the others must have wanted to reach the Anadyr´ as soon as possible. The 17th-century documents emphasize that as a rule the Russians sailed along the shore. Therefore it is to be presumed that the islands which Dezhnev and his men saw are Yttygran and Arakamchechen – a suggestion, incidentally, made by Ogloblin some seventy years earlier[4] – islands which one would pass closely in rounding the Chukotskiy Peninsula. On one of them Eskimos lived in the not too distant past. However, scientific caution persuades Polevoy not to press this thesis too hard. If neither of these islands, nor the Diomedes, qualifies, the islands might be some others near the Chukotskiy Peninsula.[5] Later he suggests that Alaska might be one of the islands, though documentary proof to support this suggestion is lacking.[6]

With several of the identifying features of the great rocky nos now associated with Kresta Bay, Polevoy is convinced that Dezhnev learned

---

[1] Belov (*RM*, p. 272, note 3) explains the phrase *v russkuyu storonu* (on the Russian side) thus: 'in the direction of the Kolyma, to the north along the northern coast of the Chukotskiy Peninsula, the route along which Dezhnev came'.

[2] *ORZPM*, pp. 405, 406. [3] Polevoy, 1962b, p. 151; 1965a, p. 108.

[4] See p. 218 above. [5] 1962b, p. 151.

[6] 1965a, p. 109. He repeats this thesis in an unpublished article written in 1979.

of them from having visited that bay. This conclusion leads in turn to a change in the chronology of the voyage, and to the further conclusion that Dezhnev, not Ivanov, has to be considered as the first discoverer of that bay, in 1648, not 1660. In all probability, Polevoy writes, the expedition was not in Bering Strait on September 20 when the Russians engaged in a fight with the Chukchi and Alekseyev was wounded, but near Kresta Bay.[1] This relocating of the fight eliminates the great disproportion of chronology according to which the expedition took 93 days to cover the 2,000 km from Sredne-Kolymsk to the Bering Strait (maybe only 70 days from the mouth of the Kolyma River) and just eleven or twelve days from there to Cape Olyutorskiy. If the fight occurred near Kresta Bay, it becomes obvious that the expedition passed through the strait considerably earlier than heretofore believed, probably in August 1648. Moreover, Polevoy does not think that the winds and currents that prevail around Cape Chukotskiy could have carried the koches as far south as Cape Olyutorskiy whereas those in the vicinity of Anadyr´ Bay could have carried the two boats south of that area.[2]

Such are Polevoy's conclusions and arguments, advanced in the conviction that nothing Dezhnev says about the nos can be limited to Cape Dezhneva alone.[3] They add up to a far-reaching re-interpretation of the voyage and its events. How valid are they?

We begin our critique with his interpretation of the phrase 'between north and northeast'. It is, I am convinced, the correct one. Dezhnev's phrase applied to the position of the nos, not the direction of its axis as Müller, Berg,[4] Belov,[5] and others understood it. The critical word is 'lies'; Dezhnev does not say 'extend' or 'stretches' or 'points'.[6] He

---

[1] 1962b, p. 151 if the fight of September 20 occurred on Cape Dezhneva, it would have had to be on the northern or southern side of the lowland connecting the mainland and the mountainous and rocky head of the cape, whose steep-to sides make landing dangerous. Too, one has to ask whether enough Chukchi would have lived on or near the cape to do battle with some 40 or even 50 Russians.

[2] 1962b, p. 151.   [3] 1965a, p. 106.

[4] 1946, p. 32.   [5] 1973, p. 117.

[6] In light of the new explanation given by Polevoy about the location of the great rocky nos based on Lavrentsova's corrected text it becomes of interest to note that Müller on two occasions approached this modern interpretation, but on each occasion combined an incorrect element with a correct one. In his 1737 article, written at Yakutsk, he stated that the nos 'extended far into the sea in a northeasterly direction, then turned to the south'. Here the first element is wrong, the second correct. In his 1758 account he quoted Dezhnev's words as copied in Yakutsk: 'It lies between north and northeast and turns in a circle toward the Anadyr´.' In this case the first element is correct and the second wrong. But even though he quoted Dezhnev correctly in the first element, Müller evidently retained the understanding evidenced in the 1737 statement, to judge by his maps. Meanwhile, why in his 1758 account did he ignore the turning south? The most likely explanation is that at Yakutsk he had Dezhnev's original report before him, whereas in

was trying to place the nos relative to the lower Anadyr´, to the sandspit with its rookery at the entrance to Anadyr´ Bay where he had discovered valuable walrus tusks, so he specified the compass directions which mark the western and eastern limits of the nos. To be sure, they are not as precise as degrees of longitude, but they carry a rough accuracy. When this mode of location is used, Cape Dezhneva is eliminated, for while it is northeast of the Anadyr´, it is not directly north longitudinally. It is to be noted that not only Yakutsk cossacks used this method of geographical placement, but so did Aleksey I. Chirikov, one of Bering's lieutenants on his first voyage into the north Pacific. He placed the non-existent Shalatskoy Nos between 'N and NW' relative to their vessel's course.[1]

The corrected sentence that the nos turns abruptly southward toward the Anadyr´ effectively disqualifies Cape Dezhneva as the great rocky nos and lends substantial support to Polevoy's choice of the Chukotskiy Peninsula. Though the southern side of Cape Dezhneva does turn southward, it does so gradually, first to the southwest, then south, toward Cape Chukotskiy, which faces south, not east like Cape Dezhneva. Cape Dezhneva is situated 8° of longitude east of the mouth of the Anadyr´ (about 575 km or 355 miles) along the 65th parallel and only $1\frac{1}{2}$° of latitude (165 km or 100 miles) north of that point. Quite clearly the Anadyr´ lies much more west than south of Cape Dezhneva. On the other hand, the western limit of the Chukotskiy Peninsula is situated to the north of the mouth of the Anadyr´ River. In one respect, however, Polevoy's argumentation needs qualification. He writes that the mouth of the Anadyr´ is directly (*pryamo*) south of Kresta Bay. Actually it is much more southwest, about 4° of longitude or 190 km (115 miles) along the 65th parallel. It is the entrance to Anadyr´ Bay that is almost due south of Kresta Bay.

Though Polevoy makes little of the feature that the nos 'extends far into the sea', that feature suggests a large landform like the Chukotskiy Peninsula as much as, and very likely more than the much smaller Cape Dezhneva. To be sure, Cape Dezhneva extends farther into the sea than any of the other capes along the Arctic coast east of Cape Shelagskiy and those south of Cape Dezhneva (excluding possibly Cape Chaplina), and if the other features added up to a cape rather than a peninsula, this extent would be a confirming attribute; but the

writing the later account, as many as two decades later, he had to depend on the erroneous copy and had forgotten or overlooked the earlier description.
[1] Fisher, 1977, p. 88.

other features add up more to a peninsula than a cape. The problem is to determine what Dezhnev meant by 'far'. Does a cape 15 to 20 km long extend 'far into the sea'?[1] In the same report (document 9) he states that from the coast to the Anadyr´ (80–100 km or 50–60 miles) is 'not far'.[2] By this standard one has to rule Cape Dezhneva out as the nos. On the other hand, in his second report (document 10) Dezhnev states that the Anadyr´ and the sandspit at the entrance of Anadyr´ Bay are 'far from that nos'. For this statement to become a measure of farness, we have to ask, far from which part of the nos? If only from the western boundary, the distance is about 175 km (110 miles), which we have to concede is not much greater than 80–100 km. If, however, Dezhnev here had in mind the eastern end of the peninsula, as Polevoy contends, then there is consistency in Dezhnev's use of 'far' and 'not far'. It may also be remarked that on the basis of Dezhnev's description of the nos, as already observed, Müller conceptualized on his maps a peninsula, not a cape – a peninsula that extended more than 450 km (280 miles) into the sea. Indeed he remarks that he had 'represented it still too small'.[3]

The three days-and-nights sailing distance of the nos from the Anadyr´ River and the great distance at the same time of the nos from the river do not by themselves prove the peninsular dimensions of the nos; they only create confusion by their seeming incompatibility. But by viewing the Chukotskiy Peninsula as having its near and far parts the way is opened to clearing up the confusion to a degree that viewing Cape Dezhneva as the nos does not, and that is in itself a kind of proof that the nos was a peninsula.

There is, nevertheless, one aspect of the statement about the three full days of sailing which is not cleared up by viewing the nos as having its near and far parts. Dezhnev's passage regarding the sailing time from the nos as corrected by Lavrentsova reads: 'A good run from the nos to the Anadyr´ River is three days-and-nights and no more. To go from the coast to the river is not far because the Andir´ River empties into a bay.' Müller, in paraphrasing this passage (document 2) added two phrases and miscopied a third: '*With a good enough wind* one can sail from the cape to the Anadyr´ River in three days-and-nights, and *by land* it is likewise *no farther* because the Anadyr´ empties into a bay' (emphasis added). 'With a good enough wind' and 'by land' are

---

[1] Kotzebue thought so (p. 216 above).

[2] In the Müller copy of Dezhnev's report this reads 'no farther'. Lavrentsova corrected it to 'not far'.

[3] 1758a, p. 281; 1758b, Tom VIII, p. 405; 1761, p. 67.

interpolations; 'no farther' is one of the mistakes in Müller's copy of the text. His version has prevailed over the years, leading to scepticism about a koch's capability to sail from Cape Dezhneva to the Anadyr´ in three days-and-nights. Berg sought to resolve the discrepancy by reading the passage to mean that Dezhnev was referring to two segments of one continuous route: 72 hours to sail from the nos to the entrance to Anadyr´ Bay and the same time to walk the 80 to 100 km from the rookery at the entrance to the bay to the mouth of the Anadyr´ River.[1] Polevoy disagrees. Noting that the cossacks would not walk between the rookery and the river mouth when faster water transportation was customary and available, he contends that Dezhnev was referring in both cases to the travelling time from the western limit of the peninsula to the river by alternate routes. Because the water route had to follow a roundabout course, it was longer than the land route and so required as much time as the land route.[2] Three years later Polevoy revised his explanation. The words 'from the coast' he takes to mean the coast adjacent to Kresta Bay, to the sandspit island Kosa Meechkyn east of it, and the 'run' was across the mouth of the bay to 'the Russian side' north of the lower Anadyr´. In other words, the coast in question is that of the nos, not the sandspit at the entrance to Anadyr´ Bay. This interpretation places the second sentence in apposition to the first, i.e. the distance covered in 'a good run' is 'not far'.[3]

I have to differ from all three explanations for the reasons that Dezhnev says nothing about a land route and that nothing in the passage associates the coast with the nos. The explanation that seems to make the most sense is this: Dezhnev is telling us that a koch can sail in three full days from the western region of the nos to the mouth of the Anadyr´, that is, to where the river empties into the Onemen estuary, the inner bay, and that even though one must sail through two bays, one can make it in that time since the distance from the ocean entrance of the outer Anadyr´ Bay, i.e. 'from the coast', to the river is not far. Otherwise the closing clause beginning with 'because' seems to be a non-sequitur. This second part of Dezhnev's passage, terse and ambiguous, remains conjectural. At the same time Müller's interpolation of 'by land' is puzzling, and his placement of the rocky promontory on his maps ignores or rejects the three days-and-nights passage.

Müller's interpolation of 'With a good enough wind' is less distorting. From its presence in the passage arises the implication that only with unusually favourable winds could the run be made in as few

<hr>

[1] 1946, p. 35.   [2] 1962b, p. 149.   [3] 1965a, pp. 107–8.

as three full days, thereby suggesting that the distance between the nos and the river was considerable. Without the phrase one can conclude that Dezhnev had average rather than exceptional speeds and shorter distances in mind.

The confusion that arose over Dezhnev's statement of a run of three full days as the distance from the nos to the Anadyr´ might have been lessened or removed had Müller's article of 1737 (document 1) been available to scholars before its publication in this century. Regarding this statement Müller wrote: 'Dezhnev declares that the Anadyr´ River is no farther from the *southern end* [emphasis added] of the Chukotskoy nos than the distance that can be run in a koch in three days-and-nights...' A glance at Müller's preliminary map of northeastern Siberia (no. 7) makes clear that he was measuring the distance of three days-and-nights from the part of the nos nearest the Anadyr´ River, and so it is implicit that in his understanding the nos had its near and far parts, as Polevoy argues. Dezhnev's statement thus becomes credible.

Polevoy finds in Popov's description of the nos of the Chukchi (document 33) further confirmation that the Chukotskiy Peninsula is Dezhnev's nos. Actually, it must be admitted, the only points on which Popov's report bears directly are the matter of the great number of Chukchi who lived on it and the mention of mountains and rivers. Given the physical characteristics of Cape Dezhneva, a rocky highland at the tip and lowland connecting it with the mainland, it could not support 'a great many', whereas the Chukotskiy Peninsula, the Nos, according to Popov, did. His figure of 2,000 or more provides a specific number of what 'a great many' means.[1] This may not seem numerous for so large an area as the peninsula, but for people living under a grazing and hunting economy it was a considerable number. Cape Dezhneva may be mountainous, but it lacks rivers.

Popov's reports does help us in other respects, the establishment of the western limits of the Chukotskiy Peninsula as seen by the Russians and the fact that they saw it as a peninsula. The nos could be reached from the lower Anadyr´. It has a big bay, beyond which Popov and his companions encountered refusal by the Chukchi to submit to Russian authority as they had rejected other Russians before them. The

---

[1] Immediately following Popov's deposition Müller quotes from another 'relation' about the Chukchi in which a population figure of 3,000 to 4,000 is given (1758a, p. 60; 1758b, Tom VII, p. 203; 1761, p. xxvi). This relation, dated in 1718, is no doubt that of Petr Tatarinov, commandant at Anadyrsk at that time, who gained his information from Chukchi visiting Anadyrsk (Fisher, 1977, p. 84, n. 17).

route from the Anadyrskiy ostrog directly to the nos took one to Matkol mountain near Kresta Bay. Thus Kresta Bay appears to have been the western entry area whether travelling directly from Anadyrsk or from the lower Anadyr'. Popov refers to this area as the nos and its inhabitants as the peninsular (*nosovyye*) Chukchi, differentiating them from the river Chukchi who lived along the lower Anadyr'. Popov does not make clear how far east on the peninsula he went; he says only that he went beyond the big bay, that is, Kresta Bay. It does not appear that he went to the eastern end of the Chukotskiy Peninsula.[1] What he learned about the islands beyond the peninsula came from the Chukchi, not his own first-hand observation. He was able to confirm the Chukchi's information by talking with natives from the islands held captive by the Chukchi. The big island which one of them mentioned and said he visited is undoubtedly Alaska.

When we turn to Polevoy's handling of the remaining features of the great rocky nos, we are on less firm ground. It is to some of these points that Belov's rebuttal pays particular attention. Polevoy's position is that in identifying the nos as the Chukotskiy Peninsula there is no call for searching for the tower and whalebones and the small river in the area near Cape Dezhneva since the cape has been eliminated as Dezhnev's nos. For Belov the contrary is the case: Cape Dezhneva is the nos whose identification as the great rocky nos is to be confirmed, and the tower and river help to do so. In Polevoy's view the association of 'the Russian side' with these two features places them in the vicinity of Kresta Bay. The logic from this premise is sound enough, but his case is not strengthened by his inability to locate the tower and river at any particular place.

The correction of Dezhnev's text in the Müller copy from several whalebone towers to a single such tower eliminates the village of Uelen as one of the landmarks.[2] It also leaves us with the question, what was the tower and where was it? Polevoy is quite insistent that the tower

---

[1] Polevoy, 1965a, p. 109.

[2] Although the Müller copy of Dezhnev's report as published in *DAI* (Tom IV, p. 26) uses *bashni*, not *bashnya*, Müller himself uses the singular in his 1758 German account, calling the structure a scaffold (*ein Gerüste*) (1758a, p. 9). The Russian translation ordinarily used by Russian writers, designates it a *bashnya* (1758b, Tom VII, p. 12). Coxe follows Müller in using the singular (1780, pp. 314, 317; 1787, pp. 254, 255), and so does Golder (1914, pp. 82, 271). Even so, Golder and the other later writers with access to both the Müller copy in *DAI* and his rendition in *Nachrichten von Seereisen* did not pick up the difference and failed to see its implication as did Polevoy. Müller's choice of the word 'scaffold' is almost unique (cf. Cook's 'stages'). It was the kind of structure he took the *bashnya* to be. Yet he omits reference to the stanov'ye. Did he write this passage when he had the original document at hand in Yakutsk, whereas it was the faulty copy taken back to St Petersburg that was published by the Archeographic Commission?

was a semi-undergound hut, about which ethnographic observers of Chukotka from Cook to Berg have written,[1] not the beacon or daymark about which Belov is equally insistent.[2] It is true that Sarychev mentions two subterranean yurts 'in a ruinous state' near Cape Baranova just east of the Kolyma, formerly occupied by Chukchi who called themselves 'Shalagy',[3] and Kotzebue,[4] Nordenskiöld,[5] and Bogoraz[6] describe these structures in somewhat the same fashion as do Berg and Polevoy, though Bogoraz's description and accompanying illustrations, as well as Nordenskiöld's illustrations, show the more modern dwellings (late 19th century) to be broad and squat with a low centre peak. He also states that the so-called jawbone huts had not been built for three generations.

Cook offers a third possible structure and use, which neither Polevoy nor Belov mentions. Cook visited Lavrentiya Bay in August 1778 and spent some time ashore in a Chukchi village. In his journal he describes their winter habitations as oval in shape, framed with wood and ribs of whales, and covered with grass and earth so that from the outside they looked like hillocks. Their summer huts were large, circular, and brought to a point at the top, framed with 'slight' poles and bones, and covered with skins.[7] Then he goes on to say:

About the habitations were erected several stages ten to twelve feet high, such as we have observed on some part of the American coast; they were built wholly of bones and seemed to be intended to dry skins, fish &c upon, out of reach of their dogs...[8]

These stages with their open structure seem best to fit Dezhnev's description whereas the semi-earthen huts with the bones mostly or entirely concealed on the outside appeared to the Englishmen as hillocks.

One possible explanation of the locale of this landmark and the little river is that Dezhnev chose them with the claim in mind of Stadukhin and Seliverstov to prior discovery of the walrus rookery at the entrance to Anadyr´ Bay. He wanted to prove that Stadukhin and Seliverstov on the voyage of 1649 had come nowhere near the sandspit, that the

---

[1] Letter to me, 30 November 1974.   [2] 1963, p. 444; 1973, p. 118.
[3] 1806, Vol. I, p. 35.   [4] 1821b, Vol. I, p. 244; 1821a, Vol. I, p. 156.
[5] 1881, Vol. II, pp. 90–1.   [6] 1904–9, pp. 178–82.
[7] Cook, 1967, pp. 412–13.
[8] Ibid. p. 413. Belov cites the account of Luka Voronin, a member of the Billings expedition (1785–95) who visited the Chukotskiy Peninsula. Voronin describes the towers of whalebones as frames in the form of a large tent not far from the earthen dwellings (Belov, 1963, p. 444). These were summer dwellings, yarangas (Innokentiy S. Vdovin, *Ocherki istorii etnografii Chukchey* [Moscow and Leningrad, 1965], pp. 49–50).

two men had not even rounded the great rocky nos, and so he mentioned landmarks found at the eastern end of the nos. Dezhnev's mentioning of these identifying features immediately follows his statement that 'Mikhaylo Stadukhin did not reach this nos' (document 10, p. 45).

The last word on this matter, however, may still be Polevoy's. In a personal communication[1] he points out what he does not mention in his articles of 1962 and 1965, and what as a Russian writing for other Russians he probably did not think needed to be pointed out, namely, that the word 'stanov'ye' refers to a temporary dwelling. This shifts the focus of our attention from the word 'bashnya' to the word 'stanov'ye'. In arguing his case Belov writes that Dal''s dictionary[2] lists 'beacon' (mayak) as one of the meanings of 'bashnya'. He ignores the word 'stanov'ye'.[3] Polevoy too seeks to explain 'bashnya' rather than 'stanov'ye'.[4] Dal' defines 'stanov'ye' as a place of temporary shelter and lists as equivalents a gypsy or nomad camp, or in Siberian and Pomor'yan usage an isolated hut or covered framework for shelter. At this point we need to re-read Dezhnev's text carefully. The revised, quite literal translation comes out 'the Chukchi made a shelter there, which is a tower from whalebones'. The word 'tower' is grammatically subordinate to the word 'shelter'; it defines the form which the shelter takes. The focus is thus moved from a tower to a shelter. This provides justification for Polevoy's explanation: The coastal Chukchi made journeys between the nos and the Anadyr'.[5] He assumes that when returning eastward across the entrance to Kresta Bay, i.e. in the open water rather than around the shore of the bay, they headed for the stanov'ye as a point of reference and rested there after a difficult voyage or trip across the ice.[6] This explanation reinforces his contention that the Russian side, the little river, and the stanov'ye were all to be found near Kresta Bay. Such a point of reference, it may be argued, would have been needed more in crossing the broad throat of Kresta Bay than in the area of coves and narrower bays of the eastern end of the Chukotskiy Peninsula. This explanation also obviates the question whether a single isolated dwelling could be some kind of permanent settlement and does away with the need to explain an isolated drying stage dissociated from habitations. On the other hand, it does conform with Belov's contention that the tower was a kind of beacon or

[1] His letter of 24 September 1978.
[2] Tolkovyy slovar' zhivogo velikorusskago yazyka, sub nomine.
[3] 1949, p. 444.
[4] 1962b, p. 148, 1965a, p. 106.
[5] 1965a, p. 118.
[6] His letter of 24 September 1978.

reference point, except that it was more than that; it was a habitation as well.

Be it dwelling, beacon, or drying stage, physical evidence that proves the one and disallows the other two is not likely to be found. A community of dwellings like Uelen is perpetuated to a degree that an isolated structure is not. Without the shelter hut or tower of whalebones identity of the little river, which may well still exist, cannot be ascertained, certainly not its precise location. We are left then to wonder why, if these landmarks of Dezhnev were in the locale of Kresta Bay, he chose ones of such low magnitude for so big a landform, why did he not point to the bay itself, the 'big bay' of his successor Ivanov, or to the 70-km long sandspit, Kosa Meechkyn Island, which stretches eastward from the entrance to Kresta Bay and along which Dezhnev would have sailed had his course taken him within seeing distance of the bay.

Polevoy's preference for Yttygran and Arakamchechen as against the Diomede Islands is difficult to confirm or reject. As long as Cape Dezhneva was believed to be the nos, the two Diomede Islands with their location opposite the cape and their labret-wearing Eskimo inhabitants appeared obviously to be the islands Dezhnev and his men saw. But now that it has become evident that the Chukotskiy Peninsula is the nos, Yttygran and Arakamchechen have to be considered. In 1962 Polevoy favoured them because unlike the Diomedes the Russians would not have had to deviate from their practice of sailing along the shore and would not have been delayed in reaching the Anadyr´ since the two islands lie on such a course.[1] But are they opposite (*protiv*) in the same sense as the Diomedes? Might they not be better described as near (*vozle*) or alongside (*posle*) the peninsula? They lie 10 to 12 km offshore, not 45. Polevoy says almost nothing about the natives inhabiting them, only that at one time labret-wearing Eskimos lived on one of them, which one he does not mention. Too, might not Dezhnev and Alekseyev have wanted to investigate the Diomede Islands for their potential in furs and walrus ivory? If they reached the strait in August instead of September, might they not have thought there was time to do so? It would not have been out of line of Dezhnev's duty to do this; and we do not know how consistently they sailed along the shore before reaching the strait. Stadukhin, it will be recalled, was ordered to investigate offshore islands on his voyage in 1649. In 1965 Polevoy backed away from his preference for Yttygran and

[1] 1962b, p. 151.

Arakamchechen and suggested that one of the islands might be Alaska, the 'big land' reported by the Chukchi in the 18th century, not then known to be a part of America. Dezhnev, he reasons, might have heard similar reports in the 17th century.[1] But this thesis leaves the second of the two Diomedes to be explained and seems to place Dezhnev and his men on one of them, as well as to suggest that three islands must have been seen. In this connection an overlooked point clouds the picture further. In his own report of 1655 Dezhnev specifies two islands; in his joint report with Semenov islands are specified, as they are in Vetoshka's report of the same year (document 11). But then in the joint report where it is said that Dezhnev and his companions saw the natives, it says 'on *an* island' (*na ostrovu* – document 10, p. 63). If this discrepancy is only a slip of the pen (a few sentences earlier the report mentions 'islands' opposite the nos), then there is a case for the Diomede Islands. If not, the statement lends credence to the case for Yttygran and Arakamchechen. Polevoy puts labret-wearing Eskimos on only one of those islands. One thing is certain, however. The two islands have to be in the vicinity of the eastern end of the nos if Polevoy's differentiation between its near and far parts is to be maintained. For the rest – much speculation without a firm conclusion.

The one remaining change in interpretation occasioned by the replacement of Cape Dezhneva with the Chukotskiy Peninsula as the great rocky nos is the chronology of the voyage. Here too our judgement has to be inconclusive. In calling attention to the elapse of only eleven or twelve days after the fight with the Chukchi in reaching Cape Olyutorskiy as against three months to reach the Bering Strait from Sredne-Kolymsk, Polevoy makes the same assumption that Golder does, that the wreck occurred on October 1.[2] But Dezhnev says only it happened after October 1.[3] We do not know how long it was after the fight that the Russians resumed their voyage, though in view of the hostility of the Chukchi one would not expect the Russians to have lingered long thereafter. We do not know how long after October 1 the voyage ended; nor do we know how long after the resumption of sailing the storm hit the two boats.

To give some guidance to our speculation let us take three periods of time elapsing between September 20 and the wrecking of Dezhnev's koch – the eleven days mentioned by Polevoy, two weeks as a middle

---

[1] 1965a, p. 109; his letter of 24 September 1978.
[2] Golder, 1914, p. 81. He says 'about October 1'.
[3] In the document: Feast Day of the Intercession of the Holy Virgin.

figure, and one month (30 days), the probable maximum period for the last stage of the voyage – and calculate the average speed to cover the distance from Cape Dezhneva to Cape Olytorskiy and Cape Navarin. If it was wrecked near Cape Olyutorskiy, the distance covered was 1,900 km (1,025 nautical miles); if near Cape Navarin, 1,300 km (700 nautical miles).[1] In tabular form the results are these:

	Cape Olyutoriskiy		Cape Navarin	
Number of days	Nautical miles per day	Knots	Nautical mles per day	Knots
11	93·2	3·9	63·6	2·6
14	73·2	3·0	50·0	2·1
30	30·2	1·4	23·3	1·0

It should be kept in mind that the last stage was not broken by shore landings and the storm might have propelled the koches more rapidly than usual. Accordingly the highest rate of knots, 3·9 and 3·0, appears feasible along with the lower figures so that the traditional understanding that the last stage of the voyage got under way in the strait is not ruled out by the disproportion between taking 93 days to cover 2,000 km and 11, 14 or 30 days to cover 1,900 or 1,300 km. Thus Polevoy's contention remains speculative, and does not provide a reliable approach for determining whether the little river and stanov'ye were at Kresta Bay.

As we come to the end of this chapter we may remind ourselves that the identification of the great rocky nos has undergone two major changes. In the hands of Müller the nos was first portrayed, in the mid-18th century, as a large peninsula extending nearly to the 75th parallel, some 280 miles northeastward into the Arctic Ocean. Two decades later captains Cook and King, as a consequence of their navigation in that area, demonstrated that such a peninsula did not exist. Impressed by the resemblence of the cape at the northeastern tip of Asia to several of the features of the nos set down by Dezhnev, they declared that cape to be the nos and named it East Cape. Full acceptance of their view did not come until the end of the 19th century when the name

---

[1] These distances have been arrived at by measuring the course along the shore on ONC C-8 and D-10. Unless the koches of Dezhnev and Alekseyev were caught by the storm off Cape Chukotskiy, it is almost out of the question that the two men would have deliberately chosen the open-sea route in search of the mouth of the Anadyr'.

of the cape was changed to Cape Dezhneva. Now within the last two decades, at the hands of Polevoy, the second major change has occurred. Once again it is viewed as a peninsula, one that does exist, the Chukotskiy Peninsula.

It is difficult to say how extensively Polevoy's interpretation has been accepted. The only published responses have been those of Belov and myself. Belov in an article in 1963 and in his *Podvig Semena Dezhneva* (1973), rejects Polevoy's thesis and stays with Berg's as modified by himself.[1] Yet Belov has gone further toward accepting Polevoy's interpretation than he seems to realize. Earlier we noted that he argues that Dezhnev had Cape Chukotskiy in mind when he stated that a koch could sail from the nos to the Anadyr´ in three days-and-nights. Thus he has Dezhnev (and himself) viewing the nos as double-pointed, as embracing the eastern face of the Chukotskiy Peninsula; but he does not explain how one can regard only the face of the peninsula as the nos and not the rest of it. How do you detach the one from the other? Nor, evidently, does he see a statement which he makes in the 1955 edition of his study on the voyage as a second step toward conceding the nos to be a large peninsula. In a paragraph in which he discusses the influence of Dezhnev's voyage he remarks that the idea of land between the Kolyma and Anadyr´ rivers which extended far into the sea in the form of a rocky or mountainous peninsula was firmly held by the traders, hunters, and service-men of the Yakutsk jurisdiction, a view which he does not reject.[2] It is difficult to believe that Cape Dezhneva fits this description. In his 1973 edition Belov takes the third step when he writes that cossacks' reference to service 'beyond the Nos (*za Nos*) meant service on the Anadyr´, that the cossacks considered the Anadyr´ to lie 'beyond the Nos, the Great Rocky Nos – the Chukotskiy Peninsula'.[3]

My response was published in an article in 1973.[4] There I stated my cautious acceptance, cautious because my initial reaction was to challenge the thesis in several details. Moreover, in an article published in 1956 I had challenged Golder's rejection of Cape Dezhneva as the

---

[1] Pages 445–6.   [2] Page 129.

[3] Page 174. Elsewhere in his discussion he labels Kamchatka a nos (pp. 169, 173). Polevoy comments that the phrase used is 'beyond the nos', not beyond several *nosy*, of which there are a number on the Chukotskiy Peninsula. In other words by not singling out any one of them Dezhnev must have in mind the one that embraced them all, the peninsula. Polevoy points out too that the phrase came into use only after 1655 when Dezhnev's report reached the Kolyma (1962b, p. 150).

[4] 'Dezhnev's voyage of 1648 in the light of Soviet scholarship', *Terrae incognitae*, Vol. v (1973), pp. 19–22.

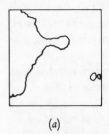 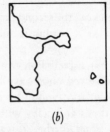 

(a)   (b)   (c)

Map 9   Three depictions of East Cape–Cape Dezhneva. (a) From Cook
and King, 1784, vol. 2, between pp. 466 and 467. (b) From Tebenkov,
1852, map 1. (c) From Defense Mapping Agency, Aerospace Center,
ONC C-8, 1973.

nos and his favouring Cape Shelagskiy, an article which Belov has cited
or paraphrased at length in support of Berg's thesis.[1] Perhaps fortunately
I took the path of scholarly caution in my article and did not endorse
Berg's and Belov's conclusions outright, a point Belov has missed, but
stated that Golder had not proved his case, which left the question open
to another explanation. Still, Cape Dezhneva appeared to me then as
the most likely promontory to be identified as the nos. Since that time,
however, I have come to find Polevoy's arguments convincing, and
I accept his identification of the Chukotskiy Peninsula as the nos.

Even before I learned of his interpretation I had become sceptical
of the applicability to Cape Dezhneva of some of the features
mentioned by Dezhnev. I could not see how it points between north
and northeast; it points east. Did it extend far into the sea? As depicted
on Cook's map and later in Tebenkov's atlas it seemed to do so, but
modern maps of the peninsula and cape make it appear less 'far' (Map
9). Too, I found it difficult to see how it could support a great many
natives. Also, it seems to me not unimportant that Müller upon
uncovering Dezhnev's description of the great rocky nos got the
impression of a large promontory, a peninsula, not a much smaller
headland like Cape Serdtse Kamen´. With the publication of Polevoy's
two articles on the new meanings to be found in the corrected versions
of Dezhnev's reports, the most convincing datum is the clarification
of the garbled passage that the nos turned around under toward the
Anadyr´. The feature of turning abruptly south toward the Anadyr´
applies uniquely to the Chukotskiy Peninsula. But a few of Polevoy's
subsumed conclusions I find inconclusive and less than persuasive. For

[1] 1957, pp. 482–5; 1973, pp. 197–8.

want of sufficient evidence they have to be considered conjectures. But their insufficiencies do not destroy his case. They demonstrate that in questions plagued with deficiencies of evidence such as we encounter in examining Dezhnev's voyage, more questions are raised than can be answered, that we are not going to obtain satisfactory answers to all our questions. In this case the ones with inconclusive answers do not arise from the crucial features. The features crucial in my mind appear conclusive.

CHAPTER 10

AFTERWARDS

The wrecking of the koch of Dezhnev and his men on the Pacific coast
of Siberia ended their voyage, and their ten weeks' march brought the
completion of their first task, the finding of the Anadyr´ River. With
their second task, the exploitation of their discovery, we are concerned
only to the extent that certain aspects of and events in this subsequent
period have a bearing on an evaluation of the voyage, both by Dezhnev
and by modern scholars. It is to these aspects and events, a number of
which are recorded in documents 10 and 11, that this chapter is directed.

Dezhnev reports that with the disappearance of half of his men after
reaching the lower Anadyr´, the survivors built boats and went up the
river and at some place on its upper course erected a tribute zimov´ye.
The precise location of their zimov´ye is not known, but it is believed
to have been in the vicinity of the modern-day Markova, on the river
about 535 km (320 miles) from the juncture of the Onemen estuary
with the Anadyr´ Bay and above the confluence with the Anadyr´ of
the Belaya River on the north and of the Mayn River on the south.[1]
This move was prompted by the fact that the lower Anadyr´ is in a
tundra region, and they needed to find forests where fur-bearing
animals lived. Presumably they made this move in the spring or summer
of 1649 when the river was again navigable. Dezhnev does not say how
they spent the winter or where the materials were obtained to build
the boats. Driftwood may have been one source.

Considering the glowing reports of sables and natives to be found
along the Pogycha-Anadyr´ River that had inspired the undertaking in
the first place, the Anadyr´ country must have been a disappointment
to the Russians. Dezhnev and Semenov in their joint report of 1655
(document 10, p. 65) provide this brief description:

The Anadyr´ River is not forested and few sables are there. There is larch
along its upper course 6 or 7 days' travel, but there are no dense forests of
any kind except birch and aspen, and from the Mayen [Mayn] there is no

[1] Belov, 1955, p. 82. A. S. Sgibnev ('Istoricheskiy ocherk glavneyshikh sobytiy v
Kamchatke, 1650–1856', Morskoy sbornik, Tom CI [1869], no. 4, p. 67) places it at 480 versts
(512 km) from the mouth of the Anadyr´. The modern town of Anadyr´ is near the mouth
of the river.

forest at all, only willows...; and the woods along the shores are not broad; all is tundra and rock. A sketch of this river: from the Anyuy River and across the mountains to the upper Anadyr´ and to the ocean, to the sandspit where the animals stretch out, the rivers which empty into it are large and small. To travel from the upper Anadyr´, from the mountains, to the tribute zimov´ye with loaded sleds [takes] two weeks or more.

Back on the Kolyma River Dezhnev's success in reaching the Anadyr´ River was, of course, not known. There the efforts were now directed to finding a route to the river by land or other rivers. In the summer of 1648 service-man Semen Motora tried unsuccessfully to find such a route.[1] The next year Nikita Semenov was sent from the Kolyma to the upper Anyuy River to bring the Khodyntsy tribes under Russian rule, which he succeeded in doing. From the hostages he captured and brought to the Kolyma it was learned that the upper courses of the Anyuy and Anadyr´ rivers were not far apart, separated by a mountain range. This information encouraged promyshlenniks to band together and ask permission to go to the Anadyr´. They requested that Motora be sent to represent the state's interest, and he was appointed to do so. On 1 March 1650 nine service-men and thirty promyshlenniks set out for the Anadyr´. All this is reminiscent of the onset of the voyage of 1648.

Shortly thereafter Mikhail Stadukhin, having returned from his unsuccessful attempt to reach the Pogycha-Anadyr´ by sea in the summer of 1649, set out with a party of his own, which included several fugitive cossacks. Carrying a commission from the voyevoda at Yakutsk, not from the commandant on the Kolyma, and superior to the others in rank, he felt entitled to assume command of any expedition in search of the Anadyr´. Arrogant, jealous, and domineering, he rode roughshod over the rights of others and was not above seizing their supplies and equipment. He soon overtook Motora and his party. He seized Motora and held him for nine days in an effort to force him under his command; but Motora refused. He reached Dezhnev's zimov´ye on the Anadyr´ on March 26, thereby learning that Dezhnev had reached the Anadyr´ first. Rather than settling in at the zimov´ye he established his own camp. Motora arrived a month later, on April 23, and joined forces with Dezhnev and his men. Stadukhin interfered in Dezhnev's collection of tribute, attacked and plundered the Anaul natives whom Dezhnev had brought under payment of tribute and killed several of

---

[1] Belov, 1955, p. 85.

them. In one attack downriver on the Anauls nine of Stadukhin's men were killed. Meanwhile, finding Stadukhin's actions intolerable and disappointed with the modest fur resources of the Anadyr´, Dezhnev and Motora and their men set off in the fall to find the Penzhina River to the south, which empties into the Sea of Okhotsk. It was rumoured to be rich in sables. But lacking a native guide, they were unable to find the trail, and after three weeks returned to the zimov´ye rather than succumb to the rigours and dangers of winter on the trail. Stadukhin likewise found the fur resources of the Anadyr´ disappointing, so in February 1651 he set off with a band of followers for the Penzhina and more southerly regions. For the next six years little is known of his activities or whereabouts, but in 1657 he emerged from obscurity when he appeared at the outpost at Okhotsk and two years later returned to Yakutsk. He did not return to the Anadyr´.[1]

Stadukhin's departure left Dezhnev and Motora free to carry on the state's business of collecting tribute, maintaining hostages, and subjugating more natives. Late in December 1651 Motora was killed in a fight with a rebellious Anaul chieftain and his tribesmen. Motora's men chose to accept Dezhnev as their leader, whereas certain other cossacks preferred Nikita Semenov, who was influential among them. Thus the dual command on the Anadyr´ continued, evidently quite harmoniously.[2]

In the summer of 1652 Dezhnev and Semenov led a party down the river in boats to the entrance of the Anadyr´ Bay[3] where they discovered a walrus resting ground or rookery, a narrow sandspit known today as Cape Geka, on the south side of the entrance into the bay. It extends about 12 km from the mainland.[4] The two leaders describe the rookery in their report of 1655 (document 10, p. 61):

Many walruses were spread out on the sandspit, and on that sandspit are the dead tusks of that animal. We service-men and promyshlenniks searched for these animals and collected the dead tusks. A great many of the animals stretch

[1] Belov, 1955, pp. 85–8, 96; 1973, p. 128; *ORZPM*, pp. 156–8, 263–4.
[2] Document 17; Belov, 1955, p. 88.
[3] Dezhnev and Semenov specify it as the mouth of the Anadyr´ River.
[4] That the rookery was found on Cape Geka and not Kosa Russkaya Koshka, a similar sandspit on the north side of the entrance to the bay (Müller [document 2] puts it on the north side), is concluded from the fact that elsewhere Dezhnev and Semenov identify it with the Koryaks, who lived south of the Anadyr´ Bay and lower Anadyr´ River. Bogoraz (1904–9, p. 685) and Innokentiy S. Vdovin (*Ocherki istorii i etnografii Chukchey* [Moscow and Leningrad, 1965], p. 107 and note 27) also identify the sandspit as Cape Geka. The adjective 'Russian' was applied to the northern spit not because Russians discovered it, but because it lay on 'the Russian side' of the bay, as mentioned earlier.

out on the point itself of the sandspit, around from the ocean side in a space of half a verst and on a slope of 30 to 40 sazhens. Not all of the animals came out of the ocean to stretch out on the land. A great many of the animals were in the ocean by the shore.

The Russians arrived at the sandspit on June 28 and departed on July 11, not lingering to explore the whole herd there because of the shortage of food and the growing lateness of the season. The report then continues:

We went four times to hunt for the animals, and they soon came out on the land. In the year 162 [1654] they came out later; the first hunting was on Il'in day [July 20]. They came ashore because the ice was carried away from the shore. Those promyshlenniks who are from Pomor'ye said that in the Russian Pomor'ye there are not so many animals as that. We service-men and promyshlenniks put 3 puds [108 pounds] of walrus tusks in the sovereign's treasury, 14 in number.

In 1653 Dezhnev and Semenov gathered materials to build a koch to take the collected furs, walrus tusks, and other items to Yakutsk by sea since it was deemed too risky to take them overland through territory of hostile natives. But the project was abandoned, as we learned in chapter 8, when they were reminded by the natives that the ice was not carried away from the shore every year, and realized that they did not have the sails and anchors equal to coping with the open sea and eddies near the shore (document 10, p. 62).

In April of the next year there arrived at the zimov'ye a new troublemaker. This was Yur'ye Seliverstov, who had been with Stadukhin on the voyage in the summer of 1649. Upon returning to the Kolyma Stadukhin had sent him the following summer to Yakutsk with the sables and walrus ivory collected on the voyage and with a report of his, Stadukhin's, activities to date (document 15). His report, written 7 September 1649 or later, recommended to the voyevoda at Yakutsk, Dmitriy A. Frantsbekov, that an expedition should be sent to exploit the wealth revealed by the voyage and stated that Seliverstov was qualified to lead it. Seliverstov arrived in Yakutsk in the winter of 1650–1 and in a petition dated 24 June 1651 provided information to the effect that he had been at sea, in a sea into which many rivers emptied: the Chukhchya River, the Kovyma River, and beyond it four more rivers, including the Nonandar[1] (Anadyr') and Chondon[2] rivers.

[1] Or Nonabora? Cf. Polevoy, 1964b, p. 22.
[2] Or Chendon. See p. 83, note 1 above.

Many peoples in several tribes lived along these rivers, and they did not pay tribute. He was prepared to bring these natives under the sovereign's dominion with the help of promyshlennik volunteers and promised to collect annually five puds of 'fish bones' in place of tribute in sables.[1] In light of this information and Stadukhin's recommendation Frantsbekov, a man of considerable entrepreneurial spirit, acceded to Seliverstov's request, investing 3,500 roubles of his own resources in outfitting the enterprise and providing him with a government koch. It is probable that it was from Seliverstov that the authorities at Yakutsk first learned that Dezhnev and Alekseyev had made some progress eastward even though two of the koches had been lost. He had no way of knowing, of course, the outcome of the voyage.[2]

Backed by the voyevoda, Seliverstov was able to recruit sixteen promyshlennik volunteers, and on 20 July 1651 he departed for the Kolyma River. Contrary winds, ice, and storms forced him to winter on the lower Indigirka. There he revealed an instability of temperament, becoming abusive and overbearing with his men. The following summer he arrived on the Kolyma by sea. Abandoned by some of his men, in the summer of 1653 he selected a new party of volunteer promyshlenniks, 32 in number, and decided not to continue his journey by sea, but to use the overland route to the Anadyr'. Late in the fall he crossed the Anyuy range and reached the Anadyrskoye zimov'ye in April 1654.[3]

On the Anadyr' Seliverstov's behaviour reverted to that on the Indigirka: he and his men pillaged and killed natives. Too, he tried to claim the authority conferred on Stadukhin, but Dezhnev and Semenov refused to submit (document 17). But particularly distressing to them was Seliverstov's action in writing a secret report to be sent to Frantsbekov at Yakutsk after a trip to the sandspit at the entrance to Anadyr' Bay. It was believed that in this report he claimed to have discovered the walrus rookery on the earlier voyage with Stadukhin. Dezhnev, of course, rejected this claim and accused Seliverstov of lying. In the report of 1655 authored by him alone (document 9) he confines himself to the statement that Stadukhin did not reach the great rocky nos. Since the nos was not far from the Anadyr', Seliverstov could not have discovered the rookery in 1649. In the other report of 1655 jointly

[1] Belov, 1955, p. 91 and 1973, p. 132, citing Portfeli Millera, *no.* 30, *list* 356.
[2] *RM*, pp. 204–6; Belov, 1955, pp. 84–5, 90–1; 1973, p. 132; Sergey V. Bakhrushin, 'Voenno-promyshlennyye ekspeditsii torgovykh lyudey v Sibiri v XVII veke', *Istoricheskiye zapiski*, No. 10 (1941), p. 177.
[3] Belov, 1955, pp. 91–2; 1973, pp. 132–3, 158.

authored with Semenov (document 10, p. 63) he says: 'Yur'ye did not write the truth because he did not reach the great rocky nos.' He then goes on to describe the nos, giving several details which he did not mention in his other report. Thus, had not Seliverstov provoked Dezhnev into this response by his false claim, we may well not have known enough about the great rocky nos to be able to identify it, however controversially. It is ironic that apparently Seliverstov decided not to send his report to Yakutsk, maybe because he learned of Dezhnev's report refuting his claim. Researchers have failed to find it among his reports, all of which were preserved in the local archives.[1]

In the same year 1654 Dezhnev led a party to the walrus rookery to collect more tusks and also to protect tribute-paying Khodyntsy from raids by nomadizing Koryaks who came north from the Penzhina region and attacked them. It was on this occasion that Dezhnev captured the Yakut woman of Fedot Alekseyev, who told him of the fate of Alekseyev, Ankudinov, and the rest.[2]

Seliverstov did not remain long on the Anadyr´. In the spring of 1655 floods wiped out six cabins and twenty storehouses at Anadyrsk. Seliverstov lost 40 puds of walrus tusks in this disaster. Then that summer on a trip to the walrus rookery, the third one made by the Russians, he lost a koch when a storm blew up from the sea suddenly, tore the koch from its anchorage, and carried it out to sea with fourteen promyshlenniks and a big load of tusks, never to be heard from again. Between the flood and loss of a koch, Seliverstov decided to return to Yakutsk. That fall he crossed the mountains to the Anyuy River and Kolyma, and in the summer went on to the Lena.[3]

In the course of his two years on the Anadyr´ Seliverstov managed to split the service-men and promyshlenniks there into two groups, those who followed and supported Dezhnev and Semenov and those who, dissatisfied with those two leaders, turned to him for leadership. It was on the basis of the instructions from the voyevoda at Yakutsk to Stadukhin empowering him to take command on the Anadyr´, but now departed, that Seliverstov tried to undercut Dezhnev and exercise that authority himself. He sent malicious reports about Dezhnev and Semenov to Yakutsk (document 17), and he attempted to carry out an order from Yakutsk to send certain fugitive cossacks back to the Lena. Dezhnev, however, had the greater support and refused to send

---

[1] Now transferred to TsGADA in Moscow (Belov, 1955, p. 92).
[2] Document 9, p. 54; Belov, 1955, p. 93.
[3] Belov, 1955, pp. 93, 94; 1973, pp. 134-5.

these men back, for they had served loyally on the Anadyr´. Seliverstov was forced to go along with Dezhnev and Semenov, who were generous enough to provide him with two koches and have him join them in the 1654 expedition to the rookery. Seliverstov's departure did not end the division, for he left one of his followers in command of his group. He tried to take charge of the collection of tribute, which Dezhnev successfully blocked, and so the dichotomy continued. Thus it was that no unified authority existed on the Anadyr´, no clear-cut definition of command.

Meanwhile, Dezhnev performed as much like a promyshlennik as a service-man. Indeed, most of his followers were promyshlenniks functioning as service-men. To be sure he collected tribute from the natives, maintained the hostages, and collected customs dues from the promyshlenniks and traders. But if the amounts he records in his report of 1655 are an indication, those collections were modest indeed (document 10, pp. 66–7), and apparently there was in general little tribute collection. It was the gathering of walrus ivory that engaged the men's main attention, and Dezhnev collected tusks for himself as well as the state.[1] This is one of the few exceptions to the primacy of sables as the main attraction for the Russian conquerors of Siberia.

Service on the Anadyr´ was proving burdensome. In the autumn of 1654 Dezhnev addressed a petition to the tsar requesting that he be paid his salary and that a successor to relieve him in command be sent (document 8). He recalled briefly his service since leaving Yakutsk, mentioned his voyage to the Anadyr´, and called attention to the hardships he had endured and the high cost of fishing and hunting equipment. It is the reference in this petition to his voyage that is his first mention of it, six years later. It was five years, however, before his request was met. His relief was Kurbat Ivanov, a cossack sotnik, who had discovered Lake Baykal in 1643 and whom we encountered above as the leader of the expedition along the southern coast of the Chukotskiy Peninsula. On 23 May 1659 Dezhnev turned the buildings, personnel, and treasury over to Ivanov and prepared to depart for Nizhne-Kolymsk and Yakutsk. At that time there were five service-men and 32 traders and promyshlenniks on the Anadyr´.[2]

Ivanov was the first regular representative of the state on the Anadyr´. He introduced a new order of affairs. He ended the division into two groups. He began a more regular collection of tribute. Promyshlenniks

[1] Belov, 1955, pp. 95–6.
[2] Belov, 1955, pp. 96–7; 1973, p. 136; Aleksey V. Yefimov in ORZPM, p. 14.

were no longer used to perform government tasks. He requested fifty cossacks so that more effective control could be exercised over the natives, and he built a stockade around the zimov'ye, thus making it an ostrozhek. The days of the more relaxed administration of Dezhnev and Semenov were over. These changes reflected Ivanov's recognition of the strategic location of Anadyrsk, and it is to be noted that it was from this outpost that the expansion into Kamchatka later occurred.[1]

Dezhnev arrived in Nizhne-Kolymsk in May 1660 with the 'bone treasury', and so after twelve years he had come full circle in his journey around the Chukotskiy Peninsula. He brought with him 150 puds (2 tons 400 pounds) of walrus tusks. These made too heavy a load for so long a voyage as that to Yakutsk for the koches then available,[2] so it was not until next summer that Dezhnev set out for Yakutsk in a government koch with the local commandant, Ivan Yerastov, who was returning to Yakutsk. They reached Zhigansk on the lower Lena that fall and Yakutsk the next spring. It was at this point that he presented to the Yakutsk officials in 1662 the petition in which he reaffirmed his voyage and gave a detailed account of his state service up to that time, noting the hardships suffered, the wounds received, the debts and expenditures incurred in this service (document 28). It is this petition which Ogloblin uncovered and which he believed confirmed Dezhnev's remarks about his voyage in his reports of 1655, thus refuting the doubts expressed by Slovtsov. In this petition Dezhnev requested payment of nineteen years of salary and grain allotments which he claimed were due him. The voyevoda dispatched the petition to the Siberian Department in Moscow with Yakutsk cossack Larion Lama.[3]

In July 1662 Dezhnev left Yakutsk in Yerastov's party, which was convoying the sovereign's treasury to Moscow. The two years that it took to make the journey were due only in part to the distance and physical difficulties. When transporting the treasury long delays were incurred by frequent inspections en route by the authorities in the more important administrative centres, inspections which could be prolonged by referrals back to Yakutsk over minor matters. The convoy reached Moscow in September 1664. On the 23rd of that month Dezhnev presented to the Siberian Department a second petition to the tsar (document 29). Much shorter than the preceding one, it briefly recapitulated his service and travels, referring to the former, and requested

---

[1] Belov, 1955, p. 97; 1973, pp. 137–8.
[2] *ORZPM*, p. 319. This source sets the weight at 130 puds.
[3] Belov, 1955, pp. 98–100; 1973, pp. 138–9.

payment of his arrears in salary. His request was considered by both the Siberian Department and, because of the amount involved, by the Boyar Duma. In January 1665 he was awarded 38 r., 22 a., 3 d. in money, and cloth worth 86 r., 17 a., 3 d. For the 39 puds of walrus tusks of his own, which he had to sell to the treasury (at less than market value), he was paid in sables worth 500 r. Given the standard of living and the value of the rouble in the 17th century, which greatly exceeded that of the 19th century rouble, Dezhnev had become a rich man, though much of his new wealth had to be used to pay off his debts.[1] Two weeks later he was promoted to the rank of cossack ataman, though in the absence in the Yakutsk jurisdiction of a vacant post calling for the rank of ataman he had to accept lesser posts after his return to Yakutsk. Before leaving Moscow he presented another petition, for permission to take his nephew with him back to Yakutsk, which was granted. He and Yerastov began the return journey early in March, escorting 'the sovereign's money treasury' to Yakutsk. They arrived there in July of the following year. A personal note that may be added is that on his return to Yakutsk from the Anadyr´ and Kolyma he found his Yakut wife, Abakayada Sichyu, still living. They had one son, Lyubima, who later served with Vladimir Atlasov, the conqueror of Kamchatka. Abakayada Sichyu died in the winter of 1666–7, and Dezhnev then married the widow of a local merchant.[2]

For the next three years Dezhnev served as commandant at the zimov´ye on the Olenek River, the region from which Alekseyev and his men had been driven in the mid-1640s; then a year as commandant on the upper Yana River. Next came a short tour of duty on the middle Vilyuy River, which turned out to be his last administrative assignment in the Yakutsk jurisdiction. In July 1670 he was named by the voyevoda at Yakutsk to command the escort taking the sable treasury for 1670 to Moscow. In his party were nine service-men and 34 promyshlenniks. The sable treasury consisted of 16,533 sable skins, 2,636 fox skins, and 16,068 sable belly strips, worth in all 47,164 r., a considerable responsibility.[3] By this time Dezhnev was the only surviving senior commander in the Yakutsk jurisdiction among his generation of service-men. Leaving Yakutsk early in the summer of 1670, he arrived in Moscow two years later. He was fated not to return to Siberia, for he fell ill late in 1672 and died in Moscow before the end of the year.[4]

[1] For the value of the rouble in the 17th century see Fisher, 1943, p. 29 and note 7.
[2] Belov, 1955, pp. 101–6; 1973, pp. 140–6.
[3] Belov, 1955, p. 111; 1973, pp. 147–51.
[4] Little is known about his death. Ogloblin writes ('Smert' S. Dezhneva v Moskve v 1673 godu', *Bibliograf*, 1891b, No. 3–4, p. 61) that the only information to survive about

Thus inconspicuously did the life of a conscientious servant of the state come to an end, far from his customary haunts and after completing an assignment of high responsibility. Now we may ask, did Dezhnev grasp the full meaning of his exploit of 1648, that it answered a question of long standing and much interest to the men of Europe, that he had marked off the easternmost limit of Siberia? Some scholars, notably Belov, have read into the evidence a considerable knowledge of the geography of northeastern Asia and the waters adjacent to it on the part of Dezhnev. As indication of this knowledge he points to Dezhnev's use of the term 'great sea-ocean' (*velikoye more-okiyan*) and to Petr Meller's map with its 'belt of land' situated in the Arctic north of the Asiatic mainland, which, Belov believes, reflects Dezhnev's and his fellow cossacks' knowledge of northeastern Siberia.[1] But one seeks in vain in the documents of Dezhnev's authorship for any statement or hint of his concept of the geography of northeastern Asia beyond his description of the great rocky nos or any suggestion of awareness of the possibility of another land mass near the nos. He must, of course, have realized that the northeastern corner of Siberia was washed on three sides by the ocean – for him the Lena Sea extended from the Lena to the Anadyr´ and that may be the reason for his use of the phrase 'sea-ocean' – but that he realized land lay to the east and that he had passed through a strait is doubtful.[2] He knew that he had found the sea route to the Anadyr´, but he soon came to

his death is found in the *okladnaya kniga* of money, grain, and salt salaries for the churchmen and service-men of Yakutsk for the year 1701: 'Semen Dezhnev – died in Moscow in the year [7]181 [1672-3]...' Polevoy informed me of a note 'Kogda umer Semen Dezhnev' in the journal *Polyarnaya zvezda* (Yakutsk), 1973, no. 3, pp. 131-2, in which it is pointed out that in August 1673 Dezhnev's death in Moscow was already known in Yakutsk. This information was reported by Stepan Shcherbakov, who left Moscow at the end of 1672. Consequently Dezhnev died at the end of 1672, not in 1673, as Ogloblin suggests. This new information does not conflict with Ogloblin's, for it must be remembered that the old Russian year 7181 began on 1 September 1672. Rather it narrows the time down to the first quarter of the year 7181, i.e. the last quarter of the year 1672.

[1] Belov, 1973, pp. 90–5; p. 175 above.

[2] Polevoy, 1964b, p. 227. The phrase 'on the great sea-ocean' appears also in ORZPM, p. 139, and on Maps 1, 3, 14, 17 and 21. This term suggests a world view of geography that on first encounter is unexpected among illiterate Russian frontiersmen in the far northeast of Siberia. The term 'sea-ocean', or more commonly in English, 'ocean-sea', originated in the middle ages in Europe and was applied to the vast body of water believed completely to surround the small area of habitable land then known to Europeans. By the 17th century it had come in the west to mean what we think of today as the system of great oceans, the high seas, in contrast to inland bodies of water like the Mediterranean and Black seas, and was falling into disuse. Its use by the Russians does indicate an awareness that the Icy Sea or Frozen Ocean, as they called the Arctic Ocean, is a part of the great ocean system. Such awareness must surely have been due at least in part to contact with foreigners, particularly the Dutch and English mariners and merchants who visited Pomor´ye and Arkhangel´sk, the main port for ocean-borne trade with the west in the 17th century, from which so many of the Russians in northern Siberia came.

realize that it was not a practicable route, particularly after the land route via the Anyuy River was discovered, and so he seems to have attached no special significance to his discovery.

One gets the firm impression, rather, from a reading of his petition of 1654, his two reports of 1655, and the two petitions of 1662 and 1664 that Dezhnev did not regard his voyage of 1648 as the outstanding event of his service, as the high point of his career. By his stating in the 1654 petition that he went to the Anadyr' by the great sea-ocean he seems to be saying that he went all the way by an extra-continental water route, not overland by rivers and portages. Can more than this be read into his remark? Meanwhile, except for the great rocky nos he tells us very little about the voyage. It is presented as the means and route by which he reached the Anadyr', as one of the occasions when he suffered material loss and great danger and physical hardship. He is building a case for compensation for arduous and zealous service rendered to the state. Too, he was bent on refuting Seliverstov's claim that he had discovered the walrus rookery at the entrance to Anadyr' Bay. So he devoted unusual attention to the identifying features of the great rocky nos in order to demonstrate that it was a nos that Seliverstov and Stadukhin could not have seen on their voyage in 1649. It is not presented as a discovery of importance, but simply as a landmark on the route he had travelled. Had not Seliverstov made his claim, it is highly doubtful that Dezhnev would have said much or anything about the nos. His main concern was that he stand high in the opinion of the authorities at Yakutsk for having discovered a highly profitable source of revenue for the state, the walrus rookery. For him that seems to have been the most important result of his voyage.[1]

Reading Dezhnev's reports and petitions, specifically the joint report of 1655 with Semenov and his petition of 1662, one's attention is drawn to the detail and length of his statements about the places where he served, the fights with the natives, the wounds received, the hostages captured, and the tribute taken – all intended, one concludes, to impress his superiors with the dangers and hardships of his service, with how well he had performed for the state. The voyage appears as one of several episodes in the course of his service, somewhat out of the ordinary, to be sure, but not to be related in the same kind of detail as his actions involving the natives, not something to be singled out for special attention as one might expect if Dezhnev had understood

---

[1] Ogloblin, 1890, p. 25. Is it significant that Dezhnev did not write his reports until after Seliverstov arrived on the Anadyr' in 1654?

the significance of it. It is possible, of course, that he grasped more of the significance than he expressed in his reports and petitions. He was illiterate and so probably not accustomed to voicing his thoughts for the record, and the records and petitions of the time were customarily concerned with the services rendered and the places discovered, the nuts and bolts of the job, to use a current expression, not with cosmographic speculation. Evidence for affirming knowledge on Dezhnev's part of the great significance of his voyage is, in short, lacking.

For others, however, knowledge of Dezhnev's voyage could have been most welcome, answering the question as it did, are Asia and America joined or separated? How soon and how well did the voyage of Dezhnev and Alekseyev become known beyond the Anadyr'. Again, as with so many of the questions raised by his voyage, the data are not explicit, or are absent or indirect. But there is enough evidence to conclude that the voyage and its implications did become known soon thereafter even though the names of its participants did not and there were distortions in the reports about it.

On the Kolyma it was known, of course, that in 1648 an expedition had set forth in search of the Anadyr' River, and Stadukhin brought back in September 1649 the news that the expedition had advanced along the Arctic coast farther than he had been able to, though losing two koches. This information, it has to be assumed, was conveyed to the authorities at Yakutsk by Seliverstov, sent by Stadukhin with the report of their voyage and the furs and walrus ivory collected by them. Seliverstov left the Kolyma in the early summer of 1650 and reached Yakutsk the following winter.[1] The later information that Dezhnev had succeeded in finding the Anadyr' reached the Kolyma late in 1654 or early in 1655, at the time when the cossack Danilo Filipov arrived on the Kolyma from the Anadyr', carrying with him Dezhnev's petition of 1654 (document 8), which reports his arrival on the Anadyr', and a pud of walrus ivory (as a sample?) for the state. The next summer he set out for the Lena, reaching Zhigansk by August 16, where he was stopped by the ice, and so continued his journey by dogs and sleds to Yakutsk, arriving there late in 1655.[2] The published documents contain no suggestion that any other individuals preceded Filipov to the Kolyma who could have brought the news of Dezhnev's success. Thus it was some seven years after the voyage when Yakutsk learned

[1] Belov, 1955, pp. 90–1; 1973, pp. 131–2.
[2] RM, pp. 119, note 1, 133; Belov, 1955, p. 90, citing Portfeli Millera, no. 31, list 98; 1973, p. 131. Filipov states that he left the Anadyr' in the year 162, which means that he left some time before 1 September 1654.

that the Anadyr´ had been found by way of a sea route around northeastern Siberia, around the great rocky nos. If one allows a year for communications to be carried from Yakutsk to Moscow, then the news of Dezhnev's voyage finally reached the capital some time late in 1656. It is likely that Frantsbekov, who was called back to Moscow in the summer of 1651, brought news learned from Seliverstov that Dezhnev and others were attempting to reach the Anadyr´ by sea, but it is difficult to see how news of their success could have reached the capital before 1656.[1] It should be added that what became known in Moscow had undoubtedly become known earlier in Tobol´sk for it was the main administrative centre of Siberia then and a repository for much information channelled through it to Moscow. And then too, Dezhnev's later journey from Yakutsk to Moscow must have afforded officials in Tobol´sk and Moscow an opportunity to learn more about the voyage.

How well and how widely Dezhnev's voyage and the conclusions to be drawn from it became known elsewhere in Russia and Siberia cannot be ascertained with any precision or certainty. Yet surely it must have become known by word of mouth in much of Siberia as the men who served on the Anadyr´ and Kolyma rivers moved about Siberia to other assignments or accompanied the sable treasury to Moscow; and it must have become known in Pomor´ye from which so many of the service-men and promyshlenniks in northeastern Siberia came and to which some of them returned. There is some evidence to support what experience tells us must have happened.

One source to which one should turn for an answer to our questions is the holographic sketch maps of Siberia made during the latter third of the 17th century. Until 1964, when the Institute of Ethnography of the Soviet Academy of Sciences published its atlas of the geographical discoveries in Siberia and northwestern America in the 17th and 18th centuries,[2] few of these maps had been published or were generally known. There are some nine maps in this atlas that deserve examination for our purpose.

Two of them, the Godunov map of 1667 (Map 10 – so called because it was commissioned by Petr Godunov, voyevoda at Tobol´sk)[3] and the map of Siberia, 1673 (Map 11),[4] depict Siberia as rectangular

---

[1] Belov, 1973, pp. 156, 159.   [2] See p. 183, note 2.

[3] *Atlas*, no. 28 and p. 18; Fisher, 1977, p. 36. The Cronman copy is in John F. Baddeley, *Russia, Mongolia, China*...(London, New York, 1919), Vol. I, between pp. cxxvi and cxxvii.

[4] *Atlas*, no. 30 and p. 19; Leo Bagrow, 'Sparwenfeld's map of Siberia', *Imago mundi*, Vol. IV (1947), facing p. 65; 'The first Russian maps of Siberia and their influence on the west European cartography of N.E. Asia', *Imago mundi*, Vol. IX (1952), pp. 84–6.

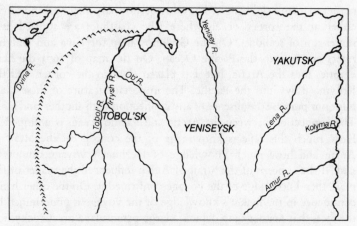

Map 10   Godunov Map of Siberia, 1667 (detail) (*Atlas*, no. 28)

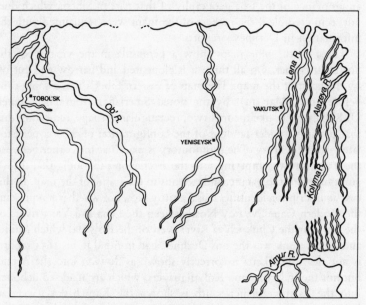

Map 11   Map of Siberia, 1673 (*Atlas*, no. 30)

in shape, the Arctic and Pacific coastlines meeting at the northeastern corner to form a right angle. They do not show any major promontories either at the corner or elsewhere (the coastlines are stylized as a succession of scallops). On the Godunov map the Lena and Kolyma rivers empty into the Pacific Ocean. On the map of 1673 the Lena empties into the Arctic, but it is placed close to the corner, and the Kolyma flows into the Pacific. The important feature of these maps is for our purpose the absence of any connection with another land mass. The connection between the Arctic and Pacific oceans is unimpeded. How much this reflects knowledge of the concept of the Strait of Anian and how much knowledge of Dezhnev's voyage cannot be said. If the concept of the Strait of Anian influenced the maker of the map, then knowledge of the voyage confirmed it. On the other hand, confidence in the maker's knowledge of the voyage is undermined by the facts that neither map depicts a large peninsula, a great rocky nos, at the northeastern corner, and that the Lena River and those east of it are shown as emptying into the Pacific Ocean. These features indicate an ignorance of the true geography of that part of Siberia which does not seem credible if the makers of the maps were acquainted with the information in Dezhnev's reports.

Three of the nine maps show a peninsula in the vicinity of the northeast corner. On all three it is elongated and narrow and cut off by the edge of the map. The map of eastern Siberia made some time before 1696 (Map 12)[1] by the noted Siberian cartographer Semen U. Remezov[2] is, like the first two, rectangular in shape, indicating that that primitive understanding of the configuration of Siberia persisted late into the century. The promontory is placed at the corner between the Yana, shown emptying into the Arctic, and the Indigirka, shown emptying into the Pacific, and extends to the frame of the map. In this case an inscription identifies it as Svyatoy Nos, but whether it represents the modern Cape Svyatoy Nos between the Lena and Yana rivers or the nos near the Chukoch'ya River west of the Kolyma, which Müller and others think was the nos Dezhnev had in mind in his 1655 reports is not clear. The Lena is correctly shown as flowing into the Arctic, but not the Indigirka and Kolyma rivers, which are made to debouch into the Pacific. Farther south is shown the Kamchatka River, an indication of the Russians' awareness of Kamchatka prior to their

---

[1] *Atlas*, no. 44; Fisher, 1977, p. 27.
[2] His career and work are discussed in Andreyev, 1960, pp. 96–148, and Leonid A. Gol'denberg, *Semen Ul'yanovich Remezov: Sibirskiy kartograf i geograf, 1642–posle 1720 gg.* (Moscow, 1965), especially chapters 2–3.

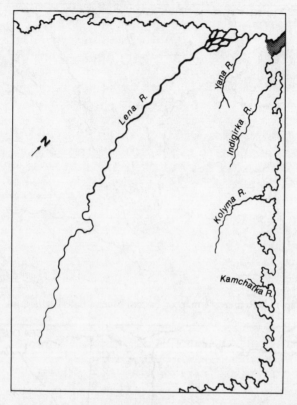

Map 12   Remezov's map of Eastern Siberia, before 1696 (detail) (*Atlas*, no. 44)

conquest of it. A second and later map of eastern Siberia by Remezov (Map 13)[1] is rectangular in shape too, but the Lena appears much farther west, the Kolyma empties into the Arctic, and the peninsula lies between it and the Anadyr´ to the south. A trail is shown connecting it with another river. The peninsula is cut off by the edge of the map, indicating that its end was not known. This depiction of a promontory at the corner of Siberia is the most accurate of the maps made thus far and conforms with Dezhnev's information. Without knowing Remezov's sources we cannot know why he depicts it thus on his second map and not on his first. The third map to show a peninsula is Spafariy's

[1] *Atlas*, no. 45 and p. 31.

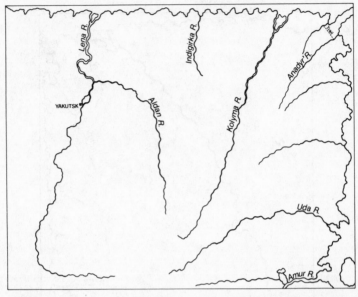

Map 13   Remezov's map of Eastern Siberia (later) (*Atlas*, no. 45)

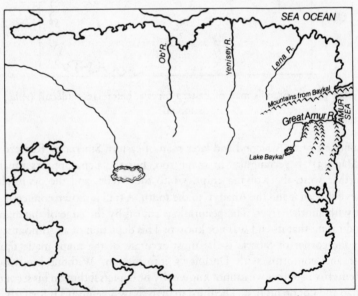

Map 14   Spafariy's map of Siberia, 1678 (*Atlas*, no. 32; Andreyev, 1960, facing p. 56; Bagrow, 1947, facing p. 69)

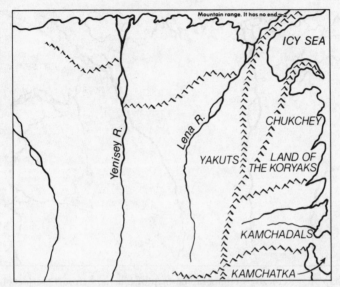

Map 15   Ethnographic map of Siberia, 1673 (*Atlas*, no. 41; Baddeley, 1919, vol. I, between pp. cxxxviii and cxxxix)

Map of Siberia of 1678 (Map 14).[1] It is portrayed as a mountain ridge extending eastward into the sea from the east coast and cut off by the edge of the map. An inscription labels it 'mountains from Baykal'. It is situated not far north of the 'great river Amur' and forms the northern limit of the 'Amur Sea'. These particulars lead to the conclusion that this promontory represents Kamchatka, even though it extends east, not south, rather than the Chukotskiy Peninsula or Dezhnev's nos, again reflecting a pre-Atlasov acquaintance with Kamchatka.

Three other maps place two promontories in the vicinity of the northeastern corner – the Ethnographic Map of Siberia, 1673,[2] Remezov's Ethnographic Map before 1700,[3] and Vinius' Map between 1678 and 1683. Andrey A. Vinius was head of the Siberian Department in Moscow. The Ethnographic Map of 1673 (Map 15) retains the rectangular shape, though it is somewhat rounded at the northeastern corner. One mountainous promontory, with the inscription 'mountain

[1] *Atlas*, no. 32 and pp. 20–1; Bagrow, 1947, facing p. 69; Fisher, 1977, p. 32.
[2] *Atlas*, no. 41 and pp. 26–7; Fisher, 1977, p. 29; Baddeley, 1919, Vol. I, between pp. cxxxviii and cxxxix (not to be confused with the map of Siberia, 1673, mentioned earlier).
[3] *Atlas*, no. 42 and p. 27; Fisher, 1977, p. 30.

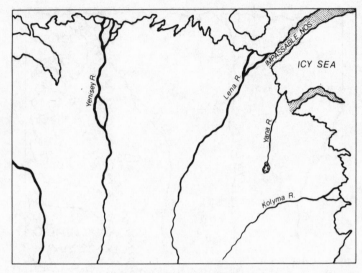

Map 16   Remezov's ethnographic map of Siberia, before 1700 (detail)
(*Atlas*, no. 42)

range it has no end', extends northeastward from the corner to the edge
of the map, and the Lena River is shown immediately west of it. A
second promontory extends in a curve into the ocean south of the first,
and the waters between the two are designated the 'Icy Sea'. Neither
the Kolyma nor the Anadyr´ River is identified. The area south of the
second peninsula is marked 'Chyukchey', and the area south of that
'land of the Koryaks'. Still farther south a mushroom-shaped Kamchatka
and the area landward of it is labelled 'Kamchadals'. Remezov's
Ethnographic Map (Map 16) is quite similar to the one of 1673 in the
configuration and placement of the two promontories. The 'impassable
nos', cut off by the edge of the map, is adjacent to the eastern bank
of the Lena, and the second promontory is just east of the Yana, both
of them considerably northwest of the Kolyma, which empties into
the Pacific, and quite removed from where one would expect
Dezhnev's nos to be shown. Their counterparts in fact do not appear
obvious. Vinius' map (Map 17) shows the two promontories extending
eastward to the edge of the map and lying astride the mouth of the
Kolyma River. Their adjacency to the Kolyma calls to mind Svyatoy
Nos west of it and Cape Shelagskiy east of it, not the Chukotskiy
Peninsula or Dezhnev's nos.[1]

[1] *Atlas*, no. 46 and p. 31; Fisher, 1977, p. 28.

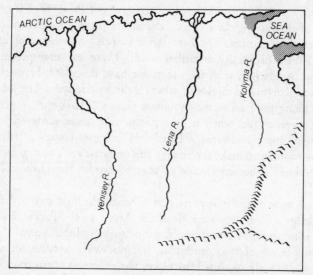

Map 17 Vinius' map of Siberia, 1678–83 (detail) (*Atlas*, no. 46)

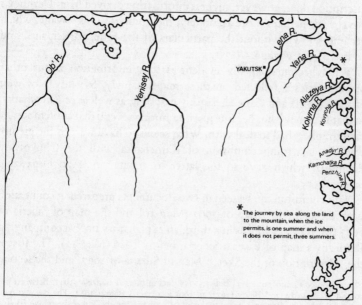

Map 18   Map of Siberia, 1684–5 (detail) (*Atlas*, no. 34)

The ninth map is the Map of Siberia, 1684–5 (Map 18).[1] It retains much of the rectangular shape of the earlier maps, though it is more rounded at the corner. The Lena River empties into the ocean at the corner, the Kolyma River farther south. There are three peninsulas, short in comparison with the others we have described, between the Lena and Kolyma, alongside of which is this inscription: 'The journey by sea along the land to the mountain (*kamen'*) when the ice permits is one summer and when it does not permit, three summers.' This statement, one may assume, is based on Dezhnev's voyage of 1648 for the one summer to make the voyage and on Ignat'yev's voyage of 1646 and Dezhnev's aborted voyage of 1647 to explain the additional two years.[2]

From these maps it appears that whereas the first two indicate a knowledge of a free passage from the Arctic to the Pacific, but not of a prominent nos or peninsula, six of them indicate knowledge of a peninsula, or of two peninsulas, but not with certainty of a free passage, and only one of them places the peninsula correctly relative to the Kolyma and Anadyr' rivers. Only the last map shows both a free passage and peninsulas, but places them west of the Kolyma. Its inscription does, however, suggest information derived from Dezhnev's voyage; or perhaps more accurately, the findings of his voyage, which became known without the particulars of the time, participants, and course of the voyage.

What becomes equally evident is that information about other promontories is reflected on these maps, namely, Svyatoy Nos west of the Kolyma and Cape Shelagskiy east of it, as well as of Kamchatka, so that Dezhnev's nos became just one among several that contemporary cartographers had to deal with. What seems to have warped the picture was the unwitting confusion of Kamchatka with the Chukotskiy Peninsula, which gave to the latter its reputation as an impassable promontory.

This confusion can be seen in two documents prepared in connection with the Godunov map of 1667 (Map 10) and the map of Siberia of 1673 (Map 11), as well as in a third, an explanatory note accompanying Remezov's map of Eastern Siberia, before 1696 (Map 12). The first is the 'Description of the Sketch Map of Siberia of 1667' and the second

---

[1] *Atlas*, no. 34 and pp. 22–3; Belov, 1955, facing p. 116; Bagrow, 1947, between pp. 70 and 71. Bagrow and Belov (1973, p. 169) incorrectly date it 1687. The copy known to us was taken by Remezov from the original preserved in the Tobol'sk archive (Belov, 1955, p. 118).

[2] Belov, 1973, pp. 163–5.

the 'Copy for the Sketch Map of the Siberian Land'.[1] In the Description of 1667 there is this passage: 'They sail in koches from the mouth of the Kalma River along the land to a rocky nos, to the southern country, in one summer when the ice permits; but when the ice does not permit, the journey to the hunting ground is three years.'[2] The resemblance to this passage of the inscription on the map of 1684–5, though longer, is apparent. The reference to the southern country and the hunting ground, presumably the walrus rookery, to be found at the end of the journey are additional facts that must have come from Dezhnev and his reports. Though this information is not noted on the Godunov map, it seems clear that it was known at the time of the making of the map.

In the 1673 Copy this information was repeated (the Copy was probably based on the Description): 'From the mouth of the Kolyma River and around the land past the mouths of the Kovycha,[3] Nanabora, Il'ya, and Dura river [corruptions of the name Anadyr'?] to the rocky barrier they reach by sail in one summer when the ice permits, and when the ice does not, they reach it in three years'[4] A later statement in the 1673 Copy says: 'Between the Nanabora and the Kovycha rivers a rocky nos extends into the sea and they go around it with difficulty.'[5] So far the nos is passable though with difficulty. But the 1673 Copy contains another statement that introduces an element of contradiction and confusion into the picture: 'There is no passage via the Amur Sea to the Chinese kingdom because there lies a mountain (kamen') around the whole land from the Mangazeya Sea [western Siberian Arctic] to the Amur, and that mountain extends into the sea, and no one can go around it because massive ice presses and mounts up, and it is impossible for a man to get over it...'[6] This impassability is asserted in the third document, the explanatory note accompanying Remezov's map of eastern Siberia, the one showing Svyatoy Nos. In it is this statement:

[1] 'Rospis' Chertezha Sibiri 1667 g.' and 'Spisok s Chertezha Sibirskiya Zemli' respectively. The latter is in Titov, 1890, pp. 41–54. The former is cited by Polevoy (1964b, p. 228) as being in TsGADA, stolbets 867. See also Belov, 1973, p. 163. The word 'Spisok' in the title of the second document, Polevoy informs me, is in this instance to be translated as 'copy', but since the copy is not of the sketch map, as a literal translation of the title would suggest, but of the 'Description', the second document will be referred to here as the '1673 Copy'.
[2] Polevoy, 1964b, p. 228.
[3] Here the name Kovycha does not seem to apply to the Kovacha River near Cape Olyutorskiy as Polevoy argues (1970c, p. 85), but to the Chaun River as Belov claims (1955, p. 117).
[4] Titov, 1890, 'Sedmaya gran', pp. 53–4; Polevoy, 1964b, p. 225–7, 243.
[5] Titov, 1890, 'Osmaya gran', p. 54; Polevoy, 1964b, p. 225.
[6] Titov, 1890, 'Pyataya gran', p. 49.

'From the upper Anadyr´ River [i.e. it can be reached from there] there is an impassable nos in the sea, and its end is not known; many natives, non-tribute paying Koryaks, Chyukchi, and Chukoty live on that nos.' The handwriting is that of someone other than Remezov so the statement may have been added by one who did not see it as the Svyatoy Nos.[1] The nos has become impassable, and confusion is added to contradiction when we read further that it 'is a day's journey across the mountain, and when one climbs it, one sees the Lena [Bering] and Amur [Okhotsk] seas.'[2] This characterization of a mountain route and reference to the Lena and Amur seas do not fit the Chukotskiy Peninsula, Dezhnev's great rocky nos.

Polevoy undertakes to clear up this confusion. He notes that the compiler of the 1673 Copy had never been in far eastern Siberia. This unfamiliarity led him in abridging certain passages to obscure their real meaning.[3] Polevoy presents persuasive evidence that the 'rocky barrier', the promontory believed to be impassable, was not the Chukotskiy Peninsula, or for that matter Cape Shelagskiy or Svyatoy Nos, as several maps suggest, but Kamchatka. There is good reason to believe that the Russians penetrated that peninsula as far south as the Kamchatka River in the 1660's;[4] and Stadukhin may have learned about northern Kamchatka after leaving the Anadyr´ in 1651. His report at Yakutsk in 1659 is open to this interpretation.[5] The mountain ridge from which the two seas could be seen and which could be crossed in one day is found on the narrow neck of northern Kamchatka adjacent to Karaginskiy Bay. Thus Kamchatka became known to the Russians long before the expeditions of Morozko and Atlasov at the end of the century, as the appearance of the peninsula and river on several of our maps testifies. However, because the Russians did not advance beyond the northern half of the peninsula and no Russians had sailed around it, the impression arose that it was impassable.

But how then did this feature of impassability become applied to the Chukotskiy Peninsula? Polevoy argues that an abridgement in the 1673 Copy of a passage from the Description gave rise to the idea that the Anadyr´ River lay south of the rocky barrier, thus figuratively displacing Kamchatka northward. Further, by the end of the sixties Russians were for several reasons no longer moving into Kamchatka, and from then on no references to a peninsula south of the Anadyr´

[1] Atlas, p. 30.
[2] Titov, 1890, 'Osmaya gran', p. 54; Polevoy, 1964b, p. 225.
[3] 1964b, pp. 226–8.   [4] 1965b, pp. 232–4.   [5] Belov, 1955, p. 169.

appear in the documents originating in the northeast.[1] On the other hand, the Chukotskiy Peninsula remained known to the Russians through its proximity to the Anadyr´ and through contacts with the Chukchi. Too, Ivanov's expedition of 1660 must have strengthened Russian awareness of the peninsula. At the same time the Anadyr´ River was often mentioned as lying 'beyond the nos'. Thus the two peninsulas appeared to be situated on the hither side of the Anadyr´ and came to be considered as one and the same, not the least by the map makers at Tobol´sk and Moscow, who had no firsthand knowledge of the far east, and so the one acquired the location of the other, and the other acquired the impassability of the one. Yet amidst all this contradiction and confusion reflected on the maps one fact stands out: at the northeast corner of Siberia there was a mountainous peninsula, and from whom else besides Dezhnev and his men could knowledge of it have come? His great rocky nos was and remained known, however distorted the information about it became and however little his or Alekseyev's name was associated with it.

The first published information pointing to the voyage appeared in the last decade of the 17th or first decade of the 18th century. In 1665 the Dutchman Nicolaas C. Witsen, later burgomaster of Amsterdam, visited Moscow, and thereafter kept in touch with many informants in Russia down to the time of his death in 1717. Müller tells us that he had the help of Vinius in obtaining information about Siberia.[2] In 1687 he published in Amsterdam a map of north and east Asia (Map 19)[3] and five years later his monumental but rare description of that part of the world, *Noord en Oost Tartaryen*, which he revised and expanded by one half, especially the geographical description, for publication in 1705.[4] In it he discusses Russian Arctic navigation, which in turn leads to a discussion of the northeastern corner of Asia and the question of the Strait of Anian. In several places in his book he mentions the Icy Cape (*Ys-kaep*), which he places on his map near the northeastern corner of Siberia. It was a tentative concept as he presented it, for the evidence he obtained was not conclusive,[5] bearing out the uncertainty we have just described. How much Witsen had to say about the Icy Cape in his first edition is hard to judge since that edition is

[1] 1964b, pp. 243, 244.
[2] Keuning, 1954, p. 99.
[3] 'Nieuwe landkarte van het noorder en ooster deel van Asia en Europa'. It is in *Atlas*, no. 33; Keuning, 1954, between pp. 88 and 89.
[4] Amsterdam, 1692; 2nd edition, 1705; 3rd edition, 1785.
[5] Fisher, 1977, pp. 29–30.

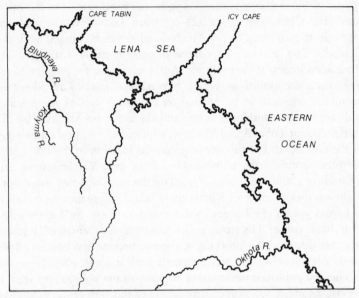

Map 19   Witsen's map of North and East Asia and Europe, 1687–90
(detail) (*Atlas*, no. 33; Keuning, 1954, between pp. 98 and 99)

so rare as virtually to be unavailable, but having shown it on his map,
he must have had something to say about it in that edition. It is from
the second edition, however, that we draw our information, and since
some of it carries references to dates after 1692, we have to conclude
that much of Witsen's information about the Icy Cape was first made
known in the west in that edition.[1]

   In the course of his remarks about the Icy Cape Witsen mentions
neither Dezhnev nor Alekseyev, but many of the details he presents bear
a striking similarity to the details provided by Dezhnev, and one or
two of them are new. In one passage he refers to an island opposite
the mouth of the Kolyma River, and then he goes on to say:

Once seven boats with Muscovite military servitors descended this river in
order to round the Icy Cape, also called the impassable cape (*Neobchodimynos*)
or remote promontory, but all of them perished, so the above-named author

   [1] It is from this version that Vladimir Yu. Vize selected the parts dealing with Russian
Arctic navigation and translated them into Russian (1949, Tom I, pp. 78–93). For
comparison of the Russian translation with the original Dutch I had access only to the 1785
edition, but in the case of the excerpts relevant to our topic the texts of the two editions
seem identical.

told me.[1] He was of the opinion that it is impossible to go around this promontory, since in both winter and summer ice is floating around and the waves are very high. In 1693, 1694, and 1695 the ice in this sea did not melt or break up...Against (tegen) this promontory are small islands in the sea where there live a special people called Czbki [Chukchi] and kbaturi [zubatnyye?], who are all hunters and live on whales, walruses, and seals, and in general they use everything yielded by the sea.[2]

Several pages farther on Witsen returns to the subject of a voyage around the Icy Cape and reproduces a letter written to him in 1698 from Arkangel'sk, apparently by a Dutchman.[3] It discusses the Icy Cape found to the north of the land of the Korils (Kuril Islands):

I talked here with a Russian who declares that last winter he was with cossacks in Moscow who had hunted for sables in the most distant parts of Siberia. They sailed in a small boat around the Icy Cape or easternmost corner (hoek), as is shown on Your Honour's map, but they went for three days before reaching the end of the corner. A strong current flowed there so that they had to hold close to shore, but they saw no ice for it was the warmest part of the summer. Thus they rounded the corner and reached the border of China.[4]

Witsen remarks that he could not vouch for the accuracy of this information, and he goes on to quote further from this letter:

A prominent Moscow merchant related to me that in Arkhanel'sk he talked with cossacks who told him that within a period of three days they had walked (afgetreden) to the end of the Icy Cape, that it is so narrow in some places one can see across it.[5] The cossacks or Muscovite soldiers were sent from Yakutsk for the collection of tribute in the land, which they customarily did in groups of ten or twenty men.

...They related further that they had had eight small boats, that four had planned to round the Icy Cape, but at its tip they met such strong whirlpools or, rather, surf, since the northern current seems to run there into the southern, that these four boats were dashed to pieces, and all the men drowned.[6]

And then there is this passage in the letter:

[1] This was Stepan I. Saltykov, voyevoda at Ustyug and Tobol'sk (1690–6).
[2] Vize, 1949, pp. 79, 83; Witsen, 1785, Vol. II, p. 668. This could not have appeared in the first edition.
[3] This too could not have appeared in the first edition.
[4] Vize, 1949, p. 83; Witsen, 1785, Vol. II, p. 676.
[5] Vize mistakenly translates this in Russian as '...[the strait] is so narrow that both the shores were seen'. The Icy Cape, not an interpolated strait, is the antecedent of the Dutch de zelve.
[6] Vize, 1949, p. 84; Witsen, 1785, Vol. II, p. 676.

In the opinion of many the Icy Cape terminated with broken islands. Fishermen (*Visschers*)[1] entered the Icy Sea from the Lena. Several supposed that they rounded this cape and reached the shore near the Kamchatka River, where they killed whales and seals. To go there and return and obtain their catch required three to three and a half or four months.[2]

Witsen's map, we might note parenthetically, exhibits some of the characteristics of the other maps we have examined. He depicts the eastern portion of the Arctic coast of Siberia as a large hump that turns toward the south to run south by east. The Icy cape extends eastward from the mainland into the ocean, separating the Lena Sea from the Eastern Sea. It is open-ended, indicating the uncertainty found in the excerpts as to whether it was passable or impassable. Of the depictions of this cape on the maps we have described, Spafariy's comes the closest to Witsen's in position, configuration, and direction. Also it is mountainous. A second cape, Cape Tabin, a carry-over in name from classical geography, is situated farther north near the corner. It is shorter than the Icy Cape, but likewise open-ended. Witsen's representation of this corner of Asia is, obviously, no better than his Russian sources.

There are several discrepancies in the foregoing extracts. For some of them explanations can be suggested. First to be noted – an omission perhaps rather than a discrepancy – is the absence of any mention of a person participating in or commanding the voyage. The passage of time, the remoteness of the region in which the voyage occurred, the greater importance of the voyage as against the participants in the minds of the informants or Witsen – any or all of these possibilities could explain the omission. We are told by both of Witsen's informants that the participants were cossacks, not promyshlenniks, no names being given. In the third excerpt the participating cossacks are reported as having been sent from Yakutsk to collect tribute and in the fourth extract the fishermen (no doubt promyshlenniks) as entering the Icy Sea from the Lena. From these data one might conclude, as later accounts were to have it, that the voyage began from the Lena River. But these statements can also be read to say where the participants came from, not where the voyage began. This is correctly reported in the first excerpt, from the Kolyma River.

That there were eight boats is, of course, incorrect, but an increase of one seems modest in information transmitted by word of mouth.

[1] Vize translates this as 'promyshlenniks', which is not wholly incorrect since promyshlenniks did engage in fishing.

[2] Vize, 1949, p 84; Witsen, 1785, Vol. II, p. 676.

The statement that four boats were wrecked in rounding the Icy Cape is not wholly incorrect. Four were in fact lost, but presumably before reaching the Icy Cape, not at it. Evidently, however, in oral tradition they came down as having been lost on the nos; but if they were lost between Kolyuchinskaya Bay and Cape Dezhneva, then they were lost on the nos, as in fact Ankudinov's koch was, though that fact is not mentioned in this account. According to the first excerpt, in which the number of boats is correctly stated, all of their occupants perished. The loss of 77 or 78 out of the 89 men who started the voyage may well have caused those informing Witsen's informants to believe that no one survived the voyage even though twenty-five did.

The reason for thinking that some of the voyagers reached the Kamchatka River, as one account reports, we have already presented (p. 192–3). The new aspect which this item of information presents is that the Kamchatka legend was not first encountered during the the conquest of Kamchatka by Atlasov, as Müller states, but seems to have been known earlier in Moscow or Pomor'ye, unless Witsen learned of it after the publication of his first edition in 1692 and before the publication of his second in 1705. In that interval Atlasov presented an account of his conquest of Kamchatka in person at the Siberian Department in Moscow in 1701.[1] The Chinese border as the terminus of the voyage is harder to explain.

The second extract presents the informant cossacks in Moscow in 1697 ('last winter') as participants in the voyage. It hardly seems likely that any of the cossacks participating in the voyage were still alive fifty years later and were to be found in Moscow. To be sure, as late as 1681 several members of Dezhnev's party, the only survivors of the voyage, presented a petition in which they told about their services, but still to be living sixteen years after that would be remarkable. Dezhnev himself had died in 1672. It has to be pointed out too that Dezhnev was the only surviving cossack or service-man. The rest of the survivors were promyshlenniks.[2] So one can not avoid doubt and has to ask if Witsen's informant misunderstood the role of these cossacks.

As puzzling as any of the information recorded by Witsen is the statement in the third extract about walking for three days to the end of the Icy Cape. The statement in the second extract that 'they went for three days before reaching the end of the corner' does not help much

[1] Nikolay N. Ogloblin, 'Dve "Skazki" Atlasov ob otkrytii Kamchatki', *Chteniia v Imperatorskom obshchestve istorii i drevnostey rossiyskikh pri Moskovskom universitete* (Moscow), Tom CLVIII (1891a), Kniga 3, [Chast'] I, p. 11.

[2] *RM*, pp. 164–5; Belov, 1955, pp. 69–70; 1973, 105.

for it does not say whether it was reached by sailing or walking, though the implication is the former. All that is said is that 'they went'. Two explanations come to mind, neither very satisfactory. The Russians could have towed their koches along the shore because of the strong currents and walked to the end, to Cape Dezhneva whose headland is connected with the mainland by a low-lying isthmus from which the waters on both sides could have been seen; or they could have reconnoitred ahead by walking and come to the end. On the other hand, the circumstance of seeing across the cape to water on each side could be a reference to the ridge on the narrow neck of Kamchatka, by then confused with the Chukotskiy Peninsula. But this too does not seem likely since the Russians had yet to reach the end of Kamchatka. Time and distance do indeed seem to have produced distortion.

Finally, just as no names are mentioned in the excerpts, so are no dates given for the events mentioned. The only dates specified are those for Witsen's informants, after 1695 for Saltykov and 1698 for the merchant in Arkhangel'sk. One is led to wonder if all this information reported by Witsen was obtained at the end of the century or whether some of it was obtained by him during his four-month stay in 1665 or from Vinius.

Though Witsen's information has its deficiencies, they are offset by other details that are remarkably close to what Dezhnev tells us, and there are even two or three bits of new information. Strong currents held the voyagers close to the shore – the typical coasting of Russian Arctic mariners. Whirlpools or eddies were encountered in the strait – it was their existence that deterred Dezhnev from making a return journey by sea to the Kolyma – and in placing them near the end of the Icy Cape Witsen's informant provides a new item of information. It took three days to reach the end of the cape according to the second excerpt – the great rocky nos extends far into the sea. Nothing is said as to where the cape began, but since the Russians regarded Kresta Bay as the western limit of the Chukotskiy Peninsula on the southern side, presumably the voyagers could have regarded Kolyuchinskaya Bay as the western limit on the northern side. In that case the distance covered in the three days is about 250 km or 150 miles. This new datum supports Polevoy's contention that the nos is the Chukotskiy Peninsula and rules out Cape Dezhneva. The Moscow cossacks reported further that they saw no ice along the cape – Dezhnev reports unusual freedom from sea ice that summer. Opposite the Icy Cape are islands inhabited by Czbki and *kbaturi*, most likely corrupted forms of Chukchi and *zubatyye*.

All this information which Witsen assembled about Russian maritime activity around the Icy Cape makes it difficult not to believe that the voyage of Dezhnev and Alekseyev, if not its participants, continued to be known at least in Moscow and Arkhangel'sk down to the end of the 17th century. Moreover, if it was still known in these two places, it must have been known in other places, namely in Siberia, in Tobol'sk, Ilimsk, Yeniseysk, and Verkotur'ye, main stops on the route between Yakutsk and Moscow, and in the towns and ports of Pomor'ye. That there was knowledge of the voyage, imperfect though it was, helps to explain why several makers of the sketch maps of northeastern Asia portrayed that region as unconnected with another land mass. Yet the knowledge was not firm enough to dispel the confusion created by the incipient knowledge of Kamchatka, thought by many until the end of the 17th century to be an 'impassable' nos situated north of its true location.

From the time of Witsen's map and book to the uncovering of Dezhnev's reports by Müller in 1736 the currency and degree of knowledge of his voyage seem little changed. The Swede Strahlenberg picked up reports in Tobol'sk of a Russian voyage from the Lena to Kamchatka. He mentioned them in this passage in his *Das nord und östliche Theil von Europa und Asia*:

in old times men crept in their boats along the shores of the ocean and other seas, from one place to another. In this way too Kamchatka...was first discovered by the Russians from the Lena River along the Arctic...When the wind in the Arctic blew from the north and drove the ice to the shore, they retired in their small craft to the mouths of rivers, but when the wind came again from the south and the ice was driven from the shore, they moved out again and thus advanced farther eastward to...Kamchatka.[1]

Kozyrevskiy in Yakutsk knew of the voyage as one to Kamchatka, and Bering brought back to St Petersburg in 1730 the report of a voyage from the Lena to Kamchatka fifty or sixty years before. The details about the voyage were sparse, and no names were associated with it in these reports. Prior to this time Bering's information seems to have been unknown in St Petersburg, perhaps because the Admiralty College was a new government department in a new capital. The Siberian Department in Moscow declined in importance after 1711, and there was little or no transfer of the information accumulated in the latter to the former. Whether by this time knowledge of the voyage still

[1] Pages 99–100.

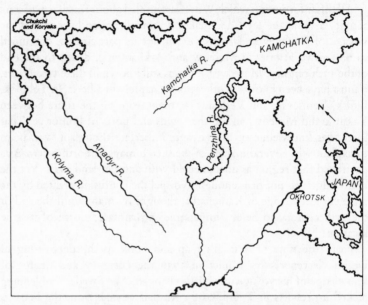

Map 20   Remezov's map of Kamchatka, 1701 (*Atlas*, no. 47)

persisted in Moscow and Pomor'ye is not clear, though the maps known or made in Tobol'sk must have been known in Moscow.[1] Meanwhile, the sketch maps of the 18th century reveal a continuing ambivalence about a passable or impassable nos at the northeastern corner of Siberia. The differences between three of Remezov's maps reflect this ambivalence. One made in 1701 (Map 20) shows a peninsula inhabited by Chukchi and Koryaks and washed by the sea on three sides;[2] a second one, made between 1706 and 1711 (Map 21), depicts an 'impassable Shalatskoy Nos';[3] whereas a third on, made between 1712 and 1714 (Map 1), is ambiguous. It shows two peninsulas north of Kamchatka with passage around them unobstructed; but there is land northwest of them that is cut off by the upper left corner of the map.[4] Similarly Kozyrevskiy's Map of Kamchatka, 1713 (Map 22), shows a free passage around two northeastern capes,[5] while the Anadyrskaya Map (Map 3), made around the turn of the century, shows a massive north directed peninsula cut off at the top by the edge of the map.[6] The so-called

[1] Leo Bagrow, 'Semyon Remezov – a Siberian cartographer', *Imago mundi*, Vol. XI, (1954), p. III.
[2] *Atlas*, no. 47; Fisher, 1977, p. 43.
[3] *Atlas*, no. 49; Fisher, 1977, p. 44.
[4] *Atlas*, no. 48; Fisher, 1977, pp. 38–9.
[5] *Atlas*, no. 50; Fisher, 1977, pp. 40, 77.
[6] *Atlas*, no. 55; Fisher, 1977, pp. 45–6.

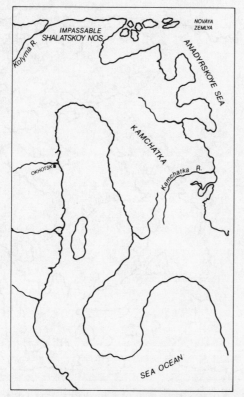

Map 21   Remezov's map of Siberia from the Yenisey to Kamchatka,
1706–11 (detail) (*Atlas*, no. 49)

Meller map carries at the northeastern corner of Siberia an elongated,
narrow, and open-ended peninsula extending eastward, reminiscent of
Witsen's peninsula at the same place.[1]

From all the foregoing evidence it becomes clear that Dezhnev's
voyage, though it became known in Russia and abroad as well, was
not identified as to time, circumstances, or participants. It remained

---

[1] Belov, 1973, opposite p. 152. If Meller drew upon Stadukhin's sketch map of 1659,
as Belov contends (1973, pp. 94–5), then one has to explain the open-endedness of the
peninsula, for surely Stadukhin must have known from Dezhnev himself that he and his
men had circumnavigated the great rocky nos.

The uncertainty of the passability of the northeastern cape carried over to the west, in
the maps of Antoine Thomas, 1690 (*Atlas*, no. 32; Fisher, 1977, pp. 33, 34); John Thornton
(Bagrov, 1952, p. 92; Fisher, 1977, pp. 34, 35); and Guillaume Delisle (Bagrow, 1952, p.
89; Fisher, 1977, pp. 35, 36).

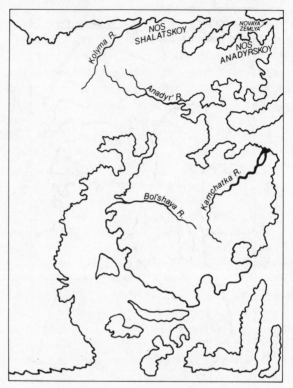

Map 22   Kozyrevskiy's map of Kamchatka, 1713 (*Atlas*, no. 50)

anonymous. In the absence of such information it was possible for the contradictory concept of an impassable cape also to gain currency and compete with the open passage concept instigated by Dezhnev's voyage. Thus it did not lead to a decisive answer to the question of the relation of Asia and America. That had to await Müller's recovery of Dezhnev's discovery.

Pre-revolutionary Russian scholars and modern Soviet scholars have been in agreement in according Dezhnev a high place in the history of geographical discovery. But some of the encomia border on the extravagant, particularly on the part of certain Soviet scholars. Yefimov, whose statements on Russian exploration and discovery can be quite original and thought-provoking, claims that Dezhnev's voyage is 'one of the major events of world history' with 'enormous historical

significance' and that it had great influence on the course of history.[1]
Petr A. Ryabchikov believes that the name of Dezhnev deserves to
stand alongside those of Columbus and Magellan, that his voyage marks
the beginning of Russian navigation in the northern part of Asia, and
that it expanded the limits of Russian dominion to include the natives
of Chukotka and the Anadyr'.[2] Belov ranks the voyage as one of the
most important of the Great Russian geographical discoveries and like
Ryabchikov places Dezhnev alongside Columbus and Magellan as a
great discoverer. Whereas Columbus discovered the new world and
Magellan sailed around its southern end, Dezhnev proved that at
its northern end the new world was independent of and separated
from Asia.[3] These strongly pro-Dezhnev sentiments are no doubt
expressed in part as a reaction to the negative opinions expressed by
Slovtsov in 1838 and Golder in 1914. Too, the official mood in the
Soviet Union after World War II when claims were being made for
Russian 'firsts' in many areas of human achievement (justifiable in
Dezhnev's case) did nothing to weaken the words of praise heaped on
Dezhnev. Now, having assembled the evidence brought forth by
Russian and Soviet scholars, much of it new, and having examined their
analyses, we are in a position to try to produce a balanced appraisal
of the importance of Semen Dezhnev's feat, for feat it was.

We begin our appraisal by reminding ourselves of what it is that
Dezhnev accomplished. He discovered the sea route from the Kolyma
to the Anadyr' River and the great rocky nos on that route, the
Chukotskiy Peninsula. He found the Anadyr' River, whose existence
had earlier become known to the Russians on the Kolyma and Lena
rivers. Four years later he and his men discovered the walrus rookery
at the entrance to Anadyr' Bay, a source of walrus ivory as valuable
as the fur resources of the Anadyr' basin, which proved to be less rich
in sables than had been reported. But one has to go further and point out
that it was not Dezhnev's discovery of the Anadyr' River by way of
the sea route that opened the way to exploitation of that river basin
and led to exploration to the south into the Penzhina and Olyutora
river basins and into Kamchatka. After Dezhnev's success in 1648 and
Stadukhin's failure in 1649 in using the sea route no one used it
thereafter to reach the Anadyr'. Thus Ryabchikov's statement about
Dezhnev's voyage as the beginning of Russian navigation in northeastern
Asia has to be amended: it also marked the end of such navigation until

---

[1] In introduction in *ORZPM*, p. 11.   [2] 1959, p. 88.
[3] 1956, pp. 162, 166; see also 1955, p. 82, and *RM*, pp. 81, 94, 95, 268–73.

Bering passed from the Pacific, i.e. from the south, into the Arctic in 1728. Moreover, Russian navigation in northeastern Siberia began before the voyage, with the voyages between the Lena and Kolyma rivers. Dezhnev's voyage was a one-time extension of those voyages. Russian dominion on the Anadyr´ became possible with the discovery of the route along the Bol´shoy Anyuy River and across portages to tributaries of the upper Anadyr´, and it was Motora and Stadukhin who opened up that route. Their discovery was not dependent upon Dezhnev's discovery. His discovery was the more remarkable, but Motora's and Stadukhin's was the more productive, for though its security was precarious often enough, the Anyuy route became the effective route for travel between the Kolyma and the Anadyr´.

How did Dezhnev view his discoveries? What importance did he attach to them? If our earlier analysis of his reports and petitions on these points is correct, he regarded his discovery of the walrus rookery as more important than his discovery of the sea route.[1] His own experience and the advice from the natives told him that the sea route was not a feasible one for communicating with the Kolyma outposts, and certainly the results of the efforts of later mariners to retrace his route bore out his judgement. Surely the loss of 85% of the men who started out on the voyage was no inducement either to Dezhnev or his associates for further use of the route, and none of them tried to use it again. Belov is nearer reality when he notes that the voyage had the important effect of diverting the Russian stream of colonization from its northeastern direction to the south, toward Cape Olyutorskiy and Kamchatka.[2] When Seliverstov arrived on the Anadyr´, it was the discovery of the walrus rookery, not the discovery of the sea route, over a good portion of which he had sailed with Stadukhin in 1649, for which he tried to take credit. Meanwhile, there is nothing in the reports and petitions of Dezhnev, Semenov, Seliverstov, and others that indicates any awareness on their part of how close to America the voyagers had come while sailing the sea-ocean or that their voyage might have disclosed the relation of Asia to another large land mass.[3] There is no mention of a 'big land' to the east such as is found in later reports of interviews with the Chukchi natives, like Popov's report in 1711.

We have seen that Dezhnev's voyage gave rise to an understanding in some quarters in Russia that Russians had circumnavigated the

[1] Ogloblin, 1890, pp. 24–5; Belov, 1973, p. 109.
[2] 1949, p. 468.   [3] Polevoy, 1964b, p. 227. See also Samoylov, 1945, p. 114.

northeastern corner of Asia, but that understanding was clouded by the conflicting notion of an impassable promontory there. This ambivalent understanding was conveyed outside Russia by Witsen in particular, and later Strahlenberg reported that voyages from the Lena occurred. Thus it was foreigners returning from Russia, not the Russians themselves, who apprised the western world that the latter had demonstrated a free passage between the Arctic and Pacific. The fact remains that Dezhnev's discovery occurred at a time when Russia was ill prepared to appreciate its significance or to communicate it to the outside world. Suspicion of foreigners, endemic in Russia, no doubt made Muscovite officials reluctant to inform foreigners of Russian discoveries. Ecclesiastical officials in particular and officials of state distrusted foreigners and their intentions. Matters of state concern were to be kept from them. In 1619, for example, the sea route to Siberia from Pomor'ye was closed to foreigners and not reopened during the rest of the century. Meanwhile, there was no trumpeting abroad of Russian discoveries. The age of Peter the Great had not yet arrived.

For nearly a century Dezhnev's voyage languished in obscurity. Then came Müller's discovery of Dezhnev's reports and his conclusion that Dezhnev and Alekseyev had sailed through the strait navigated by Bering, and this eighty years before Bering, thereby demonstrating conclusively what Bering had not demonstrated beyond a reasonable doubt, the separation of Asia and America, and answering a question to which the west had long sought an answer. Müller's rediscovery came at a much more propitious time than Dezhnev's original discovery. By then the Russian Imperial Academy of Sciences had been founded and was functioning. Among its members was much interest in a northeast or northwest passage. In the west were several noted savants equally interested in the question, and they looked to Russia as the only source for an answer to the crucial question. Furthermore, there was greater willingness on the part of the highest state officials in Russia to permit the release of information on Russian discoveries. Though some information remained confidential, they now sought recognition for Russia in the sciences as officials in the mid-17th century had not. So by virtue of Müller's rediscovery and his publicizing of it in 1758 Dezhnev acquired an importance which neither he nor his associates had thought of or aspired to. By answering an important scientific question Dezhnev had placed himself alongside Columbus, who had discovered the new world; Vasco da Gama, who had discovered the southern limits of Africa; and Magellan, who had found the route around South America. But unlike these men Dezhnev made his discovery in a part of the world from which few consequences of major or world importance could flow. Chukotka was about as far from the European Atlantic seaboard, the dynamic centre of the world in the early modern period, as a place could be. To reach it from that seaboard required a journey by sea of eighteen to twenty thousand miles. Further, it was burdened with one of the world's most inhospitable climates and lacked easily accessible resources or commodities in great demand. Not until the 19th century would European vessels penetrate the waters around the Chukotskiy Peninsula on a regular basis, from the south, not the west – in search of whales. After the initial influx of traders and promyshlenniks in the middle of the 17th century their numbers fell off as the century wore on and the original abundance of fur-bearing animals declined. Many turned to the rivers to the south, the Olyutora, Penzhina, and Gizhiga. Not only did the numbers in Chukotka decline, but in the Kolyma basin too.[1] Meanwhile, it was not until well into the reign of Catherine the Great that the Russians reached a *modus vivendi* with the hostile and stubborn Chukchi, and it was not until Captain Cook's voyage into the north Pacific that the Russian government began to give its north Pacific discoveries serious attention and thought of protection. In short, the conditions under which Dezhnev's geographical discovery might have become a great discovery were few or absent. Unlike Columbus and the others his name has not become a household word, even in the Soviet Union.

Having said all this, it still does not detract from the voyage as an achievement of men. It required fortitude, determination and steadfastness, and navigational skill in dangerous waters on the part of Dezhnev and his men – and no doubt a modicum or more of luck – to reach the Pacific shore of Siberia, and these same qualities to march ten weeks to the Anadyr´ and there to survive the winter. By so doing he added an important bit to the knowledge of the geography of the north Pacific and the limits of Asia, a bit which answered a question of concern to geographers, men of commerce, and statesmen. And, it may be noted, Dezhnev and his fellow Russians were the first Europeans to pass through the Bering Strait, at a time when conjecture, not knowledge, determined its location and configuration on the maps of his time. For all this he is to be recognized and awarded a respected place in the pantheon of geographical discoverers.

[1] Belov, 1956, pp. 181–2.

GOLDER REFUTED

We noted in chapter 1 that the American historian, Frank A. Golder, has been for more than a half century the chief sceptic and detractor of Semen Dezhnev's exploit. His chapter, 'A Critical Examination of Deshnef's Voyage', in his *Russian Expansion on the Pacific, 1641–1850*, has been more widely read among non-readers of Russian than any account by Russian or Soviet writers, and the book itself has been the source for many derivative accounts of Russian exploration and conquest in the north Pacific. It is in order therefore to examine Golder's arguments whereby he rejects the claim of Müller and others for Dezhnev's priority in sailing through the Bering Strait, thus denying Bering the honour of being the first. I made such an examination more than two decades ago,[1] but an article does not permit the extent of background for a critique that the present commentary does, and further reflection and new material, as well as the discovery of a few misreadings of Golder's arguments, justify a revision and updating of my earlier critique.

It is Golder's contention that most of the journey of Dezhnev and his companions from the Kolyma River to the Anadyr´ River was by land, that their itinerary took them nowhere near the Bering Strait. He reads the evidence to mean that their boat was wrecked not far east of the Kolyma River in the vicinity of Cape Shelagskiy, and that after wandering around for ten weeks he and his companions stumbled onto the Anadyr´ River without any clear idea of their whereabouts. Afterwards he mistook the mouth of some river which he had passed near Cape Shelagskiy to be the mouth of the Anadyr´.[2]

Golder's disputing of Dezhnev's voyage is not directed primarily at Dezhnev, who says nothing about passing through a strait, but at Müller and others who conclude from the evidence in Dezhnev's reports and petitions that his voyage did carry him through the Bering Strait. For our purpose we may group Golder's reasons for refusing to accept the traditional interpretation of the voyage into four categories. (1) The

---

[1] 'Semen Dezhnev and Professor Golder', *Pacific Historical Review*, Vol. xxv (1956), pp. 281–92. [2] Pages 71, 85–6.

documentary evidence on which the claim rests is unreliable or confusing. (2) The physical conditions prevailing in the Arctic Ocean and Bering Sea, the primitive boats and navigation methods used by the Russians, and the failure of subsequent attempts to sail eastward from the Kolyma make such a voyage inconceivable. (3) The descriptive details given by Dezhnev and his associates to identify the great rocky nos which they saw and visited are vague and apply equally well to Cape Shelagskiy. (4) There is no reference to Dezhnev and his voyage outside the reports by himself and his friends; they are ignored by his contemporaries. These categories we will examine in turn.

First, the unreliability of the documentary evidence. Golder maintains that the documentary evidence

presents peculiar difficulties owing (a) to the ignorance of the writers, the indefiniteness of the language and vagueness of the descriptions, (b) the doubtful credibility of the witnesses whose lives were made up of fighting, gambling, robbing, and killing, and (c) the character of the evidence which is ex-parte.[1]

All the documentary evidence comes from Dezhnev himself and his companions on the voyage, and according to Golder, contains contradictions.[2] Moreover, he notes, one must keep in mind that the Russians of this time had only a vague and mistaken conception of the geography of eastern Siberia.

In part Golder is right about the nature of the evidence. Much of it is indeed ex-parte and therefore needs to be corroborated whenever possible and used with care. But much historical evidence is ex-parte, and if for that reason it were rejected outright, historians would be much the poorer. Some of Dezhnev's statements do appear contradictory and inconsistent, as in the matters of the distance of the great rocky nos from the Anadyr´ and the number of boats participating in the voyage. The language is too often indefinite and the descriptions vague, but not to the extent that Golder claims. Had he sought clarification from other sources and not mistranslated a passage, the language and descriptions would have become clearer to him. Much of the difficulty in judging Dezhnev's voyage arises from his condensed language and ellipses, from the absence of explanatory and narrative detail, more notably about the part of the voyage from the Kolyma to the great rocky nos. But he does give a number of particulars about the part of the journey from the nos to the Anadyr´, and it is on these

---

[1] Page 71; cf. also pp. 75–6. [2] Pages 78, 81, 87, note 192.

particulars that Müller's conclusions rest. What Golder failed to grasp is the purpose behind Dezhnev's reports and petitions: it was not to lay claim to a pioneering voyage, but to explain to the authorities the expenses, hardships, and suffering he had undergone and the services he had performed since leaving the Kolyma. It was not to deceive as an earlier detractor, Sarychev, and Golder seem to think.[1] Golder's approach to the subject is marked by a failure or unwillingness to probe further and seek explanations of inconsistencies and contradictions, to try to give substance to vagueness. Surely this is the task of the historian. But rather than seek the degree of truth in them he chooses to see them as an excuse to dismiss the evidence as of little value.

In labelling the writers of the documents as ignorant and in attacking their credibility because of their wild and lawless mode of life Golder is himself guilty of vagueness and, in my opinion, of exaggeration. Ignorant of what? He does not say. Dezhnev and his fellow frontiersmen appear to have known their vocation and the country in which they moved as well as any comparable group elsewhere. Their on-the-spot testimony is surely as valuable as the knowledge or opinion of some armchair geographer thousands of miles from the scene in another time. Golder elsewhere seems to contradict this charge of ignorance when he argues that Dezhnev should have been able to distinguish between the Chukchi natives and the Eskimos because 'his eye was well trained, and...he had many opportunities to observe the Chukchi'.[2]

Meanwhile, to impugn the testimony of the writers of the documents on the basis of their rough and sometimes violent frontier life is to condemn by life-style. Thus, it appears, Golder would cast their testimony aside indiscriminately rather than judge it individually on the basis of a dispassionate examination. The fact is that in the few instances where there is evidence not ex-parte[3] it corroborates Dezhnev in several particulars. If one finds in the documents little by way of corroboration, one also finds little or nothing by way of refutation. The main difficulty with Dezhnev's testimony is not its unreliability, but its lack of detail that would flesh out the account of his voyage. It may be noted that such biographical information as we have about him suggests that Dezhnev was well regarded by his associates and that he was considered by his superiors as a man of integrity.[4]

As a bit of confusing evidence Golder singles out the Siberians'

[1] Page 82, note 181.   [2] Page 82, note 181.
[3] From Stadukhin (document 15) and Witsen, as related on pp. 244–5 above.
[4] Ogloblin, 1890, pp. 38–54; see pp. 123–4 above.

concept of the land east of the Kolyma.[1] He notes the Godunov map of 1667 on which the northern and eastern coasts of Siberia are shown as meeting at a right angle, and quotes the passage in Titov's collection of articles describing the mountains which extend to the sea and form an impassable cape between the Kolyma and the Anadyr´ and from which one can see both the Lena (Arctic) and Amur (Pacific) seas.[2] 'This view,' Golder writes, 'the impossibility of water communication between the Koluima and the Anadir, should be kept in mind, for it is held by all who deal with this subject during this period.' Presumably Golder is referring to men of the 17th century, not later writers. Yet, as we saw in the preceding chapter, not all who dealt with the subject then held to the impossibility of water communication between the Kolyma and the Anadyr´. Strahlenberg's and Witsen's works were as available to Golder as they have been to the present generation of scholars.

In reading those parts of Golder's chapter which deal with the physical conditions along the route of the voyage, i.e. the ice and fog, and with the primitive boats and navigation methods used by the Russians, one is persuaded that it is these which convinced Golder that Dezhnev and his associates could not have made a 2,100-mile voyage in one summer, a conclusion reinforced by the fact that all known attempts thereafter to sail eastward to the Pacific from the Kolyma River ended in failure. Not until 1878–9 was such a passage successfully made, by Nordenskiöld in a specially designed and equipped vessel.

On the basis of the evidence as adduced by Golder on this point his case is convincing, but the trouble is that he sets forth some errors of fact and draws some unwarranted conclusions. One error of fact is the distance of 2,100 miles from the Kolyma to the Anadyr´. This distance was calculated on the basis of the winding coastline distance of 1,115 miles from the Kolyma to East Cape of 1,045 miles from East Cape to the Anadyr´,[3] not on the sailing distance of 850 and 600 statute miles (1,300 and 975 km) respectively, as we noted in chapter 8.[4] Golder later conceded that the figure of 2,100 miles was an unrealistic figure and scaled it down to 1,300 miles, 800 miles from the Kolyma to East Cape and 500 miles from the cape to the Anadyr´.[5]

[1] Pages 68, 71.
[2] Titov, 1890, pp. 49, 53–4, 110; see p. 262 above.
[3] Page 78, note 177.
[4] The figure 850 miles is explained on p. 178. The figure 600 miles was reached by the same method. The latter figure differs from Berg's figure in that his is nautical miles (1946, p. 34), whereas the figure 600 is statute miles, which, when converted into nautical miles, comes out 520.
[5] Communication to the editor, *American Historical Review*, Vol. xx (1915), p. 900.

Unwarranted is Golder's contention that in leaving the mouth of the Kolyma in mid-July, which was the earliest time the Russians could have done so,[1] they could not have reached the Anadyr´ in one Arctic navigation season. But why couldn't they? If the Russians left the mouth of the Kolyma in mid-July, the seven koches would have had two months to cover the 800 miles to East Cape, which in Golder's time was believed to be the great rocky nos. There, Dezhnev says, the Russians engaged in a fight with the natives on September 20. Within this two-month period the Russians would have had to average fewer than fifteen miles per 24-hour period to cover the 800 miles.[2] The rest of Dezhnev's voyage was made in a period of two to four weeks, accelerated no doubt by the storm that separated Dezhnev's and Alekseyev's koches. Even if we accept Polevoy's contention that the fight with the Chukchi occurred not at East Cape, but farther on near Kresta bay, the average speed that would have had to be maintained over the two months is only 19–20 miles per 24-hour period. Did Golder overlook the fact that the long days of the Arctic summer facilitated round-the-clock sailing?

Golder rejects such a conclusion, however, because of the prevailing ice conditions in the Arctic Ocean and Bering Sea. He points out that seven known attempts to sail eastward from the Kolyma between 1649 and 1787 were stopped by impenetrable ice.[3] This is impressive as to the difficulties which the Russians experienced in sailing eastward from the Kolyma. Yet it may be noted that in the period 1633–48 some 40 successful voyages were made between the Lena and the Yana, Indigirka, and Kolyma rivers, along a route that carried the voyagers above 72° N latitude, higher than any point east of the Kolyma.[4] The fact remains that seven failures to reach the Pacific from the Kolyma in 238 years are not proof that in none of the other years could a successful voyage have been carried out.

Golder continues in his scepticism. He rejects the argument that because Dezhnev and Semenov in 1653 built a koch for the purpose of taking 'the sovereign's treasury' to Yakutsk, this meant that Dezhnev had come to the Anadyr´ by sea. One could then argue, he asserts, that Seliverstov also came by sea because in his report of 1655

---

[1] Page 86. Though in 1648 this appears to have been true, there is record of years when the ice broke up at the mouth of the Kolyma in late May or early June (new style) (Berg, 1946, p. 37).

[2] Koches cited by Belov (pp. 169–70 above) averaged much more than this.

[3] Page 96.

[4] DAI, Tom III, pp. 276, 277, 280–3; RM, pp. 328–31; Vize, 1948a, pp. 70–2; Ogloblin, 1903, pp. 38–62 passim.

he states that he did not know whether in the coming year he would take the tribute to Yakutsk by land or sea.[1] Golder further contends that the natives' words of caution that not every year is the ice carried from the shore out to the sea apply to the Gulf of Anadyr´, not the Arctic, since the natives with whom Dezhnev talked lived near the Anadyr´, and that they apply not to 1648, but to 1653 when he was building the koch.[2] In the same vein he writes that 'the words of Deshnef that he went from the Koluima to find the Anaduir have no weight because they were written in 1655' whereas in 1648 he was looking for the Pogycha.[3]

In responding to these arguments one would first like to ask Golder why Dezhnev, being defeated in 1648, as Golder argues, from making it all the way to the Anadyr´ by sea, should think he could do it in reverse direction in 1653 and go so far as to construct a koch. It makes more sense to think that having succeeded in 1648, he might venture to return by the sea route five years later. Meanwhile, Golder overlooks Dezhnev's remark that he and his men knew that 'the ocean is big and the eddies near the land strong' (document 10, p. 62). How better could he have known this than by having sailed the route himself? Had he been told this by the natives, would he not have said so, as he did about the ice-free year? The fact that Seliverstov, who, we know, came to the Anadyr´ by land, considered returning to Yakutsk can be interpreted just as well to mean that he was aware of the sea route and its feasibility because he knew that it was by that route that Dezhnev had come to the Anadyr´. Here Golder seems to be 'reaching' to find arguments to support his case. As for the caution of the natives, it may well be, as Golder claims, that they were referring to conditions in the Gulf of Anadyr´, not the Arctic Ocean, but the accompanying contention that it applies to the year 1653, not 1648, seems inconsistent. If it were during the summer of 1653 that the ice was being blown away from the shore, then should not that circumstance have encouraged a return to the Kolyma by sea? Though, of course, Golder could not have known this, the evidence turned up by Belov that the summer of 1648 was an unusually favourable navigation season in the Arctic argues further against Golder's contention.[4] And finally, just because Dezhnev said in 1648 that he was looking for the Anadyr´ under its incorrect name, the Pogycha, his discovery of the river under its correct name is not invalidated.

[1] *DAI*, Tom IV, p. 10.   [2] Pages 83–4.
[3] Pages 85.   [4] 1955, p. 75; *RM*, p. 331; see pp. 169–70 above.

At the time Golder wrote the standard view of the Russian koch was that it was a primitively constructed craft, ill-fitted to battle with the sea and ice; and one cannot deny that this view encouraged scepticism about the voyage as claimed by Müller and Ogloblin. But here again evidence unavailable to Golder refutes him. We have seen in chapter 8 that the Siberian koch was more than a primitively constructed vessel, that its design, born of long experience in coping with sailing conditions in the Arctic was better suited to navigation there than were most vessels of western design and perhaps more modern construction. The koch was not a boat knocked together by inexperienced mariners. It is to be remembered that Dezhnev and many of his contemporaries came to the Kolyma all or part of the way by sea from Yakutsk.

Golder also questions that enough food for ninety men over a 100-day period could have been carried in the koches. Little meat could be obtained on the Kolyma, and there probably were few provisions besides rye flour.[1] What Golder failed to appreciate is the extent to which the Russian frontiersmen depended upon fish as a source of food, as a reading of the documents attest and as to do the customs lists with their inventory of fishing equipment (documents 22 and 25).[2] To be sure, much of the information uncovered on these matters since Golder's time does not refer explicitly to Dezhnev and the other participants in the voyage, but neither do Golder's objections, and the new information does increase the credibility of the proponents of Müller's conclusions regarding the voyage.

Golder bases much of his case against Müller's interpretation on the contention that he and his followers incorrectly apply Dezhnev's descriptive details of the great rocky nos to East Cape. Golder writes: 'The defenders of Deshnef are almost willing to base their whole case on the proposition that the cape mentioned by Deshnef is East Cape'.[3] Thus, if he can demonstrate that the great rocky nos is not East Cape,

---

[1] Pages 93–4.

[2] Bakhrushin, 1951, p. 87. It is perhaps natural, if not realistic, for a 20th-century American to impute to 17th-century Russians a dependence on meat as a staple of their diet. But cattle raising existed only on a small scale in Siberia in the 17th century. Fish from the many rivers of those areas provided the protein staple. Stadukhin (document 12, p. 76) states that the service-men and promyshlenniks on the Kolyma and Pogycha rivers always ate fish. Document 10 contains some examples of the Russians' dependence upon fish as the staple of their diet, and document 26 states that the 'food on the Kovyma is fish'.

[3] Page 77. Golder appears to place Müller among the advocates of East Cape as Dezhnev's nos (p. 76), but as we have seen the nos for Müller was not East Cape (Serdtse Kamen' on his map), but his imaginary peninsula, Cape Shelaginskoy or Chukotskoy.

he has destroyed their case. To that end he argues that the directions north and northeast specified for the situation of the great rocky nos are imperfect and unreliable; and he doubts that the Siberians of that time had a compass or knew of its use. Even if one admits the description to be accurate, it applies to many other capes in northern Siberia, though he does not say which ones. He finds it preposterous that one could sail in a koch the 1,045 nautical miles from East Cape to Anadyr´ in three days, let alone walk it as Müller claimed. In fact, he says, no such cape as Dezhnev describes exists on the eastern coast of Siberia.

With this assertion in mind one wonders whether Golder had aquainted himself with the discussion by captains Cook and King of East Cape as Dezhnev's nos. If one excludes the Chukotskiy Peninsula as the nos, as everyone has before Polevoy advanced its claim, then the cape which most closely fits the ten features of the rocky nos mentioned by Dezhnev is East Cape or Cape Dezhneva, as I argued in my 1956 article.[1] Golder's arguments against East Cape rest on insufficient research. The distance of 1,045 miles we have already found Golder to have reduced to 500 miles. Witsen tells us that the Russians in the Arctic did use the compass, a statement which appears to be confirmed by the presence of loadstones in bone in Alekseyev's party (Golder can not be held for this last particular datum). We also learned that Dezhnev did not say that one could walk from the nos to the Anadyr´ in three days. Here Golder followed Müller's mistranslation, that there was an alternate land route, and repeated Müller's error when he translated Dezhnev's statement in his report of 1655 about going from the coast to the mouth of the Anadyr´ in three days.[2]

Having tried to discredit East Cape as Dezhnev's nos, Golder then undertakes to establish Cape Shelagskiy as that nos. The passage in which he endeavours to do this begins by stating that in his report Dezhnev attempts to explain to the officers at Yakutsk just where his cape lies, and to help them he gives them a landmark, the Kolyma. That is acceptable, but Golder does not mention a second landmark, the Anadyr´ River: Dezhnev says that the nos is between the Kolyma and the Anadyr´. Golder then goes on to say:

The cape, [Dezhnev] says, is not Sviatoi Nos, west of the Koluima, but another cape east of that river. Which one? There are many, all unknown to them. Under the circumstances one would naturally name the one nearest the Koluima, or the most northerly, or the most dangerous.

[1] Page 291.   [2] Pages 282, 287.

But would one 'naturally' name the nearest, or the most northerly, or the most dangerous? Why not the longest, or the rockiest, or the one nearest the Anadyr´ River, the other landmark? One can not escape the conclusion that Golder chose his features with an eye to those that best identified Cape Shelagskiy. Golder continues:

East Cape comes under neither of these heads. In describing a new country one does not pass by the nearer and more important points to speak of similar places farther removed and less important. Shelagski Cape is farther north, more dangerous, and nearer the Koliuma than East Cape.[1]

Golder assumes that Dezhnev is describing a new country, but he is not. He is describing a great rocky nos situated on the route to the Anadyr´. If it happens to be nearer the Anadyr´ than the Kolyma, then so be it. Why Cape Shelagskiy was more important that East Cape Golder does not explain, unless it was because it is farther north, more dangerous, and nearer the Kolyma than East Cape. But for all Golder knew East Cape was dangerous too. Moreover, Dezhnev could not have known that East Cape was farther south and less dangerous unless he had come to know of its existence. The validity of Golder's arguments based on a comparison of the two capes has to stand on the premise that Dezhnev knew of both of them, and Golder does not believe that he did. In short, Golder's arguments here are self-serving.

Farther on Golder quotes from Dezhnev's report as follows: 'In the year 1648, September 20, in going from the Koluima River to the sea...the Chukchi in a fight wounded the trader Alexeef.'[2] From it Golder draws this conclusion:

Taken as it stands, and there is no reason why it should be read in any other way, the statement means that on that late day Deshnef was not very far from the Koluima, and therefore by October 1, about the time he was wrecked, he could not possibly have reached East Cape, and, it goes without saying, the Anaduir.[3]

The reasoning behind this statement when standing by itself is hard to follow. It is a non-sequitur. Golder tries to fill the gap in this reasoning by referring to the statement in the report of Vetoshka and others (document 11) that the great nos lies 'in front of' the place where Stadukhin turned back in 1649 and by commenting: 'Since Stadukhin had gone only about seven days from the Koluima, it follows that the cape in front of Stadukhin can not have been very far from the Koluima.' Given Golder's scepticism about the sailing qualities of the

---

[1] Page 77.   [2] Page 81.   [3] Page 81.

koch, he no doubt believed that Stadukhin's koch could not have gone very far in seven days even though it sailed with sails unslackened. Since the cape lay 'in front of' the place where Stadukhin stopped, it could not have been far from the Kolyma. But Golder's interpretation of 'in front of' to mean a short distance is not necessarily correct. The Russian word is *vperede*. 'Ahead' or 'beyond' better renders the meaning of the word, and they imply an indefinite distance rather than the immediate proximity suggested by 'in front of'. In reading the documents that relate to Russian activity in northeastern Siberia and along the Arctic seaboard, one becomes aware of a deficiency, namely, that writers say little about the distance between points and indicate distance in the most general terms.[1] When Vetoshka reported that the great rocky nos lay ahead of the stopping point of Stadukhin and his party, he could have meant any distance from a few to a few hundred miles. The probable fact is that he did not know how far ahead the nos was situated. In light of this argument Golder's attempt to place the great rocky nos close to the Kolyma becomes unconvincing.

Finally, Golder dismisses the Diomede Islands as the locale of the labret-wearing Chukchi. The islands, he writes, are not opposite East Cape and are very far from it, far enough at least to make it impossible to observe from the sea just what ornaments the inhabitants wore. If Dezhnev did stop at the islands, he used up precious time and was not where he should be if he were looking for a river.[2] According to Vrangel', Golder adds, there are two small islands near Cape Shelagskiy, which qualify it as the nos. On the point of the Diomede Islands Golder's contention does find some support in the similar questioning, if not outright rejection, of those islands by Polevoy. But he does not see the two islands near Cape Shelagskiy as their replacement. Golder finishes this discussion by calling attention to the piles of whalebone noticed by Vrangel' in the vicinity of Cape Shelagskiy, which he takes to be the tower of whale bones mentioned by Dezhnev.[3]

One is constrained to note that Golder neglects several of the identifying features of the great rocky nos. He mentions only five of the ten. The northerly and northeasterly location and the turning

---

[1] An exception is the three days-and-nights' run from the great rocky nos to the Anadyr'.

[2] Pages 81–2.

[3] Page 82. For the reference to the two islands and the piles of whalebone Golder cites Wrangell, *Siberia and Polar Sea* (London, 1840), pp. 325 and 327. But I find no record of a work of that title by Vrangel'. Since the place and date of publication are the same as for his *Narrative of an expedition to the polar sea* and the passages for which pp. 325 and 327 are cited occur on pp. 339–40 and 342 of the *Narrative*, one has to conclude that that work is the one cited and erroneously titled and paginated.

around toward the Anadyr´ apply, he says, to many capes. The two islands and the tower of whalebones apply to Cape Shelagskiy. The three days-and-nights' sailing distance from the Anadyr´ River does not apply to East Cape, and presumably not to any other cape in northeastern Siberia. The other five features he ignores in their application to East Cape and Cape Shelagskiy, or for that matter to any other cape. Such are the nature and extent of Golder's discussion of the matter that is at the heart of the question whether Dezhnev passed through the Bering Strait.

One may further comment that Golder does not explain why it took Dezhnev and his men more than three months, from 20 June to early October, to travel from Nizhne-Kolymsk to the alleged point of shipwreck near Cape Shelagskiy. To travel 220 miles (355 km) in two and a half months is at the rate of three miles a day. At that pace would not Dezhnev and Alekseyev have decided to give up and return to the Kolyma, as they did the year before? Had they been shipwrecked in early October near Cape Shelagskiy, would 'cold and hungry men' have wandered aimlessly to the south for ten weeks rather than try to return to the Kolyma? Had they started from Cape Shelagskiy, would they not have come upon the Anadyr´ farther up river rather than near its mouth as Dezhnev reports. Moreover, he states that the koch was wrecked 'beyond the Anadyr´' (document 9)[1] and that he passed the mouth of the Anadyr´ on his voyage (document 28), statements which Golder dismisses as mistaking one of the 'many' rivers near the Kolyma for the Anadyr´. How Dezhnev could have mistaken the much smaller rivers which debouch into the Arctic near the Kolyma for the much larger Anadyr´ Golder does not explain; and Dezhnev and his men could hardly have become so disoriented as not to know on which side of the Anadyr´ they arrived, that is, the south or right bank – hence they had been wrecked beyond the Anadyr´ – or on the north or left bank – to conform with Golder's thesis. The fabric of Golder's thesis is indeed loose and fragile.

It is further testimony to the quality of Golder's scholarship that he misrepresented Müller's account of what happened to the men in Alekseyev's koch. According to Golder Müller told of Alekseyev's koch being wrecked in Kamchatka.[2] But as we saw in chapter 8, Müller reported that it was the survivors of Alekseyev's and Ankudinov's

---

[1] Incidentally Golder mistranslates Dezhnev's phrase 'on the forward end *beyond* the Anadyr´' as 'on the forward end *of* the Anadyr´' (emphases added). Neither phrase is very clear, but Golder's is the less clear.　　　　[2] Page 84.

parties, those who escaped from the attack of the Koryaks, that legend has fleeing to Kamchatka, including Fedotov's alleged son. It was Krasheninnikov, not Müller, who put Alekseyev in Kamchatka. Yet Golder attributes this 'mythological account' to Müller, despite the fact that he correctly rendered Müller's statement on the episode in Appendix A of his book.[1]

The fourth category in Golder's argumentation is the absence of any reference by contemporaries of Dezhnev to the voyage. We saw in the last chapter that although no reference to Dezhnev or Alekseyev by name appears in the literature of the 17th and early 18th centuries, there are references to a voyage from the Lena to Kamchatka that can hardly be other than the voyage of Dezhnev and Alekseyev. Witsen learned of it from a man in Arkhangel'sk, Strahlenberg in Tobol'sk, both of whose books were available in Golder's time; and Bering learned of the voyage, probably in Tobol'sk, though this fact did not become known until recently. It would be a telling argument against Golder's contention if it could be demonstrated that Popov's report of the Chukchi's having been visited by Russians from the sea (document 33) refers to Dezhnev, but in light of Ivanov's voyage and effort in 1660 to obtain tribute from these natives and several Russian excursions there in the 1680s and 1690s[2] Popov's report is inconclusive on this point. To some modern historians it seems puzzling, given the interest then in the question of an Asian-American strait, that Dezhnev's voyage received so little attention. But it must be remembered that the interest of the Russians at this time was in finding new areas of fur-bearing animals or other natural products to exploit, not in answering questions of global geography. Too the Russians distrusted foreigners and did not tell them all they knew. Perhaps more important is the fact that no use was made of Dezhnev's sea route, and in time the fur resources of northeastern Siberia become depleted and the Russians turned their attention elsewhere. Also the appearance of the concept of an impassable barrier in Chukotka cast doubts on the reports of the voyage. And finally, it must be remembered that Dezhnev stressed in his career not the voyage, but the discovery of the walrus rookery at the entrance to Anadyr' Bay. His description of the great rocky nos was his means of situating it in relation to Stadukhin's voyage, not to another continent. Under these circumstances what happened in a remote part of the world could become poorly remembered and Dezhnev's name lost.

[1] Page 281.   [2] Polevoy, 1965a, p. 105, note 2.

As one goes through the arguments and evidence against Golder, one is struck by how much of the refutation of his views is based on from his ignoring or careless use of evidence that was available to him at the time. The refutation does not have to depend upon what Soviet scholars have turned up, though of course the new information has made the case against him much more convincing. Meanwhile, his ill-founded conclusions have provided added incentive to more than one Soviet scholar to probe the archives and to seek explanations of the puzzling aspects of the voyage. Thus we now know much more about the voyage, or, if not the voyage itself, about its background and antecedents – the great activity in northeastern Siberia in the mid-17th century, the considerable maritime operations between the Lena and Kolyma rivers, the widespread interest in the Pogycha–Anadyr´ River – and the resources of the participants, as well as the boats they used. Such questions as the identity of the great rocky nos and the fate of those in Alekseyev's koch have been probed more thoroughly. All of this supports Dezhnev's proponents and further undercuts Golder's position. That position turns out to be ex-parte, to have been hastily conceived and put together. It bears out the judgement of the anonymous reviewer of his book in the *American Historical Review*[1] – he turns out to be the Alaskan specialist and naturalist-historian, William Healey Dall[2] – who said of the chapter under discussion that 'the argument partakes too much of the nature of special pleading to be convincing'. The book itself, he concludes, 'is lacking in the workmanship to be expected of a trained historian'. Dezhnev and his fellow voyagers deserved better from Golder.

[1] Vol. xx (1915), pp. 626–7.
[2] Paul Bartsch et al., *A bibliography and short biographical sketch of William Healey Dall* (Washington, D.C., 1946), p. 88.

BIBLIOGRAPHY

Adelung, Johann C.
1768 *Geschichte der Schiffahrten und Versuche, welche zur Entdeckung des nordöstlichen Weges nach Japan und China von verschiedenen Nationen unternommen worden, zum Behufe der Erdbeschreibung und Naturgeschichte dieser Gegenden entworfen*...Halle.

Alekseyev, Aleksandr I.
1966 *Gavriil Andreyevich Sarychev.* Moscow.

Andreyev, Aleksandr I.
1937 'Trudy G. F. Millera o Sibiri' [The works of G. F. Müller on Siberia], in: Gerhard F. Müller, *Istoriya Sibiri* [History of Siberia] Moscow and Leningrad, Tom I, pp. 57–144.

1940 'Zametki po istoricheskoy geografii Sibiri XVI–XVII vv.' [Notes on the historical geography of Siberia of the 16th–17th centuries], *Izvestiya VGO* (Leningrad), Tom LXXII (1940), pp. 152–7.

1959 'Trudy G. F. Millera o vtoroy kamchatksoy ekspeditsii' [Works of G. F. Müller on the Second Kamchatka Expedition], *Izvestiya VGO* (Leningrad), Tom XCI, pp. 3–16.

1965 *Ocherki po istochnikovedeniyu Sibiri* [Outlines in source studies of Siberia], Vypusk vtoroy: *XVIII vek (pervaya polovina)* [18th century (first half)], Moscow and Leningrad.

Andreyev, Aleksandr I., ed.
1944 *Russkiye otkrytiya v tikhom okeane i severnoy Amerike v XVIII–XIX vekakh* [Russian discoveries in the Pacific ocean and north America in the 18th–19th centuries]. Moscow and Leningrad.

1952 *Russian discoveries in the Pacific and in North America in the eighteenth and nineteenth centuries; a collection of materials.* Translated from the Russian by Carl Ginsburg. Ann Arbor.

Armstrong, Terence E.
1952 *The northern sea route; Soviet exploitation of the North East Passage.* Cambridge, Eng. [Scott polar research institute, Special publication, No. 1.]

1979 'Cook's reputation in Russia', *Captain James Cook and his times* (Robin Fisher and Hugh Johnston, editors; London and Vancouver, B.C.), pp. 121–8, 248–50.

Atlas   *Atlas geograficheskikh otkrytiy v Sibiri i severo-zapadnoy Amerike*
XVII–XVIII vv. [Atlas of geographical discoveries in Siberia
and northwestern America in the 17th–18th centuries]. Edited
by Aleksey V. Yefimov. Moscow, 1964. [AN SSSR, Institut
etnografii.]

Baddeley, John F.

1916   Review of: Frank A. Golder, *Russian expansion on the Pacific,*
1641–1850, in *The geographical journal* (London), vol. XLVII, pp.
468–70.

1919   *Russia, Mongolia, China*...2 vols. London and New York.

Baer, Karl E. von

1872   *Peter's des Grossen Verdienste um die Erweiterung der geograph-*
ischen Kenntnisse. St. Petersburg. [Beiträge zur Kenntniss des
russischen Reiches und der angrenzenden Länder Asiens, vol.
XVI.]

Bagrow, Leo

1947   'Sparwenfeld's map of Siberia', *Imago mundi* (Stockholm),
vol. IV, pp. 65–70.

1952   'The first Russian maps of Siberia and their influence on the
west European cartography of N.E. Asia', *Imago mundi*
(Leiden), vol. IX, pp. 83–93.

1954   'Semyon Remezov – a Siberian cartographer', *Imago mundi*
(Leiden), vol. XI, pp. 111–26.

Baker, John N. L.

1937   *A history of geographical discovery and exploration.* New edition
revised. London; reprinted, 1945.

Bakhrushin, Sergey V.

1937   'G. F. Miller kak istorik Sibiri' [G. F. Müller as historian of
Siberia], in: Gerhard F. Müller, *Istoriya Sibiri* [History of
Siberia] (Moscow and Leningrad), Tom I, pp. 5–55.

1941   'Voenno-promyshlennyye ekspeditsii torgovykh lyudey v
Sibiri v XVII veke' [Military-entrepreneurial expeditions of
traders in Siberia in the 17th century], *Istoricheskiye zapiski*
(Moscow), Tom X, pp. 167–79.

1951   'Snaryazheniye russkikh promyshlennikov v Sibiri v XVII
veke' [Working equipment of the Russian promyshlenniks in
Siberia in the 17th century], *Istoricheskiy pamyatnik russkogo*
arkticheskogo moreplavaniya XVII veka: Arkheologicheskiye na-
khodki na ostrove Faddeya i na beregu zaliva Simsa [An historical
memorial of Russian Arctic navigation of the 17th century:
Archeological findings on Faddeya Island and the shore of
Sims Bay] (Leningrad and Moscow), pp. 85–92.

1955   'Ocherki po istorii kolonizatsii Sibiri v XVI i XVII vv.'
[Outlines in the history of the colonization of Siberia in the

16th–17th centuries], *Nauchnyye trudy* (Moscow), Tom III, Chast'pervaya: *Voprosy russkoy kolonizatsii Sibiri v XVI–XVII vv.* [Questions of the Russian colonization of Siberia in the 16th and 17th centuries], pp. 11–160.

Bartsch, Paul, Harald A. Rehder, and Beulah E. Shields

1946   *A bibliography and short biographical sketch of William Healey Dall.* Washington, D.C. [Smithsonian miscellaneous collections, vol. CIV, No. 15.]

Baskin, Semen

1949   'Bol'shoy chertezh kamchadalskoy zemli' [The great sketch-map of the Kamchadal land], *Izvestiya VGO* (Leningrad), Tom LXXXI, pp. 226–38.

Beaglehole, John C.

1974   *The life of Captain James Cook.* Stanford, Calif.

Beechey, Frederick W.

1831   *Narrative of a voyage to the Pacific and Beering's Strait, to co-operate with the polar expeditions: performed in His Majesty's ship Blossom...in the years 1825, 26, 27, 28...2 vols. London.*

Belov, Mikhail I.

1948   *Semen Dezhnev, 1648–1948: K trekhsotletiyu otkrytiya proliva mezhdu Aziyey i Amerikoy* [...commemorating the tricentennial of the discovery of the strait between Asia and America]. Moscow and Leningrad.

1949   'Istoricheskoye plavaniye Semen a Dezhneva' [The historical voyage of Semen Dezhnev], *Izvestiya VGO* (Leningrad), Tom LXXXI, pp. 459–72.

1951   'Arkicheskiye plavaniya i ustroystvo russkikh morskikh sudov v XVII veke' [Arctic voyages and the construction of Russian ocean vessels in the 17th century], *Istoricheskiy pamyatnik russkogo arkticheskogo moreplavaniya XVII veka: Arkheologicheskiye nakhodki na ostrove Faddeya i na beregu zaliva Simsa* [An historical memorial of Russian Arctic navigation of the 17th century: Archeological findings on Faddeya Island and the shore of Sims Bay] (Leningrad and Moscow), pp. 63–80.

1954   'Novyye materialy o pokhodakh ustyuzhskogo kuptsa Nikity Shalaurova' [New materials on the expeditions of the Ustyug merchant Nikita Shalaurov], *Geograficheskiy sbornik Geograficheskogo obshchestva SSSR* (Moscow and Leningrad), Tom III, pp. 160–84.

1955   *Semen Dezhnev.* 2nd edition revised and supplemented. Moscow.

1956   *Arkticheskoye moreplavaniye s drevneyskikh vremen do serediny XIX veka* [Arctic seafaring from ancient times to the middle of the 19th century]. Moscow. [*Istoriya otkrytiya i osvoyeniya severnogo morskogo puti* (edited by Ya. Ya. Gakkel´, A. P. Ok-ladnikov, and M. B. Chernenko). Tom i.]

1957 'Semen Dezhnev i amerikanskaya literatura' [Semen Dezhnev and American literature], *Izvestiya VGO* (Leningrad), Tom LXXXIX, pp. 482–5.

1963 'Novoye li eto slovo o plavanii S. I. Dezhneva? (po povodu stat´i B. P. Polevogo)' [Is this the latest word on the voyage of S. I. Dezhnev? (apropos B. P. Polevoy's article)], *Izvestiya VGO*, Tom xcv (Leningrad), pp. 443–6.

1973 *Podvig Semena Dezhneva* [The exploit of Semen Dezhnev]. Moscow. This is the third and revised edition of his 1948 and 1955.

Berg, Lev S.

1919 'Izvestiya o beringovym prolive i yego beregakh do Beringa i Kuka' [Information about the Bering Strait and its shores before Bering and Cook], *Zapiski po gidrografii* (Petrograd), Tom II, Vypusk ii, pp. 77–141.

1946 *Otkrytiye Kamchatki i kamchatskiye ekspeditsii Beringa, 1725–1742* [The discovery of Kamchatka and the Kamchatka expeditions of Bering, 1725–1742]. [3rd edition.] Moscow and Leningrad.

Berkh, Vasiliy N.

1821–3 *Khronologicheskaya istoriya vsekh puteshestviy v severnyya pol-yarnyya strany, s prisovokupleniyem obozreniya fizicheskikh svoystv togo kray* [Chronological history of all the journeys in the northern polar countries, with the addition of a review of the physical characteristics of that region]. 2 Chasti. St. Petersburg.

Bogoraz, Vladimir G.

1904–9 *The Chukchee.* Leiden and New York. [Publications of the Jesup north Pacific expedition, vol. VII, Pts. 1–3 = Memoir of the American museum of natural history, vol. XI, Pts. 1–3. Issued in three parts.]

Breitfuss, L[eonid]

1939 'Early maps of northeastern Asia and the lands around the north Pacific', *Imago mundi* (Stockholm), vol. III, pp. 87–99.

Burney, James

1818 'A memoir on the geography of the north-eastern part of Asia, and on the question whether Asia and America are contiguous, or are separated by the sea', *Philosophical transactions of the Royal society of London*, vol. CVIII, Part I, pp. 9–23.

1819 *A chronological history of north-eastern voyages of discovery; and of the early navigations of the Russians.* London.

Chamisso, Adelbert von

1955 *Reise um die Welt.* Berlin.

Clark, Henry W.
1930   *History of Alaska.* New York.

Cook James
1967   *The journals of Captain James Cook on his voyages of discovery.*
        Vol. III: *The voyage of the* Resolution *and* Discovery, *1766–1780.*
        Edited by J. C. Beaglehole. 2 parts. Cambridge, Eng. [Hakluyt
        society, Extra Series, No. 36.]

Cook, James, and James King
1784   *A voyage to the Pacific ocean. Undertaken by the command of His
        Majesty, for making discoveries in the northern hemisphere. To
        determine the position and extent of the west side of North America;
        its distance from Asia; and the practicability of a northern passage
        to Europe. Performed under the direction of captains Cook, Clerke,
        and Gore, in His Majesty's ships the* Resolution *and* Discovery,
        in the years 1776, 1777, 1778, 1779, and 1780...3 vols. London.
        Vols. I and II written by Captain James Cook; vol. III by
        Captain James King.

Coxe, William
1780   *Account of the Russian discoveries between Asia and America; to
        which are added, The conquest of Siberia and The history of the
        transactions and commerce between Russia and China.* London;
        2nd edition revised and corrected, London, 1780; 3rd edition
        revised and corrected, London, 1787; 4th edition considerably
        enlarged, London, 1804.

1787   *A comparative view of the Russian discoveries with those made by
        captains Cook and Clerke; and a sketch of what remains to be
        ascertained by future navigators.* London.
        Published also as a supplement in *Account of the Russian
        discoveries...*, 3rd edition, pp. 411–56.

Dal', Vladimir I.
1912   *Tolkovyy slovar' zhivogo velikorusskago yazyka* [Explanatory
        dictionary of the living Great Russian language.] 4th corrected
        and supplemented edition. 4 vols. St. Petersburg and Moscow.

Danilevskiy, V. V.
1951   'Russkiye navigatsionnyye pribory pervoy chetverti XVII
        veka' [Russian navigation instruments in the first quarter of
        the 17th century], *Istoricheskiy pamyatnik russkogo arkticheskogo
        moreplavaniya XVII veka: Arkheologicheskiye nakhodki na ostrove
        Faddeya i na beregu zaliva Simsa* [An historical memoir of
        Russian Arctic navigation of the 17th century: Archeological
        findings on Faddeya Island and the shore of Sims Bay]
        (Leningrad and Moscow), pp. 53–62.

Delisle, Joseph N.

1752   *Explication de la carte des nouvelles découvertes au nord de la mer du Sud*. Paris.

1893   'Dezhnev', *Entsiklopedicheskiy slovar'* [Encyclopaedia dictionary], (edited by F. A. Brockhaus and I. A. Yefron; St. Petersburg), *sub nomine*.

Dezhnev, Semen I.

1948   'Otpiska Semena Dezhneva yakutskomu voyevode Ivanu Pavlovichu Akinfiyevu o morskom pokhode ego s ust'ya r. Kolymy do ust'ya r. Anadyr'' [Report of Semen Dezhnev to Yakutsk voyevoda Ivan Pavlovich Akinfiyev about his sea voyage from the mouth of the Kolyma R. to the mouth of the Anadyr' R.] (introduction by G. A. Knyazev and B. A. Mal'kevich), *Izvestiya VGO* (Leningrad), Tom LXXX, pp. 578–81.

Dolgikh, Boris O.

1960   *Rodovoy i plemennoy sostav narodov Sibiri v XVII v.* [Clan and tribal structure of the peoples of Siberia in the 17th century]. Moscow. [Institut etnografii AN SSSR, *Trudy*, vol. LV.]

Engel, Samuel

1779   *Extraits raisonnés des voyages faits dans les parties septentrionales de l'Asie et de l'Amérique ou Nouvelles preuves de la possibilité d'un passage aux Indes par le nord...Lausanne.*

1772–7   *...Geographische und kritische Nachrichten und Anmerkungen über die Lage der nördlichen Gegenden von Asien und Amerika...welchen noch ein Versuch über einen Weg durch Norden nach Indien, und über die Errichtung eines...Handels in die Südsee beygefüget ist...*Translated from the French. 2 vols. Mietau.

1765   *Mémoires et observations géographiques et critiques sur la situation des pays septentrionaux de l'Asie et de l'Amérique, d'après les relations les plus récentes. Aux quelles on a joint un Essai sur la route aux Indes par le Nord, & sur un commerce très vaste & très riche à établir dans la mer du Sud.* Lausanne.

Fedorova, Svetlana G.

1971   'Issledovatel' Chukotki i Alyaski kazachiy sotnik Ivan Kobelov' [Explorer of Chukotka and Alaska, the cossack sotnik Ivan Kobelev], *Letopis' severa* (Leningrad and Moscow), Tom V, pp. 156–72.

Fel', Sergey Ye.

1960   *Kartografiya Rossii XVIII veka* [Cartography of Russia of the 18th century]. Moscow.

Firsov, Nikolay N.

1921   *Chteniya po istorii Sibiri* [Readings in the history of Siberia]. 2 vols. in 1. Moscow.

Fisher, Raymond H.

1943   *The Russian fur trade, 1550–1700.* Berkeley and Los Angeles; reprinted, Millwood, N.Y., 1974. [University of California publications in history, vol. XXXI.]

1956   'Semen Dezhnev and Professor Golder', *Pacific historical review* (Berkeley and Los Angeles), vol. XXV, pp. 281–92.

1973   'Dezhnev's voyage of 1648 in the light of Soviet scholarship', *Terrae incognitae* (Amsterdam), vol. V, pp. 7–26.

1977   *Bering's voyages: Whither and why.* Seattle.

Gmelin, Johann G.

1751–2   ...*Reise durch Sibirien, von dem Jahr 1733 vis 1743*...4 vols. Göttingen.

Gol'denberg, Leonid A.

1965   *Semen Ul'yanovich Remezov: Sibirskiy kartograf i geograf, 1642-posle 1720 gg.* [...Siberian cartographer and geographer, 1620-after 1720]. Moscow.

Golder, Frank A.

1910   'Some reason for doubting Deshnev's voyage', *The geographical journal* (London), vol. XXXVI, pp. 81–3.

1914   *Russian expansion on the Pacific, 1641–1850: An account of the earliest and later expeditions made by the Russians along the Pacific coast of Asia and North America, including some related expeditions to the Arctic regions.* Cleveland.

Great Britain. Hydrographic Office

1959   *Arctic pilot.* 6th edition. London.

1966   *Bering Sea and Strait pilot.* 4th edition. London.

Grekov, Vadim I.

1956   'Nayboleye ranneye pechatnoye izvestiye o pervoy Kamchatskoy ekspeditsii (1725–1730 gg.)' [The earliest published information about the First Kamchatka Expedition (1725–1730)], *Izvestiya AN SSSR, seriya geograficheskaya* (Moscow), Vypusk 6, pp. 108–12.

1960   *Ocherki iz istorii russkikh geograficheskikh issledovaniy v 1725–1765 gg.* [Outlines of the history of Russian geographical explorations, 1725–1765], Moscow.

Grimsted, Patricia K.

1972   *Archives and manuscript repositories in the USSR, Moscow and Leningrad.* Princeton.

Harris, John

1744–8   *Navigantium atque itinerantium bibliotheca. Or, A complete collection of voyages and travels. Consisting of above six hundred*

of the most authentic writers...Originally published by John
Harris...Now carefully revised, with large additions, and
continued down to the present time; including particular
accounts of manufactures and commerce of each country; by
John Campbell. 2 vols. London.

Isnard, Albert

1916 'Joseph-Nicolas Delisle, sa biographie et sa collection de cartes
géographiques à la Bibliothèque nationale', *Bulletin de la
section de géographie du Comité des travaux historiques et scientifiques*, (Paris), Tome XXX, pp. 34–164.

Keuning, Johannes

1954 'Nicolaas Witsen as a cartographer', *Imago mundi* (Leiden),
vol. XI, pp. 95–110.

Kotzebue, Otto von

1821a *Entdeckungs-reise in die Süd-see und nach der Berings Strasse zur
Erforschung einer nordöstlichen Durchfahrt. Unternommen in den
Jahren 1815, 1816, 1817 und 1818, auf Kosten Sr. Erlaucht
des...Grafen Rumanzoff auf der Schiffe* Rurick *unter dem Befehle
des Lieutenants der russische-kaiserlichen Marine Otto von
Kotzebue*...3 vols. in 1. Weimar.

1821b *A voyage of discovery into the South Sea and Beering's straits, for
the purpose of exploring a north-east passage, undertaken in the
years 1815–1818, at the expense of His Highness...Count Rom-
anzoff, in the ship* Rurick, *under the command of the lieutenant
in the Russian imperial navy, Otto von Kotzebue.* Introduction
by I. F. Kruzenshtern. Translated from the German by H.
E. Lloyd. 3 vols. London.

K-r, A. [A. A. Kruber]

1898 'Semen Dezhnev i 250-letoye so vremeni otkrytiya proliva
imenuyemago Beringovym' [Semen Dezhnev and the 250th
anniversary of the discovery of the strait named after
Bering], *Zemlevedeniye* (Moscow), Knizhka III–IV (1899),
pp. 190–6.

Krasheninnikov, Stepan P.

1949 *Opisaniye zemli Kamchatki, s prilozheniyem raportov, doneseniy
i drugikh neopublikovannykh materialov* [Description of Kamchatka, with a supplement of reports, descriptions and other
unpublished materials]. Moscow.

1972 *Explorations of Kamchatka, 1735–1741.* Translated from the
Russian with introduction and notes by E. A. P. Crownhart-
Vaughan. Portland, Oregon.

Kuskov, V. P.

1966 'Byl li Fedot Popov na reke Kamchatke?' [Was Fedot Popov
on the Kamchatka River?], *Voprosy geografii Kamchatki* (Kam-

chatskiy odtel Geograficheskogo obshchestva USSR), Vypusk 4, pp. 94–100.

Lantzeff, George V.

1943   *Siberia in the seventeenth century: A study of the colonial administration.* Berkeley and Los Angeles. [University of California publications in history, vol. xxx.]

Lantzeff, George V., and Richard A. Pierce

1973   *Eastward to empire: exploration and conquest on the Russian open frontier, to 1750.* Montreal and London.

Lensen, George A.

1959   *The Russian push toward Japan: Russo–Japanese relations, 1697–1875.* Princeton.

Litke, Fedor P.

1971   *Voyage autour du monde, 1826–1829.* 3 vols., Paris, 1835; 3 vols., Amsterdam and New York.

Lomonosov, Mikhail V.

1952   'Kratkoye opisaniye raznykh puteshestviy po severnym moryam i pokazaniye vozmozhnogo prokhodu sibirskim okeanom v vostochnuyu Indiyu' [A brief description of various journeys in the northern seas and a statement of a possible passage by way of the Siberian sea to the East Indies], *Polnoye sobraniye sochineniy* (Moscow), Tom vi, pp. 416–98.

Makarova, Raisa V.

1968   *Russkiye na tikhom okeane vo vtoroy polovine XVIII v.* [Russians on the Pacific ocean in the second half of the 18th century]. Moscow

1975   *Russians on the Pacific, 1743–1799.* Translated from the Russian and edited by Richard A. Pierce and Alton S. Donnelly. Kingston, Ontario. [Materials for the study of Alaska history, vol. v.]

Markov, Sergey N.

1948   *Podvig Semena Dezhneva.* [The exploit of Semen Dezhnev] Moscow.

Masterson, James R., and Helen Brower, eds.

1948   *Bering's successors, 1745–1780: contributions of Peter Simon Pallas to the history of Russian exploration toward Alaska.* Seattle.
    Reprinted from the *Pacific Northwest quarterly*, vol. xxxviii, pp. 35–83, 109–55.

Mazour, Anatole G.

1958   *Modern Russian historiography.* 2nd edition. Princeton.

Mikhaylov, S. V.

1949   'Drevnerusskoye sudostroyeniye na Severe' [Old Russian ship construction in the North], *Letopis' Severa* (Moscow and Leningrad), Tom I, pp. 103–6.

Müller, Gerhard F.

1753 'Lettre d'un officier de la marine russienne à un seigneur de la cour concernant la carte des nouvelles découvertes au nord de la mer du Sud, et le mémoire qui y sert d'explication publié par M. de l'Isle', *Nouvelle bibliotheque germanique, ou Histoire litteraire de l'Allemagne, de la Suisse, et des pay du nord* (Amsterdam), vol. XIII, Part I. pp. 46–87.
First published separately in Berlin.

1754 *A letter from a Russian sea-officer, to a person of distinction at the court of St. Petersburgh, containing his remarks on Mr. de l'Isle's chart and memoir, relative to the new discoveries northward and eastward from Kamchatka*...London.

1758 a *Nachrichten von Seereisen, und zur See gemachten Enteckungen, die von Russland aus längst den Küsten des Eismeeres und auf dem östlich Weltmeere gegen Japon und Amerika geschehen sind. Zur Erläuterung einer bey der Akademie der Wissenschaften verfertigen Landkarte.* St. Petersburg. [Sammlung russischer Geschichte, vol. III, pp. 1–304.]

1758 b 'Opisaniye morskikh puteshestviy po ledovitomu i po vostochnomu moryu s rossiyskoy storony uchinennykh' [Description of the ocean voyages in the Icy and Eastern seas made from the Russian side], *Sochineniya i perevody, k pol'ze i uveseleniyu sluzhashchiya* [Writings and translations useful and entertaining] (St. Petersburg), Tom VII, pp. 3–27, 99–120, 195–212, 291–325, 387–409; Tom VIII, pp. 9–32, 99–129, 195–232, 309–36, 394–424.

1761 *Voyages from Asia to America, for completing the discoveries of the northwest coast of America. To which is prefixed a summary of the voyages made by the Russians in the Frozen sea, in search of a northwest passage. Serving as an explanation of a map of the Russians discoveries, published by the Academy of sciences at Petersburgh.* Translated from the High Dutch of S[taatsrath?] Muller...London; 2nd edition, 1764; reprinted, Amsterdam, 1967.

1766 *Voyages et découvertes faites par les Russes le long des côtes de la mer Glaciale & sur l'océan Oriental, tant vers le Japon que vers l'Amerique. On y a joint l'Historie du fleuve Amur et des pays adjacens, depuis le conquête des Russes*...Translated from the German...by C. G. F. Dumas...2 vols. Amsterdam.

1774 'Geographie und Verfassung von Kamtschatka aus verschiedenen schriftlichen und mündlichen Nachrichten gesammelt zu Jakuzk, 1737'. Supplement to: Georg W. Steller, *Beschreibung von dem Lande Kamtschatka dessen Einwohnern, deren Sitten, Nahmen, Lebensart und verschiedenen Gewohnheiten.* Edited by J.B.S. [Jean Benoit Scherer). Frankfurt and Leipzig.

    Beschreibung von dem Lande Kamtschatka with Müller's supplement has been reprinted with two of Steller's other works in a single volume, edited by Hanno Beck. Stuttgart, 1974.

1937–41   *Istoriya Sibiri.* 2 vols. Moscow and Leningrad. See p. 3, note 2.

Neatby, Leslie H.

1973   *Discovery in Russian and Siberian waters.* Athens, Ohio.

Nordenskiöld, [Nils] Adolf E.

1881   *The voyage of the* Vega *round Asia and Europe with a historical review of previous journeys along the north coast of the old world.* Translated from the Swedish by Alexander Leslie. 2 vols. London.

Novlyanskaya, Mariya G.

1966   *Filip Iogann Stralenberg; yego raboty po issledovaniya Sibiri.* Moscow.

Ogloblin, Nikolay N.

1889a   'K russkoy istoriografii. Gerard Miller i yego otnosheniya k pervoistochnikam' [A note on Russian historiography. Gerard Müller and his treatment of original sources], *Bibliograf: Vestnik literatury, nauki i iskusstva* (St. Petersburg), No. 1, pp. 1–11.

1889b   'K voprosu ob istoriografe G. F. Millere' [A note on a question concerning the historian G. F. Müller], *Bibliograf: Vestnik literatury, nauki i iskusstva,* No. 8–9, pp. 161–6.

1890   *Semen Dezhnev (1638–1671 gg.).* (*Novyya dannyya i peresmotr starykh*) [...(New data and reëxamination of the old)]. St. Petersburg. Also in: *Zhurnal Ministerstva narodnago prosveshcheniya,* Tom CCLXXII (December 1890), Otdel 2, pp. 249–307.

1891a   'Dve "skazki" Vl. Atlasova ob otkrytii Kamchatki' [Two "stories" of Vl. Atlasov about the discovery of Kamchatka], *Chteniya v Imperatorskom obshchestve istorii i drevnostey rossiyskikh pri Moskovskom universitete,* Tom CXLVIII, Kniga 3, Chast' I, pp. 1–18.

1891b   'Smert' S. Dezhneva v 1673 g.' [The death of S. Dezhnev in 1673], *Bibliograf: Vestnik literatury, nauki i iskusstva,* No. 3–4. pp. 60–2.

1903   'Vostochnosibirskiye polyarnyye morekhody XVII veka'; [East Siberian polar mariners of the 17th century], *Zhurnal Ministerstva narodnago prosveshcheniya,* vol. CCCXXXVII, Otdel 2, pp. 38–62.

Ogryzko, I. I.

1948   'Ekspeditsiya Semena Dezhneva i otkrytiye Kamchatki' [The expedition of Semen Dezhnev and the discovery of Kamchatka], *Vestnik Leningradskogo universiteta*, No. 12, pp. 36–47.

1953   'Otkrytiye kuril'skikh ostrovov' [The discovery of the Kuril islands], *Yazyki i istoriya narodnostey kraynego severa SSSR* [Languages and history of the nationalities of the far north of the USSR] (Leningrad), pp. 167–207. [*Uchenyye zapiski Leningradskogo gosudarstvennogo universiteta*, No. CLVII. *Seriya Fakul'teta narodov severa*, Vypusk 2].

ORZPM   *Otkrytiya russkikh zemleprokhodtsev i polyarnykh morekhodov XVII veka na severo-vostoke Azii: sbornik dokumentov* [Discoveries of the Russian land and polar sea farers of the 17th century: a collection of documents]. Compiled by N. S. Orlova; edited by A. V. Yefimov. Moscow, 1951.

Pekarskiy, Petr P.

1870   *Istoriya Imperatorskoy akademii nauk* [History of the Imperial academy of sciences]. 2 vols. St. Petersburg, 1870–3.

Podvysotskiy, Aleksandr, comp.

1885   *Slovar' oblastnogo arkhangel'skago narechiya v yego bytovym i etnograficheskom primenenii* [Dictionary of Archangel regional speech in its every day and ethnographical use]. St. Petersburg.

Polevoy, Boris P.

1962a   'O mestopolozhenii pervogo russkogo poseleniya na Kolyme' [The location of the first Russian settlement on the Kolyma], *Doklady Instituta geografii Sibiri i dal'nego vostoka* (Irkutsk), No. 2, pp. 66–75.

1962b   'Nakhodka podlinnykh dokumentov S. I. Dezhneva o yego istoricheskom pokhode 1648 g.' [The finding of the original documents of S. I. Dezhnev about his historical voyage of 1648], *Vestnik Leningradskogo universiteta*, No. 12, pp. 145–52.

1964a   'Zabytyy pokhod I. M. Rubtsa na Kamchatku v 60-kh gg. XVII veka', [The forgotten expedition of I. M. Rubets to Kamchatka in the 'sixties of the 17th century], *Izvestiya AN SSSR, seriya geograficheskaya* (Moscow), Vypusk 4, pp. 130–5.

1964b   'K istorii formirovaniya geograficheskikh predstavleniy o severovostochnoy okonechnosti Azii v XVII v. (Izvestiye o "kamennoy peregrade". Vozniknoveniye i dal'neyshaya metamorfoza legendy o "neobkhodimom nose")' [Contribution to the history of the formation of the geographical ideas about the northeastern extremity of Asia in the 17th century. (Information about the "rocky barrier". Origin and subsequent metamorphosis of the legend of the "impassable cape")],

Sibirskiy geograficheskiy sbornik (Institut geografii Sibiri i dal'nego vostoka, Sibirskoye otdeleniye AN SSSR, Moscow), Tom III, pp. 224–70.

1965a   'O tochnom tekste dvukh otpisok Semena Dezhneva 1655 goda' [The exact texts of the two reports of Semen Dezhnev of 1655], *Izvestiya AN SSSR, seriya geograficheskaya* (Moscow), Vypusk 2, pp. 101–11:

1965b   'Semen Remezov i Vladimir Atlasov (k utochneniyu datirovki rannykh chertezhey Kamchatki)' [Semen Remezov and Vladimir Atlasov (for an exact dating of the early sketch maps of Kamchatka)], *Izvestiya AN SSSR, seriya geograficheskaya* (Moscow), Vypusk 6, pp. 92–101.

1965c   'Novoye o nachale istoricheskogo plavaniya S. I. Dezhneva 1648 g.' [New information about the beginning of S. I. Dezhnev's historic voyage of 1648], *Izvestiya Vostochnosibirskogo otdela Geograficheskogo obshchestva SSSR* (Irkutsk), Tom LXIII, pp. 51–7.

1966   'Nakhodka chelobit'ya pervootkryvateley Kolymy' [The finding of the petition of the original discoverers of the Kolyma], *Ekonomika, upravleniye i kul'tura Sibiri XVI–XIX vv.* [The economy, administration and culture of Siberia in the 16th to 19th centuries] (Novosibirsk), pp. 285–91. [*Materialy po istorii Sibiri. Sibir' perioda feodalizma*, Vypusk 2.]

1970a   'O karte "Kamchadalii" I. B. Gomana' [J. B. Homann's map of "the Kamchadals"], *Izvestiya AN SSSR, seriya geograficheskaya* (Moscow), Vypusk 1, pp. 99–105.

1970b   'Soobshcheniye S. I. Dezhneva o "bol'shom kamennom nose" i proiskhozhdeniye yego lozhnogo tolkovaniya' [S. I. Dezhnev's information about the "great rocky promontory" and the origin of the false interpretation of it], *Izvestiya AN SSSR, seriya geograficheskaya* (Moscow), Vypusk 6, pp. 150–7.

1970c   'O "Pogyche"-Pokhache' (Concerning the "Pogycha"-Pokhach], *Voprosy geografii Kamchatki* (Kamchatskiy otdel Geograficheskogo obshchestva SSSR), Vypusk 6, pp. 82–6.

Polonskiy, Aleksandr. S.

1851   'Pervaya kamchatskaya ekspeditsiya Beringa, 1725–1729 god' [The First Kamchatka Expedition, 1725–1729], *Otechestvennyya zapiski* (St. Petersburg), [Series 3], Tom LXXXV, otdel viii, pp. 1–24.

Robertson, William

1777   *The history of America.* 2 vols. Dublin; also London, 1777.

Russia.   Arkheograficheskaya kommissiya
DAI   *Dopolneniya k aktam istoricheskim* [Supplement to the historical
            documents], 12 vols. St. Petersburg, 1846–72.
PSI   *Pamyatniki sibirskoy istorii XVIII v.* [Monuments of the history
            of Siberia of the 18th century]. 2 vols. St. Petersburg, 1882–5.
1875   *Russkaya istoricheskaya biblioteka* [Russian historical library] 39
            vols. St. Petersburg, 1875–1927.
Russia.   Sobstvennaya Yego Imperatorskago Velichestva kantselyariya
1830   *Polnoye sobraniye zakonov rossiyskoy imperii s 1649 goda* [Com-
            plete collection of laws of the Russian empire from 1649]. 44
            vols. St Petersburg.
1979   *Russkaya tikhookeanskaya epopeya.* Compiled by V. A. Divin,
            K. E. Cherevko, and G. N. Isayenko. Khabarovsk.
RAE   *Russkiye arkticheskiye ekspeditsii XVII–XIX vv. Voprosy istorii
            izucheniya i osvoyeniya Arktiki* [Russian Arctic expeditions of
            the 17th–19th centuries. Questions in the history of the study
            and annexation of the Arctic]. Edited by Mikhail I. Belov.
            Leningrad, 1964. [Arkticheskiy i Antarkticheskiy nauchno
            issledovatel'skiy institut.]
RM   *Russkiye morekhody v ledovitom i tikhom okeanakh. Sbornik
            dokumentov o velikikh russkikh geograficheskikh otkrytiyakh na
            severo-vostoke Azii v XVII veke* [Russian seafarers in the Frozen
            and Pacific oceans. Collection of documents about the great
            Russian geographical discoveries in northeastern Asia in the
            17th century]. Edited and compiled by Mikhail I. Belov.
            Leningrad and Moscow, 1952. [Arkticheskiy nauchno-
            issledovatel'skiy institut.]
Ryabchikov, Petr. A.
1959   *Morskiye suda: Istoriya razvitiya i sovremennyye tipy sudov* [Sea
            vessels: History of their development and contemporary
            types of vessels]. 2nd edition. Moscow.
Samoylov, Vycheslav A.
1945   *Semen Dezhnev i yego vremya. S prilozheniyam otpisok i
            chelobytnikh Semena Dezhneva o yego prokhodakh i otkrytiyakh*
            [Semen Dezhnev and his times. With an appendix of Semen
            Dezhnev's reports and petitions about his journeys and
            discoveries]. Moscow.
Sarychev, Gavriil A.
1806–7   *Account of a voyage of discovery to the north-east of Siberia, the
            Frozen ocean, and the North-East sea.* Translated from the
            Russian. 2 vols. in 1. London; reprinted, Amsterdam and New
            York, 1969.
1952   *Puteshestviye po severo-vostochnoy chasti Sibiri, ledovitomu moryu*

i vostochnomu okeanu [Journeys along the northeastern parts of Siberia, the Icy sea and Eastern ocean]. Edited by N. N. Zubov. Moscow.

Sauer, Martin
1802   *An account of a geographical and astronomical expedition to the northern parts of Russia, for ascertaining the degrees of longitude of the mouth of the river Kovima; of the whole coast of the Tshutski, to East Cape; and the islands in the Eastern Ocean, stretching to the American coast, performed by command of Her Imperial Majesty Catherine the second, empress of all the Russias by commodore Joseph Billings, in the years 1785, etc. to 1794.* London.

Sgibnev, A. S.
1869   'Istoricheskiy ocherk glavneyskikh sobytii v Kamchatke 1650–1856' [Historical outline of the principal events in Kamchatka, 1650–1856], *Morskoy sbornik*, vol. CI, No. 4, pp. 65–142; vol. CII, No. 5, pp. 53–84, No. 6, pp. 37–69; vol. CIII, No. 7, pp. 1–129, No. 8, pp. 33–110.

Shokal'skiy, Yuliy M.
1898   'Semen Dezhnev i otkrytiye beringova proliva' [Semen Dezhnev and the discovery of Bering Strait], *Izvestiya Imperatorskago russkago geograficheskago obshchestva* (St. Petersburg), vol. XXXIV, pp. 495–500.

Slovtsov, Petr A.
1886   *Istoricheskoye obozreniye Sibiri* [Historical review of Siberia.] 2 vols. Moscow and St Petersburg, 1838–44; 2nd edition, 2 vols. in 1, St Petersburg.

Sopotsko, A. A.
1978   'Vakhtennyye zhurnaly korabley V. I. Beringa', *Izvestiya VGO* (Leningrad), Tom CX, pp. 164–70.

Spasskiy, Grigoriy I
1821   'Istoriya plavaniy rossiyan iz rek sibirskikh v ledovitoye more' [History of the voyages of Russians from the Siberian rivers in the Arctic ocean], *Sibirskiy vestnik*, 1821, Chasti XV–XVI, pp. 17–28, 79–90, 120–32, 233–6, 270–81; 1822, Chasti XVII–XVIII, pp. 39–48, 117–28, 185–96, 305–14, 379–98; 1822, Chast' XIX pp. 167–80.

Stepanov, N. N.
1949   'Stepan Petrovich Krasheninnikov i yego trud "Opisaniye zemli Kamchatki"' [Stepan Petrovich Krasheninnikov and his work 'Description of Kamchatka'], in: S. P. Krasheninnikov, *Opisaniye zemli Kamchatki* (Moscow and Leningrad), pp. 13–84.

1950   'Pervyye russkiye svedeniya ob Amure i gol'dakh' [The first

Russian knowledge of the Amur and the Gol'dy], *Sovetskaya etnografiya*, No. 1, pp. 178–82.

Strahlenberg, Philipp Johann Tabbert von

1730   *Das nord und östliche Theil von Europa und Asia, in so weit solches das gantze russische Reich mit Sibirien und der grossen Tatarei in sich begreisset, in einer historisch-geographischen Beschreibung der alten und neuern Zeiten, und vielen andern unbekannten Nachrichten vorgestellet...* Stockholm.

1738   *An historico-geographical description of the north and eastern parts of Europe and Asia; but more particularly of Russia, Siberia and great Tartary; both in the ancient and modern state...* Now faithfully translated into English. London; re-printed, New York, 1970.

Teben'kov, Mikhail D., comp.

1852   *Atlas severozapadnykh beregov Ameriki ot beringova proliv do mysa Korriyentes i ostrovov aleutskikh s prisovokupleniyem nekotorykh mest severovostnochago berega Azii* [Atlas of the northwestern shores of America from the Bering strait to Cape Corrientes and of the Aleutian islands with the addition of several places on the northeastern coast of Asia]. [St. Petersburg.]

Titov, Andrey A.

1890   *Sibir' v XVII v. Sbornik starinnykh russkikh statey o Sibiri i prilezhashchikh k ney zemlyakh* [Siberia of the 17th century. A collection of old Russian articles about Siberia and the lands adjacent to it]. Edited by G. Yudin. Moscow.

United States Navy. Hydrographic office.

1951   *Sailing directions for the, east coast of Siberia. Mys Otto Shmidta to Sakhalinskiy Zaliv (Sakhalin Gulf)*. 2nd edition. Washington. [Hydrographic office publication No. 122a].

Vdovin, Innokentiy S.

1965   *Ocherki istorii i etnografii Chukchey* [Outlines of the history and ethnography of the Chukchi]. Moscow and Leningrad.

Vize, Vladimir Yu.

1948a   *Morya sovetskoy Arktiki; ocherki po istorii issledovaniya* [Seas of the Soviet Arctic; outlines of the history of exploration]. 3rd edition. Moscow and Leningrad.

1948b   *Russkiye polyarnyye morekhody iz promyshlennykh, torgovykh i sluzhilykh lyudey XVII–XIX vv. Biograficheskiy slovar'* [Russian polar mariners of the 17th to 19th century: promyshlenniks, traders and service-men. A biographical dictionary]. Moscow and Leningrad.

1949   'Novyye svedeniya o russkom arkticheskom moreplavanii v

XVII veke' [New information about the Russian Arctic voyages in the 17th century], *Letopis' severa* (Moscow and Leningrad), Tom I, pp. 78–93.

Vrangel', Ferdinand P.

1840 *Narrative of an expedition to the Polar sea, in the years 1820, 1821, 1822, & 1823. Commanded by lieutenant, now admiral, Ferdinand von Wrangell, of the Russian imperial navy.* Translated from G. Engelhardt's German translation of the then unpublished Russian manuscript. Edited by Major Edward Sabine...London.

1885 *Ferdinand v. Wrangel und seine Reise langs der Nordküste von Sibirien und auf dem Eismeere.* Edited by L[isa Vrangel] Engelhardt. Introduction by A. E. Nordenskiöld...Leipzig.

Witsen, Nicolaas C.

1785 *Noord en oost Tartaryen: behelzende eene beschryving van verscheidene tartersche en nabuurige gewesten, in de noorder en oostleykste deelen van Aziën en Europa; zedert naauwkeurig onderzoek van veele jaaren, en eigen ondervinding ontworpen, beschreven, geteekent, en in 't licht gegeven...*[North and east Tartary: containing a description of several Tartar and adjacent regions in the northern and easternmost parts of Asia and Europe; designed, described, drawn up, and published on the basis of many years of research and personal experience...] New edition. 2 vols. Amsterdam.

Yefimov, Aleksey V.

1948 *Iz istorii russkikh ekspeditsiy na tikhom okeane (pervaya polovina XVIII veka)* [From the history of Russian expeditions on the Pacific ocean (first half of the 18th century)]. Moscow.

1950 *Iz istorii velikikh russkikh geograficheskih otkrytiy v severnom ledovitom i tikhom okeanakh XVII-y-pervaya polovina XVIII v.* [From the history of the great Russian geographical discoveries in the north Arctic and Pacific oceans in the 17th and first half of the 18th century]. Moscow.

Zagoskin, N. R.

1910 *Russkiye vodnyye puti i sudovoye delo v dopetrovskoy Rossii* [Russian waterways and shipping in pre-Petrine Russia]. Kazan.

Zelenin, A.

1898 'Yakutskiy kazak Semen Dezhnev. K 250 letnemu yubileyu otkrytiya beringova proliva' [Yakutsk cossack Semen Dezhnev. Commemorating the 250th anniversary jubilee of the discovery of Bering strait], *Nauchnoye obozreniye* (St Petersburg), Kniga 12, pp. 2181–93.

INDEX

Abuses of service-men, 55, 57–8, 145, 241–2, 244

Academy of Sciences, 9, 21, 275; archives of, 40, 41, 42; documents from, nos. 3, 4, 6–8, 11, 13–17, 21, 32; members sent to survey Siberia, 2–3; map of 1758 of, 205–7, 209; atlas of, 205; published Müller's 1758 account and map, 5; sponsored tricentennial of Dezhnev's voyage, 19

Adelung, Johann Christoph, 7–8

Administrative Senate, 55; adopted Bering's proposal, 2

Admiralty College, 5; adopted Bering's proposal, 2; a new government department, 269

agents: Fedot Alekseyev, Afanasiy Andreyev, Ivashko Yakovlev Chirka, Ivan Dmitriyev Sinitsyn, Luka Sivorov – all q.v.

Akinfiyev (Akinfeyev), Ivan Petrovich, voyevoda at Yakutsk (1651–August 1654), 52, 56, 82

Alaschka (island), on Stählin von Storcksburg's map, 210

Alaska, 214, 216, 231; as one of islands seen by Dezhnev, 224, 235

Alay (Olay), Oymak (Yukagir) chieftain, 93, 104; defeat of, 93–4; paid tribute, 94, 131; son Kinita, 104, 131; location of camp of, 133, 134

Alazeya (Olozeyka) River, 134; became known, 32, 105; Dezhnev served on, 107; zimov'ye built on, 125, 135; as depicted on map, 253

Aldan River, 125

Alekseyev, Fedot, identified, 142; also known as Kholmogorets and Popov, 91, 142; activities of – before 1647, 142–3; aborted voyage (1647) of, 27, 33, 143, 145; 1648 voyage of: initiated by, 105–6, 158; departed on, 27; second in command of as customs agent, 150, 158, 159; composition and size of party of, 147,

148, 155; employees of, 91; koch of, 153; travel document of, 89, document 22; petitioned for Dezhnev's service, 106; goods carried by, 91; fight with Chukchi and wounding of, 23, 34, 52, 226; separated from Dezhnev, 28, 34, 52, 182, 185; death of, 54, 88, 190; Yakut woman of, 29, 37, 54, 65, n. 1, 88, 150, 184; alleged son of, 29, 38, 191, 192; nephew of, 91, 192; legend of – in Kamchatka, see Fedotov legend

Aleutian Islands, 214, 216

Alexander I, 13

America, joined with Asia, 2, 12, 26, 212; separated from, 118, 197, 213, 275; Dezhnev and others unaware of, 274, cf. 249; route to, 202

Amosov, Fedot, 26

Amur River, 138, n. 1, 257; on maps, 256, 261

Amur Sea, 256, 257, 261, 262

Anabar River, 171

Anadyr', modern town of, 240, n. 1

Anadyr' Bay (sometimes the river), Anadyr' River empties into, 228; down near the sea, 53, cf. 289; sandspit and rookery at entrance to, see sandspit at mouth of Anadyr'; relation to great rocky nos, 219, 222, 227, 228, 244; length of, 219; distance from Anadyrsk, 240; bordered by 'Koryak side' and 'Russian side', 191, 225, 229

Anadyr' (Anandyr', Onandyr') River, 55, 109–25 passim, 143, 145, 151–9 passim, 197, n. 1, 236, n. 1, 238, 250, 273, 277, 282–7 passim; early knowledge of, 33, 36, 49, 57; first known as Pogycha, 140; description of, 65, 73, 240–1; empties into bay, 54; discovered by Dezhnev, 106, 107; location of tribute zimov'ye on, 240; fishing grounds on, 61; lower part of, 230–1; few sables on, 73; bordered 'Russian side', 225; distance of – from great rocky/Chukotskoy Nos: far, 72,

Dezhnev (*cont.*)
  and unmentioned by navigators after
  Cook, 215–17; high praise of – by Soviet
  scholars, 272–3; appraisal of, 273–6; *see
  also* voyage of 1648
Diomede Islands, 219, 234; not Dezhnev's
  two islands, 225, 286
distances: Anadyr' to Cape Navarin, 188; to
  Cape Olyutorskiy, 187, 189; to western
  boundary of Chukotskiy peninsula, 228;
  to Kamchatka River, 194; to Kresta Bay,
  223, 227; to Matkol, 189; upriver to
  Markova, 240; mouth of – to Anadyr'
  Bay entrance, 219, 228; Arakamchechen-
  Yttigran offshore, 234; of Cape Dezhneva
  (dimensions), 210, n. 1, 228; Cape
  Dezhneva (East Cape) to Anadyr' Bay,
  219, 222, 227, 280, 284; to capes Navarin
  and Olyutorskiy, 236; to Chaunskaya
  Bay, 176, n. 3; Diomede Islands to
  Uelen, 225; East Cape to Diomede
  Islands, 234; to Cape Prince of Wales,
  210; Indigirka to Alazeya and Yana, 169;
  mouth of Kolyma to Nizhne-Kolymsk,
  130; to Sredna-Kolymsk, 134; Sredne-
  Kolymsk to Nizhne-Kolymsk, 131;
  Kolyma to Alazeya, 134, 169 and n. 2; to
  Anadyr', 171, 280, 284; to Cape Dezhneva (East Cape), 176, 178, 280; to
  Chaunskaya Bay, 179; to Indigirka, 169;
  to Kolyuchinskaya Bay, 176; to Yakutsk,
  170, to Zhigansk, 171; of Müller's
  Chukotskoy Nos (dimensions), 207, 228;
  Nos to Anadyr', 207; Svyatoy Nos to
  Khromskaya Bay, 169; Yakutsk to
  Svyatoy Nos, 169
documentary collections, 40–2
Dolgikh, Boris O., 131; on first Russian
  outpost on Kolyma, 129; on locale of loss
  of two koches on 1648 voyage, 174, 175,
  180, 181
dumb trade, 32, 44, 45, 141; locale of, 174,
  179
Dunay, Konstantin, commandant on
  Kolyma (1655–7), 135
d'yaks at Yakutsk, *see* Peter G. Stenshin and
  Osip Stepanov

East Cape, 13; easternmost point of Asia,
  114, 215; so named by Cook, 8, 116, 211;
  identified and described by him and
  King, 8, 210; also by Kotzebue, 10, 216;
  dimensions of, 210, n. 3; depicted on

maps, 238; as Dezhnev's great rocky nos,
  8, 18, 110, 116–18, 213, 215, 217; name
  changed to Cape Dezhneva, 17, 217, n.
  1, 218; not great rocky nos, 283, 284,
  285; not circumnavigated by Dezhnev,
  17, 277, 285; *see also* Cape Dezhneva
Engel, Samuel, 7
equipment, 51, 81, 186–7; prices of, 91,
  97–9, 103
Eskimos, mistaken for Chukchi, 116, 174,
  219, 225; on Bering Strait islands, 225,
  234; met by Stadukhin, 181

Faddeya Island, 167
Fedotov, Vaska, mistaken for Fedot Alekseyev's alleged son? 192
Fedotov legend, as reported by Müller, 29,
  38, document 18, 191–2; misrepresented
  by Golder, 287–8; as recounted by
  Krasheninnikov, 86–8, 192–3; espoused
  by modern scholars, 193; critique of,
  192–6; encountered before Atlasov, 267
Fedotovshchina (Fedoticha, Feodoticha,
  Fedotovka) River, name given to Nikul
  River, 38, 85, 87, 191, 192, 194; tributary
  of Kamchatka, 29, 38, 86, 87; wintering
  place of Alekseyev or son, 29, 38, 86, 87,
  192, 195
Fel', Sergey Ye., on L'vov-Anadyrskaya
  map, 200, n. 2
Filipov, Danil, delivered reports to Yakutsk,
  50, 52, 55, 56, 251 and n. 2; served with
  Seliverstov, 69
firearms, *see* weapons
fish, 53, 69, 185; staple of diet, 76, 100, 283
  and n. 2; white vs. red, 65, 73; many on
  Kolyma, 125; supply at Sredne-Kolymsk
  inadequate, 135; on Yemokon, 125;
  fishing grounds on Anadyr', 61; fed to
  hostages, 61, 65, 73
fishing equipment, 65, 73, 100; cost of, 81,
  82, 91, 97, 98
fish tooth bone, 45, 54, 80, 82, 106, 183, 198;
  items made from, 45, 76; *see also* walrus
  tusks
Foma, promyshlennik in Fedot Alekseyev
  legend, 86
fondy, 40
food, grain (flour) 81, 82, 91, 97, 98; meat,
  283, n. 2; shortage of, 100, 133; on
  voyage (Golder), 283; of Chukchi, 113;
  of nearby islanders, 114; *see also* fish
Frantsbekov (Fronsbekov), Dmitriy A.,

Vetoshka (cont.)

11, 172, n. 1, 198; wounded, 60; pledge of – for goods, 67; description of great rocky nos by, 72, 198

Vinius, Andrey A., identified, 257; map of, 257, 258, 259; assisted Witsen, 263, 268

Vinsgeim, Kristian N., editor of *Notes to the St. Petersburg Gazette*, 24; edited Müller's 1737 account, 24–5

Vize, Vladimir Yu., accepts legend of Alekseyev in Kamchatka, 193; translations of excerpts from Witsen's *Noord en Oost Tartarye*, 264–6

Vlas'yev, Vasiliy, commandant on Kolyma (August 1648–1650), 48, 56, 57, 60, 71, 78, 90; instructions from Yakutsk voyevoda to, document 26, 127–8, 132, 150; replaced Gavrilov, 139; on Yana and Indigirka and arrest of, 49, 145

Vologda, 121

Voronin, Luka, see tower of whalebones

voyage from Lena to Kamchatka, 288; report of, 1, 2; discussed by Müller and Bering, 4, 204; mentioned by Strahlenberg, 269; by Krasheninnikov, 86, 87, 192; by Kozyrevskiy, 193, by Witsen, 265, 266

voyage of 1647, 33, 148; initiated by Alekseyev, 45, 143; Dezhnev's participation in – requested, 45, 143; number of men on, 45; departed from Sredne-Kolymsk, 143; stopped by ice, 49, 51, 144; Gavrilov's reports about, 45, 46, 144

voyage of 1648, 1; documents describing – discovered by Müller, 4, 275; described by Dezhnev, 51, 52, 106; Müller's accounts of, 4–6, 27–8, 33–4; Ogloblin's treatment of, 16; Berg's, 18; Belov's, 19; publicized, 7–9, 13–15; controversy over, 11–13, 15, 17–18; materials relating to, 19–21; mentioned by Stadukhin, 79, 154, 172, 173; by Krasheninnikov, 87, 88; initiated by Alekseyev, 33, 146, 158, 160; membership of expedition, 147–51; Dezhnev's participation in – requested, 105–6, 146–7, 159; ownership of koches on, 151–3; number of, 27, 33, 153, n. 3, 153–4, 172; supplies and equipment carried, 155, 187; economic objective of, 155–6; place of origin of, 156–8; mode of navigation used, 166–8, 225; no log book or journal for, 169; number of participants, 150, 184; first

stage (to mouth of Kolyma) departure of, 161, 170; second stage (along Arctic coast), 170–82; ice conditions during, 170–1; elapsed time and distance of, 171; loss of four koches during, 170, 172–3; where? 173–82; wrecking of Ankudinov's koch, 34, 63, 173, 182; third stage (to Dezhnev's landfall), 182–5; fight with Chukchi, 182; where? 182–5, 226; separation of Dezhnev and Alekseyev, 185; wrecking of Dezhnev's koch, 185; what was salvaged, 186–7; where koch wrecked? 34, 52, 185, 187–9; march to Anadyr', 28, 34, 106, 182, 189–90; 12 men lost on Anadyr', 53, 106, 185–6; fate of Aleseyev, see Alekseyev; first knowledge of voyage, 79, 244, 251–2; subsequent knowledge of – in Yakutsk, 251; in Moscow, 252; elsewhere, 252, 254, 260, 261, 263; mentioned by Witsen, 264–6; commentary on, 266–9, 288; by Strahlenberg, 269, 288; interest in, 6–9, 13–15; decline of interest in, 214–15; intermittant interest in, 215–17; revival of, 16, 218; importance of voyage, 272–4 275–6; to Dezhnev, 249–51, 274

voyages east of Lena, 169–70, 274, 281, 283; Vlas'yev ordered to make one, 100; of Novoselov, 126, 146, n. 1, 169; of Stadukhin, 79, 91, 104, 126–7, 172; of Seliverstov, 80, 243, 244

voyevodas, defined, 43, n. 1; at Yakutsk: Ivan Petrovich Akinf'yev, Dmitriy A. Frantsbekov, Matvey B. Glebov, Ivan Fedorovich Golenishchev-Kutuzov, Petr Petrovich Golovin, Vasiliy Nikitich Pushkin, Kiril Osipovich Suponov – all q.v.

Vrangel', Ferdinand P., 15; identified, 13, 180; explorations of, 13; wrote account of Dezhnev's voyage, 14; on place of turnaround of Stadukhn's 1649 voyage, 180, 181; accepted East Cape as great rocky nos, 215; mentions two islands near Cape Shelagskiy, 286

walruses, on island near Kolyma, 75, 77; on Arctic coast, 79–80, 181; in Pomor'ye, 61, 243; on Anadyrskoy Nos, 113, 223; hunted for food, 65, 265; an object of worship, 75; rookeries of: at mouth of Anadyr', see sandspit; discovered by Dezhnev, 37, 61, 63, 72, 74, 273; visited